The Open Economy

EDI Series
in Economic Development

EDI Series in Economic Development

Maxwell L. Brown, *Farm Budgets: From Farm Income Analysis to Agricultural Project Analysis.* Johns Hopkins University Press, 1979.

James E. Austin, *Agroindustrial Project Analysis.* Johns Hopkins University Press, 1981.

William Diamond and V. S. Raghavan, editors, *Aspects of Development Bank Management.* Johns Hopkins University Press, 1982.

J. Price Gittinger, *Economic Analysis of Agricultural Projects.* 2d ed. Johns Hopkins University Press, 1982.

Gerald M. Meier, editor, *Pricing Policy for Development Management.* Johns Hopkins University Press, 1983.

J. D. Von Pischke, Dale W Adams, and Gordon Donald, editors. *Rural Financial Markets in Developing Countries.* Johns Hopkins University Press, 1983.

J. Price Gittinger, *Compounding and Discounting Tables for Project Analysis.* 2d ed. Johns Hopkins University Press, 1984.

K. C. Sivaramakrishnan and Leslie Green, *Metropolitan Management: The Asian Experience.* Oxford University Press, 1986.

Hans A. Adler, *Economic Appraisal of Transport Projects: A Manual with Case Studies.* Revised and expanded edition. Johns Hopkins University Press, 1987.

Philip H. Coombs and Jacques Hallak, *Cost Analysis in Education: A Tool for Policy and Planning.* Johns Hopkins University Press, 1987.

J. Price Gittinger, Joanne Leslie, and Caroline Hoisington, editors, *Food Policy: Integrating Supply, Distribution, and Consumption.* Johns Hopkins University Press, 1987.

Gabriel J. Roth, *The Private Provision of Public Services.* Oxford University Press, 1987.

The Open Economy

Tools for Policymakers in Developing Countries

edited by
Rudiger Dornbusch
and
F. Leslie C. H. Helmers

Published for The World Bank
Oxford University Press

Oxford University Press

NEW YORK OXFORD LONDON GLASGOW
TORONTO MELBOURNE WELLINGTON HONG KONG
TOKYO KUALA LUMPUR SINGAPORE JAKARTA
DELHI BOMBAY CALCUTTA MADRAS KARACHI
NAIROBI DAR ES SALAAM CAPE TOWN

Manufactured in the United States of America
First printing May 1988

Library of Congress Cataloging-in-Publication Data

The Open economy : tools for policymakers in developing countries /
edited by Rudiger Dornbusch and F. Leslie C. H. Helmers.
    p.   cm.—(EDI series in economic development)
Includes bibliographies and index.
ISBN 0-19-520656-8   ISBN 0-19-520709-2 (pbk.)
  1. Developing countries—Economic policy—Case studies.
I. Dornbush, Rudiger, 1942–   . II. Helmers, F. L. C. H. (Frederik
Leslie Cornelius Hazlewood), 1929–   . III. Series.
HC59.7.0529 1987
338.9'0091724—dc19   88-5176

Contents

Preface

THE ECONOMIC DEVELOPMENT INSTITUTE (EDI) of the World Bank has several objectives. One is to teach officials in the developing world the principles and practices of project analysis. Another is to familiarize government officials with current issues of economic policy. To meet these objectives, the EDI organizes courses and seminars in cooperation with its partner institutions in the developing world. In addition, the EDI makes its materials available for independent study. In principle, EDI materials are written in nontechnical language so that they will be understandable to interested persons outside the economics profession.

This volume was produced at the request of EDI. The editors drew up an outline of the aspects of economic policy concerning an open economy and assembled a team of economists to write about the issues. The book does not offer specific policy prescriptions for every conceivable situation a country might face, but the writers give valuable advice based on their experience. Although intended for use in courses and seminars at EDI and its partner institutes, the study should also be of interest to government officials and policymakers in the developing world who want to have an overview of the various policy issues. Professional economists may also find it useful.

The editors would like to express their thanks to the fourteen other authors who contributed to this volume. They all welcomed with enthusiasm the idea of producing in nontechnical language a guide to the issues facing an open economy, and all met the deadlines for their own contributions.

Numerous persons gave support or advice or constructive critical comments. Unfortunately, the list of indebtedness has become too long to be produced here. An exception may be made, however, for Sonia Hoehlein, Carman Peri, and Marshall Schreier, who processed the manuscript in record time.

One of the editors, F. Leslie C. H. Helmers, died on March 3, 1988, just before this book went to press. An economist's economist, he brought economic analysis to bear on topical problems of public management in such a way that the noneconomist could understand and apply the concepts developed, and he helped developing countries build their own capacity for economic management. His contributions to this volume and to the work of the Economic Development Institute and of the World Bank are gratefully acknowledged.

1

Introduction

F. Leslie C. H. Helmers

DIFFERENT ECONOMISTS writing about a subject inevitably have, in addition to different styles, nuances, and judgments, different perceptions of the economic background of the reader. In addition, they sometimes use different terminologies. To give the interested noneconomist reader a basic understanding, this book begins with the present overview, and a discussion in chapter 2 of how the real exchange rate is used as a policy instrument. Four appendixes deal with data sources and basic economic concepts. Readers familiar with real-exchange-rate analysis and basic economic concepts need not read chapter 2 and the appendixes.

No summary can do justice to a writer's views. The following paragraphs therefore present only a few salient aspects of the various chapters in this volume.

Part I deals with policy issues and policy tools. In chapter 3, which sets the tone, Dornbusch derives the basic balance of payments identity, which provides the unifying theme for the following chapters. The identity equation shows that a current account surplus has three guises. It is at one and the same time (a) the excess of the nation's income over its expenditures, (b) the excess of the nation's exports of goods and services over its imports, and (c) the net increment to the nation's foreign asset holdings.

If national income exceeds domestic expenditures, then the surplus manifests itself as an excess of current foreign exchange inflows over current foreign exchange outflows, or (in other words) as a surplus in the current account of the balance of payments. Conversely, if domestic expenditures exceed national income, then current foreign exchange outflows exceed current foreign exchange inflows, and the current account of the balance of payments will show a deficit. Surpluses or deficits in the current account of the balance of payments of course mean that the country's foreign assets position has improved or deteriorated, respectively. It is also self-evident that, if there is a surplus, the country

1

must build up its foreign exchange reserves, lend abroad, or invest abroad. The converse also holds: if there is a deficit, foreign exchange reserves are being drawn down, or foreigners must finance the deficit.

The equality of the three separate ways of measuring the current account surplus or deficit is an ex post identity that holds at every and any level of domestic activity. Labor may be unemployed or fully employed; exports and imports may be at low levels or at high levels, depending on the openness of the economy. In all cases, the basic identity will be valid. The interesting aspects appear if one analyzes how one moves from one equilibrium to another. Basically, this book considers the different policy measures that can be taken to move from one situation to another and the different effects.

In principle, three types of policy measures, corresponding to the three guises of the current account can be distinguished. Expenditure-changing policies, such as fiscal and monetary policies, directly affect the level of economic activity. They act on the national income and domestic expenditure part of the basic equation. Expenditure-switching policies, such as trade and exchange rate policies, change the pattern of economic activity. These policies lead to changes in the composition of production, spending, and foreign exchange flows. Finally, financial policies toward the rest of the world concern capital flows, debt management, and the net foreign assets position of a country. In addition, there are the so-called structural policies, the objective of which is to enhance the efficiency of domestic production processes. These policies are not, however, discussed in this volume because this study deals principally with balance of payments issues.

The order of the chapters in this book follows closely the above-mentioned typology of policy instruments. After chapter 3, which provides the basic framework, Krugman in chapter 4 gives an overview of expenditure-changing and expenditure-switching policies. In chapters 5, 6, and 7, Dornbusch, Fischer, and Collins explain issues of real exchange rate, multiple exchange rates, and trade policies. In chapters 8 and 9, external financial policies are discussed by Williamson and Fishlow. In chapter 10, Bruno discusses the order in which the different policy instruments should be used. Finally, in chapter 11, Harberger provides persuasive documentation that small economies do as well as large economies and that professional economists' policy prescriptions lead to better economic progress. The five country studies in Part II review the types of policies the countries have actually followed in the recent past.

1. Policy Issues and the Main Policy Tools

After Dornbusch sets the stage in chapter 3, Krugman starts in chapter 4 with a detailed account of the type of external adverse disturbances a country can encounter and then reviews the difference between expenditure-reducing and expenditure-switching policies. The objective of both types of policies is to transform a deficit in the current account of the balance of payments into a surplus. The former policies have the disadvantage that cutting domestic expenditures may cause the economy to enter into a recession and that consequently unemployment may increase; moreover, private investment may be reduced to such an extent that future growth may be jeopardized. In contrast, expenditure-switching policies, which increase the domestic prices of the internationally traded goods, will curtail imports and stimulate exports so that the economy can continue to grow. The problem here, however, is that the price increases of imports as well as of export goods sold in the home market may lead to a demand for wage increases. This demand may lead to an inflationary spiral, which may make import goods again attractive and production of export goods less profitable, so that the effects of the policy will be negated. It becomes immediately clear that the objective of expenditure switching is not only to increase the nominal prices of the traded goods but also to increase their real prices. The real exchange rate therefore emerges as an important policy instrument. Krugman sees the need to combine nominal increases in the prices of traded goods with expenditure-cutting policies to curtail domestic demand or to reform the labor market to permit increases in real prices. He recognizes that political reality may lead policymakers to stray from policies of strict economic efficiency.

In chapter 5, Dornbusch discusses the question of overvaluation. He introduces a number of real-exchange-rate indexes. Basically, each of these indexes tries to measure in real terms the international competitiveness of the domestic producers of traded goods. A very powerful concept is to define the real exchange rate as the ratio of domestic wages, say, pesos per hour, to the nominal exchange rate in pesos per dollar. In this case the real exchange rate is defined as simply the domestic wage in dollars. If wages in dollars are high, then domestic producers of tradables will have difficulty competing with imports and producing export goods because neither type of activity will be very profitable in competition with the world market. A high real exchange rate, as defined here, means that the exchange rate is overvalued: the high value of domestic currency, reflected in the high wage rate in dollars, leads to high imports and low exports. This definition is very powerful because it quickly conveys an understanding of how difficult it sometimes is to move from an overvalued currency (with real wages that are above the level at which labor supply equals labor demand) to an equilibrium level with significantly lower wages.

In the remaining part of chapter 5, Dornbusch emphasizes again the importance of the real exchange rate as a policy instrument. He also discusses in detail how a domestic currency can become overvalued and reviews all the possible adverse impacts on the economy. In addition, a number of detailed country experiences are reviewed. His conclusion may be put in this way: no automatic mechanism will ensure that exchange rates will not become misaligned. The real exchange rate must therefore be considered an important policy guideline.

Fischer's chapter 6 complements Dornbusch's review in chapter 5. After a brief discussion of different exchange rate arrangements, Fischer provides helpful guidelines to determine whether the domestic currency is overvalued. Also, Fischer points out that a devaluation must be accompanied by restrictive macroeconomic policies to ensure that domestic price and wage increases do not offset the effects of a nominal devaluation. According to Fischer, "every successful stabilization program has been preceded by an unsuccessful attempt in which the government sought to stabilize purely by fixing the nominal exchange rate, without taking accompanying macroeconomic measures."

In chapter 7, Collins discusses multiple exchange rates and quantitative restrictions. These policies have been introduced for a variety of reasons. The objective behind special nominal exchange rates or special restrictions, for example, may be to favor certain food or energy imports and to keep prices in these sectors low. It may be to stimulate the domestic production of some types of exports or some types of import substitutes or to protect an infant industry. Countries may also introduce a series of special rates and restrictions in hopes of curtailing total imports and capital outflows and improving their balance of payments. Collins points out, however, that other effects of these policies can make them very harmful. In particular, they alter relative prices, and they affect the government budget. They create distortions in the incentive system and can be very difficult to enforce, thereby encouraging illegal activity. Collins concludes that these special measures are not appropriate remedies for large and persistent balance of payments deficits. They will not, for example, enable a country with a substantially overvalued exchange rate to postpone devaluation indefinitely but may in fact exacerbate the problem. Collins identifies some situations in which the special policies can be useful. Capital controls, for example, can provide an effective buffer against disruptive speculative capital flows.

In chapter 8, Williamson deals with foreign exchange reserve policies. When a country experiences, say, an export boom, how much of the extra foreign exchange receipts should it add to its foreign exchange reserves and how much should it spend on imports? The answer depends on how far the country may wish to diverge from the long-run equilibrium path—that is, the path along which the country produces its normal, maximum output level (internal balance) while the balance of payments is also in equilibrium (external balance). Williamson leads us step by step through the different considerations, such as the size of the external shock, the costs of reserve depletion, the opportunity cost of holding reserves, the speed of adjustment, the type of exchange rate regime, the structure of the balance of payments, the opportunity for foreign borrowing, and so on. In the final analysis, the speed of adjustment is a very important factor because countries that cannot adjust quickly will need to hold relatively large reserves. The strategy proposed by Williamson is that, except in special circumstances, countries should target reserves at 30–40 percent of a year's imports. In addition, a continuous review should seek to determine whether divergences from internal and external balance are occurring and whether within a time frame of five years the reserve targets can again be reached in cases of shortfall.

In chapter 9, Fishlow provides a historical overview of international capital movements and makes the important point that, from a historical perspective, the present debt of the developing countries is not high. Its maturity, however—six to ten years—is much shorter than that of the pre–World War I debt. Furthermore, the debt is expressed in U.S. dollars, and much of it has floating interest rates. For these reasons and others, several developing countries at present have problems paying off their debts.

In general, the developing countries coped well with the first oil-price shock of 1973, but they had problems with the second oil-price shock of 1980. The reasons were that since 1980 countries worldwide had followed restrictive monetary and fiscal policies, which led to a decline in the developing countries' export earnings at the same time as interest rates rose worldwide. The developing countries continued to borrow, but the new debt was used to a large extent to service the old debt at higher interest rates. Often when there was some inflow of foreign exchange, capital flight emerged and caused much of it to disappear. Serious debt servicing problems started to appear in 1982, especially for Mexico. The response consisted of a rescheduling of debt combined with restraints on domestic demand, mainly on investments.

It became clear, however, that continuation of expenditure-reducing policies would lead to intolerably low consumption levels. Fishlow therefore welcomes the 1985 plan of U.S. Treasury Secretary James Baker, which again stresses growth. Specifically, the Baker plan seeks for the developing countries an enhancement of the productivity of domestic assets through liberalization and through more capital lending from external official and private bank sources. Fishlow endorses the overall thrust of the plan but believes that more resources than planned should be made available to the fifteen debtor countries in greatest trouble and that a greater diversity in internal liberalization strategies should be welcomed because this will ensure a greater internal commitment to the implementation of liberalization. He sees the need for an active import-substitution strategy in developing countries to curtail imports. (Appendix D offers a different point of view.) In the final part of his analysis, Fishlow also makes the point that financial openness cannot be pursued as a substitute for effective adjustment policies. Capital inflows may temporarily resolve balance of payments deficits, but a country must effectuate real adjustments in order to solve the problem in the longer run.

Numerous studies have shown that growth will be higher in countries that follow open-economy policies than it will in closed economies. The explanation for this phenomenon is basically very simple: when the economy is opened up, domestic production processes will become competitive with those of the rest of the world, thus ensuring enhanced efficiency. Suppose we are at a relatively closed stage, characterized by high tariffs, quantitative restrictions, foreign exchange controls, and so on. How should we go about liberalizing the economy? Bruno addresses this question in chapter 10. Bruno makes the important point that adjustment in the financial markets may be very fast, whereas the response of exports and import-substitute producers to changes in the real exchange rate tends to be sluggish. Rapid liberalization may thus lead to high unemployment costs, and in such cases Bruno favors a gradual approach to the liberalization of commodity flows while maintaining controls on capital flows. The latter are necessary because massive short-term capital inflows may lead to an unwanted appreciation of the domestic currency, which will result in increased imports and reduced exports. In Bruno's view, the wrong order of liberalization of markets has in many cases caused crises, and he argues strongly that the liberalization of goods markets should precede the liberalization of capital markets. Bruno also reviews the stabilization attempts in high-inflation countries. In such cases, he concludes that the approach should consist of policies that provide not gradual disinflation but very fast disinflation, because prolonged contractionary monetary and fiscal policies will entail substantial unemployment.

Finally, in chapter 11, Harberger argues persuasively that small developing countries (as a cutoff rate he takes countries with a 1983 population of less than 20 million) should economize on the use of governments because they have relatively few trained officials. Policies should therefore be simple and robust. At the same time, however, the many ties among and within the small leadership elite require the policymaker for the sake of survival to take into account the many special interests of the educated elite. Can we expect to find special interest pressures so large that most small developing countries will have inferior economic growth? Far from it! Harberger's review shows that one small group of small countries has done badly but also that a much larger group has done relatively well. Furthermore, according to his review, the small countries with policy weaknesses show symptoms similar to those revealed by larger countries with policy weaknesses.

2. Country Studies

Part II of the volume consists of five country studies, which review briefly the types of policies these countries have followed in recent years.

Although Argentina had a spectacular growth during the first three decades of this century, its performance deteriorated substantially during the 1940s and 1950s. Cavallo contends that the reason was mainly the effect of trade distortions and domestic currency overvaluation. Very elucidating too is Cavallo's analysis of the period 1956–84, which shows that economic policies rather than external shocks led, through large fluctuations in the real exchange rate, to several stagflation crises.

Simonsen reviews Brazil's economic policies. Brazil could be considered to have been an open economy until 1929, but with the collapse of coffee prices in that year, Brazil started a thirty-five-year period of inward-looking policies. Emphasis on investments and diversification led to high growth rates, but the economy became more and more closed. Imports as a percentage of gross national product (GNP) fell from about 24 percent in 1929 to less than 6 percent in 1964, when a major change in policy emphasized real-exchange-rate adjustments. The results were spectacular through 1973, the year of the first oil-price shock, and remained very good because of external borrowing through 1980, the year of the second oil-price shock. At about that time, it became apparent that Brazil's external debt was becoming a problem. Subsequent adjustments resulted in a severe decline in investment. The crucial issue in Brazil will be to maintain growth by restoring the savings ratio to its old levels.

From 1965 to 1986, Indonesia has had a spectacular economic performance matched by only a small number of other countries. To a large extent, Gillis and Dapice ascribe this to the very sensible real-exchange-rate policies followed by the Indonesian government. Although Indonesia's exchange rate strategy may be characterized as outward looking, trade strategy has turned inward looking since 1973, when import quotas and bans were imposed on automobiles, motorcycles, some textiles, and newsprint. The protection of domestic industry by means of quantitative restrictions accelerated after 1980: by 1984, some 22 percent of imports had some form of restriction. One possible explanation for Indonesia's success, offered by Gillis and Dapice, is that the deft management of exchange rate policy and the economic cushion provided by petroleum earnings enabled Indonesia to withstand the protectionistic excesses.

Park looks critically at the development process in the Republic of Korea. Like many other authors, Park argues that Korea's spectacular economic progress has been due to its outward-looking strategy, in particular its export-led industrialization. Unlike other authors, however, he argues that this progress took place in a regime that was not laissez-faire but highly centralized and interventionist, a regime in which the government gave high priority to export promotion. In addition, he believes that Korea's highly educated and disciplined work force, together with massive foreign assistance, paved the way for Korea's outstanding growth. As negative results of these policies he sees too much concentration of economic power in a few hands and an excessive susceptibility to external shocks. He believes that the pursuit of economic growth has led to too much borrowing from abroad. In retrospect, Park feels that if Korea had relied more on market mechanisms than on interventionist policies, it would have prevented some misinvestments in heavy industries.

Cardoso and Levy review Mexico's economic policies. During the "Mexican miracle" period from 1956 to 1970, gross domestic product (GDP) grew at 6.7 percent a year. The government budget had small deficits or surpluses, and the average inflation rate was only 3.8 percent a year. Investment increased from 14 percent to 23 percent of GDP. Although absolute poverty decreased, some authors criticized the policies during this period for not having improved relative income distribution.

The "shared development" policies during 1971–76 emphasized the public sector as the engine of growth and import substitution by means of protection. The public deficit rose from 2 percent of GDP in 1971 to 10 percent in 1976. Public debt increased from $7 billion in 1971 to $21 billion in 1976.[1] Substantial deficits in the current account of the balance of payments made an adjustment program necessary, which was, however, abandoned when oil production and exports came on stream.

The oil euphoria caused many problems. Between 1977 and 1981, the domestic currency was allowed to become more and more overvalued. Exports increased spectacularly because of oil exports, but imports increased even more so. Current account deficits soared, and the public debt tripled. A substantial capital flight ensued. In 1982, the budget deficit reached a peak of 17 percent of GDP; inflation reached 60 percent. As Cardoso and Levy write, "overvaluation and budgets deficits proved to be a deadly combination."

In 1982, Mexico could no longer service its debt, and a massive adjustment program was undertaken. Between 1982 and 1986, public investment was reduced by some 60 percent in real terms; similarly, real wages were reduced by more than 30 percent. The adjustment process is still going on. The lesson to be learned is that "imbalances allowed to accumulate for too long are extremely painful to correct."

3. Not Policy Miracles

This volume covers a number of important issues faced by open economies and discusses how to deal with them. One disadvantage of this approach is, perhaps, that too much attention has been paid to problems and not enough to the very positive aspects of an open economy. For it is widely acknowledged that by opening up its economy, welcoming new technology, and competing with the rest of the world a country will become a genuine partner in worldwide progress.

Another issue that has not been treated in this volume, as mentioned above, is the attempts of many developing countries at present to enhance the productivity of their domestic capital. Unviable government plants are being closed, subsidies are being abolished, and in many cases efforts are being made to have the market mechanism replace government interventions. Although this volume does not treat, or deals relatively lightly with, such matters and the ongoing debt crisis, this fact does not in any way diminish their importance.

One last point: From this volume, as from many studies of economic policy, the reader may garner the impression that it is easy to determine the right economic policies to follow at any moment and that it is a rather straightforward matter to implement them. Reality is far different. Indeed, no country in the world has always followed the right economic policies. It is hoped, however, that this study has shown that it does not take policy miracles to produce good results. If major policies are largely in the right direction, then economic performance is likely to be quite successful.

Note

1. "Billion" refers to 1,000 million throughout. The symbol "$" refers to U.S. dollars unless otherwise specified.

2

The Real Exchange Rate

F. Leslie C. H. Helmers

ONE MAJOR LINE that is central to many (and present in all) of the discussions and reviews in this volume is the importance of the real exchange rate. This chapter provides an overview of how the concept of the real exchange rate may be used. The nominal-exchange-rate concept remains important because we need it for the analysis of debt issues, of the process of short-run market-clearing under flexible rates, and of many other problems. For the analysis of trade and current account balances, however, the nominal concept must be replaced by a real-exchange-rate concept.

There are two main reasons for working with a real exchange rate. First, there is a need to work in real terms to put the analysis of trade and current account movements on the same basis as the analysis of real supply, real demand, and real price of a single commodity. This is not difficult to understand. If export revenues increase in nominal terms just as much as the costs of producing the exports, for instance, then nothing has changed in real terms, though substantial changes may have occurred in nominal terms.

Second, there is a need to introduce some discipline into the analysis of the current account in a world that has many different exchange rate systems. We have the fixed-exchange-rate system, which does not contemplate devaluation of the domestic currency, but under which we in fact observe intermittent devaluations in many countries. We also have the clean-floating exchange-rate system, whereby the domestic currency is allowed to find its own level without any government intervention. In addition, there is a pure crawling-peg system, which contemplates frequent changes (say, once or twice a month) in the nominal rate in order to adjust for the inflation differential between the country concerned and the outside world. In other words, under this system the target is to fix the real exchange rate.

In practice, none of the three systems is pure. Multiple exchange rates are common in the fixed system, government interventions often take place in the floating system, and divergences from an absolute real-exchange-rate target are frequent under crawling-peg systems. Furthermore, the domestic currency may be tied to the U.S. dollar or to a basket of currencies of the main trading partners. In addition, there may be quantitative restrictions on the amounts of foreign exchange that the residents of a country are allowed to use for certain purposes. Real-exchange-rate analysis has the virtue of providing a common framework within which one can analyze current account movements under many different systems.

1. The Real Exchange Rate as the Price of Foreign Exchange

The real exchange rate can be defined in several different ways, as indicated in the previous chapter. One key distinction is whether the exchange rate is viewed as the price (measured in units of local money) of foreign currency or as the value (measured in foreign currency) of the local monetary unit. Some countries quote their official exchange rates in one way, some in the other. So, too, do authors. In the present volume, Bruno, Cavallo, Simonsen, and Gillis and Dapice base their definition of the real exchange rate on the first approach. Thus they measure the number of units of domestic goods (in real terms) per unit (that is, per real dollar's worth) of foreign output. This type of index may also be viewed as the price of a real dollar measured in real domestic currency units. Looked at in this way, the real exchange rate is nothing more than the relative price variable in a simple supply-and-demand analysis in which the quantity of real dollars demanded or supplied is expressed as a function of its real price.[1]

There are many other distinctions one might draw among the different views of and approaches to the real exchange rate. Most particularly, such distinctions would deal with the various alternative indexes that can be used to deflate the local currency component and the foreign currency component of the real exchange rate. For example, important insights flow from the use of the wage rate as the deflator of the local currency component. This use automatically makes the real exchange rate connote a real-wage-rate index (or its reciprocal), and it makes clear how policies influencing the real exchange rate often carry important political overtones and how they intertwine with wage policies (in those countries where that term is meaningful). Both Dornbusch and Fischer emphasize wages as a relevant deflator in a real-exchange-rate measure, at least for some important purposes.

The second way of measuring real exchange rates—the value of the domestic currency, measured in foreign money—is used by Dornbusch, Krugman, Fischer, and Cardoso and Levy in the present volume. This way of expressing the real exchange rate is simply the mirror image of the first, so no conceptual issues are involved.

In discussing the second approach, however, the above-named authors use a framework centered on the market for nontradable goods. To complement their approach, this chapter presents the framework of the foreign exchange market for the analysis of real exchange effects so that the reader will be familiar with both types of analysis. As will become evident, real-exchange-rate analysis in the context of the foreign exchange market is similar to standard microeconomic analysis of commodity markets.

2. Analysis of the Real Exchange Rate

Our treatment of real-exchange-rate effects is built on a series of assumptions that have traditionally been made in order to render the analysis more manageable. First, we assume that the world prices of imports and exports in dollars are given, that the country's imports and exports do not change these prices, and that the state of the world economy does not change. In addition, we take the tariff structure of the country as given. To avoid confusion, we will use the following terminology. For the domestic currency unit we take the rupiah, for the foreign currency unit the dollar. When more rupiah are paid for a dollar, we will say that the exchange rate increases or rises and that the rupiah depreciates or devalues. Vice versa, when fewer rupiah are paid for a dollar, the exchange rate falls or declines, and the rupiah appreciates or revalues.

Consider now figure 2-1. On the horizontal axis are measured the quantity of demand and supply of real dollars (for example, dollars deflated by the U.S. wholesale price index). On the vertical axis is measured the real exchange rate—that is, real rupiah per real dollar. The formula for the real exchange rate E is:

$$E = \frac{E_n/P_d}{\$1/P_w}$$

where E_n is the nominal exchange rate, P_d is the domestic price deflator (for example, the domestic consumer price index), and P_w is the deflator for the U.S. dollar (for example, as above, the U.S. wholesale price index).[2] Appendix C presents further details about this concept.

Figure 2-1 presents functions representing the demand for ($\overline{DD}$) and the supply of ($\overline{SS}$) foreign exchange. These functions should not be taken as simple supply and demand curves—in fact, they reflect a far subtler concept. The best way to think about these curves is to conceive of them as reflecting alternative equilibrium situations in the foreign exchange market. The intersection point of the curves reflects a situation in which there is no net movement of capital (or of the central bank's monetary reserves of foreign currency) in either direction.

Figure 2-1. Demand for and Supply of Real Dollars: Interaction between Capital Flows and the Real Exchange Rate

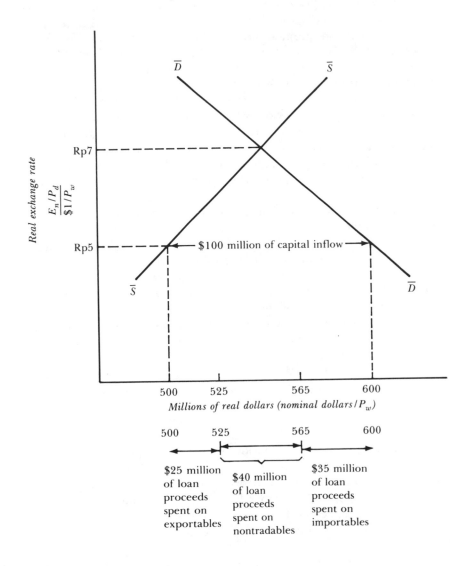

If Rp7 is the equilibrium real exchange rate for no net movement of capital, a real exchange rate such as Rp5 per dollar would reflect an equilibrium with a capital inflow of, say, $100 million (or with a reserve loss of like amount). Either the capital inflow or the reserve loss will reflect a situation in which total national expenditure exceeds total output.

We can now contemplate a situation in which, starting from an equilibrium real exchange rate of Rp5, the situation is modified so that the new equilibrium real rate is Rp7 to the dollar. In the simplest description of such a scenario, foreigners, having up to now been content to lend the country in question, say, $100 million a year, now decide to make new loans only to the extent that old ones are amortized. That is, the country's line of credit from abroad, which in the past had been expanding at the rate of $100 million a year, now stops increasing.

The first consequence of this drying up of foreign credits will be that those entities that were previously borrowing from abroad will have less money (real purchasing power) to spend. They will accordingly cut back their purchases, presumably by a like amount. Part of this cutback in spending will reduce the demand for exportables, part will reduce that for importables, and still another part will typically fall on the nontradables sector.

The reduction in home demand for exportables (here assumed to equal $25 million) will tend to increase actual exports and add to the available supply of foreign exchange. The reduction in home demand for importables (here taken to be $35 million) will quite clearly reduce the demand for imports and hence for foreign exchange. But these two effects will suffice to eliminate the initial trade deficit only in the case where the full proceeds of the loan were spent on the two classes of tradable goods. Most likely, the borrowers would spend some part of the loan on nontradables. In the present example, such spending amounts initially to $40 million.

When part of the loan was initially spent on nontradables and the supply of new loan money dries up, there will also be a reduction (by the domestic currency counterpart of $40 million) in the demand for nontradables. The result will be a pair of disequilibria, fully "compatible" with the assumption that total domestic spending equals total income produced plus the net inflow of funds from abroad. On the one hand, there will be, at the old real exchange rate of Rp5 to the dollar, a gap ($40 million in figure 2-1) between the demand for and supply of foreign exchange. On the other hand, corresponding to the excess demand for tradable goods will be an excess supply of nontradables, itself the outcome of the reduction in demand for that category of goods.

To equilibrate both markets, a relative price adjustment is required. This is the movement of the real exchange rate from Rp5 to Rp7 to the dollar. The rise in the real exchange rate will reduce the supply of and stimulate the demand for nontradable goods, thus eliminating the excess supply in that market. At the same time it will stimulate an expansion in the production of tradables (by making the production of both exportables and importables more profitable), while curtailing their demand through a rise in their relative price.

The full adjustment to the cessation of the net capital inflow will have taken place when the real exchange rate has moved up to Rp7.

Note that in the above scenario no explicit policy is required to cut back expenditures. That problem is directly solved by putting no new loan money into the borrowers' hands. All that is needed in this case, therefore, is an expenditure-switching policy (typically a devaluation of the currency) to produce the required rise in the real exchange rate.

Other scenarios are more complicated and may entail the use of both policies. The easiest case to treat is identical to the above, except that the government is assumed to be the entity that initially borrowed. Now, when the loan funds are no longer forthcoming, some explicit decision will typically be required to bring about a cutback in expenditures by the amount of the fall in net foreign borrowing. In this case, a combination of expenditure-reducing and expenditure-switching policies would be required to carry the economy to its new equilibrium at a real exchange rate of Rp7 to the dollar.

A third scenario is one in which the central bank jumps into the breach, as it were, and uses new credits to support the same outlays as those previously financed by foreign loans. The easiest variant of this scenario occurs with a fixed exchange rate. In such a case, the same trade deficit that was previously financed by foreign loans is now financed by a loss of international reserves of the banking system. Once the step is taken to replace foreign loans by domestic credit expansion, a combination of expenditure-reducing (in this case stopping credit expansion) along with expenditure-switching policies (a real devaluation) is now required in order to reach the new equilibrium.

A fourth scenario is like the third but does not entail an initial capital inflow from abroad. That is, from the beginning an excess of domestic spending over domestic production is financed in a direct way by the creation of new credit in the banking system but in a more fundamental way by the loss of foreign exchange reserves. (Note that there is no trade deficit nor any ex post excess of spending over production in this case, unless reserves are drawn down. Otherwise, the credit expansion spree will produce only inflation, which of course would have to be accompanied by a devaluation or a flexible exchange rate or new trade restrictions in order to avoid a reserve drain.)

In a sense, the fourth scenario is the most common among developing countries. In a country pursuing a fixed-exchange-rate policy, international reserves provide a sort of cushion, which allows a degree of independence in monetary and fiscal policy. If such a country engages in a spurt of deficit financing and if the spurt is reversed quickly enough, the final result may be merely a once-and-for-all loss of reserves. What is critical in this case is that the process should not go on so long that wages and other domestic costs rise to a level that is difficult if not impossible to reduce.

The scenario in this simple case would be that a spurt of credit expansion (either to the private or to the public sector) would cause the demands for exportables, importables, and nontradables *all* to shift to the right. This shift would cause (a) a deficit in the current account owing to increased imports and reduced exports and (b) a rise in the relative price of nontradable goods, that is, a fall in the real exchange rate. To rectify this situation in a sufficiently timely way, the only policy needed is to eliminate the spurt of credit expansion. This will shift the demand curves for importables, exportables, and nontradables back to their initial positions, and the country will be none the worse for the experience, apart from the loss of reserves that occurred in the interim.

In the above simple case no expenditure-switching policy is required. Because the entire "problem" came from expenditure generation, all that is needed to cope with it is expenditure curtailment. Readers should not consider this case as some sort of esoteric rarity. Quite to the contrary, it is part of the normal existence of any economy which successfully pursues a fixed-exchange-rate policy for any extended period.

The fifth scenario occurs when the fourth scenario gets out of hand. In this case, the credit expansion lasts so long that it has significant effects on nominal wages and other costs. The supply curves of all three categories of goods therefore shift upward and the nominal supply prices increase for given quantities. In this case the simple reversal of credit expansion will not do the trick because supply shifts have intervened. The easiest way to deal with this case is expenditure curtailment, together with devaluation, with the former policy working to curtail the current excess of expenditure over income and the latter one working to effectuate the needed amount of expenditure switching.

3. Expenditure Reducing and Expenditure Switching

The objective of the expenditure-reducing policy is to leave GDP unchanged while reducing domestic expenditures on consumption goods C and on investment goods I so that exports X minus imports M can rise.

One way of achieving this objective is for the government to reduce its expenditures on consumption goods and investment goods. Another way is to force the private sector to reduce its expenditures. In theory, wages could be reduced in order to cut private consumption, but in practice, political reasons make this almost always unfeasible. Tax increases are also possible but are difficult to implement, particularly in the short run. Another, more feasible policy is to restrict bank loans to the private sector so that private investment is curtailed. In principle, then, in some ways expenditures on C and I (and therefore on M, because M forms part of C and I) can be reduced.

Unfortunately, domestic expenditure-reducing policies have many negative side effects. Reduced expenditures on C and I, and therewith on M, will lead to unemployment and excess capacity in the C and I industries. The export industry X will not be able to absorb the freed resources immediately because the adjustment process takes time. Furthermore, if prices and wages are inflexible, then the export industry may not expand at all, because its profitability does not increase. Thus, although indeed there will be some improvements in the balance of payments because of reduced imports, GDP will very likely decline. In other words, expenditure-reducing policies may well lead to a recession.

Let us consider now how expenditure-switching policies work. To do so we must understand how the different types of domestic industry will be affected. In principle, we can distinguish four types of industries. First, there are the import-competing industries. They satisfy part of the domestic demand for importables, whereas the remaining part is provided by actual imports. Thus, when the rupiah price of imports increases, imports will decrease, whereas the import-competing industries will expand production (until the marginal resource cost equals the new higher import price in rupiah). Second, there are the exportables industries, whose production satisfies domestic demand as well as export demand. When the export price in rupiah increases, they will increase production (until the marginal resource cost equals the new higher export price in rupiah). The higher price for the products of these industries reduces domestic demand, so that production will be diverted to exports. In addition, exports will increase because of the production expansion. Third, there are industries producing goods and services only for the domestic market, but these products may become internationally traded if the exchange rate changes. Imports may take place if the rupiah price of imports falls substantially, for instance, and exports may take place if the rupiah price of exports increases substantially. Finally, some industries produce only pure home goods and services, which are not tradable at all, such as transport, construction, electricity, and many banking and insurance services. Both the third and the fourth type of industries may be considered producers of home goods or noninternationally traded goods.

Consider now what happens if the real exchange rate rises. Imports as well as export goods sold in the domestic market become more expensive. The reduced demand for these goods will be switched to import substitutes and home goods because both are relatively cheap. In addition, exports will increase because they become more profitable. In sum, there is a reduction in the demand by residents for foreign-produced goods and an increase in demand by residents, as well as increased foreign sales of domestically produced goods. Another way of expressing the switching effect is to say that the increase in the price of traded goods (imports and exports) switches domestic demand from the traded goods to home goods.

Figure 2-2 presents the effects of the expenditure-switching policies. The increase in the real exchange rate leads to movements along the supply and demand curves for real dollars. The result of these movements is that the balance of payments deficit, which is equal to D at a real exchange rate of Rp5 to a dollar, is being converted to a surplus S at a real exchange rate of Rp8 to a dollar. In this case, in contrast to the expenditure-reducing policy, we see that the expenditure switch caused by the increase in the real exchange rate does not lead to unemployment. In fact, we will see a resumption of growth because the export industries will expand, as will the import-substitute and home-goods industries.

The slopes of the supply and demand curves determine to what extent the real exchange rate needs to be raised to turn a deficit into a surplus. These slopes represent the responsiveness of trade to expenditure switching, and this will, of course, differ from country to country. In other words, the structural differences between countries determine the magnitude of required changes in the real exchange rate for balance of payments improvements.

Figure 2-2. The Effect of Expenditure-Switching Policies

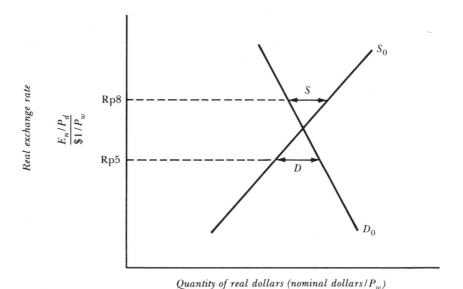

Quantity of real dollars (nominal dollars / P_w)

A problem is how to ensure that the real exchange rate rises. Suppose we increase the nominal exchange rate (more on this point below). Traded goods then become more expensive in nominal terms. In addition, however, the domestic price level will rise. As a result there will be demands for wage increases. In many countries, wages are indexed to the general price level, and a vicious circle may then begin: the general price increase leads to wage increases, which lead to further price increases, and so on. Such processes may in the end produce no increase at all in the real exchange rate. In such cases, expenditure-switching policies need to be combined with expenditure-reducing policies so that a general inflationary spiral can be averted and the real exchange rate can indeed rise.

4. Floating and Fixed Exchange Rates

The real exchange rate is the instrument for changing the expenditure patterns of a country. This statement applies to whatever exchange rate regime the country follows, although the mechanisms will be different. To illustrate, I will review briefly how floating- and fixed-exchange-rate systems work.

Variants of floating-rate regimes are now common for the leading industrial countries. Two conditions are necessary for effective operations of a floating-exchange-rate regime: first, there must be a well-developed market for the domestic currency, and second, there must be a well-developed internal capital market. The first condition is obvious; the second condition is necessary for control of the money supply and therefore of the real exchange rate. Suppose we want to increase the real exchange rate. In this case the central bank will buy outstanding bonds, or expand credit. Because the purchase price of the bonds will be given to residents, the money supply will be increased, thereby enabling residents to bid more rupiah for a dollar. When factors of production are idle, the increased money supply will not result in a general price increase, and the real exchange rate will thus go up. When the economy is operating at full capacity, the increased money supply will also lead to price increases, and the increase in the nominal exchange rate will thus be negated to a certain extent by the general price increase. When the economy is operating at full capacity, of course, there is no sense in overheating the economy.

International capital movements also affect the real exchange rate under a floating-exchange-rate regime. Figure 2-3 illustrates this point. There is a current deficit at Rp5 per dollar equal to a quantity of real dollars denoted by D, which is covered by a capital inflow. Thus the total supply of real dollars is indicated by the broken line, and the market mechanism has ensured that, at a price of Rp5 to a dollar, supply is equilibrated with demand. A capital inflow, of course, may be initially

Figure 2-3. The Real Exchange Rate and Capital Inflows

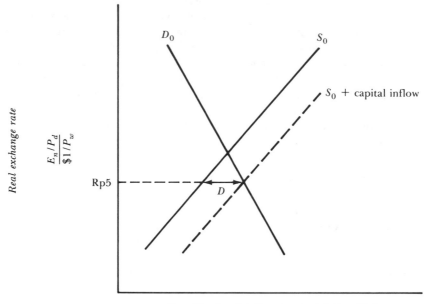

Quantity of real dollars (nominal dollars/P_w)

larger or smaller than the current account deficit (and similarly, of course, for capital outflows as compared with current account surplus). When the capital inflow exceeds the amount that is compatible with the prevailing real exchange rate, the rupiah price per dollar will decrease. Given the internal price level, the real exchange rate will fall. Consequently, importers will demand more dollars and exporters will supply fewer dollars. Expenditures will exceed income, and there will be a new larger equilibrium current account deficit at a lower real exchange rate.

Unfortunately, floating-exchange-rate regimes have their problems too. Recent experiences have shown that short-term capital movements are often quite large and spurious. Because capital flows affect the real exchange rate, overshooting or undershooting of real-exchange-rate targets because of the speculative capital movements occurs often.

Let us consider now a fixed-exchange-rate regime. This type of regime is at present used mainly by developing countries whose currencies have no outside market and whose internal markets are weak. The money supply is a function of the government deficit, central bank policies with respect to the commercial banks, and international capital movements. Suppose we want to increase the real exchange rate. In this case the government must set the domestic currency at such a level that the devaluation exceeds the expected inflation rate, which is, of course, determined by the money supply.

Just as in a floating-exchange-rate regime, increased capital inflows will lead to a fall in the real exchange rate. The mechanism is different, however. Whereas in a floating-rate regime additional capital inflows lead directly to a lower price for the dollar in the foreign exchange market, in a fixed-exchange-rate regime the additional capital will lead to an increase in the money supply so that prices will rise and the real exchange rate will fall.

Thus the way in which real-exchange-rate adjustments take place depends on the exchange rate regime a country has. In principle, under a floating-exchange-rate regime, domestic money supply and foreign exchange flows determine the real exchange rate in the foreign exchange market, whereas under a fixed-exchange-rate regime adjustments take place through devaluations and movements of the domestic price level.

The supply and demand curves of foreign exchange shift when foreign or domestic incomes change. A contraction of world income, for instance, shifts the supply curve to the left, and as discussed earlier, a contraction of domestic income shifts the demand curve to the left. In addition, there are shifts peculiar to the foreign exchange market. Table 2-1 provides in shorthand notation an overview of such shifts.

Table 2-1 may be summarized as follows. As in any supply-and-demand analysis, the real exchange rate will change if the underlying supply and demand curves shift. Furthermore, the change in the real exchange rate will be in the same direction whatever the exchange rate regime may be. If there are large autonomous capital inflows, the real exchange rate will fall. If the world price of exports increases, the supply curve will also shift to the right and the real exchange rate will fall again. A decrease in the world price of imports, however, may cause the demand curve to shift either to the left or to the right, depending on the elasticity of demand. In this case, the effect on the real exchange rate cannot be determined a priori. Abolition of import duties, however, will increase the demand for real dollars so that the demand curve shifts to the right and the real exchange rate rises (figure 2-4). Abolition of export duties makes exports more attractive so that the supply curve shifts to the right and the real exchange rate falls (figure 2-5). The same effect occurs if exporters become more efficient. Thus the more efficient exporters are, the lower the real exchange rate will be.

I do not wish to draw policy conclusions from the above analysis because in doing so I would duplicate the points made by the other writers in the next chapters. Still, a few pointers may be useful:

- Expenditure-switching policies often need to be complemented by expenditure-reducing policies.

Table 2-1. Examples of Real Exchange Rate Movements under Floating- and Fixed-Exchange-Rate Systems

Floating exchange rate	*Fixed exchange rate*

Capital inflows

Capital inflows affect the real exchange rate only to the extent that they are spent on nontradable goods and services. This rule is logical: if the inflow of dollars is spent only on the outflow of dollars caused by the current account deficit, then no monetary expansion occurs. Only to the extent that capital inflow is spent on nontradables will there be a monetary expansion (the central bank issues rupiah for the dollar inflow). This assumes, of course, that the central bank does not sterilize the inflow by issuing bonds (not possible in developing countries without domestic capital markets).

The excess supply of dollars causes the real exchange rate to fall.	The excess supply of dollars leads to an increase in the general price level. The real exchange rate falls.

Increase in the dollar price of exports or reduction in the real production cost of exports

The supply curve of dollars shifts to the right.

The increased supply of dollars causes the real exchange rate to fall.	The increased supply of dollars (converted by the central bank into rupiah at the fixed exchange rate) leads to a monetary expansion, which increases the general price level. The real exchange rate falls.

Increase in the dollar price of imports

When the demand for dollars (to be used for imports) is inelastic (for instance, when importers want the dollars whatever the price), then the demand curve for dollars shifts to the right.

The increased demand for dollars leads to a rise in the real exchange rate.	The increased demand for dollars means that more rupiah will be converted into dollars. The domestic monetary contraction leads to a fall in the general price level. The real exchange rate rises.

When imports have an elastic demand, the demand curve shifts to the left.

Table 2-1 (*continued*)

Floating exchange rate	Fixed exchange rate
The reduced demand for dollars leads to a fall in the real exchange rate.	Fewer rupiah will be converted into dollars. The domestic monetary expansion leads to a rise in the general price level; the real exchange rate falls.

Reduction or elimination of import duties

Total expenditures minus import duties represent what importers spend on dollars for imports. When import duties are reduced, importers can buy more dollars for the same total expenditures. Thus the demand curve shifts to the right.

The increased demand for dollars leads to a rise in the real exchange rate.	More rupiah will be converted into dollars. The domestic monetary contraction causes the general price level to fall; the real exchange rate rises.

As shown in figure 2-4 (where t_m stands for import duties as a fraction of c.i.f.[a] imports), the real exchange rate rises from E_0 to E_1. Importers are better off because their real exchange rate falls from $E_0 (1 + t_m)$ to E_1. Exporters are better off because their real exchange rate increases from E_0 to E_1.

Reduction or elimination of export duties

Export duties are just like resource costs in that they represent necessary outlays for exporters. Hence, lower export duties reduce the outlay required for a given quantity of exports. Thus the supply curve shifts to the right.

The increased supply of dollars leads to a fall in the real exchange rate.	More dollars will be converted into rupiah. The domestic monetary expansion leads to a rise in the general price level; the real exchange rate falls.

As shown in figure 2-5 (where t_x stands for export duties as a fraction of f.o.b.[a] exports), the real exchange rate falls from E_0 to E_1. Exporters are better off since their real exchange rate increases from $E_0 (1 - t_x)$ to E_1. Importers are better off since their real exchange rate falls from E_0 to E_1.

a. c.i.f. = cost, insurance, and freight; f.o.b. = free on board.

Figure 2-4. Elimination of Import Duties

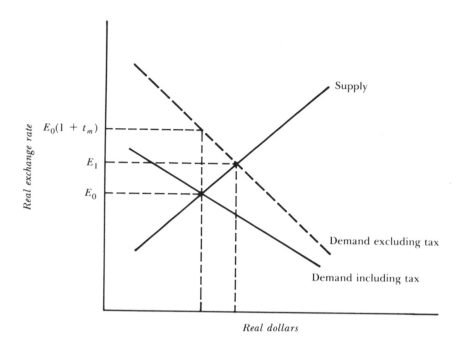

Real dollars

- The longer one waits to implement a devaluation (once the situation calls for it), the more harmful the adjustment process will be.
- Because large speculative capital inflows (by causing a decline in the real exchange rate) will negate the effect of a devaluation, immediate liberalization of capital flows may not be in the best interest of a country.
- Liberalization of import duties or other import restrictions will lead to a rise in the real exchange rate, thus providing incentives to export industries.
- Reduction or abolition of export duties is an appropriate way to increase the supply of dollars and to reduce a balance of payments deficit. A devaluation combined with the elimination of export duties will not need to be as severe as when export duties are left unchanged.
- Opening up the economy typically leads in the long run to a fall in the real exchange rate.

Figure 2-5. Elimination of Export Duties

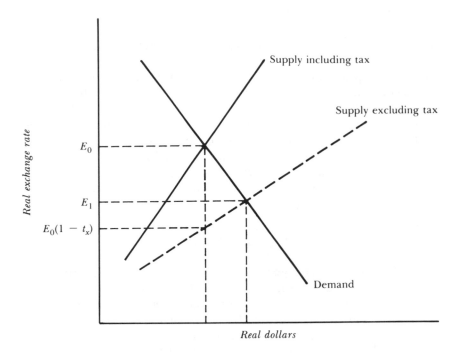

This last point needs to be emphasized. When the economy is opened up, efficiency, especially of exporters, increases. As a result the real exchange rate falls over time. Is this good or bad? It is good, of course, because it means that fewer real resources are necessary to earn a certain standard of living. This point also elucidates the static and dynamic aspects of real-exchange-rate policies. In a static situation, we need to increase the real exchange rate so that more real resources can be devoted to exports and import substitutes. In a dynamic situation, the consequence is that the economy becomes more open to outside competition and that domestic industries will become more efficient. Therefore, gradually (or sometimes quickly) the real exchange rate can fall over time.

The broad analysis presented here is no substitute for the detailed expenditure-switching analysis discussed in many chapters in this volume. Still, the broader analysis makes clear why, for instance, Bruno is worried that capital inflows may offset the effects of a devaluation or why increased protectionism leads to a fall in the real exchange rate.

Both types of analyses—and this point is probably the most important—explain why real-exchange-rate adjustments can lead to a restoration of growth as well as of external balance.

5. Effects of Changes in the Real Exchange Rate

To provide a practical context for the preceding analysis, I will discuss in this section the relationship between the real exchange rate and the trade balance for the five countries used as examples in Part III of this book.[3] I use the most basic definitions (see appendix C for a review of real-exchange-rate indexes). The real exchange rate is expressed here as the price in real domestic currency units of a real dollar. For the domestic price deflator I use the domestic consumer price index; for the dollar deflator I use the U.S. wholesale price index. Thus the formula for the real exchange rate is:

$$E = \frac{E_n/P_d}{\$1/P_w} = \frac{E_n \cdot P_w}{P_d}$$

where E is the real exchange rate, E_n is the nominal exchange rate, P_d is the domestic consumer price index, and P_w is the U.S. wholesale price index. The data are readily available in *International Financial Statistics* (IFS). The nominal exchange rate E_n is found in the *rf* line, the domestic consumer price index in line 64, and the U.S. wholesale price index in line 63. All indexes have their base of 100 in 1980. The real exchange rate is thus expressed as the price in 1980 domestic currency for a 1980 dollar.

Because we are interested in the effects of the real exchange rate on exports and imports, we use the trade balance instead of the current account balance, which includes the factor payments to abroad. This trade balance in current dollars is reported in line 77 ac d of the IFS. By deflating line 77 ac d by the U.S. wholesale price index, we find the real trade balance expressed in 1980 dollars.

The data used in the five country examples cover the period 1973 through 1985 and are presented in graphic form in figure 2-6. The left vertical axis shows the real exchange rate (note, however, that the inflation zeros before the decimals have been omitted for Argentina and Brazil); the right vertical axis presents the real trade balance in billions of 1980 dollars.

The reader will notice that there is a remarkable relationship between the real exchange rate and the real trade balance, although sometimes with a time lag for the latter. As the analysis in the preceding section suggested, when the real exchange rate increases, exports increase and imports fall, and thus the trade balance improves. The analysis of such movements along the supply and demand curves, how-

Figure 2-6. Real Exchange Rate and Real Trade Balance, 1973–85

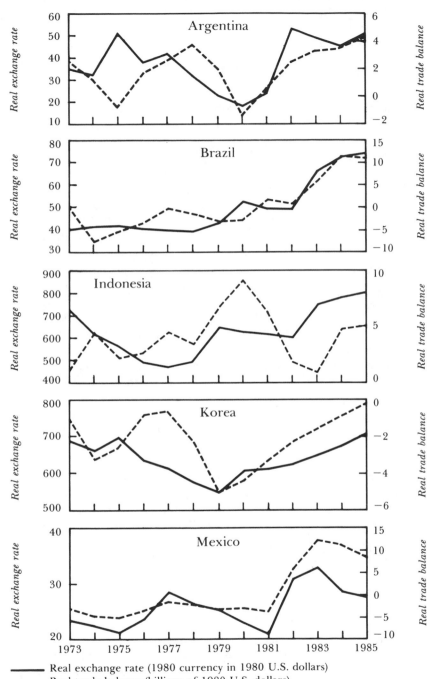

Real exchange rate (1980 currency in 1980 U.S. dollars)
Real trade balance (billions of 1980 U.S. dollars)

Source: IMF, *International Financial Statistics.*

ever, must be complemented with an analysis of supply and demand shifts that are due to autonomous factors, such as oil price increases. The types of real-exchange-rate policies and external factors influencing the trade balances of the five countries are highlighted below.

Argentina

To understand Argentina's policies, we must consider the government deficits as reported in line 80 of the IFS. In 1969, the government deficit as a percentage of GDP was at the low level of 1.2 percent. Since then, the deficit increased until it reached a high of about 10 percent of GDP in 1975. To a large extent, the deficit was monetized and the consequent inflation rate reached a peak of 443 percent in 1976. By devaluing the domestic currency more than the inflation rate, Argentina was able to achieve a steady rise in the real exchange rate until 1975. The trade balance did not present noteworthy problems except those due to outside shocks. The sharp deterioration in 1975, for instance, was caused by the worldwide recession, which caused Argentina's earnings from merchandise exports to fall in real dollars by some 31 percent (a shift to the left of the supply curve).

From 1975 through 1980, the government deficit was reduced to about 3 percent of GDP. At the same time, the domestic currency was strengthened (that is, the real exchange rate was reduced) to help combat inflation. Indeed, the two measures reduced the inflation rate to 101 percent in 1980, but as figure 2-6 shows, the trade balance deteriorated to an unsustainable level.

Policies changed again in 1981. Since then, the government deficit increased again (it reached 11.8 percent of GDP in 1983), borrowing from abroad accelerated, and import controls which had been abolished during 1978–80 were reinstated. The inflation rate increased and reached 672 percent in 1985. Depreciation of the domestic currency at a rate greater than that of inflation allowed the real exchange rate to rise so that the trade balance could improve, which indeed occurred to a significant extent. Because of the large external debt built up over a period of heavy foreign borrowing, however, net factor payments to abroad amounted to about 10 percent of GDP and 67 percent of exports in 1984, making it difficult for Argentina to service its debt.

Brazil

In contrast with Argentina and Mexico, Brazil has almost always had its government budget in equilibrium. The unique feature of Brazil is that from 1968 to 1979 it had a crawling-peg system combined with wage indexation. The target was to fix the real exchange rate. Indeed, as figure 2-6 shows, from 1973 through 1978 the real exchange rate was very stable.

The quadrupling of oil prices in 1974 led to a trade deficit of almost $8 billion in 1980 dollars as compared with equilibrium in 1973. To deal with this problem, the authorities did not want to adjust the real exchange rate but increased subsidies to exporters (thereby causing a shift of the supply curve of real dollars to the right) and imposed higher import duties (thereby shifting the demand curve for real dollars to the left). Indeed, the measures helped and the trade balance improved. This improvement was further helped by a jump in export demand for coffee in 1976. In 1977, the trade balance was again in equilibrium.

Bad crops of soybeans in 1978 and 1979 and rising imports led to trade deficits measured in 1980 dollars of about $1.5 billion in 1978 and $3.1 billion in 1979. The government raised the real exchange rate by about 30 percent, and the trade balance became slightly positive in 1981 and 1982. This shift was not enough, however. The past borrowing needed to finance the balance of payments deficits had resulted in increased interest payments to abroad. In 1981 and 1982, factor payments to abroad amounted to about $10 billion and $13 billion (in 1980 dollars), respectively.

Instead of raising the real exchange rate in 1981 and 1982, Brazil financed the deficits by heavy short-term borrowing. When the supply of external credit became tighter because of Mexico's debt crisis, Brazil had to raise the real exchange rate, which it did in February 1983 by some 30 percent. The results were spectacular: in 1984, the trade balance had a surplus of more than $11 billion (in 1980 dollars), and the current account of the balance of payments was in equilibrium for the first time in many years.

Indonesia

The Indonesian regime is a fixed-exchange-rate system with emphasis on adjustments when the real exchange rate gets out of line. Government deficits have not been a stimulus to inflation because deficits, if they occurred, were always relatively small.

In 1971 Indonesia devalued the rupiah from Rp378 to Rp415 to the dollar. The inflation rate, however, which was only 4 percent in 1971, was allowed to increase to a peak of 33 percent in 1974; it was brought down to 7 percent in 1978. As a result, the real exchange rate declined during the entire period 1971 through 1977. Fortunately, the trade balance did not deteriorate because oil prices increased in 1973. In 1974, real dollar earnings (in 1980 dollars) from oil exports rose by some 170 percent, and the trade balance reached a comfortable $4.4 billion (in 1980 dollars). Although the world recession in 1975 caused earnings to fall, the trade balance remained very positive through 1978, and foreign exchange reserves continued to rise. As Gillis and Dapice point out in their country study, there was no pressure to devalue because of inadequate foreign exchange or a poor trade balance.

Nevertheless, the heavy dependence on oil (in 1977 oil accounted for 67 percent of export revenues), the stagnation of the rubber industry, and the need for diversification into labor-intensive export industries led the authorities to devalue the currency at the end of 1978 to the level of Rp625 to the dollar. The results were spectacular: in 1979, non-oil exports increased in real terms by some 36 percent. Further increases in oil prices in 1980, and slow growth of imports because of the higher real exchange rate, resulted in 1980 in an all-time high surplus in the trade balance of about $9.2 billion and in the current account balance of about $2.9 billion.

The surpluses were not, however, sterilized (Indonesia has no internal capital market), nor was aggregate demand contracted. The money supply and domestic credit therefore increased tremendously. Because import controls had been loosened after the devaluation of 1978, imports surged in 1981 and 1982, so that inflation rates were held to the modest levels of 6 percent and 9 percent, respectively. The real exchange rate was not pushed up, however, and by the end of 1982, increased imports and stagnating exports had reduced the trade surplus to only $1.7 billion (in 1980 dollars), or a drop of $7.5 billion from the high in 1980. Similarly, the current account balance deteriorated and showed a deficit of $4.8 billion in 1982. Capital started to flee the country.

A devaluation of almost 40 percent took place in the second quarter of 1983. The results became already apparent in 1984 when the trade balance moved to a surplus of $4.8 billion and the deficit in the current account balance settled at $1.8 billion (1980 dollars).

Republic of Korea

Korea's success story is well known. What is less well known, however, is that Korea has consistently had deficits year after year amounting to several percentage points of GDP in its current account of the balance of payments. From the early 1950s through the mid-1960s, these deficits were mainly financed by foreign aid flows and thereafter by direct equity investments and foreign lending. Nonetheless, in 1973, the foreign debt was still at a very comfortable level: interest payments amounted to slightly more than 2 percent of export revenues.

The oil-price increases in 1973 (given an inelastic demand for oil) caused imports in 1980 dollars to jump by some 40 percent (the demand curve for dollars thus shifted to the right). The trade balance deteriorated from a deficit of $1.1 billion in 1973 to a deficit of $3.3 billion in 1974 (in 1980 dollars). In 1975, Korea devalued its exchange rate from W400 to W484 to the dollar. It kept that rate until 1980 and the result was, of course, that the inflation, which reached a high of 25 percent in 1975 and fluctuated thereafter between 10 percent and 18 percent, pushed the real exchange rate down. The result was to be expected. After an improvement in the real trade balance in 1976 and 1977 due to the world's economic recovery, the deficit in the trade balance reached $5 billion in 1979.

Korea had learned its lessons well. Immediately after the second oil-price shock in 1980, the currency was devalued from W484 to W600 to the dollar. Furthermore, contractionary aggregate demand policies curtailed imports so that the trade balance improved almost immediately.

The early 1980s were quite inflationary for Korea. The government deficit, which was at the low level of 1.3 percent of GDP in 1978, rose to a peak of 3.5 percent in 1982. The inflation rate, which had jumped to 31 percent in 1980, was still at 21 percent in 1981. By devaluing the currency more than the inflation rate, however, and by curtailing domestic expenditures, Korea was able to increase its trade balance while reducing its inflation.

By 1984, the government deficit had been reduced to 1.1 percent of GDP, and the inflation had fallen to the low level of 2.3 percent. Furthermore, the deficit in the trade balance had been reduced to less than $1 billion (in 1980 dollars), and the current account deficit was only slightly larger. Interest payments on the foreign debt amounted to about 7 percent of export earnings, still a comfortable level.

Mexico

Mexico had a very successful economic record from the mid-1950s until the early 1970s, when things got out of line. The government deficit, which was about 1 percent of GDP in 1970–71, increased to almost 5 percent in 1975. The deficit was financed by increases in the money supply, which caused the inflation rate to rise from about 7 percent in 1970–71 to about 20 percent in 1974–75. The nominal exchange rate during this period was fixed at 12.50 pesos to the dollar, but the real exchange rate fell because of the inflation. Consequently, the trade balance deteriorated. A very substantial devaluation took place in 1976, when the new exchange rate was set at 22 pesos to the dollar.

During 1976–81, budget deficits were lowered to the level of about 3 percent of GDP except in 1981 when the deficit jumped to 6.7 percent. The inflation rate reached a peak of 29 percent in 1977, dropped to 17 percent in 1978, and then rose to 28 percent in 1981. The real exchange rate declined steadily. The trade balance, however, which had improved substantially in 1977 because of the devaluation, did not deteriorate, because Mexico's oil sector had become a significant export earner. Exports, measured in real dollars, increased three and one-half times between 1976 and 1981. Unfortunately, the declining real exchange rate also led to substantial increases in imports, so that during the entire period 1976–81 the trade balance remained negative. The policy error during this period was that the real exchange rate was not pushed up by further devaluations combined with cuts in domestic expenditures to maintain a positive trade balance. If the error had been avoided, the substantial borrowings that became necessary to finance the balance of payments deficits could have been prevented.

The rest of the story is well known. In 1982, Mexico had difficulty in paying off its debt. Furthermore, the fiscal deficit increased to 15 percent of GDP and the inflation rate to 59 percent. Massive devaluations in 1982 and 1983 pushed up the real exchange rate. Indeed, the trade balance became largely positive for the first time in many years. Unfortunately, the real exchange rate was again allowed to decline in 1984 and 1985, and the real trade balance started to deteriorate. The collapse in oil prices, which started in November 1985, exacerbated Mexico's problems further.

Notes

1. The analysis in this chapter goes back a long time and may be found in pre–World War II European textbooks. Classic articles include Fritz Machlup, "The Theory of Foreign Exchange," *Economica,* vol. 6 (1939), pp. 375–397, and Gottfried Haberler, "The Market of Foreign Exchange and the Stability of the Balance of Payments: A Theoretical Analysis," *Kyklos,* vol. 3 (1949), pp. 193–218.

Also writing in the classic tradition is Arnold C. Harberger, at whose suggestion section 2 in this chapter was included. The author wishes to acknowledge his great debt to Harberger's analysis, particularly as found in the following papers prepared for the Economic Development Institute of the World Bank: "Trade Policy for a Developing Country" (July 1984), "Trade Policy and the Real Exchange Rate" (March 1985), "Issues of Tariff Policy" (April 1985), and "Applications of Real Exchange Rate Analysis" (June 1986).

2. The quantity of real dollars (the horizontal axis) multiplied by real rupiah per real dollar (the vertical axis) gives us real rupiah earnings or real rupiah expenditures. For imports, for instance, the real rupiah expenditures would be found as follows:

$$\frac{N}{P_w} \cdot \frac{E_n/P_d}{\$1/P_w} = \frac{N \cdot E_n}{P_d}$$

where N stands for the nominal dollar expenditures, P_w is the U.S. wholesale price index, E_n is the nominal exchange rate, and P_d is the domestic consumer price index. Each point on the supply and demand curves thus corresponds to a certain level of real rupiah earnings and expenditures, respectively.

3. The graphical analysis presented in this section is similar to Cavallo's analysis in chapter 12, figure 12-7 in this volume, and Harberger's analysis in "Applications of Real Exchange Rate Analysis" (paper prepared for the Economic Development Institute of the World Bank, June 1986; processed). The Dornbusch analysis in chapter 5 of this volume is, of course, also applicable. The only difference is that the analysis in this chapter takes reciprocal form, as contrasted with the Dornbusch analysis.

Part I

Policy Issues and the Main Policy Tools

3

Balance of Payments Issues

Rudiger Dornbusch

THERE ARE, broadly speaking, three reasons for discussing the policy issues of an open economy. First, policymakers need to understand the environment in which they operate. Open-economy issues arise every day. Second, policymakers need to make judgments as to where the economy is moving—whether opportunities are opening up or closing down. Third, policymakers need to make decisions. For each of these reasons, it helps to know something about the main relations and regulations of an open economy.[1]

Throughout this chapter I will adopt the perspective of a small country, namely, a country that takes as given the economic activities occurring in the rest of the world. The external activities are exogenous to the home country's policies, and they provide an environment in which policy is set. The first task is to identify this external environment.

1. An Overview of Linkages

Figure 3-1 shows a schematic overview of the economy. Three kinds of markets are identified. At the center is the market for goods. Goods may be either traded or nontraded. Traded goods enter international trade and are divided into exportables and importables. Nontraded goods, by contrast, are not traded, though they may have the potential of being traded. The labor market is the key factor market. The assets markets are represented by the money and credit markets.

The schematic presentation shows that the markets are interrelated. The rest of the world (ROW for short) influences each of these markets. The task is to identify the influences of the rest of the world on the home economy.

Figure 3-1. An Overview of the Economy

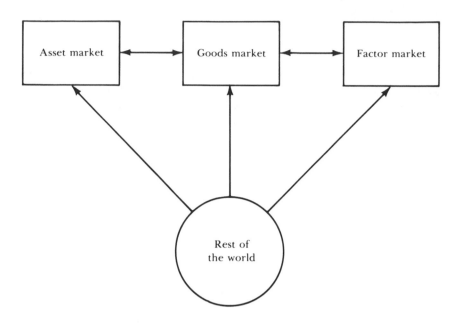

The Goods Market Linkages

Trade in goods is the most obvious link with the rest of the world. A country exports part of the goods produced at home and imports some final consumption goods, machinery, and industrial inputs. This trade establishes linkages in two ways. The rest of the world influences the prices at which we trade in world markets. For certain groups of goods, the ROW also determines the volume of our export sales.

We can highlight the effects of ROW on our goods market in different ways. We can speak of prices and quantities separately for exports and for imports. We can also speak of revenue derived from export sale and import spending. We can speak of the terms of trade (the ratio of export to import prices) or of the purchasing power of our exports (the amount of imports that our exports can buy). Each of these ways expresses the interdependence in goods markets.

Consider the example of Brazil. Table 3-1 shows a number of price and income measures. The export and import price indexes, for instance, allow a comparison over time of the dollar prices of what was received per unit of export and what was spent on a unit of import. Brazil's dependence on the world economy is quite apparent in the case of oil. When world oil prices rise, Brazil must pay more per barrel, and the economy must adjust to that higher cost. If the world price of soya

Table 3-1. Trade and Income Measures in Brazil, 1979–84

Item	1979	1980	1981	1982	1983	1984
Export price	94	100	94	88	84	85
Coffee	108	100	89	69	68	72
Soya	111	100	110	97	94	114
Import price	78	100	111	107	102	97
Oil	60	100	113	117	102	99
Terms of trade	121	100	85	82	82	88
Export value						
(billions of U.S. dollars)	15.2	20.1	23.3	20.2	21.9	27.0
Export volume	81	100	120	110	126	150
Purchasing power of exports	97	100	104	94	107	138

Source: Central Bank of Brazil, *Bulletin.*

rises, Brazil as a net exporter of soybeans enjoys the benefit of selling at a higher price. The price increase will affect the economy through a number of channels.

The terms of trade (TOT) measure gauges the behavior of export relative to import prices.

$$(3\text{-}1) \qquad \text{TOT} = \text{Export price}/\text{Import price}$$

This index is of interest because it focuses on the question of whether our export prices have done well relative to import prices. The relative price matters because a doubling of export prices would help little if, at the same time, import prices tripled. The TOT measure is one of the most important indicators of external shocks to the economy. An improvement in the terms of trade is a good thing; a deterioration is an adverse shock. For Brazil, 1979–84 represents a period of adverse terms of trade. But what is a big or a small deterioration? What should one make of the 27 percent (88/121) deterioration during 1979–84? The cost of a terms of trade deterioration can be measured by the following formula:

$$(3\text{-}2) \qquad \text{Cost of TOT deterioration} =$$
$$\text{Percentage TOT change} \cdot \text{Imports}/\text{GDP}$$

This expression measures the burden of the increased cost of imports as a fraction of income or GDP. In Brazil, the ratio of imports to GDP is about 10 percent, and hence the cost (or benefit) of the terms of trade change would be equivalent to the loss of about 3 percent of a year's output. The 3 percent constitutes about half of the growth in a good year. The formula makes it clear that a terms of trade improvement—a positive terms of trade change—represents a gain in real income. This simple measure makes it easy to calculate the cost on the back of an envelope; it is simply the import/income ratio times the percentage change in the terms of trade.[2]

The TOT measure of exposure to the world economy takes into account only prices, not quantities. It does not make allowance for the fact that, even though our export prices may have done poorly, when compared with import prices, our export volume may have increased greatly. A measure that takes into account export volume is the purchasing power of exports. It is defined as the product of the terms of trade and the index of export volume.

(3-3)   Purchasing power of exports = TOT · Export volume

Even if the terms of trade decline, a sufficient increase in export volume can make up for it in the sense that we can afford the same amount of imports. It thus seems a handy measure to judge the influence of the world economy. Still, that is not really the case. The increased export volume must come from somewhere: increased effort, reduction in home consumption, or increased productivity. Only in increased productivity is there an unambiguous benefit to the economy. In the first two cases, the ability to import more has some domestic cost.

In one case, however, equation 3-3 does give an indication of some benefit. For some of the goods exported by developing countries, markets are not perfectly competitive, so that there are abnormal or excessive profits. In such a case, increased export volume is an unquestioned blessing because every extra unit sold brings excess profits; the level of demand does matter. Just as a barber likes to see a long queue of customers, so do our exporter-oligopolists.

Table 3-1 shows conflicting answers provided by equations 3-2 and 3-3. The TOT measure indicates that the world economy has an adverse influence on Brazil. The purchasing-power-of-export measure, because of strong growth in trade volume, shows a gain. Though there is no general rule about which measure to pick, it helps to be a bit skeptical of the purchasing-power measure.

The impact of world prices and volume of trade has so far been discussed in terms of costs or benefits, but other aspects are important from a policy point of view. Changes in world prices, whether favorable or unfavorable, will not only affect the economy by changing the standard of living but will also exert a direct impact on inflation and resource allocation. For example, if the price of an exported good that is an important item in the cost of living, rises, the price increase can have an important effect on consumer prices and may spread first to wages, and then to industries far away from the initial sector where the disturbance occurred.

The resource-allocation channel works in the following fashion. When a sector's price rises, the industry will increase its profits and will try to expand. Firms or farms will try to attract more resources to increase production, sales, and profits. They will take resources away from other sectors that cannot afford to pay the higher wages. Increased export prices in some industries will thus draw resources from elsewhere: from import-competing industries, from other export industries, and from the nontraded-goods sector. These reallocations of resources often pose important issues for public policy.

Factor Markets Linkages

There are two factor markets linkages of a country to the rest of the world. The first is international mobility of labor; the second is mobility of capital.

Labor mobility has become an important feature of the past decade. Migrations have taken place from the poorer countries of Europe to the richer ones, from Central America and Mexico to the United States, and from neighboring countries and places as far away as Korea to oil-producing states in the Middle East. These labor movements, whether short term or more permanent, affect the economy through a number of channels. First, they influence the labor supply in the home country. Second, through remittances, they influence the home country's income. Finally, in a longer-term perspective they may be an effective way of training labor.

Capital mobility may take one of three forms. The home country may borrow abroad by issuing debt. The country may receive foreign equity in existing firms. The country may also permit direct investment. These three forms are very different indeed. Borrowing sometimes locks a country into a fixed debt service arrangement. The debt crisis of the 1980s highlighted in an extreme fashion how changes in world interest rates, by changing debt service obligations, shocked debtors. If their investment had been financed predominantly by equity rather than debt, the interest rate shock would have been less severe to the debtors.

Assets Market Linkages

The assets market linkages arise from the fact that some people choose to hold their wealth abroad despite legal and even physical obstacles. The less stable the finances of a country are, and the lower the rewards associated with holding assets, the more likely capital is to flee abroad.

The idea is very simple: if an asset holder in the United States can get a return of 10 percent a year, but an asset holder in Mexico can get only 3 percent, and if in Mexico the exchange currency depreciates by 50 percent a year, who will hold pesos? Everybody will try to hold a maximum of liquid assets in U.S. securities. This course of action may not be practical for many people whose wealth is too small to permit them to approach U.S. financial institutions. They may simply hold dollar bills.

In Argentina, for example, the public holds an estimated $3 billion in U.S. currency.[3]

The international linkage of asset markets is, perhaps, the most immediate and strongest of the linkages. When prices in a country get out of line with those abroad, it may take a while before they make a strong impact on the economy. But when interest rates adjusted for exchange depreciation get out of line, there is an immediate, highly visible pressure from capital flight. Reserves will be lost or the exchange rate will drop.

Controls on international capital flows might seem an effective way to break this international linkage when it becomes a burdensome restraint on policy. Such controls do not always work, however. Capital mobility is, therefore, a fact policymakers must recognize and learn to live with.

2. Basic Accounting Concepts

Macroeconomics is organized around the accounting concepts of production, income, and expenditure. These concepts and the accounting relationships between them, called budget constraints, provide important insights.

Two basic identities stand in the foreground:

(3-4)   Value of output produced = Value of incomes paid out

(3-5)   Value of income received = Expenditure + Saving

We start with the definition of gross national product (GNP) as the value of income received by residents from the factors of production they own anywhere in the world. Gross domestic product (GDP), which is complementary to GNP, is the value of output produced in a country by all the collaborating factors of production, whether they are domestically owned or owned by nonresidents. A third relation links domestic production, incomes received by residents, and net factor payments from abroad (NFP):

(3-6)   GNP = GDP + NFP

NFP will tend to be positive for a country like Pakistan where substantial remittances from workers located abroad are the rule. Conversely, in a country that has a large external debt contracted by firms to finance capital accumulation, NFP will be negative so that income falls short of the value of output.

The Current Account, Income, and Spending

The next relationship involves the current account, income, and spending. The current account measures net receipts (surplus) or net payments (deficit) for goods and services, including unilateral transfers. The net receipts of domestic residents are simply total receipts less total payments by residents, because intraresident receipts and payments cancel from the totals within the country. Thus total receipts less total payments is equal to net receipts from the rest of the world:

(3-7)   Current account = Total receipts − Total payments

Total receipts are equal to income received by residents—which is GNP plus transfers. Total payments are expenditure on goods or services, denoted by *E*, plus transfers made. Thus the current account (CA) is equal to GNP plus net transfers (NTR) less expenditure (*E*).

(3-8)   CA = GNP + NTR − *E*

One can also look at the current account in terms of saving, investment, and government budget. For that purpose we recognize that the total income plus net transfers received by residents is either saved (*S*), paid in taxes (*T*), or consumed (*C*)—that is, GNP + NTR = *C* + *T* + *S*.[4] Total expenditure is the total of government spending (*G*), household consumption spending (*C*), and investment spending by firms (*I*)—that is, *E* = *G* + *C* + *I*. Substituting these expressions on the right hand side of equation 3-8 yields:

(3-9) $CA = (S − I) + (T − G)$

Identities 3-8 and 3-9 are critical to the understanding of external balance issues. They state:

- Current account deficits reflect an excess of expenditure over income. To correct a deficit, expenditure must be cut or receipts must be increased. The effectiveness of any proposed policy to improve the external balance must be evaluated in terms of equation 3-8 to judge whether it can achieve the objective.

- Improvements in current account can be brought about only if saving rises relative to investment or if the government budget surplus (*T* − *G*) improves. If policies cannot achieve either one of these two objectives, directly or indirectly, the external balance cannot be expected to improve.

- Identity 3-9 shows a direct link between the budget surplus (*T* − *G*) and the external balance. A deterioration in the budget, unless it is offset by increased saving or reduced investment, will make the current account worse.

These statements are important because payments issues are often regarded as trade problems. A country might, for example, think that an export subsidy is a good way to improve the current account. But is that really true, once we look at (3-9)?[5]

Financing the Current Account

A current account deficit means that spending exceeds income. The deficit must be financed by running down external assets or by adding to external debt. There are three chief ways of financing a deficit:

- Running down foreign exchange reserves
- Borrowing from banks, foreign governments, or international organizations such as the World Bank or the International Monetary Fund
- Capital inflows in the form of direct or portfolio investment

The stock of net foreign assets (NFA) is equal to all claims by residents on the rest of the world less all claims by foreigners on domestic residents. Then the current account is equal to the change in net foreign assets:

$$(3\text{-}10) \qquad \Delta \text{ NFA} = \text{CA}$$

The identity in equation 3-10 simply states that bills must be paid. A surplus of income over spending means that we make, in one form or another, claims on the rest of the world. Such claims may mean dollar balances in banks in New York or London, apartments in Miami or Geneva, and IOUs. A deficit means we are borrowing or selling off assets; foreigners may acquire a domestic firm, the central bank may run down reserves, or an international bank may make a loan to finance the deficit.

It is clear from equation 3-10 that it is not sound in the long run to show deficits. The net assets will vanish or will become negative, and there will be a lingering question as to how to pay the bills in the end.

The Noninterest Balance

We are often interested in knowing whether a country obtains resources from the rest of the world or whether it transfers its resources abroad. The chief difference between net resource flows and the current account comes from factor payments, specifically interest payments. We are, therefore, interested in the noninterest current account (NICA). The noninterest current account surplus is equal to the current account surplus less net factor payments (NFP) received from abroad:

$$(3\text{-}11) \qquad \text{NICA} = \text{CA} - \text{NFP}$$

When interest payments are large, a current account deficit will signify that a country is actually transferring resources abroad (see table 3-2). Most of the interest will be paid out of a surplus in the noninterest

Table 3-2. Latin America's External Balance Deficit, 1977–85
(percent of GDP)

Year	Current account	Noninterest current account
1977–82	3.8	0.6
1983–85	0.8	−4.7

Source: IMF, *World Economic Outlook.*

account, but the surplus will simply not be enough to pay all the interest due, so that the overall balance will be in deficit.

After 1983, when credit rationing was introduced, Latin American debtor countries could no longer finance their interest bills through additional borrowing. They had to earn the interest. The overall current account deficit became almost zero; as a result a large noninterest surplus earned the foreign exchange needed to pay the interest bill. In other words, Latin America was making net resource transfers to the creditor countries.

3. Policy Instruments

The chief instruments at the government's control are:

- Fiscal policy
- Financial policy
- Commercial policy
- Exchange rate policy

Fiscal Policy

Fiscal policy encompasses a government's spending, transferring, and taxing decisions and its policies on public sector enterprises. Many issues concerning fiscal policy fall in the area of public finance; three are particularly important.

The first issue concerns the impact of fiscal policy on production and consumption. What incentives are offered by the government's spending or tax policies to produce home goods against traded goods or to consume home goods against traded goods? A government, for example, may levy a tariff at the port to raise revenue. The fiscal effect of a tariff may be that it encourages the production of importables, discourages the consumption of tradables, and has a systematic impact on trade. The impact of fiscal devices, such as advance deposits for imports, would be similar.

The second issue concerns absorption or aggregate demand. A change in fiscal policy that results in increased spending, higher transfers, or reduced taxes will affect aggregate demand and hence the allocation of resources and the external balance.

The third issue concerns the financing of imbalances in the budget. The deficit can be financed by borrowing domestically through public debt issues; by borrowing externally from banks, governments, or international agencies; and by levying an inflation tax.

In domestic borrowing, there is a danger that increased financing of the government budget deficit may preempt others from using these resources, may increase interest rates, and may hence reduce investment. The decline in investment, if it should occur, will affect the competitiveness of the economy in the long run. In foreign borrowings, the future costs of debt servicing not being apparent, governments may overborrow and may sink in a debt crisis. The danger of inflationary finance is the most visible in that it leads to inflation, high inflation, and occasionally hyperinflation. Because inflation tax reduces private spending, however, it does not leave behind the burden of debt for the future. Of course, inflationary finance is not a good strategy. Deficit financing and money printing will most certainly invite portfolios to shift out of money. Vast reserves of foreign exchange would be lost if the central bank attempted to defend the existing exchange rate; if it did not, the exchange rate would collapse. In this sense, borrowing abroad is a less visible way of running deficits. The exchange rate crises may simply be postponed, of course, until credit rationing in the world market suddenly opens a foreign exchange gap.

Recently, in the aftermath of the debt crises, privatization of the public sector has become an important feature of fiscal policy. There is nothing particularly attractive about selling—or not selling—public firms to foreign investors. If the price is the present value of future profits, then selling off the firms involves trading cash on the barrel for giving up future receipts. Having a fire sale of public sector enterprises to pay off foreign debts is in all likelihood a poor proposition.

In the area of public sector pricing, the government plays an important role with clear impacts on the external balance. If public sector goods are sold at subsidized prices, the implied budget deficit will show up—one way or another—in a deterioration of the external balance. This deterioration may occur because the government buys in the world market at a high price and sells domestically at a low price. It may also happen in much more indirect forms: because the subsidy raises demand for government-produced goods, resources are drawn into their production. These resources would otherwise produce for export or produce import-competing goods. By being drawn into the subsidized activity, they close one foreign exchange gap but open up another. Thus, even if government pricing appears far away from the external sector, resource linkages on the production side or the implicit income subsidy on the spending side make sure that a subsidy finds its way into an external deficit.

Financial Policy

The government's policies concerning the financial system have a pervasive influence on the external balance. Asset holders can shop in the world financial market for the most attractive rates of return. They will not hold domestic assets unless returns (after tax) are sufficiently attractive compared with those abroad. To be sufficiently attractive the yield on domestic assets must not only equal the yield abroad but also take into account the expected depreciation of the currency and a risk premium. The risk premium reflects the fact that asset holders are averse to risk and need compensation for taking a gamble on the home assets. The risk may be associated with politics or simply with uncertainty about the exchange rate.

The standard for interest rate policy, therefore, is that the rate of return on large investments (i) should equal the interest rate abroad (i^*) plus expected depreciation (x) plus a risk premium (R):

$$(3\text{-}12) \qquad\qquad i = i^* + x + R$$

Equation 3-12 provides a benchmark. Large departures from this level of interest rate will inevitably lead to capital movements and hence to either reserve losses or exchange rate problems. Holders of small deposits, however, certainly cannot expect the same rate on their deposits as those in New York—or even a positive real interest rate, for that matter.

Positive real interest rates do not necessarily mobilize savings for investment. In a growth-oriented policy, the government should seek to tax money holders through low interest to make more resources available to investing firms. The payment of low rates does not mean that investment funds are allocated inefficiently. To say so would be the same as saying that funds can be allocated efficiently only if the price is set so high that nobody wants to borrow. It would also be a mistake to keep the rates of return on money extremely negative; to do so would encourage a shift into foreign money, would result in a loss of inflation-tax revenue, and would create exchange rate problems.

A question about dollarization that is frequently asked is: should a government routinely offer foreign currency deposits and condone the use of dollars for payment by its citizens? Should this be taken as a first step or as a last resort to prevent a black market in foreign currency? The answer is quite unambiguous: a country that maintains reasonable economic stability should discourage residents from shifting into and using dollars. Even as a last resort, a shift to dollars is a very expensive way of buying quasi stability for a month, two months, or a year. It is better to make the hard adjustments quickly.

If a government regulates positive real interest rates on deposits, it inevitably raises the costs of capital to firms. The lending rate of financial institutions is related to the deposit rate. The loan rate will exceed the deposit rate by a factor that depends on the reserve requirements, taxes, and profit markups. The regulation of high deposit rates therefore inevitably pushes up loan rates. If the high deposit rates serve primarily to pay depositors higher incomes rather than to lead them to save more, then the regulated rates serve to transfer incomes from investing firms to consuming households. Even though it may not occur, this fact must be borne in mind when we toy with the idea of high deposit rates.

Government credit policy affects resource allocation in an important way. If one sector (say, agriculture) is favored by credit, it will draw resources away from other sectors. If agriculture is developed to save foreign exchange, the resources into agriculture may come from export or import-competing industries. Often the foreign exchange problem is shifted around because we fail to recognize that external balance problems involve not only the level of spending relative to income but also the composition of spending and production.

Commercial Policy

The government sets tariffs, quotas, and export taxes and subsidies in part as fiscal devices and in part to affect resource allocation. Because of macroeconomic considerations and immediate balance of payments objectives, an export subsidy may often be preferred to devaluation or a quota preferred to a tariff. The resource costs of a poorly managed commercial policy, however, can be very expensive in the long run. In this area what is good and helpful in the short run and in the long run can create intense conflicts.

Three rules of thumb should be followed to establish a sound commercial policy. First, in principle, commercial policy should not replace exchange rate policy. Second, trade quotas should be placed only when there is a very good excuse. Third, to minimize the effect on inflation, an export subsidy may sometimes be chosen over devaluation. But the overriding concern in commercial policy should be to watch for distortions that might arise on account of tariffs, quotas, and subsidies. Distortions are easier to create than to undo.

Exchange Rate Policy

Exchange rate policy cannot be considered independently of fiscal policy. If the budget deficit is financed by inflationary money creation, then only a crawling-peg exchange rate system is sustainable. Under such a system, the exchange rate is depreciated at a rate approximately equal to the difference between home and foreign inflation.

In contrast, if a deficit is financed by debt, exchange rate policy becomes more difficult. Current borrowing finances a deficit in the external balance and allows a high real exchange rate. But when debt servicing starts, a real depreciation is necessary to improve the external balance. Failure to move the exchange rate implies overvaluation and borrowing to finance exchange rate misalignment, and that means wasting resources.

The choice of the "right level" of the exchange rate is, perhaps, the most critical decision in an open economy because it has a visible impact on income distribution. A wrong exchange rate policy is expensive. An undervalued exchange rate depresses the standard of living and results in current account surpluses. An overvalued exchange rate artificially raises the standard of living above the level of productivity and finances it by incurring external debt. Politically, an overvalued exchange rate may be very popular; it is also very expensive once the bills arrive.

A question frequently posed is whether it is sensible for a government to use different exchange rates for various kinds of transactions. Different rates may apply to basic versus luxury goods, traditional versus industrial goods, and current account versus capital account transactions. The same arguments that were made about commercial policy apply here. For macroeconomic reasons, such policies may be helpful in some circumstances, but they do have resource costs. Of course, the introduction of distortions by itself need not be an argument for ruling out multiple exchange rates immediately. Considerations of unemployment and inflation, which might be lessened by such policies, may weigh much more heavily than the disadvantage of distortions. International institutions tend to favor unified rates. A highly complicated exchange rate structure is certainly counterproductive.

4. Determinants of Growth

The standard of living in a country is governed by two factors: the physical productivity of labor and the terms of trade. Let us measure the standard of living as the purchasing power of the income produced by an hour of work. Labor productivity is the amount of output per hour worked and is denoted by α. The price of domestic output is P, and the consumer price index is Q. The purchasing power of an hour of work is then:

(3-13)   Standard of living $= \alpha \, P/Q$

The consumer price index is a function of domestic prices and import prices. Suppose it is an (exponentially) weighted average

(3-14) $$Q = P^{1-b} \cdot (P^*)^b$$

where $1-b$ is the share of domestic goods in spending. Substituting in (3-13) yields

$$(3\text{-}13a) \qquad \text{Standard of living} = \alpha \, (P/P^*)^b$$

The formula shows there are two ways of increasing the standard of living. The first is to have an increase in labor productivity. If an hour of work produces a larger amount of output, then it produces a higher consumption level. This statement is true whether we consume the output ourselves or sell it abroad in exchange for other consumption goods.

Labor productivity can be increased by a better allocation of resources. If we shift resources out of industries where their productivity is low into those where it is high, then the economywide average productivity and standard of living must increase. The market economy will ordinarily bring about this change. Activities with high productivity can afford to pay more for factors and therefore can manage to win labor away from inefficient uses. But there are exceptions to the market mechanism. The government may artificially maintain labor in low-productivity areas by distorting prices and policies, including commercial and exchange rate policies. The government sector itself is often regarded as a user of low-productivity labor. The second way of increasing labor productivity is through capital accumulation and technical progress. Of these two, technical progress is by far the more important source of growth, but also the one less well understood.[6]

The second determinant of the standard of living, as shown in equation 3-13a, is the terms of trade. An increase in the prices at which we sell, relative to those at which we buy (P/P^*) raises our real income. This point is obvious, for example, for an oil-producing country when oil prices increase. An hour of oil extraction produces so many barrels. If the price of oil is up relative to the price of other things, then a given amount of extraction work will make the oil producers better off.

For many developing countries, fluctuations in the terms of trade are the dominant source of changes in the standard of living. Much of their income is derived from primary commodities. As exports of commodities become a smaller share of GNP, fluctuations in the real prices of commodities receive less weight in the determination of income. Even so, major changes in the terms of trade, such as those that occurred during 1979–85, continue to be an important source of changes in the standard of living.

A source of change at first sight not captured in equation 3-13a comes from the level of utilization of resources. If we regard α as the average productivity in the economy of all those willing to work, however, then unemployment will appear as a reduction of average productivity. An increase in the level of utilization of resources will raise economywide productivity.

In the short term, changes in resource utilization and in the terms of trade dominate changes in the standard of living. In the long term, technical progress and capital formation receive emphasis. But changes in the standard of living in both periods depend on the policy environment that the government creates. There may well be tradeoffs that favor stable long-run policies over aggressive day-to-day management of the economy. It is also clear that both long-run and short-run policies are necessary if the private sector lacks the courage or resources to take a long-run view.

Argentina and Australia offer the best example of contrasts (see table 3-3). At the turn of the century and until World War I, both countries were developing rapidly and compared well with the economic progress in industrial countries. By 1980, however, Argentina's economy had been severely affected by decades of mismanagement, whereas Australia's moved consistently ahead. Between 1953 and 1983, Argentina grew at an average annual rate of 2.2 percent and Australia at 4.2 percent. The 2 percent difference in the economic performance of the two countries was caused not by differences in resources but by differences of politics and policies.[7]

5. Some Mistakes To Be Avoided

The list of mistakes to be avoided is endless. The problem is that no clear set of rules can easily be applied to any policy situation. Any shock to the economy brings the policymaker opportunities to lessen the costs of resource allocation and unemployment. In addition, however, it tempts him or her to exploit an opportunity for political purposes. Resource allocation that is a little bit worse but provides a more equal distribution of consumption and opportunities does not have to be condemned. Economics does not require that efficient resource allocation take precedence over social considerations.

In economics, as in other fields, there is often more than one way to skin a cat. Other things being equal, we should pick the one that raises

Table 3-3. Average Annual Rate of Growth in Argentina and Australia, 1900–83

Country	1900–29	1929–50	1953–83	1973–83
Argentina	4.8	2.2	2.2	0.6
Australia	2.1	3.7	4.2	2.3

Sources: Argentina Instituto Nacional de Estadísticos y Censos, *Censo Nacional de Población y Vivienda* (Buenos Aires, various issues); IMF, *International Financial Statistics;* and Arthur Smithies, "Economic Growth: International Comparisons: Argentina and Australia," *American Economic Review,* proceedings, vol. 55, pt. I, 1965, p. 30.

consumption for some without lowering that of others. A lot of policies that seek to make people better off in fact end up being ineffective and expensive (for example, deficit spending).

The usefulness of economics resides in two areas. First, it helps us understand which tools can be used for what purpose, what their main effect is, and what the side effects are. Second, economics has a long case history of outcomes ending badly: overvaluation, deficit spending, excessively rapid liberalization, financing of capital flight, high real interest rates, excessive protection, and more.

There are at least three countries that can be held up as examples for having done things right for a long time: Brazil, the Republic of Korea, and Turkey. Korea and Brazil have achieved average growth rates of 4 percent to 6 percent in per capita income for thirty years, figures that should attest to the fact that something is being done right. Turkey achieved a rapid turnaround after several years of severe mismanagement. There are, of course, many problems in these countries, but one fact stands out: they had made a commitment to avoid bottlenecks in the foreign exchange area to prevent the economy from slowing down or collapsing.

Notes

1. A good review of basic economics, including tools such as index numbers, growth rates, and graphs, can be found in any of the modern textbooks. See especially William Baumol and Alan S. Blinder, *Economics,* 2d ed. (New York: Harcourt Brace Jovanovich, 1982); and William Nordhaus and Paul Samuelson, *Economics,* 12th ed. (New York: McGraw-Hill, 1985). An intermediate-level treatment can be found in Rudiger Dornbusch and Stanley Fischer, *Macroeconomics,* 3d ed. (New York: McGraw-Hill, 1984).

2. The formula in equation 3-2 has a solid economic interpretation as the cost or benefit of changes in the terms of trade. It can be shown that it is the amount of compensation someone would need to buy the same bundle of goods after the price change as before. Suppose you import goods worth 20 percent of GDP and import prices rise 30 percent, so that the cost of imports is up by 6 percent of GDP. If you were to receive the same amount in compensation, you could afford to buy what you bought before, even at the higher prices.

3. See C. L. Ramirez-Rojas, "Monetary Substitution in Developing Countries," *Finance & Development,* vol. 23 (June 1986), pp. 35-38.

4. Tax payments here are understood as net taxes, that is, taxes net of all domestic transfer payments made by the government.

5. Yes!

6. A fascinating study by William Baumol suggests that much of growth is catching up on countries that are technically ahead; see "The Catching up Hypothesis" (New York: New York University, Starr Center, October 1985; processed).

7. See Lloyd Reynolds, *Economic Growth in the Third World, 1850–1980* (New Haven, Conn.: Yale University Press, 1985); Angus Maddison, *Phases of Capitalist Development* (Oxford, Eng.: Oxford University Press, 1982); and R. C. O. Matthew, ed., *Economic Growth and Resources,* vol. 2 (London: Macmillan, 1980).

4

External Shocks and Domestic Policy Responses

Paul Krugman

NO DEVELOPING country can or should isolate itself from the world economy. The benefits of outward-looking policies that take advantage of the possibilities for international trade and capital flows are well understood in economic theory and are also demonstrated by development experience. By linking itself to the world economy, however, a country also exposes itself to external shocks—that is, it can experience economic disturbances that originate in events outside the country. Coping with such external shocks is often the most crucial test facing policymakers in developing countries. The purpose of this chapter is to describe the main forms of external shocks to which developing countries are vulnerable and to review some of the issues involved in policy response to these shocks.

The chapter is in four parts. The first part provides an "anatomy" of external shocks. It describes and illustrates the chief ways in which disturbances in the rest of the world affect the economies of developing countries. The second part analyzes the most important policy options available to countries that experience an adverse external shock. The third part discusses some of the pitfalls frequently encountered as countries attempt to cope with adverse shifts in the world economic environment. The fourth and last part has some concluding remarks.

1. Anatomy of External Shocks

By any standard, the international economic environment since 1970 has been highly volatile and uncertain. Figures 4-1–4-4 illustrate the major changes in the world economy:

- The world business cycle: The industrial countries experienced two major recessions, both deeper than anything seen since the 1930s.

Figure 4-1. Rate of Growth of Real GDP in Industrial Countries

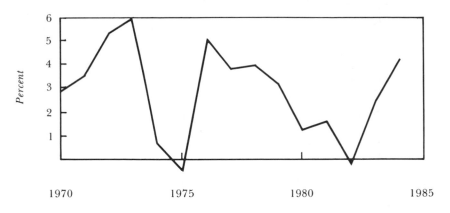

Source: IMF, *International Financial Statistics.*

Figure 4-2. Real Commodity Prices
(1980 = 100)

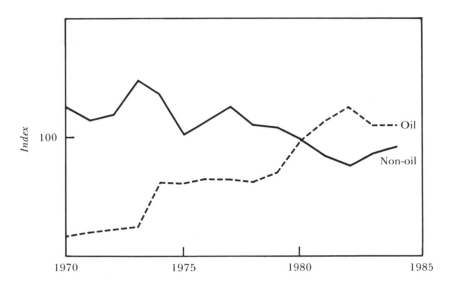

Source: IMF, *International Financial Statistics.*

Figure 4-3. Inflation and Interest Rates

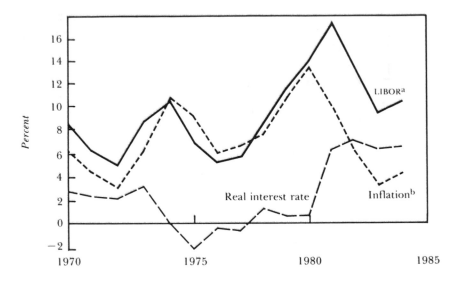

a. London interbank offer rate.
b. U.S. consumer price index.
Source: IMF, *International Financial Statistics.*

Figure 4-4. U.S. Dollar Exchange rate

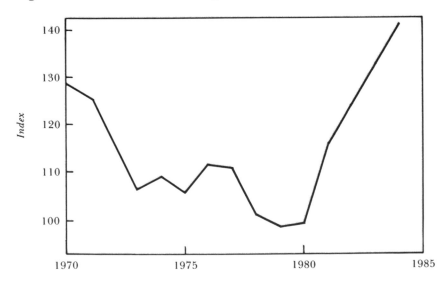

Source: IMF, *International Financial Statistics.*

- Commodity prices: Oil prices rose sharply in 1973–74, then again in 1979–80. Prices of other commodities experienced a dramatic boom in the early 1970s but have fallen in the 1980s in spite of economic recovery in the industrial nations.
- Exchange rates: The dollar fell sharply against other industrial country currencies during the 1970s, then rose equally sharply during the 1980s.
- Inflation and interest rates: Inflation in the industrial countries rose during the 1970s, then fell in the 1980s. Interest rates also rose in the inflationary 1970s but not as much as inflation, so that the 1970s were a golden era for debtors. Interest rates have failed to fall in the disinflation of the 1980s.

Given these sharp swings in virtually every aspect of the international economy, it is not surprising that the problem of dealing with external shocks has been a central preoccupation of policy in developing countries.

To understand the nature of this problem, we need to do more than catalog the disturbances in the world economy. We need to focus on the specific channels through which an unstable world economy affects developing countries. Most of this chapter focuses on adverse shocks, that is, on shocks that either reduce the foreign exchange earnings of an economy or increase its payments to the rest of the world. Developing countries also sometimes experience favorable shocks, which are not without their dangers; I discuss these dangers briefly in the next part.

An unstable world environment can adversely affect developing countries through either international goods markets or international capital markets. Within these broad categories, shocks in the goods market can take the form of declines in export demand, with a subsequent decline in the price of exports and, in some cases, constraints on the volume of exports. Alternatively, declines in world supply of important commodities, notably oil, can raise the price of some imports into developing countries. Some shocks can be viewed as either import or export shocks. The dollar's rise from 1980 to 1985 was an export shock if one measures prices in other currencies and an import shock if one measures prices in dollars. In any case, we can often summarize the net effect of external shocks to both imports and exports by looking at a country's terms of trade, defined as the average price of its exports divided by the average price of its imports.

In the capital market, both price and quantity can move adversely. Countries that have borrowed extensively on international markets are adversely affected by increases in interest rates. These debtors are also affected by inflation rates. A rise in world (not domestic) prices tends to reduce the real value of foreign debt; thus a fall in inflation amounts to an adverse shock. A useful summary indicator of the combined effect of

interest rates and inflation rates on the burden of debt is the real interest rate, the difference between the interest rate and the inflation rate.
In addition to changes in the cost of debt, countries sometimes find
themselves constrained in the quantity of borrowing that they can
undertake. When countries that have been borrowing heavily for development are faced with a slowdown in the rate at which they are able to
continue that borrowing, the adjustment can be very difficult.

Let us consider these different shocks in more detail.

Shocks Arising from the Goods Market

Shocks can arise from the export market as well as from the import
market.

EXPORT SHOCKS.   Historically, the largest single source of export-
market shocks to developing countries has been the business cycle in the
industrial countries. The rate of growth in industrial countries affects
the exports of developing countries in two ways. The first is through
commodity prices. When industrial countries grow rapidly, their
demand for raw materials also grows and usually leads to a rise in commodity prices relative to prices of manufactured goods. Conversely,
recessions in the industrial countries generally reduce commodity
prices. Despite growth in manufactured exports from some nations,
most developing countries continue to be net exporters of raw materials
and net importers of manufactured goods; the negative effect of industrial country recessions on commodity prices is therefore an adverse
export shock.

Manufactured exports from developing countries are also affected by
the business cycle in the industrial world but in a slightly different way.
In commodity markets, prices move to clear the market; that is, sellers
can always sell as much as they want at the going price. If the volume of
exports falls when demand declines, it is because the price has become
unattractive to potential suppliers, not because of an inability to sell. In
the case of manufactures, however, prices tend to be somewhat sticky.
The result is that, although manufacturers' prices may also fall when
demand falls, the price may not fall enough to clear the market, and volume falls not only because firms choose to supply less but also because
they are unable to sell as much as they would like. Consequently, for
developing countries that are substantial exporters of manufactures,
their export prices alone may not reveal the full extent to which their
economies have experienced an adverse shock to export demand.

The recent behavior of commodity prices differed from that of the
past. From 1982 to 1985, the industrial countries experienced a recovery that, though disappointingly weak in Europe, was quite strong in the

United States. Despite this recovery, commodity prices as a whole have risen only slightly from their levels at the depth of the recession. The reasons for this failure of commodity prices to recover are disputed, but two contributory factors are clear. One is the rise in the dollar; the other is the rise in real interest rates.

In addition to the effects of the world business cycle, which affect all markets, exports of developing countries can be affected by other events beyond their control. Many small countries rely heavily on a few commodities for export revenue, and fluctuations in the markets for these commodities—which may be largely unrelated to the general world economic picture—can therefore have a large impact on particular nations. A case in point is sugar, whose price on world markets has fallen to record lows in real terms in recent years. This decline probably has little to do with the overall state of the world economy. Instead, it is due to protection of high-cost sugar producers in consuming nations and the growing availability of substitute sweeteners. Although the decline in sugar prices results from factors peculiar to that crop, it has had serious adverse effects on sugar-exporting countries, especially in the Caribbean.

IMPORT SHOCKS. Although most developing countries are net exporters of commodities, even countries that export some commodities import others. Supply shortfalls or other factors that cause prices of particular commodities to rise can also constitute an adverse external shock to importers of these commodities. An important example was the surge in world food prices in the first half of the 1970s. From 1971 to 1974, an accidental combination of factors conspired to triple world wholesale prices for foodstuffs. The causes included harvest failure in the U.S.S.R. and the disappearance of Peru's offshore anchovy population; speculation in food stocks may have contributed as well. For food-exporting countries, such as Argentina and Brazil, the unexpected rise was a windfall, but for the many food-importing developing countries, the rise posed a significant problem.

The principal import shocks of the period since 1970 have been surges in the price of oil. (For oil-exporting countries, these were of course export shocks.) The causes of the rise in oil prices during the 1970s are still far from completely understood. Whatever the reasons, however, for oil-importing developing countries, the two major oil price increases posed one of the most central policy problems of that decade.

EXCHANGE RATES AND TRADE. Movements in the exchange rates between industrial countries can have important effects on the prices of exports and imports in developing countries. The direction of these effects depends on which currency one uses to measure prices. When the dollar rises against European currencies, both the import and the export prices of developing countries normally fall when measured in dollars but rise when measured in European currencies.

If import and export prices of developing countries were affected equally by movements in the dollar, a rise in the dollar would have no net impact: if one chooses to reckon prices in dollars, an adverse export shock would be matched by a favorable import shock. To put it more succinctly, a rise in the dollar need not affect developing countries' terms of trade. Experience suggests, however, that the effects of exchange rate changes on developing country export and import prices are not equal. When the dollar rises, dollar import prices of developing countries seem to fall less than their export prices. Thus the net result is that the adverse export effect outweighs the favorable import effect: a rise in the dollar worsens the terms of trade in developing countries. This point is well illustrated by Brazil's experience from 1980 to 1984, when the dollar rose 44 percent against an average of other industrial country currencies. In dollar terms, Brazil's export prices fell by 13 percent, whereas import prices fell by only 2 percent.

The reasons for this unequal effect are not entirely clear. A possible explanation is that, whereas prices of commodities are highly flexible, prices of manufacturers are often somewhat inflexible. Because the dollar is the world's premier international currency, even manufacturing exporters outside the United States may be reluctant to have volatile prices in dollars and may therefore fail to cut their prices when the dollar rises. Econometric evidence suggests that the rise of the dollar may be an important factor in the failure of commodity prices to rise during the 1982 to 1985 recovery.

THE TERMS OF TRADE.   For most developing countries, the overall effect of external shocks transmitted through the goods market can be summarized by the change in the terms of trade, defined as the ratio of the average price of a country's exports to the average price of its imports. When a country's terms of trade decline, any given volume of exports pays for a smaller volume of imports. To compensate for this decline, a country must do one of three things: increase its export volume, reduce its import volume, or increase the rate at which it borrows abroad. If the country does borrow abroad or has engaged in such borrowing in the past, it becomes exposed to shocks originating in the capital market.

Shocks Originating in the Capital Market

The main factors here are the cost of borrowing, as determined by interest and inflation rates, and the constraints on international borrowing.

INTEREST RATES. The international borrowing by developing countries is almost entirely denominated in the currencies of industrial countries, mostly in the U.S. dollar. Thus the principal measure of the cost of debt to these countries is the interest rate on dollar loans.

A rise in the current interest rate raises the cost of any increases in a country's debt. Whether it also increases the burden of existing debt depends on two factors: whether the debt is at a fixed or floating rate and, if the debt is at a fixed rate, the maturity of the debt.

The distinction between fixed- and floating-rate borrowing is the following: a fixed-rate loan establishes a definite interest rate when the loan agreement is signed. A subsequent rise in world interest rates is the lender's problem. A floating-rate loan, in contrast, has an interest rate that is revised periodically in the light of recent world interest rates. Typically such loans specify the interest rate as a premium over the London interbank offer rate (LIBOR), a dollar interest rate widely viewed as a sort of world standard. If LIBOR rises, the interest rate paid by countries that have borrowed on floating rates rises as well. Clearly the distinction between fixed- and floating-rate loans is a question of who bears the risk of interest rate volatility.

The "maturity of debt" refers to the length of time to repay. If a country has borrowed at short maturities, even if it does not increase the total value of its debt, it will have to roll over a substantial part of its debt every year, taking out new loans to pay the principal on old loans. For countries that have borrowed at fixed interest rates, the shorter the maturity, the more rapidly an increase in world interest rates will be reflected in a higher average interest rate paid on existing debt.

Both the choice between fixed- and floating-rate debt and the maturity of debt vary widely among developing countries. Broadly we can distinguish two groups among countries whose levels of debt are high relative to national income. The first group consists of low-income countries, particularly in Africa, that have borrowed extensively from official lenders, including the World Bank. These countries generally have debt at fixed rates with long maturities. For this reason, the average interest rate on these countries' debt lags far behind changes in current market rates, insulating them to a large degree from the direct effects of interest rate volatility. The second group consists of middle-income countries, particularly in Latin America, that have borrowed heavily from private commercial banks. The banks were unwilling to bear the risk of uncertain interest rates, and thus these countries have debt that is mostly floating rate and of short maturity.

For a country in the latter group, an increase in world interest rates clearly constitutes an adverse external shock: interest payments increase, and these increased interest payments, like a deterioration in the terms of trade, must be met by some combination of increased exports, reduced imports, or increased borrowing. The experience with such interest rate shocks is discussed below, but the inseparable issue of inflation rates needs to be considered first.

INFLATION AND DEBT.   In assessing the ultimate burden of a debt, what matters is not the money value of the debt but the extra exports or forgone imports that will be necessary to generate the foreign currency to repay it. If the dollar prices of exports and imports rise because of world inflation, the burden of repaying any given dollar debt will become smaller. Thus in assessing the change in a country's debt position over time, we should look not at the change in money value but at the change in the value of the debt in terms of the prices of the country's imports and exports. To put it another way, inflation reduces the real value of a country's debt, and this gain should be subtracted from interest payments in calculating the cost of a country's debt.

During the 1970s, the dollar prices of most goods traded on world markets rose rapidly, so that much of the real value of existing debt was eroded by inflation. This situation reversed itself in the 1980s, but the reversal is best examined in the context of a joint analysis of interest and inflation rates.

THE REAL INTEREST RATE.   The combined effect of interest and inflation rates on the debt burden may be measured by looking at the interest rate minus the inflation rate, the real interest rate. The role of interest rate and inflation rate changes in the determination of this real rate over time are illustrated in figure 4-3. The striking feature of this chart is the shift from an environment highly favorable to debtors in the second half of the 1970s to a highly favorable one in the 1980s. From 1975 to 1979, LIBOR, the standard for many international loans, averaged 7.8 percent. At the same time, world inflation, as measured by the rate of increase in world export prices in dollars, averaged 8.9 percent. Although developing countries that borrowed on the international market generally had to pay some premium over LIBOR, the real interest rate on international loans was still negative. From 1980 to 1984, in contrast, the corresponding interest and inflation rates averaged 13.0 and 1.2 percent, respectively. Thus heavily indebted countries, especially those with extensive floating-rate or short-maturity debt, were faced with a dramatic increase in the real cost of their debt. It is thus not surprising that a debt crisis occurred in 1982–83. The most immediate symptom of the crisis, however, was the emergence of constraints on borrowing, which constituted a shock over and above that to the cost of debt.

CONSTRAINTS ON BORROWING.   Increases in the cost of debt are not the only way in which capital markets can be a source of adverse external shocks to national economies. In addition to rises in cost, restrictions on availability have been a major problem for some countries.

The characteristic situation is one in which potential lenders lose confidence in a country's ability to repay its debt and become unwilling to lend. If the country has until that point been borrowing extensively, it is abruptly forced to expand exports or cut imports, a process likely to be costly. The problem is particularly severe if the country already has large foreign debt and this debt is of short maturity. In that case, the country will usually have been accustomed to rolling its debt over, borrowing to repay principal. To be suddenly forced to meet debt service from current revenues will pose a difficult and in some cases quite literally impossible problem of adjustment. Because crises of confidence usually occur when a country has experienced adverse external shocks, the effect is to compound the problem.

A Case Study: Brazil, 1979–84

We have now reviewed the main kinds of adverse external shocks that developing countries face. To give a more concrete view of these shocks, we consider a particular case that—to the country's misfortune— illustrates all of the shocks. The case is that of Brazil, which suffered an extraordinary deterioration of its external environment from the late 1970s to the early 1980s.

Table 4-1 gives some summary data on Brazil. During the 1970s, Brazil was a success story of the developing world. Extensive foreign borrowing both helped Brazil achieve a high rate of economic growth and was itself encouraged by that growth. Given the rapid growth of the economy and the inflationary world economic environment, most observers, including international bankers, saw Brazil's position as fundamentally strong.

Table 4-1. External Shocks to Brazil's Economy
(percent)

Item	1974–79	1979–84
Rate of increase of export prices in U.S. dollars	7.1	−1.5
Rate of increase of import prices in U.S. dollars	8.1	4.6
Change in terms of trade in percent	−5.2	−30.5
Average LIBOR[a]	7.8	13.0
Average real interest rate[b]	−0.7	14.5

a. London interbank offer rate.
b. LIBOR minus rate of increase of Brazilian dollar export prices.
Source: IMF, *International Financial Statistics.*

Things began to go wrong in 1979. Essentially, Murphy's Law seems to have applied: everything that could go wrong did. All of the adverse external shocks I have described happened to Brazil in the 1980s. Specifically:

- Export shock: The recession in industrial countries and the decline in real commodity prices after 1979 hit Brazil hard. Despite its progress in industrialization, Brazil is still primarily a commodity-exporting country, and its export prices fell relative to those of the world as a whole.

- Import shock: Brazil is dependent on imported oil; in fact, oil accounted for more than half of imports by 1983. When oil prices surged after 1979, Brazil was a heavy net loser.

- Terms of trade: The combined effect of the adverse shocks to exports and imports was a 30 percent decline in Brazil's terms of trade from 1979 to 1984.

- Real interest rates: Brazil's foreign debt was high relative to that of other developing countries: 270 percent of exports in 1980–82 two and one-half times the average for all developing countries. Furthermore, Brazil's debt was mostly floating rate and at short maturities. The increase in world real interest rates thus found Brazil extremely vulnerable.

- Constraints on borrowing: As the extent of the adverse external shocks became apparent to lenders in the early 1980s, willingness to lend to Brazil vanished. A virtual cutoff of new loans in the fall of 1982 forced Brazil to adopt a harsh adjustment plan.

2. Policy Response to External Shocks

External shocks demand a policy response for two reasons. The first, and usually most urgent, is that an adverse shift in the world economic environment produces a balance of payments problem. Whenever the central bank of a country establishes an official value for the currency it issues, a fall in the receipts of domestic residents from abroad or an increase in their payments to foreigners leads to a drain on the bank's foreign exchange reserves. Because foreign reserves are limited, this situation necessitates some kind of policy response. Even if the central bank does not try to establish an official value and allows the exchange rate to float—a rare policy in developing countries—the effect of adverse external shocks may be to produce an unacceptably large depreciation of the currency.

The second reason for policy response is that adverse external shocks inevitably have repercussions in the domestic economy. Some of these effects come directly. A decline in export demand will reduce income and employment in export sectors, and this decline will in turn reduce demand for the products of industries that serve the home market. An increase in interest payments on foreign debt may worsen the government budget deficit if the debt is public or threaten the solvency of domestic firms if the debt is private. Often even more important than these direct repercussions are the indirect repercussions of the policies that are undertaken to cope with the pressing issue of the balance of payments.

In coming to grips with these problems, governments face three levels of choice. First, they must decide the extent to which the external shocks should be met by financing or by adjustment—that is, by borrowing to make up for declines in export revenues, increased import prices, or higher interest payments or by attempting to increase exports and reduce imports. Second, to the extent that adjustment is called for, governments must decide on the degree to which they rely on expenditure reduction or on expenditure switching—that is, on cutting public and private demand or on trying to shift that demand, and the demand of foreigners as well, from foreign-produced goods to domestically produced goods. Finally, expenditure switching can be attempted either through devaluation or through commercial policies—that is, by increasing the price of foreign exchange or by using import quotas, export subsidies, and other policies to promote or restrict particular imports and exports. Thus, to understand the policy problem of countries that experience adverse external schocks, it is necessary to examine each of these levels of choice in turn.

Financing versus Adjustment

The issues here apply to unfavorable as well as favorable shocks, and the policy responses depend to a large extent on the availability of foreign capital.

THE CHOICE OF RESPONSE IN CASE OF UNFAVORABLE SHOCKS. Suppose that a country experiences an adverse external shock of any of the kinds described above. The immediate need will be to stop the drain on the central bank's foreign exchange reserves. One option that can work for a time is to replace the loss in reserves by borrowing abroad—either from private lenders in world capital markets or from official lenders such as the International Monetary Fund (IMF). This strategy of financing the balance of payments deficit resulting from an external shock makes sense as long as the shock seems likely to be only temporary and likely to reverse itself before the implied borrowing becomes unsustainable. If the shock looks temporary, a government may also try to offset the domestic repercussions, for example, by using tax cuts or public expenditure to sustain domestic demand.

If the shock does not appear temporary, however, it must be met by adjustment. That is, the country must compensate for the loss of receipts from abroad or the increased burden of payment by making offsetting adjustments elsewhere. Exports must increase or imports must be reduced or both.

The case for meeting adverse external shocks with financing rather than adjustment should be obvious. Adjustment policy is a matter of choosing between unpleasant alternatives. To adjust to an adverse shock inevitably requires a cut in living standards and often turns out to involve some sacrifice of longer-run growth prospects as well. Clearly, to incur these costs unnecessarily for a shock that is only temporary would be a mistake.

Trying to meet a permanent or long-lived shock by financing, however, not only postpones the necessary adjustment but also makes that adjustment harder because of the additional debt accumulated during the interval. The problem, of course, is that it is often unclear how sustained an external shock will turn out to be. Faced with that uncertainty, countries often opt initially for a mix of financing and adjustment.

It is also true that, even when a substantial degree of adjustment is called for, this adjustment may be easier to accomplish given time. Increases in exports, in particular, require time to build plants and establish new markets. Thus a period of transitory financing is often a feature of strategies whose ultimate aim is adjustment.

In principle, it is as bad to overadjust and underfinance in response to an adverse external shock as it is to underadjust and overfinance. In practice, because financing initially seems easier than adjustment, governments typically fail to pursue sufficiently vigorous adjustment policies until too late. Counterexamples are hard to find. India in the mid-1970s seemed at the time to be an example of too little financing and too much adjustment. Not only did India not respond to the recession of 1974–75 and the increase in the price of oil by increasing her borrowing, she actually shifted from a mild trade deficit to a substantial surplus. This shift would ordinarily be considered excessive. Still, given the subsequent massive shift in the world economic situation toward an inhospitable environment for debtors, India's policy does not look so bad in retrospect.

RESPONDING TO FAVORABLE SHOCKS.   Most of this chapter focuses on the problem of adverse external shocks. The financing-versus-adjustment issue also applies, however, to favorable shocks, and consideration of the issue in this context may help clarify the nature of the problem.

Suppose a country experiences a favorable external shock, such as a rise in the world price of a major export commodity. The government of that country is then faced with a choice. Financing, in this case, would mean using the additional export revenue to retire existing foreign debt or to acquire foreign exchange reserves. Adjustment would mean pursuing policies, such as more ambitious public works or exchange rate appreciation, that lead to increased imports and reduced exports. If the improvement in the country's prospects turns out to be sustained, a financing strategy will have wasted time and failed to use the new opportunities as productively as possible. If the country adjusts to a favorable external shock that turns out to be transitory, however, adjusting back may be painful and disruptive.

The 1970s, unfortunately, provide a number of examples of countries that allowed themselves to become accustomed to an improvement in their external environment that turned out to be only temporary. A good example is the Côte d'Ivoire, whose principle exports are coffee and cocoa. The coffee boom of 1976–77, which dragged cocoa prices up as well, led to a short-lived 60 percent improvement in the Côte d'Ivoire's terms of trade. The government responded with a massive, not too carefully conceived program of public investment. The subsequent fall in beverage prices led to substantial difficulties, even though the Côte d'Ivoire's terms of trade at the end of the 1970s were still considerably better than they were at the decade's start.

SOURCES OF FINANCING. A country can use finance rather than adjust to an external shock only if it has a source of financing. For countries that have large foreign exchange reserves, this situation is not a problem. Middle Eastern oil-exporting nations, for example, accumulated large reserves during the 1970s and are able to postpone adjustment to the slump in the oil market by drawing down those reserves. Most developing countries are not in that position, however, and must rely on borrowing abroad.

Broadly speaking, a country can draw on two major sources of finance following an external shock. The first is borrowing from official sources, of which the IMF has traditionally been the most important. The other is borrowing from private sources, especially commercial banks.

Developing countries that are able to borrow from private sources usually turn to these sources first and to official loans only when necessary. One reason is that the IMF as a matter of internal policy lends only when it is needed, and a mild or obviously transitory shock does not qualify. (An exception is the IMF's Compensatory Financing Facility, which is explicitly designed to lend when countries experience temporary falls in export prices.) The other reason is that the IMF lends only when the borrowing is part of a comprehensive package of policy changes, and countries do not relinquish their policy autonomy unless they have to. From 1979 to 1982, for example, Brazil attempted to respond to its adverse external shocks by borrowing from commercial banks and was unwilling to turn to the IMF.

When external shocks are severe enough, however, countries are obliged to turn to official finance. The reason is not that the volume of required finance is too large for private lenders but that private lenders become unwilling to lend at all. What happens next is not that official finance fills the gap but rather that official finance is provided under an agreement by the country to adjust and that this agreement provides private lenders with the assurances that they need to resume lending. The bulk of the financing may still come from private sources, but the leadership comes from the IMF.

The important point is that, when the IMF is called in, the choice between financing and adjustment—and to some extent the choice about the policy instruments used to achieve adjustment—is no longer purely in the country's hands and is instead to a large degree dictated by the IMF.

Expenditure Reduction versus Expenditure Switching

When a country does attempt to adjust to an external shock, it faces a second choice, this time relating not to objective but to method. The aim is to improve the trade balance. On one side, this may be done by policies such as tax increases, cuts in government spending, and restrictions on the credit created by the banking system. These policies reduce spending in the domestic economy, which lowers demand for imports and, by releasing resources from industries serving the domestic market, may in an indirect way lead to increased exports. Alternatively, policies such as export subsidies, import controls, and devaluation may be used to encourage both indigenous and foreign residents to switch their spending from foreign to domestic goods, thus raising exports and cutting imports.

Each of these two methods has undesirable side effects. On the one hand, expenditure-reducing policies, by reducing the demand for domestic goods as well as imports, typically lead to unemployment and excess capacity. The immediate economic and social costs can be large; furthermore, much of the burden often falls on investment, which reduces the economy's future growth prospects. On the other hand, expenditure-switching policies invariably have an inflationary impact. Unless such policies are accompanied by at least some expenditure-reducing policies, the inflationary impact quickly erodes any improvements in the trade balance. Even when this is not the case, the inflationary consequences of expenditure-switching policies are often serious and complicate otherwise successful adjustment programs.

To understand the tradeoff between these two kinds of policies more thoroughly, we need to examine more specifically the policy options available to governments.

EXPENDITURE-REDUCING POLICIES. An expenditure-reducing policy reduces the overall level of spending by domestic residents. Some of this reduction in spending will stem from reduced spending on imports, which will in a direct way help a country adjust to an adverse external shock. Expenditure-reducing policies are also important as a way of curbing what would otherwise be unacceptable and perhaps self-defeating inflationary effects of expenditure-switching policies.

Governments can seek to reduce the overall level of spending by residents in three ways. Governments can reduce their own spending, cutting government programs or reducing public investment. They can induce cuts in private consumption by raising taxes or cutting subsidies. Or private borrowing can be constrained by limits on credit creation by the banking system.

All of these policies have an unpleasant side effect. In addition to reducing expenditure on imports, they reduce demand for domestic goods and thus lead to unemployment and excess capacity. This consequence can be mitigated by combining the policies with expenditure-switching policies, as described below. Beyond this common feature, however, the various types of expenditure-reducing policies differ in important ways. Cuts in government programs, of course, mean scaling back or eliminating the objectives of those programs. Ideally, only wasteful and unjustified items would be cut, but life is not usually ideal. Tax increases or subsidy cuts strike directly at the living standards of the population and sometimes provoke strong political reactions. Credit restriction is less immediately a source of distress but has serious longer-run consequences because it strikes primarily at investment and thus at the economy's longer-run growth prospects. A disquieting feature of the recent adjustment efforts of Latin American countries is that severe credit restraint has sharply reduced investment as a share of GNP; this reduction in investment qualifies any optimism that one might gain from the impressive improvement in trade balances.

EXPENDITURE-SWITCHING POLICIES. The term "expenditure switching" refers to the spending of both indigenous and foreign residents. Attempts to cut imports without an overall cut in domestic spending require that indigenous residents shift their demand from foreign to domestic products. Attempts to increase exports require that foreign residents do the same.

The main policy instruments with which governments attempt to switch expenditure are devaluation, on the one hand, and commercial policy—tariffs, quotas, export subsidies—on the other. Whichever tool is used, however, certain common problems arise.

The main problem of expenditure-switching policies is that they tend to be inflationary. This aspect is very apparent when such policies are pursued by an economy that is operating at or near capacity. Increased demand as exports grow and indigenous residents shift from foreign to home goods will, in this case, push against limited supply and drive up the prices of domestic goods.

Even when the economy is not near capacity, expenditure-switching policies typically have at least an initial inflationary effect on the prices of imported goods. If this increase in import prices leads to a demand for wage increases, and these wage increases are then reflected in domestic prices, the result will be an upward ratcheting of the inflation rate.

Inflation is undesirable in itself and can, in addition, defeat the adjustment process. Suppose that either devaluation or commercial policy is used in an attempt to improve the trade balance and that the result is an acceleration of inflation. The inflation will lead to a growing real appreciation of the domestic currency, which will undo the very expenditure-switching effects that were the aim of the policy. If a country then applies further expenditure-switching measures, the process will be repeated and can lead to ever-accelerating inflation.

The best answer, although still an unsatisfactory one, lies in a combination of expenditure-switching and expenditure-reducing policies.

THE POLICY MIX.   Consider an economy that is operating more or less at full capacity when it experiences an adverse external shock and whose government either decides to adjust to the shock or is forced to adjust because of inability to finance as much as it would like. How should the government choose between expenditure-reducing and expenditure-switching policies?

Pure reliance on expenditure-reducing policies amounts to putting the economy into a recession so as to cut imports. This approach will work, but it is a very costly way to improve the trade balance because it typically involves sacrificing several dollars' worth of domestic output for every dollar's worth of domestic output for every dollar's worth of import reduction. Reliance on expenditure-switching policies alone will be inflationary and will not work for very long. The answer, then, is to use both types of policy.

Suppose for a moment that inflation would be a problem only if demand exceeded the economy's capacity and also that the government could calculate the effect of its policies with a good deal of precision. Then the government could fine tune its policies as follows: use expenditure-switching policies to reduce imports and increase exports by the desired amounts and use expenditure-reducing policies to cut domestic demand by just enough to keep overall demand for domestic products from exceeding capacity. This textbook solution would produce a one-time jump in import prices but would then leave the economy continuing to produce at full capacity with an improved trade balance. The policy would not be painless. Expenditure-reducing policies involve real costs, and expenditure-switching policies also reduce real incomes; but the policy would achieve its aims at relatively low cost.

In practice, however, adjustment programs are almost always more costly and lead to at least a temporary economic downturn and excess capacity and to at least a temporary acceleration of inflation. One reason is uncertainty. Governments are not sure enough about the effect of their policies to fine-tune them and, when they finally do decide to adjust to an external shock, often prefer to err on the side of too much adjustment rather than too little. The main reason, however, is that inflationary impacts of expenditure-switching policies do not, unfortunately, occur only when the economy is at capacity. To control inflation, countries resort to harsher expenditure-reducing policies than the textbook solution would suggest, and thus they suffer recessions and excess capacity.

Devaluation versus Commercial Policy

Some kind of expenditure-switching policy is a vital part of the adjustment to an adverse external shock. The choice of which policy to use is, however, often a controversial one. The simplest policy is devaluation—an increase in the price of foreign currency. It is an across-the-board expenditure-switching policy that both encourages exports and discourages imports. It raises export prices and encourages increased supply, whereas the increase in import prices discourages demand. The problem is that these price increases contribute directly to inflation and may also affect income distribution in ways that are undesirable and politically difficult.

The alternative to the across-the-board incentive for expenditure switching provided by devaluation is a program of more detailed interventions to promote particular exports and discourage particular imports. The presumed advantage of such programs of commercial policy is that they can reduce the inflationary impact of adjustment by concentrating on limiting "inessential" imports, and they can achieve adjustment with smaller adverse effects on income distribution than is possible with devaluation. In practice, these advantages often turn out to be illusory, but commercial policies remain a key part of many countries' adjustment efforts.

DEVALUATION.   Devaluation has two highly desirable features as an expenditure-switching policy. The first is that it is administratively simple. Changing the price at which the central bank converts foreign exchange into domestic currency does not require a new set of regulations or a bureaucracy to enforce them and thus creates no incentives for evasion or corruption. The second advantage is that devaluation is a decentralized incentive that allows the economy to take advantage of all possible means of adjustment: export growth as well as import reduction, untraditional exports as well as traditional, cuts in "essential" imports (which may prove to be not as essential as one thought) as well as in inessential ones. Sustained devaluations often produce adjustment in ways that were unexpected and would not have happened under a more centralized policy.

This favorable view must be qualified in two ways. The first is that, to be effective, a devaluation must lead to a depreciation of the real exchange rate, not simply of the nominal rate. In other words, devaluation must more than offset the difference between domestic and world inflation rates and must not itself lead to offsetting increases in domestic wages and prices. Brazil, despite continuous exchange rate depreciation, has actually achieved virtually no real devaluation of its currency.

The second qualification is that devaluation has effects on income distribution that often make it politically unattractive. This statement is particularly true in commodity-exporting countries that have pursued strategies of import-substituting industrialization. In these countries, a devaluation means a rise in the price of exports, which typically benefits the agricultural or raw material–producing sector, and an increase in the price of imports to both firms and workers in the industrial sector. From a humanitarian point of view, this income distribution effect may seem either a plus or a minus, depending on the characteristics of each sector. Since such countries have in effect already made a political decision to support the industrial sector, however, the politics are nearly always unfavorable.

COMMERCIAL POLICIES.   The alternative to the across-the-board incentive of a devaluation is selective commercial policies. These include import quotas, exchange controls, and export subsidies.

Import quotas and exchange controls are similar in their effects. A system of import quotas places direct restrictions on the quantities of particular goods or classes of goods that can be imported. A system of exchange controls achieves much the same result by requiring that foreign exchange be turned over to the central bank and then by restricting the availability of foreign exchange for particular imports. The effect is to enforce a reduction in imports by direct government mandate. Export subsidies are payments made to exporters, which can selectively encourage particular exports that a government believes will respond to this incentive.

All these policies, like devaluation, raise domestic prices and thus feed inflation. Quotas and exchange controls, in reducing the domestic availability of imports, drive up their prices. Export subsidies, by diverting production to foreign markets, raise the home prices of export goods. The hope of governments, however, is that by pursuing such selective policies they can restrict the domain of price increases to less sensitive areas—avoiding basic consumption goods, for example, or avoiding providing bonuses to wealthy owners of resources.

The problems are the converse of the advantages of devaluation. Commercial policies introduce administrative complexity, which can encourage evasion and fraud. An extreme example is Turkey in the late 1950s, where evasion of exchange controls reached such proportions that legal international transactions virtually disappeared. Furthermore, commercial policies provide only narrow incentives, denying the possibility of creative responses, such as domestic production of essential imports or development of new exports. The worse feature of commercial policies as a response to external shocks is that they have a way of becoming permanent because they create groups with a vested interest in their continuation.

THE MIX OF DEVALUATION AND COMMERCIAL POLICIES. Economic analysis suggests that, from the standpoint of efficiency, the optimal mix of devaluation and commercial policies in expenditure switching is all of one and none of the other. Governments rarely follow this advice, however. In part their failure to do so may reflect lack of faith in the effectiveness of devaluation, although such lack of faith is not justified by experience. For the most part, however, it reflects the political considerations mentioned above.

There is something of a parallel between the adjustment-financing choice and the devaluation–commercial policy choice. Governments often finance first, then adjust only when this position becomes untenable. When they adjust, they often rely on commercial policies first, then devalue only when these become unworkable. Persuading countries to do the right thing from the beginning is one of the main tasks of international organizations.

Brazil Again

Earlier I used Brazil as an example of a country that had experienced severe external shocks. Table 4-2 shows some of the ways in which Brazil coped with those shocks.

Table 4-2. Financing and Adjustment in Brazil, 1978–84

Item	1978	1981	1984
Current account balance (billions of U.S. dollars)	−7.0	−11.8	−4.2
Trade balance (billions of U.S. dollars)	−2.4	−0.8	11.8
Change in export volume over previous three years (percent)	14.8	61.9	25.0
Change in import volume over previous three years (percent)	−3.6	−5.6	−28.1
Real exchange rate[a] (1978 = 100)	100	108	110
Rate of growth of real output over previous three years (percent)	6.8	4.0	0.7

a. Wholesale prices in U.S. dollars deflated by world export prices.
Source: IMF, *International Financial Statistics.*

The first question is that of financing versus adjustment. Brazil went through two phases. From 1980 to 1982, Brazil opted for a mix of financing and adjustment. The current account deficit rose, financed by increased borrowing from commercial banks, but it rose by far less than the size of the external shocks. Import volume fell sharply, exports rose despite the world recession, and Brazil's trade balance improved despite a sharp worsening in the terms of trade. In late 1982, however, this mix became untenable because of a loss of creditor confidence. Brazil was then forced to go to the IMF, and, under the IMF-sponsored plan, the balance of policy shifted heavily toward adjustment. The country began to run a massive trade surplus, despite unfavorable terms of trade, to offset the rise in interest payments.

Adjustment in Brazil was achieved through both expenditure-reducing policies and expenditure switching. A combination of budget tightening and credit restriction led to a virtual cessation of growth in domestic demand in the first half of the 1980s. At the same time, imports were cut relative to GDP, and export growth was faster than in the late 1970s. The reason for harsh expenditure-reducing policies may be seen in the fact that the inflation rate accelerated to triple-digit levels. Without the restraint on domestic demand, this inflation would surely have been even worse.

Brazil's expenditure-switching methods were, however, not what economists would recommend. Brazil's real exchange rate hardly changed over the period. Thus the improvement in trade performance was achieved through exchange controls and export subsidies.

3. Additional Problems

I have now cataloged the major sources of external shocks to developing countries and have set out a framework for thinking about the policy response. The fact is that after an adverse external shock the path of policymakers is rarely smooth. Even when the policies are sensibly chosen, the process of coping with an adverse shift in the world economic environment usually runs into a few potholes. This is, of course, even more likely when the initial policy response is not sensible. The final part of this chapter describes some of the pitfalls that countries attempting to cope with adverse external shocks encounter.

Every country has problems in dealing with external shocks that are to some degree unique. Nonetheless, certain common problems have afflicted a number of countries after adverse changes in the world environment. These are the problems of reduced growth rates, inflation, and capital flight.

Reduced Growth

Countries that experience adverse external shocks often experience a sharp slowdown in their domestic economic growth. Brazil's economy grew at an average rate of about 7 percent a year from 1973 to 1980, then grew less than 1 percent in total from 1980 to 1984. This growth took place with a growing population, a sharp deterioration in the terms of trade, forced cuts in imports, and an expansion of exports. The result was a drastic reduction in the per capita resources available for domestic use, whether consumption or investment. Probably these were about 15 percent lower in 1985 than they had been in 1979, in a country that had been accustomed to rapid growth.

Much of the slowdown in growth that takes place in such cases reflects reduced use of an economy's capacity rather than a slowdown in the growth of that capacity. A slowdown in the use of capacity is in the long run less of a problem than a slowdown in the growth of potential output because it may be followed by a compensating period of rapid growth as the economy takes up the slack. Thus in Chile the drastic fall in output of 1974–76 brought on by the government's adjustment policies was followed by four years of rapid growth as the economy returned to trend. The short-run social costs and political risks of a decline in capacity utilization, however—which among other things mean a rise in unemployment and underemployment—are surely greater than a slowdown in potential growth.

Even if these short-run costs are discounted (where the short run may easily be five years or more), the adjustment to external shocks seems in many cases to compromise long-run prospects as well. The most disturbing feature here is the tendency for expenditure cuts to fall disproportionately on investment. The reason is partly that expenditure cutting via credit restriction is easier politically than reductions in government spending or tax increases and partly that the excess capacity which results from expenditure restriction itself deters investment.

How could the costs of adjustment in slower growth be reduced? One answer would be to use more financing and less adjustment. If the external shock is long-lived, however, this will involve an unfeasible accumulation of debt; indeed, if potential lenders see the shock as permanent, a country will not have the choice of extra financing in any case. Conceivably, some countries whose situation is particularly desperate could have their problems lightened by a write-down of debt, but this is not a usual option (and not one that can be used very often!).

The better answer is to rely less on expenditure reduction and more on expenditure switching. In the textbook solution discussed earlier, the mix of expenditure-reducing and expenditure-switching policies is fine-tuned so as to achieve adjustment without creating any excess capacity. With fine-tuning, a slowdown in growth is not an inevitable consequence of adverse external shocks. East Asian developing countries have maintained growth since 1980 despite external shocks arguably as severe as those of Latin America. But this is not something that only Asians can do. Latin America itself turned in a quite creditable growth performance during the 1930s despite a radical worsening of the external environment.

Many governments nonetheless respond to external shocks with drastic expenditure-reducing policies and are reluctant to go too far on expenditure-switching policies, especially devaluation, largely from fear of inflation.

Inflation

Many countries that experience external shocks also experience a surge in inflation. Brazil's inflation rate soared from under 50 percent in the late 1970s to over 200 percent in 1984. This increase was, if anything, less drastic than that experienced by other Latin American debtors.

This acceleration of inflation operates by a simple mechanism. The countries that have experienced drastic accelerations in inflation typically have wages that are indexed to consumer prices with a short lag. Suppose that such a country devalues as an expenditure-switching measure. The devaluation will immediately raise the prices of imports and other traded goods. Because wages are indexed, they will rise in turn: these wage increases will be passed on in increases in domestic prices. These price increases will then lead to further wage increases. The inflation will cause a real appreciation that erodes the effects of the devaluation, necessitating another; and the process continues.

The acceleration of inflation may have serious social costs. Inflation at a few percentage points a year has few measurable costs, but inflation rates in the hundreds or thousands of percentage points a year lead to substantial resources wasted in inefficient transactions and speculation, destroy the basis for rational economic decisions, and damage the credibility of all government policies. To limit this inflation, governments resort to expenditure-reducing policies. These policies allow the needed adjustment to take place with less inflationary expenditure-switching policies and, by depressing domestic demand, tend to limit the pass-through of wages into prices. The problem is that the reliance on expenditure reduction then cuts severely into growth.

How can this dilemma be made less painful? Some contribution can be made by better-conceived expenditure-switching policies. Whatever the intended effects of exchange controls and other commercial policies, they are probably more inflationary for any given trade balance target than devaluation because they are less efficient. The most important change, however, must be to break the wage-price spiral. Effective adjustment policy may thus require reform of labor market institutions as well. Recent adjustment policies have included such measures as the deindexing of wages, on the one hand, and the imposition of temporary wage-price controls, on the other. Such policies are difficult to implement and often fail; the costs of adjustment in their absence are nonetheless so high that a good case can be made for trying them even with a substantial risk of failure.

Capital Flight

No discussion of the problems of coping with external shocks to developing countries can be complete without mention of the problem of capital flight. In a number of cases, the problems of financing and adjustment have been greatly exacerbated by a flow of private funds abroad. Such capital flight worsens the tradeoff between financing and adjustment. For any given degree of adjustment, the government must secure additional financing, and thus the external debt grows more rapidly. If financing is constrained, capital flight forces a more stringent adjustment.

In some cases, the magnitude of capital flight has been such that it dominates the picture. From 1979 to 1982, Argentina experienced capital outflows of $19.2 billion while increasing foreign debt by $26.5 billion—that is, 65 percent of the borrowing went to allow Argentine residents to acquire foreign assets rather than to finance imports. Mexico's experience was only marginally less extreme. For once, Brazil was spared the worst: capital flight was only a marginal factor in its accumulation of debt.

These massive capital flights occurred under similar circumstances. In each case, a combination of adverse external shocks and the legacy of past policy mistakes made adjustment inevitable, but governments used external financing to postpone this adjustment. Residents anticipating

future devaluation and exchange controls, shifted funds out of the
countries. In so doing, they made the eventual adjustment problem
much more difficult.

There are basically two ways to avoid the problem of capital flight.
The first is to adjust promptly when the eventual necessity for adjustment is clear, so as not to present speculators with a policy course that is
clearly not credible. The threat of speculation provides an additional
reason for not falling into the short-term, easy course of postponing
adjustment and relying on financing to deal with external shocks.

Once capital flight has begun, however, even a government determined to bring the economy under control may find it hard to persuade
speculators of that determination, and their lack of confidence can be
self-fulfilling. The only answer during a difficult adjustment period
may be controls on international capital movements.

4. Conclusions

Adjusting to external shocks is never easy or painless. A country that
experiences severe external shocks has done well if it escapes with only a
temporary recession and a temporary bout of inflation, rather than a
sustained reduction in growth prospects and a permanent shift to
higher inflation rates.

This chapter began with a review of the main sources of external
shocks to developing countries. In addition to providing a guide to some
of the likely sources of future external shocks, the extensiveness of the
list should have made it clear that no country can realistically attempt to
insulate itself from all potential adverse external shocks. The world
economy is sufficiently volatile in a sufficiently large number of ways
that to participate in that economy is unfortunately to risk a subsequent
unfavorable surprise.

The key to coping successfully with an unfavorable external shock is a
realistic understanding of the problem and a willingness to make hard
choices. I have noted three levels of choice. First, countries must decide
whether to finance or to adjust—that is, whether to borrow abroad on
the assumption that the shock is temporary or to seek to increase
exports and cut imports. Second, to the extent that countries choose to
adjust, they must decide on the mix of expenditure reduction and
expenditure switching—that is, decide when to cut spending and when
to switch spending from foreign to domestic goods. Third, in promoting expenditure switching, they must decide whether to rely on devaluation or on commercial policies that make detailed interventions in
international trade.

Economic analysis does not always dictate each choice unambigu-
ously. The choice between financing and adjustment depends on how

long an external shock will last, something which differs for each case—
although it is probably a good idea for governments to bend over backward to avoid an inherent temptation to postpone adjustment too long.
The choice between expenditure reduction and expenditure switching
depends on the ability to control inflationary pressures—again something that varies with each case and that is usually highly uncertain until
it has been tried. Only the last choice is fairly clear: economic analysis
says that devaluation is preferable to more complex commercial policies. Even here, political realities may force the most technocratic of
governments to stray from strict efficiency.

What I provide here, then, is less a cookbook with explicit recipes
than a road map that indicates the problems associated with each possible route.

5

Overvaluation and Trade Balance

Rudiger Dornbusch

OVERVALUATION of the exchange rate is a serious problem in many developing countries. It not only makes imports artificially cheaper for consumers and exports relatively dearer for producers but also reduces the external competitiveness of a country and thereby causes losses of domestic production, employment, and fiscal revenues.

The main causes of overvaluation are expansion in domestic demand (possibly as a result of increased government spending), loss of export revenue (because of a drop in the price of commodity exports), and deficits in the external balance (because of increases in import costs). If the exchange rate remains overvalued for even a year or two, countrywide speculation on devaluation can ruin the economy and can result in massive flight of capital abroad.

Countries with overvalued currencies are generally unprepared for a rapid turnaround. There is no easy way to correct misaligned exchange rates. Some Latin American countries, ravaged by triple-digit inflation rates, have experimented with crawling pegs. Other countries elsewhere have tried floating their exchange rates or pegging them to currency baskets.

This chapter begins by summarizing the effects of overvaluation and offering definitions and measurements of real exchange rates. It then analyzes various disturbances that bring about trade deficits and overvaluation, describes the impact of overvaluation in goods, factor, and asset markets, and traces the experiences of six countries that overvalued their exchange rates. Various exchange rate options are given, and there is discussion of the special problems of undervaluation.

1. Effects of Overvaluation

The problems of an overvalued exchange rate can be highlighted by the experiences of Chile during 1978–81. Initially, there was no problem in financing large deficits by borrowing abroad. Moreover, large structural changes in the economy, including drastic trade reform, obscured an overvalued peso. It was difficult to tell what the equilibrium real exchange rate should be and whether the real exchange rate was in fact appreciating. In hindsight, however, the overvaluation became massive and had destructive effects on the economy.

The real exchange rate for Chile appears below; the index year is 1978. The real exchange rate is expressed as an index of domestic prices to the prices of import goods. Real appreciation is defined as an increase of domestic prices relative to import prices, and this pattern appears quite clearly in the data. Between 1979 and 1981 the real exchange rate appreciated by more than 30 percent.[1]

1978	1979	1980	1981	1982
100	99	110	130	109

What happened? Early in 1979 the Chilean government, having introduced budget and trade reforms over the past few years, decided to tackle inflation. The exchange rate was fixed at thirty-nine pesos to the dollar and was kept at that level through 1981, even though inflation in Chile in 1979—running at 33 percent—was well above the level in the United States and other industrial countries. The inflation level did drop to less than 10 percent in 1982, but this reduction was achieved at the cost of a deterioration in the external balance. Imports increased by more than $2 billion. Unemployment increased sharply as a result of a loss in the competitiveness of the domestic industry. After several exchange depreciations in 1982, inflation went back up to more than 25 percent within a year.

The Chilean experiment is quite a typical illustration of what happens when, for one reason or another, the exchange rate gets out of line. The main effects of overvaluation are:

- A loss in external competitiveness: This loss leads to an increase in imports and a reduction in exports. Even if the resulting trade deficit can be financed by reserves or borrowing, it may be unwise to give up these resources or to incur increased external liabilities that will ultimately need to be serviced by trade surpluses.
- Loss of domestic production, employment, and fiscal revenues: Firms that can no longer profitably compete with imports or produce exports for the world market will cut production first and, if overvaluation persists, will stop production. The result will be a loss of jobs and tax revenue.
- An ultimate devaluation: This measure is often forced upon policymakers by an external balance crisis. Asset markets (which include grocers, traders, and others) will anticipate devaluation and

will therefore shift to dollars and other foreign currencies if these are freely available, or they will speed up imports of underpriced goods and withhold exports that will fetch higher domestic prices. These shifts into quasi-dollars mean (a) a loss of some foreign exchange to the country, (b) a subsidy to importers, and (c) a windfall gain for exporters.

- Adverse effects on domestic financial markets: Traders will try to borrow in domestic currency to finance the buildup of imports or to carry stocks of exports that are held off pending devaluation. Interest rates will be pushed up and will hurt other sectors. If the overvaluation persists, many industries may go bankrupt speculating. If banks fail because of speculation, the government may have to incur heavy costs to bail out the financial system.

One might think that, although all these things are possible in principle, they do not really occur. Not so. The problems faced in Chile were repeated in various forms in Argentina, Israel, Mexico, and Peru.

2. Definitions of the Real Exchange Rate

An economy has thousands of prices—for imported goods, for exports, and for goods that do not enter international trade (haircuts, restaurant meals, and so on). These prices vary individually over time, but their trend collectively equals the aggregate rate of inflation. An important pattern other than inflation is brought out by looking at the ratio of prices of home goods or nontraded goods (the terms are used interchangeably) to the prices of traded goods. This ratio is one of the measures often used to calculate the real exchange rate:

$$(5\text{-}1) \quad \text{Real exchange rate} = \frac{\text{Price of home goods}}{\text{Price of traded goods}}$$

The real exchange rate affects the allocation of resources in the economy. An increase in this rate will make home goods more expensive and will encourage consumers to substitute the less expensive traded goods for home goods. Relative prices do affect household spending patterns. Consumers reallocate their budget and buy more of those goods that have become relatively cheaper.

A policy of overvaluation makes imports artificially cheaper for consumers but dearer for producers. Producers will produce less traded goods either because they cannot break even in traded goods or because there is more profit in home goods.

Few countries have good data, or indeed any data, on home goods. However, countries do maintain statistics on the consumer price index (CPI), wholesale prices, GDP deflators, and export and import prices. We are interested in the price of traded goods in terms of home goods. As a proxy for the latter, we may use the GDP deflator even though it includes some traded goods together with home goods. If the prices of traded goods rise more than the prices of home goods, this imperfect measure will still indicate the direction in which the real exchange rate moves.

Traded goods can be subdivided to make further distinctions. Oil-importing countries, for example, may want to separate oil and non-oil import prices to ensure that changes in world oil prices do not obscure the effects of changes in the prices of imported non-oil goods (manufactures, for example) relative to domestic goods. Similarly, traditional exports (agricultural or mining) may need to be separated from nontraditional exports (mainly manufactures).

In the end, because there are many real exchange rate measures, the distinction between home goods and traded goods might be considered lost. Such is not the case. The refinements merely serve to bridge the conceptual distinction between home goods and traded goods and to link the empirical problems of measurement on the one hand and special issues for certain traded goods (for example, oil and commodities) on the other hand. The difficulty lies in trying to obtain one single number—the real exchange rate—to indicate profitability for all firms in the traded goods sector. The firms may produce peanuts or manufactures for export or may produce cars or textiles to compete with imports. The same number is also sought to guide households on the relative price of home goods and traded goods. The difficulty in finding one single number is further complicated by the absence of satisfactory statistics.

To avoid some of these problems, it has become common to measure competitiveness by comparing not home goods with traded goods, as in equation 5-1, but the dollar prices of manufactures in the domestic market with the dollar prices of manufactures in the export markets. This measure is known as the real exchange rate in manufacturing.

$$(5\text{-}2) \quad \left[\begin{array}{c} \text{Real exchange} \\ \text{rate in} \\ \text{manufacturing} \end{array} \right] = \left[\frac{\text{Price of manufactures in domestic market}}{\text{Price of manufactures in export market}} \right]$$

In table 5-1, the index of real exchange rate compares the relative prices of a country's exports with those of other countries. The index measures the external competitiveness of a country, not the internal resource allocation (between traded goods and home goods). A rise in this index, for example from 98 to 106 in Peru in 1984, represents a real appreciation or a loss in international competitiveness in exports.

The behavior of real exchange rates differs. In Taiwan and Hong Kong, for example, the variations in real exchange rates are very small; in Mexico and Brazil, they are sizable. Among the large Latin American debtor countries, real exchange rates depreciated 25 percent to 30 percent in the early 1980s. This gain in competitiveness compensated for

Table 5-1. Real Exchange Rate in Manufacturing in Selected Economies, 1982–86

(1980–82 = 100)

Economy	1982	1983	1984	1985	1986
Argentina	76	81	80	71	63
Brazil	112	86	86	85	79
Chile	97	89	90	79	72
Colombia	105	104	99	86	72
Hong Kong	99	102	100	106	100
Indonesia	100	111	97	96	86
Israel	99	108	118	107	100
Korea, Rep. of	101	103	96	89	79
Malaysia	99	105	119	116	108
Mexico	82	78	92	90	73
Peru	104	98	106	97	100
Philippines	101	106	107	114	104
Taiwan	103	97	96	93	86
Turkey	104	95	91	91	82
Venezuela	109	116	86	93	91

Note: The figures for 1986 are projections.

Sources: Data for this group of semiindustrial countries and for all industrial countries are reported monthly in the publication *World Financial Markets* of Morgan Guaranty Trust Company of New York. The International Monetary Fund reports real-exchange-rate measures in its monthly publication *International Financial Statistics* under the heading "Cost and Price Comparisons for Manufacturing." Unfortunately, the Fund does not report data for all developing countries. Both sources provide data that, despite their imperfections, are the best available for policy analysis.

earlier overvaluation of the currency and helped the countries earn the dollars needed to withstand the effects of the oil and the debt shocks. Turkey, to take another example, faced trade imbalances in the late 1970s and went through stabilization programs that resulted in a gain in external competitiveness. Generally, behind every big movement in the real exchange rate is an external balance crisis. Correcting misaligned exchange rates is one way of correcting imbalances in payments.

Even though manufacturing real exchange rates are a very useful instrument for analyzing a country's competitiveness, they have their limitations. First, they refer only to exports; the competitiveness on the import side is not known. If a country gains competitiveness on the export side, import-competing domestic firms will probably also be competitive with foreign suppliers of the home market. It is also quite possible, however, that a country sells to one major market (say the United States) and imports predominantly from another (say Japan). Changes in the dollar/yen exchange rate affect competitiveness on the import and export sides differently. A gain in competitiveness on the export side may be offset by a loss in competitiveness on the import side.

Second, the export prices in equation 5-2 are those of industrial countries, and equation 5-2 therefore refers to a country's competitiveness with industrial countries, not with other developing countries. Brazil's gain or loss in competitiveness, for example, is measured relative to Europe, Japan, and the United States, not relative to Mexico and Taiwan. Brazil's competitive position among other developing countries may be important, especially when these countries are undergoing structural changes.

Third, structural manufacturing is only a small part of the traded goods sector. It would be little comfort for a country to know that it has not lost its competitiveness in manufacturing when its traditional exports have lost the edge.

To measure the competitiveness of traditional exports, we must examine the relationship between prices and costs. In agriculture, for instance, the prices at which agricultural output is sold in the world market are given. An individual producer's ability to compete effectively in producing for export will depend on whether prices are higher than costs. Costs include wages, materials, (including imported inputs such as fertilizers), and taxes or duties on exports.

The competitiveness of traditional traded goods industries can be defined as:

$$(5\text{-}3) \qquad \left[\begin{array}{c} \text{Competitiveness of} \\ \text{traditional exports} \end{array} \right] = \left[\dfrac{\text{Domestic cost}}{\text{World price}} \right]$$

whereby both price indexes are measured in the same currency.

The measure of competitiveness in equation (5-3) highlights the supply side of the economy. Whenever costs get out of line with prices, firms will cut production to avoid losses. If wages are increased but the exchange rate is not depreciated, firms will experience cost increases that cannot be covered by the going prices. Profit margins, slim in the first place, will be reduced, and the profitability of production for export will fall. Firms will reduce output and employees. These statements apply to exports and to traditional goods that compete with imports.

We have seen a variety of measures trying to capture various aspects of competitiveness. The objective is to find a few indicators that tell us which way incentives are tilting: are consumers diverted from home goods to traded goods? Are firms discouraged from producing traded goods, or are they losing out relative to foreign suppliers? Are firms in traditional industries facing costs that have gotten out of line with the prices they face in world markets? There is no perfect indicator, and the same indicators may not be appropriate to each country. For some, manufacturing is the main issue; in others, commodity production may be paramount. But in each instance the question is much the same: which way are resources being shifted?

Overvaluation has many faces: manufacturing exports become over-priced in world markets relative to the prices of competitors; traded goods are overly cheap for domestic consumers; traded goods sell at prices too low to make production worthwhile, and their costs of production are too high to compete effectively with imports. The net result, through one channel or the other, is a large import bill and small exports. This situation is a problem for two reasons: first, instead of output reductions, entire industries disappear; second, the persistent trade deficit leads to a debt buildup that will ultimately have to be financed by trade surpluses. The very industries that are supposed to earn the debt service, however, are destroyed by lack of profitability.

3. Effects of Disturbances

Figure 5-1 presents a simple conceptual framework relating to the market for foreign exchange. The real exchange rate is measured on the vertical axis and the level of import spending and export revenue in the economy on the horizontal axis. The real exchange rate is defined here

Figure 5-1. Conceptual Framework of the Foreign Exchange Market

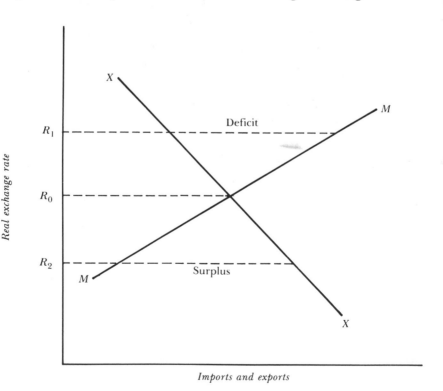

Imports and exports

as the ratio of wages to the exchange rate.[2] The wage is measured as so many pesos per hour of work and the exchange rate as pesos per dollar. The real exchange rate is thus simply the wage in dollars.

The level of the wage in dollars determines the international competitiveness of the country's economy because it determines the costs of the country's industries and hence its ability to sell in world markets. The wage in dollars also determines the ability of home industries to compete with imports. The lower the wage in dollars, the better the country will be able to sell abroad and to compete with foreign suppliers in the home market.

The schedule *MM* shows import spending. The higher the real exchange rate, or the wage in dollars, the more will be spent on imports. First, with a high wage in dollars, home producers cannot effectively compete with foreign firms in the domestic market. Second, if wages in dollars are high, other things being equal, the power of the local population to purchase imports will also be high. For these reasons, *MM* is upward sloping.

The schedule *XX* shows export earnings. A high real exchange rate will render home firms uncompetitive in world markets. Home producers of manufactures cannot compete with low-wage foreign firms, hence they earn little export revenue. Domestic producers of traditional exports, who face world prices, cannot cover their costs and hence do not produce much. Conversely, when wages in dollars are low, home producers are highly competitive and earn considerable export revenue. For these reasons, *XX* is downward sloping.

The trade deficit is simply the horizontal distance between import spending and export revenue. At a real exchange rate, R_0, there is equilibrium; at R_1 there is trade deficit; at R_2 there is surplus. R_1 is clearly an overvalued exchange rate unless the trade deficit is financed, for example, out of aid. The equilibrium real exchange rate, R_0, provides external balance. If there are no aid flows and no service transactions, external balance means trade balance equilibrium. When there are service transactions, they are added to import spending (debt service, transport, and so on) and to export revenue (tourism, remittances from workers abroad, and so on).

The framework of analysis developed here is useful for a review of how disturbances—such as a loss of export revenue, a domestic overexpansion, increased import costs, and domestic cost increases—affect the trade balance and the real exchange rate.

Loss of Export Revenue

When a country suffers a loss of export revenue—for example, when world prices of an export good fall—the export revenues decline at each level of the real exchange rate. The schedule *XX* shifts to the left (see figure 5-2). At the initial real exchange rate, say, R_0, there is now a trade deficit. Import spending exceeds export revenue.

There are a number of possible reasons for the shift in the *XX* schedule. First, recession could reduce demand in an important market, or the real income of customers in that market could decline, say, because of a drop in oil prices. As a result, sales and revenues may drop even though competitiveness remains unchanged.

Second, competitors may get ahead by reducing their dollar costs and prices. So even though the country's wage rate and costs in dollars remain unchanged, competitors cut into its sales. Third, countries that have highly specialized exports may find that the world demand for their products has declined. The replacement of copper by optical fibers in long-distance transmission, for example, has had a devastating impact on the export earnings of copper producers.

The deficit in the external account might be financed by borrowing from commercial banks or by using the foreign exchange reserves. The important question to be asked, however, is whether the deficit is transitory or permanent. If it is transitory, commercial borrowings can cover the deficit; if it is permanent, adjustment is inevitable, and the sooner it

Figure 5-2. Trade Deficit and the Real Exchange Rate

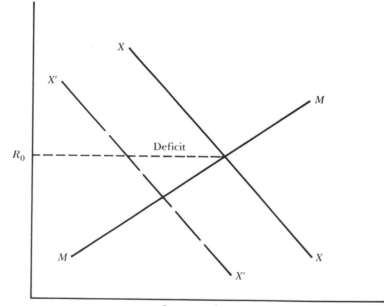

is initiated, the better it is. The trouble, of course, is that initially every adverse disturbance looks transitory, and every favorable one seems permanent. Consequently, adjustment comes too late and becomes more expensive than necessary. Unfortunately, there is often no easy way to tell whether the external disturbance is permanent or transitory.

Overexpansion

Another disturbance, and one that leads to overvaluation, is an expansion in domestic demand. If the government increases spending—through such means as public works projects, a cut in taxes, and an increase in subsidies or transfer payments—more money ends up in people's pockets. The increased spending has two effects. On the export side, export revenue is reduced at each real-exchange-rate level as XX shifts to $X'X'$ (see figure 5-3). Firms that exported before will sell more of their goods in the home market to meet the increased demand. On the import side, households spend more on all goods, including imports. As a result, MM shifts to $M'M'$, showing higher import spending at each level of the real exchange rate. At R_0, a deficit now needs to be financed.

Figure 5-3. Overvaluation and Structural Adjustment

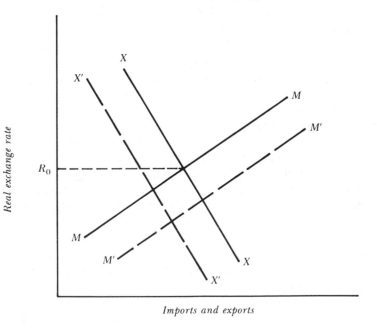

Imports and exports

Increased Import Costs

When import costs increase—because of an oil price increase, for instance—the schedule *MM* shifts to the right to *M'M'* (see figure 5-3). At each level of the real exchange rate, more payments have to be made for imports, hence at R_0, the initial real exchange rate, there will now be a deficit in the external balance. If the external shock is of a transitory nature, it may be easy to finance the deficit; if it is permanent, adjustment measures will need to be initiated rapidly.

Domestic Cost Increases

Increases in domestic cost are frequently not offset by appropriate depreciation in the exchange rate. When home wages rise, for example, the exchange rate may be held constant, so the wage in dollars increases. This corresponds to a move from R_0 to R_1 in figure 5-1. On the export side, revenues decrease because traditional export industries can no longer compete at current world prices. The profit margins of these industries are cut, and production is reduced. Producers of manufactures find that the prices that cover their costs leave them uncompetitive in world markets. They sell less, and their export revenue drops. These statements are true both for the producer of textiles and for a country that is a tourist spot. On the import side, an increase in home wages in dollars will increase imports of traditional goods. In fact, a net food exporter might become a net importer.

Countries that maintain fixed exchange rates against a major currency even when their domestic inflation rate is higher may face special problems of disequilibrium. Nothing may happen in the short run, but over time the currency will become overvalued. A difference of 2 percent to 3 percent in the inflation rates between a country that is pegging its currency and the country to whose currency it is pegged will result in a large overvaluation over time.

This kind of problem arises particularly for a country that is in a currency area (dollar, sterling, or franc) and has a formal, or at least longstanding, commitment to maintain the exchange rate with the major currency. The Dominican Republic's exchange rate, for example, is fixed to the U.S. dollar under its constitution. For nearly a decade, however, the domestic price level in that country has been getting increasingly out of line with the price level in the United States, so that there has been a massive overvaluation.

This peculiar case of fixed exchange rates poses many difficult questions. Is it possible to roll back the overvaluation by containing wage increases and encouraging growth in productivity to bring costs in line with prices abroad? Or is devaluation a better remedy because the loss in competitiveness over the years is too large to be reduced gradually?

4. Goods, Factor, and Asset Markets

Overvaluation can have detrimental effects on the goods, factor, and asset markets.

The Goods Market

Overvaluation means that firms producing goods in competition with foreign firms are at a handicap. They have higher costs than foreign firms and must hence charge higher prices. The alternative is to cut profit margins or cut production levels to lower costs, both on the export side and on the import side, in manufacturing as well as in traditional goods.

An interesting effect of overvaluation on the output of tradable goods occurs from the input side. A large portion of international trade happens in inputs—steel, chemicals, semifinished goods, and fertilizer, to name a few. A firm that produces finished goods will purchase these inputs in addition to using labor and capital. When the exchange rate becomes overvalued, imported inputs cost less than domestically produced inputs and even domestic labor. Domestic firms will therefore tend to substitute imported inputs for domestic inputs or labor. An agricultural enterprise, for instance, might use more fertilizer and less labor. An industrial firm might not conserve petroleum or steel as eagerly. In the construction sector, prefabricated houses might be imported—to use an extreme example—rather than being built by domestic labor. Even if the houses are not prefabricated, they might have imported plumbing, appliances, or furniture. The result will be a larger import content for the whole economy, which will worsen the trade balance.

Overvaluation also affects the choice of firms. Large multinational firms have learned to split the production process into different stages. The parts of a car—engine, transmission, windows, and so on—might come from different countries and be assembled finally in one location. To be part of the circuit, a country must be competitive—that is to say, it must have low wages in dollars.

When the exchange rate gets out of line, the country will be written off the supplier list or will stop being the assembly location for the region. Assembly operations are extremely sensitive to dollar wage movements. The northern part of Mexico, for instance, is a free trade area. U.S. firms bring in duty-free semifinished goods for assembly by low-wage Mexican labor. The finished goods are then exported, duty free, to the United States. Mexico competes with Puerto Rico and Asian countries in being an assembly location. When the Mexican wage in dollars rises, revenue and employment begin to decline.[3]

What is true of intermediate goods also holds true for final goods and services. Tourism is a case in point. When dollar wages in a country rise, and when accordingly the local costs of a vacation rise, the inflow of tourists declines, especially if a particular location has close competitors. (Close competitors exist, for example, in the Caribbean and the Mediterranean regions). Tourists, like everybody else, go shopping for bargains. Overvaluation may soon mean that hotel rooms go empty, nightclubs are deserted, and souvenir shops go broke.

The extent to which overvaluation cuts into export revenue and increases the import bill depends on a number of factors. Two are particularly important. The first is the persistence of an overvaluation. A brief spell of a few months hardly means any trouble because everybody does take some time to shift away from habitual supply sources in search of bargains. A period of a year or two, however, is clearly so long that much and even all of business can be very seriously affected.

The other factor of importance is the degree of substitutability between a country's goods and those supplied by competitors. If the goods are totally homogeneous—say, cotton shirts from Hong Kong or from Singapore—then overvaluation can mean a quick, dramatic loss of markets or rapid import penetration. In contrast, if goods are highly differentiated, as is the case for sophisticated manufactures (Rolls Royce or Mercedes Benz cars), there may be more leeway and less cause for alarm. Part of the reason is that firms in these industries, because they tend to be less than fully competitive, have profit cushions with which they can absorb a loss in competitiveness. But for developing countries the rule is more nearly that the goods are highly homogeneous and that there are plenty of foreign producers ready to take away their markets. Hence overvaluation becomes a serious issue much more rapidly and on a much larger scale.

Factor Markets

Factor markets are the mirror image of the goods markets. If production falls, so will the demand for factors of production. The demand for labor will be particularly affected. Overvaluation will cause firms in the traded goods sector to cut back on employment. Mines, farms, factories, other enterprises, and the tourist industry will all employ fewer workers.

There are also secondary effects. When the traded goods sector is doing poorly, activities in the rest of the economy will also be curtailed. The workers in the traded goods sector who become unemployed will have less money to spend and will reduce their demand for many of the nontraded goods produced. Firms in the nontraded goods sector will be forced to cut production and employment, causing declines in output and employment throughout the economy. Because of the multiplier effect, the initial loss of the single job will trigger the loss of perhaps two or more jobs. This loss can be translated into a substantial economywide employment problem. And the employment problem can lead to a budgetary problem.

Over the long run, sustained overvaluation will lead to disinvestment. Investors finding their capital no longer profitable may want to invest elsewhere. As a result, jobs, export earnings, or import-competing production disappears. This situation may be acceptable to a country with a small traded goods sector because it can finance the deficits easily, but few countries, if any, are in such position. It is more likely that, after a few years of financing overvaluation by borrowing, the country runs out of luck (or money), and adjustment will be called for. Now the country will have to pay not only for all its imports, but also the interest on all the debt incurred in the meantime. The adjustment will be easier if the country has a strong export sector, with plenty of capacity, and an equally strong import-competing sector.

Experience has shown that countries with overvalued currencies are generally unprepared for a rapid turnaround. After a few years of overvaluation, the trade sector may be run down, firms may close, and foreign companies may shift their operations abroad. It will take a long period of undervaluation to attract resources into the traded goods sector and start it off again.

Some critics may not find this distressing scenario persuasive. After all, agriculture or mining cannot leave, nor can factories go abroad. But it is a grave error to follow this line of reasoning. Agriculture can be run down by failure to fertilize, to irrigate, or to maintain land. Mines can be shut down or allowed to decay. Machinery can be allowed to deteriorate because maintenance is not worth the expenditure; it can even be dismantled and sold abroad. Multinational companies can easily close down their operations and shift to another country or region with better policies.

Uncertainty about the real exchange rate can be as detrimental to the sustenance of a viable traded goods sector as overvaluation. Firms that hold capital assets must constantly guess the future profitability of their operations. If there is substantial uncertainty about a government's ability to maintain a reasonable exchange rate or to make timely adjustments, then investment and capacity will fall off.

Financial Markets and Speculation

Sooner or later every overvaluation comes to an end. A massive balance of payments crisis and a big devaluation or exchange rate collapse are usually the end results. If the overvaluation is large and persistent, everybody in the economy becomes a speculator. Speculation on an ultimate devaluation affects the economy in several ways.

- The country becomes a betting parlor. People want to borrow in home currency to buy underpriced imports or to store exports. Those who have the means will want to buy foreign assets whether they are dollars or real estate abroad. The clamor for dollars and quasi dollars will push up interest rates until they reach levels at which lenders are compensated for the expected exchange depreciation. If the overvaluation is 30 percent and is expected to last a year, interest rates can be expected to remain at 30 or 40 percent.

- If the government holds off on devaluation—and in fact it might— the speculators who borrowed to buy dollars or hold traded goods will incur big losses. Many of them may be unable to pay their bills and may go bankrupt. The banks that loaned speculators money may be unable to collect the interest, and if they had borrowed abroad to make loans to the speculators, the banks may default on paying interest too. If depositors find out that the banks are in trouble, they will stage a run that will force the central bank to step in to save the banks. Public funds may have to be transferred to the banks to cover their losses.

- Often the government will assure the public that the exchange rate is just right. There will be no devaluation! Policymakers in Chile, Argentina, and Israel argued this point. But the public does not believe it. The government responds by giving exchange rate guarantees to banks that borrow abroad and bring in money to finance the deficit. The government will also guarantee the exchange rate for importers. In the end, devaluation does occur after all. At that time the government finds that the exchange losses incurred from its guarantee may be as large as 5 percent or 10 percent of GNP. The consequences are huge deficits, deficit finance, inflation, and therefore even more depreciation, perhaps all the way to hyperinflation. Such was the experience of Argentina in 1982-85.

- Capital flight is a regular side effect. A doubtful public will try to shift into foreign goods or assets. To defend the reserves, the government will attempt to restrict access to foreign exchange. At that point, firms will underreport their export earnings and will overstate their import spending and keep the difference in accounts abroad. It is unlikely that this underreported income will ever come back. Capital flight takes other routes too. Tourist revenues do not find their way to the central bank, foreign income goes unreported, and currency is smuggled out and sold abroad. The scope for capital flight is unlimited. Some $30 billion is estimated to have been taken out of Argentina and Mexico each in the past decade.

• Remittances from abroad will be reduced. If nationals employed abroad anticipate a devaluation, they will reduce their remittances and will even withdraw their capital. For some countries, remittances from abroad are an important source of foreign exchange. For Turkey, these remittances amounted to 27 percent of its merchandise exports in 1983.[4]

Temporary Fixes

Governments are generally reluctant to devalue their currencies. They prefer temporary "fixes" to fundamental adjustments. The fixes may include a general "temporary" import duty, selective duties on "unnecessary imports," and quotas on luxury goods to restrict particular imports. These measures are generally expensive and ineffective. The import duties often fall on intermediate goods or on materials that are used to produce exports or import-competing goods. If the country has no rebate policy, competitiveness for these industries will be reduced even further.

Governments in mismanaged economies are chronically short of revenue. Import protection therefore looks like a good policy. A tariff gives extra revenue, whereas an export subsidy costs revenue. Such protection is undesirable, however. It introduces a wedge between the costs and benefits of an extra dollar of resources in the export and import sectors. In the protected sector, dollars are earned, under the cover of protection, at a higher resource cost than they could be earned in the export sector. Exports are thus discriminated against on the production side. On the demand side, consumers pay too much for imports, which are now expensive because of protection, and too little for exportables, of which more should be exported to earn scarce foreign exchange. A uniform import tariff and an equal rate of export subsidy would be more sensible but would be seen as a devaluation.

In the short run, the costs of protection are probably not expensive, but if protection persists, they may be. High tariffs for some industries, rather than a small devaluation for all industries, will lead to inefficient industries. Once the currency is devalued, the excess protection given to some industries can be trimmed. Because these industries were the ones that received protection in the first place, however, they are unlikely to want to lose it now.

The costs of overvaluation stem not only from the misallocation of production but also from the fact that firms devote too much resources to "rent seeking."

Politics

When extended overvaluation leads to heavy foreign borrowing and the flight of capital abroad, it can become a hot political issue. If

overvaluation persists, the risk of losing domestic capital through con-
versions into foreign exchange becomes great. Over an extended
period, the rich of the private sector will build up assets abroad even as
the government increases foreign borrowings to finance the
overvaluation. External debt increases.

At some point, overvaluation will become unsustainable. Foreign
loans will no longer be available. Trade deficits will not only need to be
eliminated but will also have to be turned into surpluses to help repay
the bill for the dollars sold to the rich. (The rich probably got their
money abroad by underinvoicing exports, overinvoicing imports, or
purchasing underpriced imported goods such as cars, boats, planes, and
real estate in places lilke Miami and Hong Kong.) Thus workers' real
wages will need to be cut to gain a trade surplus to pay the bills of the
rich.

The longer an overvaluation lasts, the more controversial subsequent
policies will be. A profitable traded goods sector will have to be created
by cutting real wages and by keeping them low. Initially, these low wages
will yield super profits for firms without resulting in any extra export.
Firms need to be enticed by big profits to expand investment. But excess
profits can be a touchy political isssue.

An overvalued exchange rate is popular in the beginning. Wages are
high in real terms, and they seem to purchase a large piece of the artificially enlarged pie. Still, the cash register keeps running up the bill,
which must ultimately be paid. By this time those workers who still have
jobs, being accustomed to high wages, are unlikely to accept any suggestion that wages are artificially inflated by overvaluation. Strikes will be
the rule, and cutting real wages will be extra difficult.

5. Country Experiences

The problems countries face when they fail to make timely adjustments
in real exchange rates are highlighted by the experiences of six countries below.

Mexico

In 1979, the world price of oil increased sharply for the second time in
less than a decade. Mexico, although not a member of the Organization
of Petroleum Exporting Countries (OPEC), was one of the beneficiaries
of the oil price increases. Revenue from oil exports increased from $4
billion in 1980 to almost $10 billion in 1981 (see table 5-2). The
increased revenue provided some leeway for a relaxed exchange rate
policy and for a more ambitious pursuit of public spending priorities.
But current account deficits were allowed to widen, the real exchange

Table 5-2. Overvaluation of the Exchange Rate in Mexico, 1979–85
(1981 = 100)

Item	1979	1980	1981	1982	1983	1984	1985
Current account deficit as a share of GDP	−4.1	−4.4	−5.8	−3.7	3.7	2.3	0
Budget deficit as a share of GDP	7.4	7.9	12.4	15.0	7.8	5.0	7.5
Noninterest budget	n.a.	n.a.	7.4	5.9	−6.3	−6.6	−5.0
Public investment	n.a.	n.a.	9.6	8.0	5.7	5.3	4.9
Debt as a proportion of GDP	n.a.	33	31	31	39	43	51
Real wage index	n.a.	n.a.	100	105	76	73	67
Real-exchange-rate index	86	91	100	72	68	80	79
Oil revenue (billions of U.S. dollars)	n.a.	3.9	9.8	13.8	16.7	15.2	16.4
Per capita growth	6.7	5.8	5.4	−3.1	−7.8	1.1	1.3
Inflation rate	20	29	27	61	92	66	60

n.a. Not available.

Source: Bank of Mexico, *Economic Indicators.*

rate to appreciate, and budget deficits to mount. External deficits were financed by borrowing; the national debt increased significantly. Even though oil revenues increased fourfold (between 1980 and 1985), servicing and amortization of the debt remained a problem. When commercial banks refused to roll over loans in 1982, a payments crisis developed. The peso had to undergo depreciation, and wages had to be cut (both in real terms). An estimated $30 billion of capital was taken out of the country, financed by the central bank from the current account surplus.

The spending boom left an extraordinary adjustment problem. Even drastic adjustments in the noninterest budget were insufficient to make ends meet. Because capital flight is difficult to stop, even at the best of times, in a country with 3,000 miles of open border to the United States, a drastic cut in real wages was necessary to generate a trade surplus. This is an extraordinary situation: a drastic cut in real wages was necessary to generate a trade surplus with which to finance capital flight (because of continued overvaluation) and to repay bank loans.

The beginning of a decline in oil prices in early 1986 has worsened Mexico's problems. The options are limited. Further cuts in private and public investment will not advance economic growth. If the right price incentives are offered, production and trade may increase, and the problems may be minimized. A big devaluation can quickly restore growth and external balance. The standard of living will decline, but at least the economy will be set on a course of improvement. If there is a lack of confidence in economic recovery, however, in part because the necessary adjustments are so large, further cuts in real wages when there are initially no results will be difficult to implement.

Mexico's difficulties arose from economic mismanagement and bad luck. A good opportunity to rectify many of the difficulties was allowed to slip by after the decline of the oil prices.

Indonesia

As an oil and commodity exporter, Indonesia profited from the price increases of the 1970s. The light manufacturing industries, however, were taxed by an overvalued rupiah and increasing domestic costs. Once commodity prices started declining and oil revenues no longer increased, the current account began to deteriorate. Soon economic activity began to decline. Real depreciation of the rupiah helped bring prices in line again. Some of the key macroeconomic variables are shown in table 5-3 and details of Indonesia's external balance policies appear elsewhere in this book (see chapter 14).

Korea

The Republic of Korea is frequently cited as a success story in adjustment. As table 5-4 shows, the large deficits accumulated in the current account in the early 1980s were narrowed in subsequent years. One conclusion that can be drawn from the Korean example is that countries wanting to sustain a high growth rate cannot afford to run into external balance constraints. An exchange rate policy must be forward looking to ensure that the current account deficit does not get out of line.

In Korea's case, there was no large real depreciation to turn the external balance around. Lower world interest rates after 1982 and a decline in commodity prices helped correct the external imbalance, but to maintain the competitiveness of manufactures, some depreciation was needed.

Turkey

A number of factors helped Turkey become another successful case in adjustment. One of them was correcting an overvalued exchange rate. The dramatic export growth of 1981–82 demonstrated that adjustments of the real exchange rate can, in some cases, yield fast growth in exports (table 5-5). Often the results are slower.

Table 5-3. Key Macroeconomic Variables in Indonesia, 1979–85

Item	1979–81	1982	1983	1984	1985
Real growth	7.0	2.2	4.2	n.a.	n.a.
Current account deficit as a share of GDP	1.7	–5.9	–7.8	–2.5	n.a.
Real exchange rate index (1981 = 100)	96	105	78	71	67

n.a. Not available.
Source: Bureau of Indonesian Statistics, *Indikator Ekonomi.*

Table 5-4. Korea's External Adjustment, 1977–84

Item	1977–79	1980	1981	1982	1983	1984
Real growth rate (percent)	9.6	–4.8	6.6	5.4	11.9	8.4
Current account as a share of GDP (percent)	–5.7	–8.5	–6.8	–3.7	–2.1	–1.6
Real exchange rate index (1981 = 100)	92	96	100	103	97	96

Source: Bank of Korea, National Accounts, 1987, and *Monthly Statistical Bulletin.*

Table 5-5. Key Macroeconomic Indicators for Turkey, 1978–84

Item	1978–80	1981	1982	1983	1984
Real growth (percent)	–0.5	4.1	4.5	3.4	5.9
Export growth (percent)	3.0	62.2	36.1	8.4	20.6
Real exchange rate index (1982 = 100)	122	109	100	98	96

Source: Central Bank of Turkey, *Quarterly Bulletin.*

Of course, the exchange rate policy alone was not responsible for strong export growth. Recovery of the export markets in this case also helped. A sustained commitment to export-led growth, however, is necessary if the world economy is to be used as a vehicle for economic growth.

Dominican Republic

The exchange rate in this country is legally at par with the U.S. dollar. To maintain the fixed rate requires careful management of the economy. Specifically, the trend of prices cannot be allowed to get out of line with that of the United States. It is difficult to maintain equilibrium when a variety of shocks—from hurricanes to sugar price declines—take their toll.

As prices in the Dominican Republic rose faster than those in the United States, the fixed exchange rate got increasingly out of line (see figure 5-4). The government was forced to use a parallel market exchange rate for an increasing range of trade to avoid a trade crisis. The consequence, however, was distortions in the economy. Exports that used the parallel rate were remunerated, whereas others were implicitly taxed. Imports that passed through the parallel market were taxed, whereas those that used the fixed rate were implicitly subsidized.

With discrepancy between the two rates growing, devaluation was inevitable. To delay it meant high real interest rates.

**Figure 5-4. The Free-Market Premium
and the Relative Price Level in the Dominican Republic**

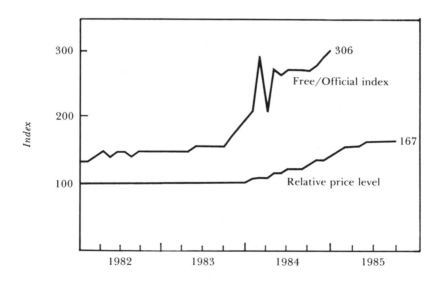

Source: Central Bank of the Dominican Republic, *Monthly Bulletin.*

United States

Perhaps the United States is one of the grossest experiences in overvaluation. It is illustrative to consider this case because it highlights the point that an ability to finance huge deficits in the world capital market may, in the end, be a serious source of trouble.

During 1980–85, the U.S. dollar appreciated in real terms by more than 40 percent because of a tight money policy and huge budget deficits. When high interest rates followed, capital flowed into the United States and pushed up the price of the dollar in world currency markets. With wages and prices less than fully flexible, the dollar got overvalued, and overvaluation put the U.S. current account into a large deficit. From 1980 to 1985 the current account moved by 3.5 percent of GNP toward deficit, or by $130 billion.

The U.S. deficit had dramatic negative effects on manufacturing. Imports increased sharply, and export growth decreased. Between 1981 and 1985, exports (at constant prices) declined by 6 percent, whereas imports increased by 51 percent. Employment in manufacturing fell sharply. The farm sector—an export industry—faced severe financial difficulties. The U.S. Congress reacted to these events by threatening protection.

By 1986, the dollar was less overvalued, but there was still concern that the overvalued dollar might have accelerated a loss in competitiveness in many U.S. industries. Plants were closed, and industries moved to countries with lower wages. Some fear that these international relocations might be irreversible if compensatory measures are not taken. As a result, the U.S. real wage will have to fall substantially if the level of competitiveness is to be gained to earn the dollars needed to service debt. The problems of the United States are no different from those of Mexico or any other country that allows its exchange rate to be badly misaligned.

6. Exchange Rate Rules

How can a country avoid exchange rate misalignment? Is the right answer to fix the exchange rate relative to a major trading partner, say, the United States or Japan? Or is the right policy advice to have a flexible exchange rate or a managed exchange rate following a simple, definite rule?

There is no simple answer, and the same answer is often not appropriate for different countries. When exchange rates among major industrial countries were fixed and world inflation was low, the answer was much less complicated. The choice was basically between a fixed rate for those countries that had good inflation performance or a crawling peg for countries whose inflation made it impossible or inadvisable to maintain fixed rates.

Crawling Pegs

Under a crawling peg regime, the currency is devalued at very frequent intervals by relatively small amounts. Each devaluation is randomly timed and of random magnitude so as to avoid building up speculation. The average rate of depreciation, however, equals the inflation differential between the country and the major trading partners. The crawling peg rule thus amounts to fixing the real exchange rate.[5]

Crawling pegs are very common today, particularly in Latin America. The reason is that a country with a 100 percent or 1,000 percent rate of inflation has no chance to maintain a fixed exchange rate. A policy of occasional devaluations has very detrimental effects on traders. As the exchange rate becomes overvalued, traders increasingly anticipate the next devaluation. Importers will try to speed up their purchases so as to take advantage of the low rate, whereas exporters will hold off sales to get the better price following the next devaluation. With imports and exports increasingly underpriced, import-competing industries will cut back production and exporters will hold off producing. Financing anticipated imports will push up interest rates, as will the carrying of stocks of exportables. Thus credit moves increasingly to finance speculation on the devaluation and away from other business.

Clearly this state of affairs is counterproductive. Because devaluations must occur, on average it is much better to make them small, frequent, and random so that they remain uninteresting for speculators. In this manner trade flows follow a regular pattern set by comparative advantage rather than by the political timetable that dictates the pattern of major and traumatic exchange rate realignments.

Another important reason for the automaticity of a crawling peg is political. Governments simply do not like the idea of devaluation. Any time is a bad time for a devaluation, and hence there is a tendency to postpone the inevitable. If on average devaluation is postponed, however, then on average the exchange rate will be overvalued. The trade sector will be weakened, and speculation will be needlessly encouraged. Much better to make the devaluations a routine operation in the central bank rather than a cabinet decision. There can be no question that Brazil's ability to adjust to the debt and oil shocks is in no small part due to a tradition of nearly twenty years to use minidevaluations as a way of sustaining external competitiveness.

It is clear, however, that a policy of maintaining a constant real exchange rate is sometimes not good enough. Such a policy helps in that it keeps a high inflation rate from interfering with external competitiveness, but it may not be sufficient to sustain the external balance. Thus after an adverse shock—for example, an oil price increase or increased debt service because of higher world interest rates—a real depreciation will be required. It is therefore essential to recognize that a crawling peg in itself is only a partial assurance of good exchange rate policy. Thinking must go beyond offsetting inflation differentials to look at the level of the real exchange rate that assures a comfortable external position. In Brazil's case that required a policy of repeated real depreciation to cope with the two oil shocks and the debt shock, as the figures shown below indicate.[6]

	1970–73	1974–78	1979–82	1983–85
Real exchange rate	122	107	88	76

The Brazilian real depreciation, two maxis apart, was achieved by two simple devices. The first, throughout the 1970s, was to base the minidevaluations on the differential between U.S. and Brazilian inflation. The weakening of the dollar gave Brazil a gain in the overall real exchange rate, in which Europe has a considerable weight. The second device was to base the depreciation not on manufacturing prices but on a much more comprehensive index. In countries with high productivity growth, manufacturing prices show much less inflation than the overall price level. Accordingly, choice of the inflation of the overall price level as a benchmark meant that each year an extra few percentage points of real depreciation were built in.

Baskets

Apart from inflation differentials, trade patterns also matter for exchange rate policy. When exchange rates among major industrial countries move a lot, then it becomes unwise, in most cases, to tie oneself to one currency or the other. Very few countries are so specialized in their trade flows that they should look just at the dollar or the yen or the European currencies. Concentration on a single major currency may be good policy for the Caribbean, where U.S. tourism dominates, or for Mexico, but it is clearly not appropriate for Korea or for Malaysia.

The appropriate exchange rate policy here consists in finding a simple rule that ties the crawling peg to the differential between home inflation and the weighted-average inflation of the major trading partners and competitors. The weighting in principle is that of trade flows both on the export side and on the import side. The appropriate arrangement will differ in each case, and it is important to take into account the particular trade pattern and commodity structure. But the principle is very easy: to avoid being caught by a strengthening, say, of the dollar, as a result of pegging the dollar.

When a basket of currencies is pegged, the risk that a rise in the dollar or the yen will bring about overvaluation is avoided, and trade is sheltered, at least to some extent. Thus Korea, for example, follows a basket policy, because on the import side there are significant imports from Japan and on the export side there is large trade with Europe and the United States. If Korea pegged to the dollar, with a crawling peg, the real rate would behave just like the U.S. dollar, and in the 1980s Korea would have experienced a devastating real appreciation.

Freely Flexible Rates

It is often argued that any kind of managed exchange rate risks getting out of line. Why not let markets freely determine rates rather than allowing administrative decisions and political considerations to risk bringing about highly damaging misalignments? The argument sounds good and seems reasonable for the market for fresh fish, but not for the foreign exchange market.

The experience with fully flexible rates, even in the thickest markets, such as that for the dollar, is very mixed. Although administrative decisions may easily misprice foreign exchange, so can speculators. When the exchange market is left to trade flows and speculators, major and unwarranted exchange rate movements may very well take place. These quickly spill over to prices of traded goods and from there to wages and to the budget. It may be extraordinarily difficult to maintain macroeconomic stability when external balance shocks, political shocks, or simply a bad day in the foreign exchange market produce such waves.

Flexible exchange rates may be appropriate for major currency blocks, but they are certainly a poor idea for an individual developing country.

7. Undervaluation

In concluding this chapter I briefly raise the question of undervaluation. Is there any risk to having an exchange rate that creates a large trade surplus and a very strong traded goods sector? It is difficult to see that this is a serious risk. There are nevertheless four considerations.

The first is that trade and current account surpluses come at the expense of a domestic absorption of resources. A country that builds up current account surpluses will be acquiring external assets. This increase in net assets might take the form of building up reserves, paying off debts, or allowing indigenous residents to buy financial and real assets abroad. Reserve buildup is certainly, within limits, a reasonable objective. As discussed in chapter 8, reserves act as shock absorbers and are thus well worth having.

Paying off debt may occasionally be a good idea, particularly if the interest burden is believed to exceed the productivity of investment in alternative uses. More often than not, however, it is wiser to invest at home. The reason is that it is difficult to borrow when trouble comes. Thus it is better not to repay debt prematurely when things are going well. As a rule, investment opportunities in developing countries can be expected to have a rate of return well in excess of interest rates on external debt. Hence investment at home should be preferred to debt repayment.

It is a very poor policy to run current account surpluses so as to finance private capital export. It is certainly not reasonable for residents of poor countries to buy U.S. Treasury bills in preference to investing resources in their own countries so as to raise productivity and the standard of living. There is no economic justification for such portfolio investments. Capital export may be hard to stop, but it most definitely should not be an objective of public policy. The use of an undervalued exchange rate to earn the foreign exchange with which to finance capital exports (this should often really be called capital flight and tax evasion) is the opposite of good development strategy.

The second consideration concerns the question of growth. Is it true that countries with an undervalued real exchange rate produce a better growth record? It is certainly true that an undervalued rate will be better than an overvalued rate. But having an undervalued rate simply means sailing under the wind. The issue is the tradeoff between consumption and investment, not the tradeoff between domestic and foreign investment. To have strong growth on a sustainable basis is essential for investment. High levels of investment require high domestic saving. Some investment can of course be externally financed, and doing so entails current account deficits, but the major part must come from domestic saving. To have high investment at home, firms must have confidence in a sustained profitability of production, both for the home market and for export and import substitution. Overvaluation would thus certainly be a problem. Undervaluation, however, means that resources are transferred abroad rather than invested at home.

The third consideration involves risk and asymmetries between good and bad news. It is always possible to give up a gain in competitiveness, but it is much harder to become competitive at short notice to deal with bad news. According to this argument, countries should try to take advantage of any transitory gain in competitiveness and lock it in rather than give it away. When oil prices decline for an oil importer there should be no real appreciation, and when world demand picks up for a commodity exporter the real exchange rate should not be allowed to appreciate. This is sound advice, even though it will be difficult not to distribute the benefits of an external improvement in the form of higher real wages. This reasoning takes us to the final point.

The real exchange rate has a counterpart in the real wage. When the real exchange rate is such as to make a country particularly competitive, then it is also almost invariably the case that real wages are low and that the profitability of traded goods sectors is high. Conversely, a real appreciation means a gain in the purchasing power of labor and a loss in profitability for capital invested in the export and import-competing industries. Thus real-exchange-rate policy is also income distribution policy. If the real exchange rate is kept undervalued, income can be redistributed toward capital in the traded goods sector and away from labor. The appropriate policy may involve fostering high investment. This policy is believed to be the recipe for the strong European growth that occurred, especially in Germany, in the 1950s and 1960s.

When the different considerations are weighed, the answer is not obvious. There are plausible reasons for maintaining an exchange rate in a position that keeps a country supercompetitive. The only inadmissible reason is that the currency should be undervalued so as to make it possible to finance capital outflows.

If the general considerations do not allow us to formulate a conclusion, there are nevertheless two clear-cut cases. Both involve transitory good fortune.

One case arises when a country has an extended but temporary windfall: it finds oil or is adjacent to an oil-producing nation that attracts its labor force and thus makes available a large flow of remittance payments for a few years. Such was the case for Turkey, Pakistan, and even Korea, which benefited from the labor shortage of the oil-producing countries in the Middle East. In such a case, should the real exchange rate be allowed to appreciate in the period of largesse? Clearly, foreign exchange is plentiful, and on that account is there a reason to keep wages low?

The answer, without any doubt, is that the real exchange rate should not be allowed to appreciate. The large foreign exchange inflows may be very transitory, and even if they last for a few years they will ultimately dry up. When they do dry up, it is essential that there remain a traded goods sector in a position to earn the foreign exchange to keep the country going. Allowing an appreciation would certainly deteriorate prospects for the traded goods sector and lead to low investment or even disinvestment. The right policy in this case is to maintain the traded goods sector and to promote investment. One means of doing so is to run budget surpluses and provide investment incentives.

The other case of interest involves short-term cyclical fluctuations in commodity prices. When the price of one of the major exports of a country rises, is that an occasion for real appreciation? Once again, the answer is no. Even though there is no foreign exchange shortage, it is wise to keep the real exchange rate for manufacturing at a level that, across commodity cycles, yields a comfortable external balance. To keep cyclical fluctuations in an important export product from upsetting the economy, a cyclical tax should be introduced.

When commodity prices are high the government should tax the commodities, and when prices are low the government should subsidize them. Thus both the budget and the foreign exchange reserves will then move with the commodity price, whereas the economy will not. Such a system is used in Malaysia to offset the impact of rubber price movements on the economy. It is a sensible system for any economy in which commodity exports play an important role and in which it is also essential to keep manufactures from being jolted around by the good and bad fortunes of a particular export sector.

Notes

1. Vittorio Corbo and Jaime de Melo, "Liberalization and Stabilization in Chile: 1974–82," World Bank, Development Research Department, Washington, D.C., 1983; unpublished manuscript.

2. Foreign wages are considered as given, so that changes in domestic wages measured in dollars also cause changes in external competitiveness.

3. See Joseph Grunwald and Kenneth S. Flamm, *The Global Factory* (Washington, D.C.: Brookings Institution, 1985), and William Cline, *Exports of Manufactures from Developing Countries* (Washington, D.C.: Brookings Institution, 1984).

4. See World Bank, *The World Development Report 1985* (New York: Oxford University Press, 1985).

5. See John Williamson, ed. *Exchange Rate Rules* (New York: St. Martin's Press, 1981), and Peter Wickham, "The Choice of Exchange Rate Regime in Developing Countries," *IMF Staff Papers*, vol. 32 (June 1985), pp. 248–88. The latter includes extensive references.

6. Central Bank of Brazil, *Bulletin*.

6

Devaluation and Inflation

Stanley Fischer

DEVALUATIONS, like visits to the dentist, are widely feared, are sometimes necessary, are generally put off longer than they should be, inflict pain for some time, and often do good.

Devaluation becomes necessary when the currency is overvalued or will become overvalued unless action is taken. Overvaluation occurs when the nominal exchange rate is held fixed, or adjusted too little, in response to overexpansion of the domestic money supply or to increases in import or domestic costs. Overvaluation can also develop gradually if the nominal exchange rate is held fixed, whereas domestic inflation outpaces foreign inflation.

In this chapter, five devaluation topics are discussed: (a) alternative exchange rate arrangements, (b) alternative exchange rate indicators, (c) how devaluations work, (d) asset market problems, and (e) the inflationary economy.

1. Exchange Rate Arrangements

Many different types of exchange rate arrangements are possible, ranging from more or less permanently fixed rates to freely floating rates.[1]

Fixed Exchange Rates

Between the end of World War II and 1973, most countries had their exchange rates fixed against the U.S. dollar. The system was known as the adjustable peg. Although the exchange rate against the dollar was pegged at any one time, the level of the peg was occasionally changed. The U.K. pound sterling, for instance, was exchanged at 4.86 against the U.S. dollar until 1949; devaluation in 1949 reduced the exchange rate to $2.80 per pound. A further devaluation in 1967 lowered the rate to $2.40.

Governments were willing to buy and sell foreign exchange at the official exchange rate. When the demand for foreign exchange at the existing exchange rate exceeded the supply in the market, the government (usually the central bank) would draw down its reserves to make available the difference. The level of the reserves was one indicator of the government's ability to maintain the exchange rate. Heavy reserve outflows were a sign that the exchange rate might have to be devalued. Governments could also borrow foreign currencies to defend the exchange rate. They could restrict access to the foreign exchange market by tightening exchange controls at times when the currency was under attack.

The period of the Bretton Woods system saw a remarkable expansion of world trade.[2] But as countries began to follow policies that were incompatible with the maintenance of constant exchange rates, the system became increasingly crisis prone during the 1960s and collapsed in 1973. Because German inflation was lower than that of the United States, for instance, the dollar was becoming progressively overvalued relative to the mark. The mark was revalued in 1969, but revaluation was not enough. Further revaluations followed in 1970 and in later years.

The development of international capital markets increased the capital flows among countries and made it difficult for governments to hold exchange rates during the 1960s. When it became clear that a devaluation was imminent, capital would flow out of a country, reserves would be depleted, and devaluation would speed up.[3] Exchange controls were not sufficient to stop the flows. Ways were found to get around the controls. Foreign financial investments in the country, which were not subject to exchange controls, could be moved out; payments for imports could be speeded up; and receipts from export sales could be delayed.

Governments could have changed their macroeconomic policies to protect the exchange rate. They could, for instance, have tightened monetary policy to raise domestic interest rates and make it more attractive to keep funds in the country.

Some countries initiated monetary and fiscal policies to prevent devaluations. (Examples include the United States in the early 1960s and the United Kingdom from 1964 to 1967.) Governments regarded devaluation as a sign of failure and were anxious to avoid it. Yet when the policies needed for an external balance (restrictive monetary policy, for instance) clashed with the needs of domestic policy (monetary expansion, for example), devaluation became more attractive. In particular, after an election, devaluation could be blamed on the economic misdeeds of the previous government.

As long as the inflation rate in the United States was low, other countries could hold their exchange rate against the dollar only if they too maintained a low inflation rate. Thus the United States provided a nominal anchor for prices worldwide. During the 1960s, however, the U.S. inflation rate increased, and the value of the link to the U.S. dollar as a means of keeping down domestic inflation weakened. For that reason Germany had to revalue the mark in 1969; it was operating at a lower inflation rate than the United States.

Once it became clear that countries, including the United States, were not willing to run their macroeconomic policies with the main goal of keeping the exchange rate constant, and given the large capital movements, the Bretton Woods system was doomed. It broke down in 1973. That marked the end of fixed exchange rates among the major currencies (especially the U.S. dollar, the Japanese yen, the German mark, and the British pound), but fixed-exchange-rate arrangements were maintained among smaller groups of countries. Several countries in Francophone Africa belong to the franc currency area; their currencies are pegged to the French franc. Eight European countries maintain the European Monetary System, in which exchange rates are held within narrow bands and are occasionally adjusted. More than thirty countries peg their currencies to the U.S. dollar. In all these cases, countries are operating adjustable peg systems, which indicate their willingness to adjust their macroeconomic policies to some extent to defend the exchange rate. Controls on capital flows are in operation in many of these countries.

Optimal Currency Areas

In most modern economies, the domestic currency is issued by the central bank. But there is no inherent need for a country to have its own currency. It could adopt the stable foreign currency of a major trading partner as the legal tender in the country. Notes and coins could be imported or borrowed. The use of a stable foreign currency ensures the stability of domestic prices and is thus a benefit to the user country.

Instead of using a foreign currency directly, a country could issue a domestic currency that is backed one for one by foreign currency. The balboa, for example, is the official Panamanian currency, but it exchanges one for one for the U.S. dollar, and dollars circulate freely. The same arrangements are found in Liberia, where the Liberian dollar is the currency. The value of local currency could also be fixed with reference to a certain weight of gold. The country could issue domestic bills against the gold reserves.

The free circulation of a foreign currency at a fixed exchange rate against the domestic currency is one way of fixing the exchange rate of the domestic currency irrevocably. Because the exchange rate cannot be changed, there is no possibility of destabilizing the economy by speculating about future changes.[4]

The issue of whether to fix a currency's exchange rate definitively is often put in terms of the formation of a currency area—an area in which a single currency circulates freely. Mobility of capital and other factors of production within this area is essential for the currency area to be successful.

For a small country, the benefits of using a foreign currency are low rates of inflation over long periods. The cost to the government of using a foreign currency is the waiver of the right to print its own money. The amount of revenue obtained from seigniorage, or the right to issue money—sometimes called the inflation tax—is unlikely to exceed 1 percent of GNP in an economy with a low rate of inflation. In some rapidly growing countries, in which the demand for money increases rapidly, governments may obtain revenue of as much as 5 percent of GNP through the issue of money, without creating high inflation. At high rates of inflation, governments generally collect 3–4 percent of GNP through the inflation tax.

The inflation tax, however, can easily be used to excess. As the inflation rate rises, people begin to move from money into real estate, consumer durables, or foreign currency. The shift from money means that the government obtains fewer resources from printing money. In response, the government may step up the rate at which it creates money, thereby increasing the inflation rate further. Eventually there may come a point at which the government obtains less revenue at a high inflation rate than it did when inflation was lower. In addition, inflation has other costs for the economy. Some governments are therefore willing to give up the inflation tax as a potential source of revenue by using foreign money. There are other, less costly ways of keeping inflation rates down, however. The creation of an independent central bank with explicit powers to maintain reasonable stability of the value of money is one such way.

Crawling Peg

The crawling-peg exchange rate is a middle course between fixed and floating rates. The government fixes the exchange rate on any one day but over time moves the rate in a preannounced fashion. A country's economy that is inflating 20 percent faster than that of its major trading partner, for instance, may announce a "crawl" of 20 percent a year. The exchange rate may be moved daily or weekly by an amount corresponding to 20 percent depreciation over the course of the year.

The crawling peg combines the flexibility needed to accommodate different trends in inflation rates between countries while maintaining relative certainty about future exchange rates relevant to exporters and importers. The disadvantage is that the crawling peg—like the fixed exchange rate—leaves the currency open to speculative attack because the government is committed on any one day or over a period to a particular value of the exchange rate.

Crawling pegs were used in the mid- and late 1970s in countries with moderate to high inflation rates; these included Argentina, Brazil, Israel, and Portugal. In Argentina, domestic inflation was higher than desired, so the preannounced exchange rate (called the tablita) became increasingly overvalued until eventually, when it was too late, it had to be abandoned. It was too late because the economy had gotten used to low-priced imports, and capital owners had taken advantage of overvalued exchange rates to buy U.S. dollars. Capital flight had ensued.

Despite such difficulties, a crawling peg can be a useful exchange rate when a country has higher inflation than its major trading partners and therefore cannot credibly fix the exchange rate, but wants to give its exporters and importers relative certainty about future exchange rates. In countries with strong domestic capital markets, an alternative to the crawling peg is for the government to provide forward exchange cover or exchange rate guarantees for exporters.

Currency Pegs

The question in currency pegs is the currency or currencies against which the rate should be held fixed. In many cases this is no real issue. When a small economy has a dominant trading partner, such as the Caribbean countries with the United States, the peg will be against the dominant currency. In other cases, where countries import to and export from several foreign countries, the exchange rate can be tied to a basket of currencies, with weights reflecting the shares of the countries in foreign trade.

When the directions of capital and current account transactions differ, deciding on a peg can be complicated. A country may, for instance, export to and import from Europe, the Pacific, and the United States about equally, but may deal mainly with American banks and use U.S.

dollars for international transactions. If the exchange rate is fixed to the U.S. dollar to simplify capital account transactions, movements in the dollar exchange rate will affect the country's real exchange against major trading partners. The real effective exchange rate of the U.S. dollar appreciated by about 30 percent between 1980 and 1985; the current account of the United States deteriorated correspondingly. Any country that fixed its exchange rate against the dollar would have suffered the same fate. For that reason, it is preferable to fix the exchange rate against a basket of currencies reflecting trading patterns in goods and services.

Flexible Exchange Rates

A flexible exchange rate may change from day to day or even minute to minute. The degree of government intervention in the foreign exchange market varies. At one extreme is a system of clean floating, in which the government does not intervene. The United States, for instance, kept out of the foreign exchange markets between 1981 and 1985, but such forbearance is rare.

More usually, the government has some exchange rate target and intervenes to attain it. This phenomenon is called a managed, or dirty, float. Unlike the crawling peg, however, the exchange rate target is frequently not explicit; it may be changed or abandoned without official acknowledgment. Figure 6-1 shows the range of exchange rate arrangements, from most fixed (at the top) to the most flexible (at the bottom).

During the Bretton Woods period, two arguments were presented in favor of flexibility. The first was that flexible rates would insulate countries from macroeconomic policies pursued abroad, giving them more

Figure 6-1. Exchange Rate Arrangements

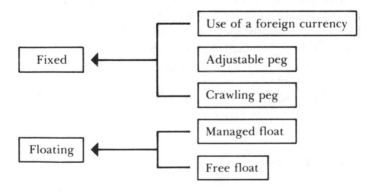

policy independence. The second was that speculation would ensure substantial exchange rate stability by reducing the variability in the price of the foreign currency.

Neither of these arguments has been borne out in practice. It has become quite clear that the effects of both monetary and fiscal policies are transmitted internationally under flexible rates. The insulation argument would apply only to the effects of monetary policy changes if prices were freely flexible. Because prices are not fully flexible, however, monetary policy has real effects on interest rates and on output that are transmitted between countries. There is no way of avoiding the transmission of shocks between economies that trade in goods and assets. With regard to the second argument, the floating-exchange-rate system has seen major movements in exchange rates that have later been reversed.

Large exchange rate movements are no proof that speculation is destabilizing. Large shifts in the dollar exchange rate, for instance, can be related to fiscal policy shifts between the United States and its trading partners. But the exchange rates of even major currencies can change by as much as 20–30 percent within a year. These changes would be regarded as large devaluations were they brought about through official decisions. In response to large exchange rate shifts, in particular the appreciation of the dollar from 1980 to 1985, the finance ministers of the five largest Western economies announced in September 1985 their intention of working together to reduce exchange rate fluctuations.

Because exchange rate movements affect trade and domestic inflation, countries are unlikely to initiate domestic policies without paying attention to the behavior of the exchange rate. They are likely to intervene in the exchange markets from time to time in the hope of moving the exchange rate in the appropriate direction. The days of clean floating are gone; dirty floating is in. It is also clear that large economies are unlikely to coordinate their policies closely enough to return to an adjustable peg or to a fixed-rate system. Rather, the world will gradually move to a system with three major international currencies and associated blocs: the U.S. dollar, the German mark (with associated European currencies), and the Japanese yen. Smaller countries will then have the option of tying their currencies through an adjustable peg to any one currency, to a basket of these currencies, or to a basket of other currencies or of floating against all currencies. Smaller countries will also have the choice of allowing their currency to float freely or of intervening in a managed float.

2. Exchange Rate Indicators

The dangers of overvaluation were spelled out in chapter 5. But how is a country to know when the currency is overvalued and when a devaluation is needed? And why the emphasis on overvaluation rather than on undervaluation?

The fundamental criteria for judging the appropriateness of the exchange rate are the present and prospective levels of the current account. If the current account deficit is "unsustainable"—that is to say, if it cannot be financed by drawing down reserves or through borrowing—or if reasonable forecasts show that it will be unsustainable in the future, devaluation will be necessary sooner or later.

By this criterion, it is possible that a devaluation should take place even if the current account is not at present in deficit. By the same token, if a current account deficit is merely temporary—because it is the result of a short-term disturbance such as an exceptionally poor export crop—devaluation may not be needed. The difficulty is in knowing whether any given deficit is temporary and therefore can perhaps be financed, or is long term, in which case a devaluation is needed. A variety of indicators can be used to make this judgment.

The Current Account

The primary indicator is the current account deficit. Large actual or projected current account deficits—or, for countries that have to make heavy debt repayments in the future, insufficiently large surpluses—are a call for devaluation.

When should a devaluation take place if the current account is not currently in difficulties but will be so at a later date? It is preferable to devalue the currency before the problem arises so that production and consumption in the domestic economy can begin to move in the right direction. In this respect, gradual adjustment may be more difficult than a one-time devaluation because gradual adjustment exerts continuing pressure to reduce the real wage.

The current account is not always a good indicator because it reacts relatively slowly to changes in the real exchange rate. The J curve best describes the effects of a devaluation on the current account. At the time of a devaluation, the economy is at the left-most point on the J curve. Immediately after the devaluation, the current account may worsen as the economy travels to the bottom of the J. The worsening occurs because imports have mostly been contracted for and will be paid for in the foreign currency. Because foreign currency is now more expensive, the value of imports in domestic currency will rise. The value of exports, however, will increase only slowly. As the value of exports increases and that of imports falls, the current account will improve and the economy will end up at the top of the J, at a level higher than when it began. In a large economy, such as that of the United States, devaluation may take more than a year to improve the current account. The effects will generally be more rapid in smaller, more open economies.

The Real Exchange Rate

The real exchange rate is frequently used as an indicator of the need for devaluation. When the real exchange rate appreciates, current account difficulties may lie ahead. The real exchange rate is often calculated by comparing the relative costs of manufactures in two countries. An alternative measure is to compare wage levels within the country with those abroad, adjusted for productivity. Note that the calculation of the real exchange rate from relative wage levels places emphasis on the behavior of wages—indeed an appropriate emphasis when considering the exchange rate.

The larger the increase in domestic cost relative to foreign cost, the more likely a devaluation is to be needed. It is common to compare the current real exchange rate with the level at some date in the past when the current account was thought to be in satisfactory condition.

Foreign Exchange Reserves

Falling reserves are another indicator of devaluation to follow. Reserves can fall for two reasons. One is that the current account is in deficit; another is that asset holders—domestic and foreign—are moving out of the domestic currency into foreign currencies. As they lose confidence in the maintenance of the exchange rate, the pressure on the reserves increases. Unless controls on capital flows are strong, pressures from private asset holders may force a devaluation well before the government is willing.

These asset holders are frequently called speculators. They are indeed speculating that the domestic currency will be devalued. It is possible, however, that the asset holders have understood the fundamentals of economics better and more quickly than the government. Governments sometimes react by refusing to devalue to teach speculators a lesson. If the fundamentals are right and on the side of the government, such a decision may be a success. If the government is wrong, it will ultimately have to devalue anyway, in which case it would have saved itself a lot of money by devaluing earlier rather than engaging in a Don Quixote battle with speculators.

Because foreign exchange reserves can be augmented by borrowing, and because central banks have tricks for making them look larger than they are, reserves may not be a good guide for outsiders. But the government should not be fooled by the manipulation of reserves; it should insist on a full accounting from the central bank of the actual drain from the private sector on reserves.

If a devaluation is inevitable, the government should not prolong the agony and help enrich the speculators by trying to delay the devaluation.

Foreign Debt

The reserves can be maintained by foreign borrowing. Thus a rapidly increasing debt may be another sign of a currency heading for trouble. Foreign debt, however, may also be the counterpart of productive domestic investment that may later generate the foreign exchange needed to repay the loans. Thus debt is an ambiguous indicator of the need for devaluation.

Useful as these indicators are—particularly as a warning of dangers that are not yet clear in the current account—the best way to make decisions about the exchange rate is to attempt to forecast the balance of payments for the next four to five years on the assumption that the exchange rate is held constant. If, under this assumption, the current account goes into serious and unsustainable deficit, the need for a devaluation is clear.

Undervaluation

The discussion has focused on devaluation rather than on revaluation because undervaluation of a currency in a small developing country is rare; it also has less serious consequences than overvaluation. When the currency is undervalued, the country is running a current account surplus that is larger than needed and is reducing the standard of living of its citizens below the sustainable long-run level. The political pressures are generally in the direction of overvaluation rather than undervaluation. Nonetheless, some countries have kept their exchange rates deliberately undervalued in an attempt to open up foreign markets and develop exports, relying on export growth to lead domestic growth. Japan may have followed such a strategy in the late 1970s and early 1980s.

3. How Does Devaluation Work?

A reduction in the real exchange rate reduces imports and increases exports, thereby leading to an improvement in the current account (see figure 6-2). Behind this account lie several steps.

Devaluation and the Terms of Trade

The terms of trade are the price of exports relative to the price of imports. It is natural to think that a devaluation worsens the terms of trade by increasing the price of imports while leaving the price of exports, measured in domestic currency, unchanged. Devaluation does change the terms of trade for medium-size or large countries. It is possible, however, for a devaluation to leave the terms of trade of a small

Figure 6-2. The Effects of Devaluation

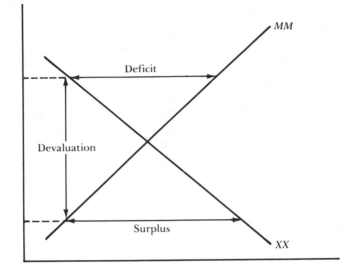

Imports and exports

country unaffected. Consider a small country exporting a single primary commodity, say, copper. The dollar price of the export and the dollar price of imports are both set in world markets. When the small country devalues its currency, both prices in domestic currency change in proportion to the devaluation. The terms of trade are thus unaffected.

If imports do not become more expensive relative to exports, how does devaluation work? The answer lies in the distinction between traded and nontraded goods—goods that do or do not enter into world trade. A devaluation may leave the terms of trade unaffected but can affect the price of a traded good relative to a nontraded good or a home good.

If a devaluation makes home goods cheaper relative to traded goods, the demand for home goods rises. Producers, however, want to shift toward the production of traded goods. To ensure that resources are freed to produce traded goods, the government must reduce the overall level of demand in the economy to offset the expansionary effect of the increase in the demand for home goods. I return to this point below.

Real and Nominal Devaluation

The government can change the nominal exchange rate—the domestic price of foreign currency—by announcing its willingness to buy and sell foreign currency at a particular price. The government has less control over the real exchange rate, however, which for simplicity's sake we can define as domestic production costs relative to foreign costs. If nominal domestic costs of production remain unchanged after a devaluation, then domestic costs will fall relative to foreign costs. In that case the analysis in figure 6-2 is appropriate.

Domestic costs will often increase in the wake of a devaluation, however, because some inputs, perhaps oil or machinery, are imported. Still, the main component of domestic costs is typically wages, and these may rise when there is a devaluation.

Wage indexation may make the wage increase automatic. A devaluation increases the prices of imports and therefore directly increases the domestic price level. If wages are indexed to prices, an immediate rise in wages will partly offset the effects of the devaluation.

Various measures have been used to deal with this difficulty. One has been to exclude imported goods from the index to which the wage is tied so that the wage would not automatically adjust for the major direct effect of changes in the exchange rate. Another has been to compensate for only part of the inflation (in Israel it has been 70 percent), the proportion being chosen to reflect the share of imports in the consumer price index. A third measure used has been suspension of the wage index clauses at the time of a devaluation.

Wages may also increase because of market pressures. To understand this possibility we must distinguish between alternative predevaluation situations. Figure 6-3 shows the level of domestic output and the current account. Ideally the economy is at point *E*, with output at the full employment level and the current account in balance. Devaluation is called for if the economy is substantially below the current account (CA) line. Devaluation has two effects: it switches demand from foreign to domestic goods, and it increases domestic demand.

Expenditure Switching

A successful real devaluation raises the prices of traded goods relative to those of nontraded goods. Suppose the economy is at point *A* in figure 6-3—that is, at full employment but with a current account deficit. It seems as if, with a devaluation of the currency, demand would switch from foreign to domestic goods, so that the current account problem would be solved.

A devaluation by itself, however, will move the economy from point *A* to point *B*, not *E*. Not only does devaluation switch demand, it also increases the demand for domestic or home goods. As a result, unless measures are taken to curtail aggregate demand at the time a devaluation takes place, the current account deficit will be replaced by domestic

Figure 6-3. The Current Account and Aggregate Demand

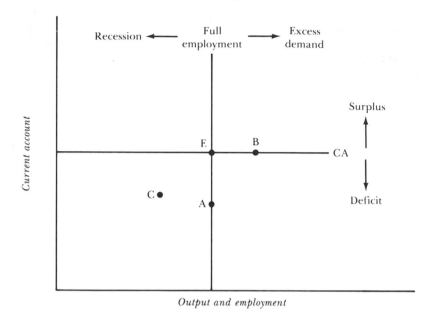

Output and employment

excess demand. The pressure of domestic demand will then cause wages to rise and will offset the effects of the devaluation.

To be effective, a devaluation should be accompanied by monetary and fiscal measures. Contractionary monetary or credit policies can squeeze domestic demand and free resources for production of traded goods. Tight fiscal policy—either an increase in taxes or cuts in government spending—will likewise reduce domestic demand. Some changes in fiscal policy that are typically undertaken to reduce the budget deficit (for instance, raising value added taxes or reducing subsidies) will be inflationary because they cause domestic prices to rise. Such measures may be inescapable, but they are better avoided if possible. The best way to avoid having to cut subsidies is not to allow them to become high to begin with.

If the economy starts from a point such as *C* in figure 6-3, then devaluation may be all that is needed to return to full employment with a balanced current account. It is relatively rare, however, for a country suffering from a current account problem to have substantially underutilized resources. More likely, a devaluation needs to be accompanied by measures that restrict aggregate demand to ensure that domestic prices and wage increases do not rapidly offset the effects of nominal devaluation.

Because even real devaluations take effect only slowly, it is often argued that they do not succeed. Evidence shows that the current account does improve after a real devaluation but that it may take a year or more for the full effects to be felt. As discussed, devaluation may not work if a nominal devaluation does not translate into a real devaluation.

4. Assets Market Problems

Several difficulties may arise in the assets market as a result of devaluation.

Linked Assets

A real devaluation increases the real value of assets whose rates of return are linked to the exchange rate. Dollar-linked or dollar-denominated accounts, for instance, may have been issued by the domestic banking system, with government support or guarantees, as a way of preventing the outflow of capital. Such accounts exist in Argentina, Brazil, and Israel. A real devaluation increases the real value of these assets, thereby adding to the inflationary effect of the devaluation.

Not much can be done beyond further tightening domestic policy to offset the inflationary effect. At times of national emergency, the government may be tempted to tax these accounts to prevent the holders from gaining when others find their standard of living reduced, but in so doing the government reduces the future attractiveness of such accounts. Capital levies have occasionally been imposed as part of emergency programs, but these generally tend not to discriminate between different types of asset.

Foreign Debts of Domestic Firms

Domestic firms may have contracted debts in foreign currency before the devaluation. A real devaluation makes it more difficult for these firms to service the debt. The firms are likely to ask the government for relief. In principle the government should leave the firms and their creditors to sort out the difficulties, but the pressures from creditors may become intense. The pressures may include implicit or explicit threats to reduce the flow of foreign credit to the country if the government does not make good on the debts of domestic firms. Difficult as it may be, the country is probably better off refusing to guarantee the private debts of firms. It is important to realize that the physical assets of a bankrupt firm—the factory and the machinery—will remain in the economy and that employment in that firm is likely to continue even if it is forced into bankruptcy.

The Capital Inflow Problem

Capital flows out of a country in anticipation of a devaluation. After a devaluation, particularly one accompanied by restrictive monetary policy, capital may begin to flow in. Restrictive monetary and credit policy will raise domestic interest rates relative to foreign rates and attract capital. In addition, domestic residents who anticipated the devaluation may now want to repatriate the capital they sent abroad earlier.

If the exchange rate is held fixed, the inflow of capital will increase the domestic money supply and tend to offset the contractionary monetary policy. If the exchange rate is allowed to appreciate, the devaluation is reversed. If the country has well-developed capital markets, it can sterilize the capital inflow by buying foreign exchange and selling domestic bonds to offset the effects of the inflow on the money supply. Where capital markets are not well developed, however, this option is not available.

One way of dealing with the capital inflow problem is to tax the inflows to offset the excess of the domestic interest rate over rates abroad.

5. Devaluation and High Inflation

High inflation rates—ranging from 20 percent a year to as high as 1,000 percent—are no longer a Latin American phenomenon; they are found in Africa and Asia and even in Iceland.

In a typical inflationary economy, the government runs a sizable budget deficit, wages are indexed, many assets are linked to the exchange rate or the price level, and the exchange rate is on a crawling peg system or some other system that permits frequent changes.

The role of the exchange rate in inflation is controversial and critical. Two facts need to be highlighted. First, fixing the exchange rate, when other prices in the economy are rising, guarantees progressive overvaluation of the currency and difficulties in the balance of payments. Second, devaluation increases the prices of traded goods and is itself inflationary. Increases in the inflation rate are often precipitated by large devaluations.

Policymakers often find themselves in a dilemma: they want to keep inflation low and the exchange rate constant or at least rising less rapidly than other prices, but they cannot allow the current account to go deeply into deficit. The result is that at first they hold the exchange rate fixed, thereby producing the current account deficit they cannot permit, then they later devalue and get the inflation they do not want.

Table 6-1 presents two examples of high-inflation countries that held the exchange rate fixed or allowed increasing overvaluation before having to devalue and then suffer from high inflation. Argentina succeeded in reducing the inflation rate by overvaluing the currency from 1978 to 1980 at the cost of a large reduction in the trade balance. The worsening of the trade balance forced depreciation of the currency in 1981, which stoked the fires of inflation. In Israel, overvaluation and worsening of the current account continued until the end of 1983, when a large devaluation began to improve the current account but resulted also in a sharp rise in the inflation rate.

For the policymakers, there is no escape from the dilemma without adjusting fiscal or monetary policies. Both the inflation rate and the current account can be improved by restrictive domestic policies (such as reductions in government spending or increases in taxes) and by restrictive monetary and credit policies. It is only when exchange rate policies are viewed as an alternative to macroeconomic policies, rather than as a complement, that exchange rates may become untenable.

As long as the government is running large deficits and increasing the money stock rapidly, the best exchange rate policy is to follow a

Table 6-1. The Real Exchange Rate, Trade Balance, and Inflation in Argentina, 1978–83, and Israel, 1981–85

Year	Real exchange rate index	Trade balance[a] (billions of U.S. dollars)	Inflation rate (percent a year)
Argentina			
1978	109	2.9	159
1979	81	1.8	152
1980	78	−1.4	101
1981	93	0.7	107
1982	129	2.8	189
1983	131	3.7	361
Israel			
1981	116	−1.7	117
1982	107	−2.7	120
1983	99	−3.2	146
1984	100	−2.4	374
1985	115	−1.0	305

a. "Trade balance" refers to current account in the case of Israel.

Sources: For Argentina, *International Financial Statistics,* and Rudiger Dornbusch, "Argentina since Martinez de Hoz," Working Paper no. 1466, National Bureau of Economic Research (Cambridge, Mass., September 1984); for Israel, Bank of Israel, *Annual Report,* 1986.

purchasing-power-parity type of rule, which keeps the real exchange rate constant at a sustainable long-run level. This policy will prevent overvaluation as well as consequent increases in the inflation rate if the currency is devalued. The temptation to use the exchange rate to reduce the inflation rate without taking accompanying macroeconomic measures is very strong because short-run success can be bought at the cost of reducing the reserves. The temptation must be resisted, however, for overvaluation episodes have been very costly for the countries that have experienced them.

Stabilization Programs

Fixing the exchange rate has been a critical component of several successful stabilization programs in high inflation or even hyperinflation economies. Exchange rate fixing is not sufficient, however; it must be accompanied by other macroeconomic measures to ensure:

- That the budget is put on a long-run course of balance between revenues and expenditures
- That monetary policy supports stabilization
- That the real wage is close to an equilibrium value
- That the real exchange rate is close to the value consistent with long-run equilibrium, as illustrated in figure 6-3

Unfortunately, every successful stabilization program has been preceded by an unsuccessful attempt in which the government sought to stabilize purely by fixing the nominal exchange rate, without taking accompanying macroeconomic measures.

The Inflation-Adjusted Budget

An inflation-adjusted budget calculates a given budget as it would be if the inflation rate were zero and tax rates or government spending were unchanged.

The most important correction to the regular budget in calculating the inflation-adjusted budget concerns the distinction between real and nominal interest rates. Nominal interest rates are high during inflationary periods to compensate lenders for the decline in the value of the money during the period of the loan. The nominal treasury bill interest rate in Mexico in the first quarter of 1986, for instance, was 76 percent. The inflation rate in the previous year was 67 percent and was expected to rise to about 70 percent. In other words, the real interest rate—that is, the nominal rate minus the expected inflation rate—was expected to be 6 percent a year.

When the normal budget is calculated, interest payments are counted as a government expenditure. If the internal national debt is, say, 20 percent of GNP and the nominal interest rate is 70 percent, then the amount of interest that must be budgeted is 14 percent of GNP. If the inflation rate were zero and the real interest rate were just 6 percent, then the budget share of interest would be only 1.2 percent of GNP.

Thus the adjustment in the interest rate would make a substantial difference in the budget deficit. In the above example, it is more than 12 percent of GNP. In practice, real interest rates tend to be high at the beginning of a stabilization program; they are likely to be lowered as inflation is brought under control. The adjustment for the reduction in the nominal interest rate accompanying reduced inflation will be large if there is any sizable national debt.

A second factor that must be taken into account in calculating the zero inflation budget is that frequently the tax system operates inefficiently at high inflation rates. A reduction in the inflation rate is likely to increase the real value of tax collection.

These two factors alone imply that the budget at a zero inflation rate will look substantially better than the measured deficit at a high inflation rate. It is, however, unlikely that no other changes will have to be made in spending and taxes. Typically, spending must be cut, often spending on subsidies, including export subsidies that have entered the budget over the years in an attempt to maintain the profitability of exports without devaluing. If the budget is not put into a position in which it can be financed without printing money or borrowing at nonsustainable rates, stabilization cannot succeed in the long term.

Supporting Monetary Policy

A successful inflation stabilization program causes a large increase in the quantity of real balances demanded. With inflation ended, businesses and individuals want to hold more money, for its value is no longer falling as rapidly as before.

Surprisingly, it is important not to hold the quantity of money constant when attempting to stop inflation. Rather the quantity of money should be increased at a rate appropriate to the increase in the quantity of real balances demanded as a result of the fall in the inflation rate. Because it is often difficult to know how much money will be demanded when there is a sudden change in the inflation rate, an automatically accommodating monetary policy should be preferred. Such a policy obtains if the exchange rate is held fixed while the quantity of money is adjusted to maintain that exchange rate or if a target interest rate is set and as much money is supplied as is needed to maintain that rate. Another option is to focus on a broad money aggregate—total domestic credit, for instance—as a target for monetary policy and to downplay shifts among various categories of assets within that total.

The Real Wage

The simplest way to calculate the equilibrium real wage is to compare its level at some point in time in the recent past at which the economy appeared to be at full employment and the current account was at a sustainable long-run level. Depending on the political situation, the trade unions could perhaps be persuaded that this is a reasonable real wage. If persuasion is impossible, it may be necessary to pursue a tighter than optimal aggregate demand policy in order to keep downward pressure on the real wage.

The Real Exchange Rate

The equilibrium real wage and the equilibrium real exchange rate are closely related. The nominal exchange rate must be set at a level such that, after all the price and wage changes have taken place as a consequence of the stabilization plan, the real exchange rate is at the right level. Achieving the right levels typically requires a substantial nominal devaluation, accompanied by smaller increases in the nominal wage to make a real devaluation possible.

If the exchange rate is to serve as a nominal anchor for the stabilization plan, then once set, it will have to remain at its given nominal level for some time, perhaps for as long as a year. Overdevaluation is therefore desirable to prevent the collapse of the plan soon after its implementation.

Wage and Price Controls

Some stabilization programs—for example in Israel in 1985 and in Brazil in 1986—have used wage and price controls to move the real wage and the exchange rate to their equilibrium levels. Such controls may be justified when stabilization is attempted in high-inflation economies, but their expected lifetime is short. Removal of these controls will trigger increases in the inflation rate unless the right aggregate demand measures have been taken in the meantime. The controls will need to be lifted because modern economies cannot operate with long-term controls even though they may be useful as part of an overall stabilization program.

Fixing the Nominal Exchange Rate

Although several accompanying measures are needed for the implementation of a stabilization package, fixing of the nominal exchange rate is often the centerpiece. A fixed exchange rate not only ensures the stability of traded goods prices but also symbolizes a government's commitment to a new policy. The successful maintenance of the exchange rate without declines in reserves or a deficit in the current account indicates the government's success in its policy. But the fixed exchange rate is merely an indicator not the cause of success. Without the appropriate accompanying macroeconomic policies, fixing of the nominal exchange rate ends in overvaluation, devaluation, and the return of inflation.

Notes

1. The International Monetary Fund publishes a summary of exchange rates of its member countries in its monthly *International Financial Statistics.*
2. The Bretton Woods system came out of an agreement at Bretton Woods, New Hampshire, in 1944. At this conference forty-five nations agreed to a comprehensive arrangement that would govern world trade and balance of payments. The establishment of fixed exchange rates was part of this arrangement. The International Monetary Fund was created to administer the payments system.
3. When capital becomes mobile, large-scale outflow of speculative capital can precipitate a devaluation even if it is not needed. Whether such destabilizing speculation took place during the Bretton Woods period of fixed exchange rates has not been documented, but large-scale capital flows did take place during periods when exchange rate adjustments were widely expected.
4. No exchange rate commitment is irrevocable, so it would be inaccurate to say that the exchange rate in Panama or Liberia, for instance, is permanently fixed to the U.S. dollar. Future governments could at some point decide to break the link with the dollar. Similarly, although exchange rates were supposedly irrevocably fixed under the gold standard, countries could, and did, go on and off the gold standard as it became more or less convenient to fix the exchange rate to gold. Because Panamanians can hold dollars freely, however, the exchange rate of the balboa is much less likely to change than the exchange rate of other currencies pegged to the dollar.

7

Multiple Exchange Rates, Capital Controls, and Commercial Policy

■ *Susan M. Collins*

COUNTRIES EXPERIENCING balance of payments difficulties face a wide and varied menu of policy options. They may change policies that govern international transactions, finance external deficits through accumulation of external debt, or alter domestic monetary and fiscal policies to increase net exports and net capital inflows. Countries typically select some combination of these alternatives.

This chapter examines the advantages and disadvantages of changing policies that govern international transactions as a means of improving the balance of payments. It does not focus on devaluation, which is discussed in detail in chapters 5 and 6 of this volume. Instead, it discusses the implications of establishing different exchange rates for different transactions, of restricting the volume of imports, and of introducing controls on international capital flows. In fact, many countries have chosen multiple exchange rates, commercial policies, or capital controls instead of (or in addition to) devaluation when they faced balance of payments problems. (More than one-fifth of the member countries of the International Monetary Fund [IMF], for example, had some type of split exchange rate in 1984.) Not surprisingly, these policies are sensible in some circumstances but may be quite harmful in others.

Venezuela provides one example of a country that has implemented a wide range of policies to influence its external accounts. The key features include differentiated exchange rates, quantitative restrictions on imports, surrender of foreign exchange earnings by exporters to the central bank, advance import deposits by importers, and restrictions on capital flows (see table 7-1).

The present chapter has two tasks. The first is to consider each policy option and to analyze how it works. The second is to examine the pros and the cons of using particular policies to achieve particular objectives. Although the primary focus will be on external objectives (balance of payments management and insulating the domestic economy from

Table 7-1. The Venezuelan Exchange Arrangement, February 1984

Bolívares per U.S. dollar	Category
Differentiated exchange rates	
4.3	Essential imports, including wheat, milk powder, and pharmaceuticals
	Debt service (registered public and public sector)
6.0	Petroleum and iron ore, exports, and imported inputs
7.5	Most other imports of goods and services
Floating rate	Nontraditional exports
	Nonregistered private debt
	Tourist expenditures and transfers
	Nonessential imports
	Capital account transactions
	Other exchange-control policies
Restrictions on payments for current transactions, including import licenses and quantity restrictions	
Advance import deposits	
Surrender requirements for export proceeds	

Source: IMF, *Exchange Arrangements and Exchange Restriction* (Washington, D.C., 1984); Republic of Venezuela Economic Memorandum, May 17, 1985.

external shocks), the discussion will necessarily touch on various internal objectives (inflation, unemployment, and income distribution). Throughout, the main points will be illustrated with reference to country experiences.

1. Overview of Policy Alternatives

To make sense of the many options, it is useful first to organize them into a few general categories and second to present a unified framework for assessing the effects of these options.

Table 7-2 presents a simple typology of the policy alternatives, distinguishing between policies with a direct impact on the current account and those with a direct impact on the capital account. (As we shall see, linkages between the two will often imply that current account policies also influence the capital account and vice versa.)

The policies that directly affect the current account are divided into five categories (see table 7-2). These policies work through different channels. Some influence the goods that are imported or exported and the volume of these transactions. Trade taxes, subsidies, and differentiated exchange rates, for example, work by directly changing relative

Table 7-2. The Policy Alternatives

Policies with direct impact on the current account
Differentiated exchange rates for commercial transactions
Trade taxes and subsidies
Quantitative restrictions (import quotas, voluntary export restrictions)
Other commercial policies (advanced import deposits, import
surcharges, nontariff barriers)
Devaluation
Policies with direct impact on the capital account
Separate exchange rates for capital account transactions
Taxes on capital account transactions
Quantitative restrictions on capital flows
Devaluation

prices. Quantitative restrictions, including import quotas, work by directly regulating quantities. These policies often involve the allocation of import licenses and therefore help determine who does the importing or the exporting. The fourth category lists a number of other commercial policies, including nontariff barriers or special rules and regulations that restrict trade flows. Because a devaluation or revaluation can be regarded as a policy that affects all imports and all exports, I include it for completeness.

Four categories are listed under policies that focus on the capital account. First, a country might split its exchange rate by establishing separate rates for current and capital transactions. Second, a country might tax or restrict capital flows. Foreign borrowing, for example, may be restricted by total volume, maturity, or usage. Third, it is often useful to distinguish between policies that influence all capital transactions and policies that have a differential impact. Fourth, a devaluation or revaluation will also influence the capital account.

These policies are widely used. As of December 31, 1984, 21 percent of IMF member countries had multiple exchange rates for commercial transactions; 23 percent of the countries had a separate exchange rate for some or all capital transactions; 37 percent imposed import surcharges; 14 percent required advance import deposits; 78 percent had restrictions on payments for capital transactions; and 81 percent required the surrender of export proceeds to the central bank.

Although there are important differences among the many policies, there are also some key similarities. If the primary objective is to improve the balance of payments, many tools are available, some focusing on the trade balance (or current account), others focusing on the capital account. In fact, the same issues arise when evaluating the advantages and the disadvantages of the alternatives. Each of the policies has important effects on the domestic economy in addition to its effects on the balance of payments. I highlight these similarities in the remainder of the section.

Consider policies that target the trade balance. To reduce a trade deficit, the policy must increase the domestic supply of traded goods relative to the domestic demand for traded goods. Individual policies do this in different ways. One part of the story is an increase in the domestic relative price of traded goods. The higher price works to reduce demand while increasing supply. Another part is a reduction in domestic demand for traded goods at each price, perhaps through quantity restrictions or through a drop in domestic income. A third part is an increase in domestic production of traded goods at each price, perhaps through the elimination of special taxes and regulations that discourage investment in certain sectors. The exact combination of these three parts differs among policies.

Each of the policies may have other important effects on the economy. Five general areas are:

- Distribution of income
- Allocation of resources
- Government revenues and expenditures
- Market structure
- Enforcement and illegal activity

Similar issues arise with the policies to improve the capital account. First, to improve the capital account, the policy must reduce relative domestic demand for foreign assets. It can do so through a change in relative prices or through shifts in the demand for foreign assets. Second, the policies will have effects on other aspects of the economy.

In some cases, the objective of policymakers is to redistribute income or to shift the sectoral allocation of resources. Often, however, the objectives are macroeconomic—for instance, balance of payments management—and the microeconomic effects are unwanted byproducts with potentially important implications for distribution and medium- to long-run growth. The critical issue for policymakers then becomes how to weigh the desired objectives against the undesired side effects in choosing policies.

Three additional points need to be made. First, it is important to stress that the precise impact of any particular policy will depend on the other elements of the policy package. It will also depend on the structure and characteristics of the individual economy. Second, the public credibility of an announced policy will figure prominently in the impact of the policy. An exchange rate change that is expected to be short-lived may have little or no impact on sectoral production and employment even if it results in a large initial change in relative prices. Third, removing tariffs while increasing other types of subsidies may result in no net change in production incentives. This inconsistency may undermine the credibility of the policy change.

Let us turn next to an analysis of individual policy tools. For each policy, the questions to ask are: what does it do, and why might a country impose it? Having discussed the policies individually, I will discuss how policymakers might choose among alternative tools to achieve macroeconomic objectives.

2. Multiple Exchange Rates and Trade Taxes

One of the most prominent features of the Venezuelan exchange arrangement of February 1984 was the different exchange rates for different current account transactions (see table 7-1). As we shall see, multiple-exchange-rate systems are nearly identical to systems of trade taxes and subsidies. For this reason the two policies are taken together, even though the focus is on multiple exchange rates. Differences between the two are noted as appropriate.

Many reasons are cited for the use of multiple exchange rates. It is claimed that a country can improve its trade balance less painfully with multiple exchange rates than with devaluation and that they provide insulation from external shocks. They have also been proclaimed useful to protect infant industries and for strategic reasons. I shall evaluate these claims at the end of the present section.

Many countries have used some type of differentiated-exchange-rate regime. Although any two regimes may have little in common, each regime can be characterized by:

- How transactions are segmented (Is there a single rate for imports and another for exports? Is there a special rate for luxury imports or a special rate for nontraditional exports?)
- How the exchange rates differ (Which rate is most depreciated, and by how much?)
- Whether each rate is fixed, managed, or floating

The next sections make five key points about multiple exchange rates. First, differentiated exchange rates work by altering relative prices. Therefore, they act in many respects like a system of trade taxes and subsidies. Second, multiple exchange rates are often used to improve the balance of payments. Compared with an across-the-board exchange rate change, they concentrate adjustment in particular sectors. Third, by altering relative prices, they also have important microeconomic consequences. Fourth, a system in which the government buys and sells foreign exchange at different rates has implications for the government budget. If, on average, the government pays more for foreign exchange than it receives, then its expenditures on trade subsidies outweigh its revenues from trade taxes. Policymakers must devise a way to finance the exchange rate system if it is to be sustainable. Fifth, the effects of a multiple-exchange regime will depend not only on how foreign transactions are segmented but also on whether the different exchange rates are fixed, managed, or freely floating and on the degree to which authorities can enforce the segmentation.

Tax and Subsidy Schemes

By establishing different exchange rates for different transactions, a multiple-exchange regime effectively taxes some goods and subsidizes others. As an example, consider the 1984 Venezuelan exchange arrangement.[1] As table 7-3 shows, wheat importers are required to pay 4.3 bolívares (Bs) per U.S. dollar in foreign exchange. Importers of transport equipment and most other goods are required to pay Bs7.5, whereas importers of alcohol and luxuries pay the free rate, which averaged Bs13.2 during 1984. This system is equivalent to one in which all importers paid Bs7.5, but certain imports were subject to additional taxes or subsidies. Wheat imports enjoyed a 42.7 percent subsidy, so

**Table 7-3. Taxes and Subsidies Implicit
in the 1984 Venezuelan Multiple Exchange Rate**

Exchange rate[a]	Export	Export tax[b] (percent)	Import	Import tax[b] (percent)
4.3 Bs/$	n.a.	n.a.	Wheat	−42.7
6.0 Bs/$	Petroleum	25.0	Imports to petroleum sector	−25.0
7.5 Bs/$	n.a.	n.a.	Transport equipment	n.a.
Free rate[c]	Bauxite	−(60–107)	Alcohol	69–107

n.a. Not available.

a. Bolívares per U.S. dollar.

b. Export and import taxes are calculated relative to the basic exchange rate of 7.5 Bs/$. A negative tax implies a subsidy.

c. The free exchange rate ranged between 12.0 and 15.5 Bs/$ during 1984, with an average rate of 13.2 Bs/$.

Source: Republic of Venezuela, *Economic Memorandum*, May 17, 1985.

that on net, wheat importers paid only 4.3/7.5, or 57.3 percent, of the full price for foreign exchange. Similarly, alcohol imports were taxed at a rate ranging from 60 percent to 107 percent during 1984.

The multiple exchange rate also applied a system of taxes and subsidies to domestic exporters. All exporters were required to remit their foreign exchange earnings to the central bank. Proceeds from nontraditional exports, such as bauxite or aluminum, were remitted at the free-market rate. Taking the average free rate, these exporters received an additional Bs5.7 per dollar relative to the basic rate of 7.5. They received a subsidy of 76 percent (5.7/7.5 = 0.76) as a result of the multiple-exchange regime.

As an alternative to an across-the-board devaluation, multiple exchange rates or trade taxes improve the trade balance by devaluing the exchange rate applicable to some transactions. In Venezuela, the new exchange regime increased domestic prices of nonessential imports and on average reduced the real value of household incomes. Both of these factors contributed to a reduction in imports. Similarly, the increased domestic relative prices of nontraditional exports were expected to stimulate production in these sectors. (In general, demand contracts quickly in response to price increases, whereas production responds more gradually.) Relative to a devaluation, the policy concentrates adjustment in some sectors and provides some insulation to other sectors. The policy will work best if these sectors are the most responsive to price changes and if other consequences are not too costly.

We have seen that a multiple-exchange-rate system works just like a system of trade taxes and subsidies in the sense that it sets different prices for foreign exchange, depending on what is bought or sold. Multiple rates and tax and subsidy schemes, however, may differ in other areas. First, the two policies may not be perceived as being equally credible or permanent by the public. If the multiple rate is announced by the central bank as one part of a macroeconomic adjustment program, for example, its credibility may be linked to the credibility of the rest of the program. Tax schemes may or may not have a history of longevity. Second, tax and exchange rate policies are likely to be administered by different institutions. One agency may be better equipped to monitor and to enforce the differentiated price structure.

Third, multiple exchange rates can be more adjustable than a tax system. If some transactions occur at a flexible exchange rate, the implicit tax or subsidy will adjust, depending on market conditions. When foreign exchange is in short supply, the flexible rate will depreciate relative to the fixed rates, thereby increasing the tax on selected imports and the subsidy to selected exports. When foreign exchange availability increases, the exchange rate will tend to appreciate, reducing the implicit taxes and subsidies.

Microeconomic Consequences

Differentiated exchange rates are nearly equivalent to a system of trade taxes and subsidies. Because these schemes may influence prices and relative profitabilities across sectors, they may have important microeconomic effects on the distribution of income and on the allocation of domestic resources.

The Venezuelan multiple-rate system, for example, helped to insulate low-income households from higher prices of basic foods. The domestic price of gasoline was also subsidized. Even after large gasoline price increases in February 1984, the domestic price remained well below world prices. The net effect of the exchange regime on the distribution of income in Venezuela is difficult to measure because it was imposed on a complex system of administered prices and import restrictions.

In general, the distributional impact of a split exchange rate will depend on specific characteristics of the policy regime and the country in question. The welfare of any particular socioeconomic group will depend on what happens to the prices of the goods it consumes and on what happens to its income and to the value of its assets. A policy that subsidizes food, for example, may reduce welfare of domestic food producers who experience a decline in income while improving the welfare of others, such as low-income urban households. The net effect on income distribution and poverty will depend on the relative shares of these groups of gainers and losers. The same policy can have very different distributional consequences, depending on the structure of the economy.

A second objective of multiple exchange rates is to stimulate domestic production of some exports through subsidies with, it is hoped, little adverse effects on production and exports of those sectors being taxed. In Venezuela, authorities hoped to expand exports of aluminum and agriculture, but it is too soon to tell how successful the policy has been in this regard. Furthermore, the Venezuelan situation is quite special in that the exports being "taxed" by the multiple-exchange-rate system are publicly owned. Petroleum, which accounts for more than 90 percent of Venezuela's export earnings, is already subject to output restrictions through membership in the Organization of Petroleum Exporting Countries (OPEC). The tax represents an internal government transfer that will not reduce incentives for petroleum production.

In general, the impact of a multiple-exchange regime on resource allocation and sectoral growth will depend first on its effects on production incentives across sectors and second on the responsiveness of output and investment to these price incentives. Production incentives are often estimated by effective rates of protection (ERP) that measure the exchange regime's effect on domestic output prices net of production costs. Three important points from the literature on ERP are summarized below.

- Quotas, production subsidies, and other policies often have important effects on domestic prices. It can be very misleading to focus only on nominal trade taxes and multiple exchange rates.
- When policies reduce production costs for a particular sector—for example, by lowering the domestic price of intermediate inputs—the sector enjoys an increase in profitability. Similarly, increased production costs reduce effective protection. The entire structure of protection must be analyzed.
- Estimates of ERP suggest that the rates are often large and vary considerably across sectors, protecting some sectors and taxing others (frequently agriculture).

Policies that result in large taxes or subsidies to domestic sectors can have significant effects on sectoral outputs and growth, particularly if these policies are expected to be long-lived. The sensitivity of output and investment to relative price changes does seem to vary, however. Investment decisions often reflect other considerations, such as the availability of technical expertise. Short-run output responses will also depend on current capacity and the ease with which producers can shift toward more profitable products or markets.

It is sometimes argued that traditional exports (often agriculture and mining) are insensitive to price changes, and that a devaluation will not increase their ability to earn foreign exchange. In addition, nontraditional exports (often manufactures) are considered to be quite responsive to price changes and therefore require an initial period of special protection to grow into viable industries. Responsiveness to price changes does vary across sectors, and there are often good reasons to protect infant industries until they are able to mature. These factors support the usage of multiple rates or tariffs while a country is adjusting structurally. But there is a danger in underestimating the responsiveness of traditional exports. The contraction of key sectors may retard economic growth and reduce foreign exchange earnings. The Jamaican experience of the 1970s provides a good example of the potential problems from policies that tax traditional agricultural exports (see appendix 1 to this chapter).

Fiscal Aspects

Multiple-exchange regimes, in which different transactions are conducted at different exchange rates, will tend to affect the government budget. Suppose the government sells importers the same amount of foreign exchange that it buys from exporters. If, on average, the government charges importers less for foreign exchange than it pays exporters, then the exchange regime subsidizes importers and worsens the budget deficit. In contrast, if importers are charged more than exporters receive, the government receipts will exceed expenditures. The counterpart of a net tax on importers is an improvement in the government budget.

The Venezuelan exchange system is illustrated in table 7-4. The first line shows that foreign exchange reserves in the central bank were $11,149 million at the beginning of 1984. Total inflows of foreign exchange in the controlled markets amounted to $16,661 million, of which $13,276 million were accounted for by petroleum or iron exports. Total outflows were $14,485 million in the three controlled markets. Finally, central bank intervention in the free market amounted to $860 million. Net of adjustments, central bank reserves increased by $1,320 million during 1984. There was an overall balance of payments surplus.

Table 7-4 also shows the domestic currency equivalent of these foreign exchange flows. Exporters receive bolívares in exchange for their

**Table 7-4. Foreign Exchange Movements
through the Central Bank of Venezuela, 1984**
(millions of U.S. dollars and bolívares)

Item	U.S. dollars	Bolívares
Net international reserves	11,149	—
Controlled markets		
Foreign exchange inflows	16,661	—
4.3 Bs/$	2,423	10,419
6.0 Bs/$	13,276	79,656
7.5 Bs/$	962	7,215
(Associated bolívar outflows)		(97,290)
Foreign exchange outflows	14,485	
4.3 Bs/$	4,981	21,418
6.0 Bs/$	2,403	14,418
7.5 Bs/$	7,101	53,258
(Associated bolívar inflows)		(89,094)
Net intervention in free market	860	—
Adjustments	4	—
End of period reserves	12,469	—

— Not applicable.
Source: Central Bank of Venezuela, Economic Memorandum, March 1985.

foreign exchange earnings. Thus dollar inflows to the controlled markets have domestic currency outflows as their counterpart. Payments to exporters, primarily in transfers to petroleum and iron companies in the public sector, amounted to Bs97,290 million for $16,661 million—an average rate of Bs5.83 per U.S. dollar. Importers paid a total of Bs89,094 million—an average rate of Bs6.15 per U.S. dollar. In other words, imports were taxed relative to exports. If all $16,661 had been sold to importers at the average rate of Bs6.15 per U.S. dollar, total inflows in domestic currency would have been Bs102,465. Because this total exceeds the Bs97,290 million outflow, the multiple-exchange-rate scheme would have helped to improve the government budget.

In assessing the impact of a multiple-exchange regime, we need to note two important balances. The dollar balance indicates whether the balance of payments is in surplus or deficit. In table 7-4, there is a surplus. The domestic currency balance indicates the impact of the multiple-exchange-rate scheme on the country's fiscal position. As a hypothetical example, suppose the total dollar inflows and total dollar outflows were both $16,661 million, with no central bank intervention in the free market. Suppose the average exchange rate for exporters remained at Bs5.84 per U.S. dollar but that all imports were at the Bs4.3 rate. Under these assumptions, the central bank would have received Bs71,642 million (4.3 Bs/$ × $16,661) from importers, but it would have paid Bs97,290 million (5.84 Bs/$ × US$16,661) to exporters. The subsidy on imports would have amounted to Bs25,648 million, which could have been paid for by increases in money creation, taxes, or government borrowing.

If the dollar value of imports were to exceed the dollar value of exports, one of four things could happen. First, foreign exchange reserves could be depleted. Second, the government could borrow abroad to finance the additional imports. Third, the government could acquire foreign exchange by buying it from the free market. If the free-market exchange rate exceeds the rates that the government charges importers, however, the third alternative is undesirable because of the adverse consequences on the budget. In the Venezuelan example, the highest price the government charged importers was Bs7.5 per dollar, but the rate the government would have to pay for dollars in the free market averaged Bs13.2. When faced with these three alternatives, governments often elect a fourth: to alter the rules of the system.

Thus an important issue that arises in multiple exchange regimes is their sustainability. A regime may be unsustainable because it worsens the budget deficit, because it implies that foreign exchange outflows exceed inflows, or both. The eventual response to an unsustainable system is to change the rules. To alleviate adverse effects on the fiscal deficit, for example, import items may be shifted to a less subsidized exchange rate. (Some essential imports, for example, may be moved to the rate of Bs7.5 per dollar.) To alleviate the problem of net foreign exchange outflow, imports may be shifted from fixed rates into the free market, or the fixed rates may be devalued.

Tradeoffs between Multiple Exchange Rates and the Balance of Payments

A multiple-exchange-rate regime can sometimes be used to improve the balance of payments while mitigating the impact of adjustment on selected population groups. These potential benefits, however, must be weighed against a number of costs. First, the system will result in an improvement in the balance of payments only if it succeeds in increasing net foreign exchange inflows. To the extent that some sectors are more responsive to price incentives than others, concentrating the relative price changes among these sectors makes sense. The expansion of some exportables, however, will be at the expense of contractions elsewhere as resources are shifted domestically. Extreme price distortions can reduce overall output growth and total foreign exchange earnings. Potential costs will tend to increase with the gap between the differentiated rates and the expected duration of the regime. Furthermore, leakages between markets will increase. Added costs from administration and corruption may be sizable.

Second, the scheme insulates targeted households by subsidizing consumption of key commodities. Like any subsidy, this one must be paid for through taxes implicit in the exchange regime, through other domestic taxes, or through increased government deficits. Attempts to subsidize a large share of the import budget will require heavy taxation with high potential costs.

A critical element in a multiple-exchange regime is that international transactions are split between different exchange markets. It can become exceedingly difficult to enforce this segmentation, however, particularly when there are large differences between the exchange rates in different markets. Exporters who must remit their foreign exchange earnings at relatively appreciated exchange rates have strong incentives to underinvoice their sales. They remit only part of their earnings at the unfavorable rate and sell the rest at a more favorable official rate, if possible, or at unofficial rates, if there are black markets for foreign exchange. Similarly, importers who have access to the appreciated exchange rate have incentives to overinvoice their imports. They can then use some of their foreign exchange to purchase imports and sell the remainder domestically. These leakages, particularly if they channel foreign exchange out of official markets, can adversely affect the country's balance of payments and fiscal positions.

Multiple exchange rates have been advocated as macroeconomic shock absorbers. In practice, they cannot insulate an entire economy from external shocks. What they can do is to concentrate the impact of shocks on particular international transactions, thereby mitigating the impact on some sectors or income groups. One alternative to achieve this objective would be to establish a special floating rate, or an exchange auction, for luxury imports. A temporary deterioration in the terms of trade, which reduces the country's export earnings, would simply reduce the quantity of foreign exchange that the central bank can auction for luxury imports. This special exchange rate would depreciate with relatively little impact on other international transactions. This system is of course subject to many of the same qualifications discussed earlier. In particular, it would not alleviate the problems of large, permanent shocks.

Other Arguments for Protection

Finally, there are three other reasons for using taxes or multiple exchange rates to protect particular sectors. First, certain sectors may be viewed as critical to national interests.

Second, an infant industry may not be viable without subsidies in the short run but may become competitive in the medium to long run, given the chance to develop.[2] Although this argument can provide strong reasons for policy intervention, it is not necessarily true that protection through a tariff or a depreciated exchange rate is the best policy. In some cases, a production subsidy will be preferable. In others, the appropriate policy will involve subsidizing key inputs. The industry may, for example, require skills and technical expertise that are initially in short supply.

Third, a country that can influence world prices of its imports or its exports can use tax or subsidy schemes to its advantage. The idea would be to restrict import demand to lower the price of its importables or to restrict export supply to raise the price of its exportables. (The OPEC countries, for example, enjoyed large welfare gains by restricting oil production to increase oil prices.) Although relatively few countries can influence import prices, many produce a large enough share of some commodity export to be able to influence market price. Any gains, however, come at the expense of losses to other countries. If they retaliate, both sides may end up losing. Furthermore, the gains may be only temporary if the higher price creates new producers, thus eroding the country's ability to control world prices.

3. Quantitative Restrictions

Quantitative restrictions (QRs) are frequently used by countries with balance of payments difficulties to regulate trade flows. Among developing countries, in particular, the use of import quotas is widespread. In addition, industrial countries have recently increased the use of many nontariff trade barriers, including quotas and voluntary export restraints (VERs). This section will focus on the effects of import quotas.

A country may seek to improve its trade balance by setting a limit on the volume or the value of some or all imported commodities. Quotas can also, however, have important effects on domestic prices, resource allocation, income distribution, profit seeking, and nonmarket activity. These factors are discussed here to show that quotas are sometimes, but not always, effective tools for balance of payments improvement. Increasing the restrictiveness of quota protection may in fact lead to a deterioration of the trade balance accompanied by accelerated inflation and slower growth.

Domestic Effects of Import Quotas

Figure 7-1 shows the impact of a quota in the Indian market for manufactures. In the absence of any domestic restrictions, they could be

Figure 7-1. Impact of Import Quotas in the Indian Market

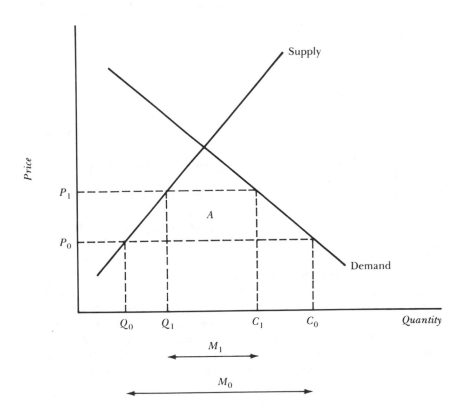

imported from the rest of the world at a domestic price P_0. Total consumption would be C_0, with Q_0 produced domestically and M_0 imported. By restricting the volume of imports $M_1 < M_0$, the quota has three effects. First, there is excess demand for imported goods, and available imports must be rationed. Second, the value of these goods in India increases from P_0 to P_1. The excess of the quota-inclusive price P_1 over the quota-exclusive price P_0 is called the quota premium. Third, domestic production will increase from Q_0 to Q_1.[3]

A system of import quotas will influence domestic prices and production. Those goods with the most restrictive quotas will see higher prices and (often) more domestic expansion.[4] These large price changes can be expected to reallocate resources (see above). Like differentiated exchange rates and tariffs, quotas tend to divert resources to protected sectors.

Quotas are also likely to have an impact on the distribution of income. First, the changes in relative prices and in sectoral output and employment will benefit some groups at the expense of others. It is difficult to generalize about the distributional impact of quotas because it will depend on the specific quota system and on the structure of the economy. Second, the quota premium implies that whoever purchases restricted goods from the rest of the world can make profits by reselling them in domestic markets. Residents who obtain licenses to import often benefit substantially from the quota system. The scheme for allocating licenses itself has important distributional consequences.

Frequently, a system of import licenses is set up to distribute the scarce imports. It is worth stressing, however, that there are problems inherent in devising such a scheme. It is difficult enough to decide the appropriate quantities of each commodity to import, given specific objectives. It is considerably more difficult to decide how to allocate these imports among individual consumers and firms. The outcome is likely to have been influenced by political pressures as much as, if not more than, by economic considerations.

An alternative allocation mechanism would be to auction the import licenses. This scheme would have the advantage of providing the government with revenues (area A in figure 7-1) arising from the difference between the domestic and the international prices. It may be less susceptible to corruption, and it introduces additional flexibility into the system. In practice, this mechanism has rarely been used.

Quota premiums are difficult to measure. Unless the quota is auctioned off, the domestic value of the scarce imports is seldom observed and must be estimated. Also, quotas are often placed on top of other taxes and restrictions. Existing estimates strongly suggest that the price effects of quotas can be substantial and that ignoring these effects can be dangerously misleading because the impact of quotas tends to vary widely across commodities. Bhagwati and Srinivasan estimated, for example, that the quota premiums for India were as high as 230 percent of the c.i.f. import value for drugs and medicines and more than 500 percent for certain food products.[5]

When the potential profits from buying restricted items abroad and selling them domestically are large, there are strong incentives to smuggle, to underinvoice imports, and to lobby for access to an import license. Possibilities for illegal activity, corruption, and wasted resources are additional distortions arising from quotas. The more restrictive the quota, the higher the quota premium and the larger the combined costs from distortions.

An additional problem with the use of quotas is that shifts in domestic demand and supply will change the quotas' restrictiveness. Because the quota premiums are not easily observable, unless the import licenses are auctioned, it is difficult to monitor the restrictiveness of each quota over time. In particular, when demand expands relatively quickly over time, a quota will become increasingly restrictive, and the implied costs of distortion will grow.

Increasing the restrictiveness of quotas may not improve the balance of payments over the medium to long run. It may substantially increase local prices of import-competing goods and domestic substitutes and thereby shift domestic production and sales away from exportables and toward the more profitable local markets. The eventual impact may be a reduction in export earnings and deterioration of the trade balance. The Jamaican experience during the 1970s provided one example of this possibility. (See appendix 1 to this chapter.)

Import Quotas versus Multiple Exchange Rates and Trade Taxes

In some respects, quotas and tariffs or differentiated exchange rates are quite similar. To see the similarity, refer again to figure 7-1. Consider protecting domestic manufacturing by placing imported manufactured goods at a relatively depreciated exchange rate so that the implicit tax raises the domestic price from P_0 to P_1. Like the quota, the tax scheme will tend to shift resources into the protected sectors and to redistribute income to domestic import competitors.

There are also many differences between quotas and tax schemes, however. One important difference is that policymakers may not know how large a tax would be required to restrict imports by a desired amount. Quotas enable policymakers to regulate volume directly. This feature can be very attractive, particularly during balance of payments crises. It helps to explain the widespread usage of quantitative restrictions.

We have already seen a number of other differences. First, quotas imply that policymakers must decide how to allocate imports. Second, the restrictiveness of quotas varies over time and is hard to measure. Third, quotas have additional redistribution effects that depend on how access to scarce imports is allocated. Fourth, quotas allocated to domestic importers do not provide the government with revenues unless they are auctioned off. Fifth, tariffs and quotas can have different effects on the market structure that can diverge considerably when markets are imperfectly competitive.

There may be important administrative differences between the two schemes. Suppose, for example, that authorities wish gradually to relax import restrictions on certain sectors. It may be easier to carry out a phased or dynamic trade policy by using quotas than by using tariffs or the exchange regime.

What can be said about whether quotas are better or worse policy choices than tariffs or multiple exchange rates? Some economists prefer tariffs because of the problems associated with changing quota restrictiveness, government revenues, and allocation schemes. In fact, the evidence for the argument that replacing quotas with tariffs stimulates economic activity is quite weak. It is difficult to evaluate the data, however, because the available episodes differ considerably in terms of other policy choices and external conditions.

On balance, a sensible view seems to be that quotas can be very useful as short-term or transitional policies. Authorities, however, should have good reasons for choosing quotas over tariffs as a long-term policy. Countries may wish to impose quotas to limit the importation of certain luxury items precisely because the implied quota premium is less visible than the required equivalent tariff. They may select quotas on administrative grounds. Depending on the structure of domestic and international markets, countries may also wish to use quotas for strategic reasons.[6]

4. Capital Controls

Almost all countries impose some restrictions on capital movements. Furthermore, a number of countries have instituted dual-exchange-rate regimes in which capital account transactions are conducted at a different exchange rate from some (or all) current account transactions. The next two sections examine capital controls and dual exchange rates. I begin the discussion of policies aimed at the capital account with some important characteristics of international capital flows. A clear understanding of the potential problems arising from capital movements will help to focus the discussion on the advantages and disadvantages of policy alternatives.

Capital Inflows and Outflows

Recall from the external accounting identity for an open economy that a current account deficit must be financed through some combination of capital account surplus and drawdown of the central bank's foreign exchange reserves.

Current account deficit = Capital account surplus
+ Drawdown of official reserves

The capital account can be divided into a number of components: direct investment, long-term loans (including public, public guaranteed, and private), and short-term capital movements. Included in short-term capital movements are private speculative capital flows. If Mexican residents anticipate a devaluation of the Mexican peso, for example, the expected returns from investing in the United States will exceed the expected returns from investing in Mexico. The result will be capital outflows. Speculative capital movements are very difficult to measure because the flows are often unrecorded and illegal. Existing estimates indicate, however, that capital flows can be very large and that they tend to be extremely sensitive to differences in expected returns across countries (see appendix 2).

Large capital inflows or outflows can create problems for the domestic economy. In a flexible exchange regime, capital outflows will tend to depreciate the domestic currency, thereby accelerating inflation and reducing real incomes. The depreciation will boost competitiveness. If the changes are expected to be temporary, however, there may be little increase in domestic output and employment. Capital inflows will lead to an appreciation in a flexible-rate regime. The U.S. experience during 1980–85 provides a stark example of the potential costs. The large and persistent appreciation of the dollar substantially reduced U.S. competitiveness. The trade balance reversed from a surplus in 1980 to a massive $100 billion trade deficit in 1984. The strong dollar has also been blamed for high and persistent levels of unemployment.

Capital flows can also create difficulties in fixed- or managed-exchange regimes. Capital outflows must be financed through reductions in official reserves or increases in foreign borrowing. Capital inflows will tend to increase domestic money growth. Higher inflation rates hurt domestic competitiveness, increase exchange rate overvaluation, and often feed expectations of devaluation.

The Argentine Experience during 1978–81

I use the Argentinian experience in 1979–80 to illustrate the problems of large capital movements in an economy with a managed exchange rate. Table 7-5 provides some information about the episode.

Table 7-5. Economic Indicators for Argentina, 1978–81
(billions of U.S. dollars)

Item	1978	1979	1980	1981
Trade balance	2.9	1.8	−1.4	0.7
Current account	1.9	−0.5	−4.8	−4.7
Increase in debt	2.8	6.5	8.0	8.5
Long-term capital and direct investment	0.4	0.5	0.9	2.0
Short-term capital and errors and omissions	−1.3	1.5	−2.4	−8.5
Inflation (percent)	174	159	101	104
Economic growth (percent)	−2.8	6.7	0.9	−6.3

Source: IMF, *International Financial Statistics,* various issues.

In 1978, the Argentine economy was experiencing severe internal and external difficulty. Real growth was stagnant, inflation stood at 166 percent, and there was an acute shortage of foreign exchange. Under Finance Minister Martinez de Hoz, Argentina instituted a new stabilization plan in December 1978.[7] A key feature of the plan was a preannounced exchange rate (a tablita) that was to depreciate at a decreasing rate. At the same time, most restrictions on capital movements were eliminated. The hope was that exposure to foreign competition would force the price inflation of tradable goods to slow down to world rates. The program's objectives were to reduce inflation and to improve the balance of payments.

The program did not work for a number of reasons. Domestic inflation remained high; the exchange rate, at its preannounced crawl, quickly became overvalued. Despite an initial period of domestic expansion, the economy went into recession and financial crisis during 1980, and the balance of payments situation deteriorated. One of the most important reasons for the program's failure was large-scale capital movements—capital inflows during 1979 and massive capital flight during 1980.

A number of reasons have been cited for the capital inflows during the first stage of the program. The sharp rise of domestic interest rates in the first quarter of 1979 implied a real rate of return (net of announced depreciation) in excess of foreign rates. The higher interest rates may be attributable to shifts in consumer behavior as a result of anticipated disinflation. In any case, the capital inflows contributed to the boom but mitigated any declines in inflation.[8] The increasing overvaluation undermined confidence in the program.

By early 1980, the direction of capital flow had been reversed. The capital flight has been attributed to a variety of sources. Growing overvaluation, external debt, and current account deficits fueled expectations of a maxidevaluation. Lack of confidence in the sustainability of the current program also stemmed from inconsistencies in the domestic policies and the persistence of large fiscal deficits. Furthermore, a new president would take office in 1981. The government accumulated an enormous external debt as it continued to defend the tablita despite capital outflows. Finally, the policy was terminated with a series of devaluations in 1981. Restrictions on capital movements were reimposed.

The Argentina example is especially interesting because of the magnitudes of the capital movements, which were much larger in the absence of capital controls. With controls in place, Argentina would probably have accumulated substantially less external debt during the period. It is doubtful, however, that the addition of capital controls alone would have made the program work.

Advantages and Disadvantages of Capital Controls

Capital controls are imposed by nearly all developing countries. Industrial countries, which tend to impose less restrictive controls, have shown a gradual trend toward reducing capital restrictions. The potentially harmful effects of speculative capital movements provide a strong argument for imposing some restrictions on capital flows. Before we conclude that capital controls are ideal, however, it is important to ask about the disadvantages of restricting capital movements and about how well capital controls work in practice.

There are arguments against capital controls on grounds of equity as well as efficiency. Controls tend to deny residents access to foreign currency, restrict their ability to protect the real value of their assets, and limit their travel and purchases abroad. For these reasons, controls can be very unpopular and are frequently circumvented. Not surprisingly, if residents view capital controls as very costly, the controls become exceedingly difficult to enforce. When there is widespread expectation of a substantial devaluation, illegal capital movements can become large. Black markets also flourish (see appendix 3).

This section has made three main points. First, potentially large and disruptive speculative capital movements provide a rationale for imposing capital controls. Second, restrictions on private capital flows, particularly on domestic ownership of foreign currency and foreign securities, are extremely widespread. Third, these controls can be very difficult to enforce, particularly when a sizable devaluation is perceived to be imminent or interest differentials are large. Capital controls should not be viewed as a means to defend an overvalued exchange rate indefinitely. They can be useful to buffer the domestic economy against large-scale private speculation.

5. Dual Exchange Rates

An alternative approach to dealing with the problem of large capital movements is to establish separate exchange rates for current and capital account transactions—that is, a dual-exchange regime. Like capital controls, dual exchange rates can help to shelter an economy from volatile capital movements. The potential benefits from dual exchange rates are sometimes overstated, however, whereas the potential disadvantages are sometimes overlooked.

There are many variants of the dual-exchange regime. A frequently discussed system has a fixed commercial rate for current account transactions and a floating financial rate for capital account transactions. The more common variant allows some current account transactions to take place at a fixed rate, while the remaining current account transactions and all capital account transactions take place at a floating rate. The systems also differ in the amount of intervention (if any) in the free market. Some dual-rate regimes maintain either two fixed rates or two flexible rates. Finally, a number of countries (for example, Venezuela) have multiple exchange rates that combine aspects of the dual rates discussed here and aspects of the differentiated rates discussed above.

How Dual Exchange Rates Work

The argument in favor of a dual exchange rate typically has two parts. First, the separate exchange rates, it is claimed, insulate domestic prices and output from the effects of capital movements. Suppose, for example, that Mexican residents would like to shift from holding domestic assets to holding U.S. dollar assets. The increased demand for foreign currency would tend to depreciate the financial exchange rate without requiring any concurrent change in the regulated rate. With no change in the commercial exchange rate, there need be no change in import prices or in the competitiveness of exports.

Second, the dual rate, it is claimed, increases central bank control over foreign exchange reserves compared with control possible in a fixed-rate regime. In terms of the previous example, the claim would be that private capital outflows do not need to be financed by a reduction in official reserves or by an increase in foreign borrowing. (The central bank would still be required to use reserves to offset current account deficits so as to defend the commercial exchange rate.)

Unfortunately, neither theory nor experience supports the view that dual exchange rates can completely insulate domestic prices or reserves, except, perhaps, in the very short run. The theoretical models stress the importance of key linkages between the two markets for international transactions. These linkages imply that dual exchange rates may mitigate the impact of short-run capital volatility, but they are unlikely to do more than postpone the impact of large, sustained capital movements. At the same time, they can create a number of potentially harmful domestic distortions.

Consider once more the example of a desired private capital outflow that results in a depreciation of the financial exchange rate. The rest of the domestic economy may be affected through at least four channels:

- Changes in domestic consumption and savings decisions
- Changes in domestic financial markets (that is, interest rates)
- Increased prices of goods traded at the financial exchange rate
- Increased leakages between markets, profit seeking, and illegal activities.

Changes in domestic consumption and savings decisions highlight the fact that depreciation of the financial exchange rate will increase the domestic currency value of foreign assets. Because they will feel wealthier, residents are likely to increase consumption at the expense of savings. To the extent that increased consumption increases imports, the current account will deteriorate, so that an offsetting reduction of reserves, a depreciation of the commercial exchange rate, or additional foreign borrowing will be required. To the extent that changes in consumption increases demand for domestic products, domestic prices will tend to rise.

Import consumption might increase for another reason. If the desired capital flight arose because of a large anticipated devaluation of the regulated commercial exchange rate, residents will try to purchase imports, especially imported durables, before the price increase occurs. The linkages between portfolio and consumption or savings decisions of private residents provide an important qualification to the view that dual exchange rates can insulate domestic reserves and prices.

The domestic economy may also be affected by changes in domestic interest rates. The exact impact of a desired capital outflow on interest rates will depend on the specifics of the dual-exchange regime, on the extent to which domestic interest rates are controlled, and on the structure of domestic financial markets. The key point here is that the existence of a flexible financial rate should not be expected to eliminate pressure on domestic financial markets, especially when interest payments are remitted at the regulated exchange rate.

As mentioned earlier, some current account transactions are usually conducted at the floating exchange rate in dual-exchange regimes. A depreciation of the financial exchange rate will tend to increase the domestic prices of these items.

Finally, as the financial exchange rate depreciates, the gap between the two exchange rates widens, increasing the incentives to shift transactions between the two markets and to exploit opportunities for arbitrage. In Belgium, for example, when the gap between the free rate and the regulated rate increased during 1980, some speculators were able to purchase foreign exchange from the central bank at the regulated rate and to resell it at the financial rate, pocketing the profits.

More generally, importers will try to overinvoice, whereas exporters will underinvoice transactions at the regulated rate, reselling foreign exchange at the depreciated financial rate. In addition to illegal activities, residents may waste considerable resources lobbying for changes in the exchange regime (that is, trying to shift the transactions that occur in each market). The combined effect of these leakages between markets may be a large deterioration of the balance in the regulated market, which adversely affects official reserves.

All of these channels imply that a dual exchange regime cannot totally insulate the domestic economy from international capital movements. It is worth stressing, however, that the strength of each channel will be an increasing function of the gap between the two exchange rates. If there is a large, sustained premium on foreign exchange in the financial market, the dual-rate system will tend to cause large distortions in domestic behavior but will provide little insulation to official reserves. Dual exchange rates will not allow a government to maintain an overvalued exchange rate indefinitely. When the premium is relatively small, however, a dual-rate system should mitigate the impact of speculative capital movements on official reserves, thereby helping the central bank to defend the fixed commercial rate.

The Mexican Dual-Exchange Regime

The Mexican dual-exchange regime provides an example of a two-tier exchange regime in which the primary objective is the reduction of private capital outflows. The system was instituted during the August 1982 debt crisis as part of a broader policy package. The country had experienced an increasing payments imbalance in the late 1970s, coupled with increasing dependence on oil exports and a massive buildup of external debt. Cumulative current account deficits during 1978–81, however, accounted for only 64 percent of total debt accumulation. Private capital outflows, in anticipation of a maxidevaluation, accounted for the remainder. The figures are most striking for 1981. External debt increased by $23.4 billion, whereas gross acquisitions of foreign assets by the private sector totaled $10.9 billion. Some basic statistics for the Mexican economy appear in table 7-6.

Table 7-6. Economic Indicators for Mexico, 1978–84
(billions of U.S. dollars)

Item	1978	1979	1980	1981	1982	1983	1984
Current account	−2.7	−4.9	−6.8	−11.7	−4.7	5.5	4.0
Foreign debt[a]	33.2	38.9	50.6	75.0	83.0	84.0	85.6
Reserve accumulation[b]							
Capital flight[c]	−0.6	−0.9	−2.8	−10.9	−9.5	−4.5	−2.7
Real growth (percent)	8.0	10.3	12.1	7.7	−1.6	−7.6	1.7
Inflation (percent)	17.5	18.1	26.4	27.9	59.0	101.8	65.5

a. Public and private external debt.

b. Change in central bank foreign exchange reserves.

c. Gross acquisiton of foreign assets by the private sector. A positive figure represents a positive acquisiton.

Source: Bank of Mexico, *Informe Anual* and *Indicadores Economicos;* IMF, *International Financial Statistics,* various issues.

In the period from December 1982 to July 1985 following the large devaluations that took place during 1982, the exchange regime consisted of a "controlled" rate and an "official free" rate.[9] Figure 7-2 illustrates the behavior of these two rates. The controlled rate applied to essential imports, all merchandise exports, and foreign debt repayments. The free rate applied to financial and all other current account transactions. The controlled rate was steadily depreciated; the magnitude of preannounced daily minidevaluations was based on inflation targets. The hope was to maintain a relatively undervalued peso to improve the non-oil current account while reducing domestic inflation. Beginning in September 1983, the daily minidevaluations were also applied to the official free rate.

I make three observations on Mexico's dual-exchange regimes. First, the central bank managed the free rate as well as the controlled rate until July 1985. By selling dollars in the dual market, the central bank could prevent the free rate from depreciating relative to the controlled rate. These sales improved the government budget measured in pesos because the free-market rate remained depreciated relative to the controlled rate during this period.

Second, the existence of the black market for foreign exchange implied that, in practice, there were three relevant exchange rates. The black market price of dollars was consistently higher than the free-market price and depreciated substantially during the second exchange rate crisis in the summer of 1985.

Third, the exchange regime was one part of a more comprehensive policy package. Other measures included fiscal contraction, a nationalized banking system, strict import controls (with some relaxation

Figure 7-2. Mexican Exchange Rates, 1982–86

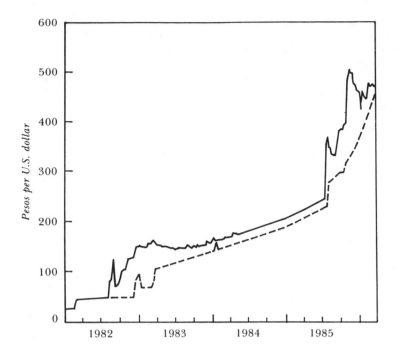

Source: Bank of Mexico, *Indicadores Economicos.*

beginning in 1984), and a variety of policies to adjust domestic relative wages and prices.

Before discussing the effectiveness of the dual-rate regime in controlling capital flight, I may usefully summarize Mexican economic performance since 1982. During 1983, Mexico experienced significant declines in real growth and employment. The balance of payments improved dramatically, however, so that foreign exchange reserves grew surprisingly large. During 1984–85, there was a moderate improvement in real growth, but the current account deteriorated as oil prices declined and the U.S. economic recovery slowed. Furthermore, Mexican inflation continued to exceed targets. Nominal exchange rate adjustments did not keep up with domestic inflation. From the first quarter of 1983 to the fourth quarter of 1984, the controlled rate appreciated by 18 percent in real terms, while the free rate appreciated by 37 percent. These factors, combined with further private capital outflows as residents perceived that additional devaluations were imminent, led to a second exchange crisis in July 1985. New policies included modification of the dual-rate regime to a managed float in the controlled market and a flexible rate in the free market.

The Mexican exchange regime seems to have contributed to a reduction of private capital outflows but to have been unable to prevent an acceleration of capital flight as economic conditions deteriorated in 1985. During 1983–84, private capital outflows were substantially below the peak levels observed during 1981–82 but remained high relative to pre-1980 levels. The reduction can be explained in large part by the 1982 maxidevaluations; as a result the peso was widely believed to be undervalued during 1983. The dual-rate regime did imply a relatively larger devaluation of the rate applicable to financial transactions. The Mexican split rate system could not prevent all capital outflows because the official free rate was managed. An increase in foreign exchange demand would result in additional foreign exchange to the free market supplied by the central bank.

With the two exchange rates moving in tandem by predetermined amounts, the free rate did not adjust to market pressures. In particular, the rate of depreciation did not accelerate as market confidence deteriorated during 1985. Estimates suggest that capital flight increased substantially during this period.

Evaluating Dual-Exchange Regimes

Although one must be careful not to overstate the potential benefits of a dual exchange rate, the policy can be useful. First, by partially insulating domestic reserves from short-term international capital volatility, dual exchange rates can be viewed as a type of speculative shock absorber, but one that is not appropriate for large, sustained capital movements.

In many respects, a dual-exchange regime resembles a system of capital controls, just as there are parallels between tariffs and import quotas. Capital controls prevent net capital outflows by imposing quantitative restrictions. A dual-exchange regime prevents net capital outflows through a depreciation of the financial exchange rate. Because the domestic currency price of foreign assets increases, the depreciation acts like a tax on capital outflows. Like capital controls, dual exchange rates do influence the domestic economy, and the leakages, distortions, and illegal activities increase with the opportunities for arbitrage. When these opportunities become large, the costs of either capital controls or dual exchange rates may substantially outweigh any benefits.

When the financial rate is flexible, dual exchange rates have an advantage over capital controls in that the implied tax on international capital movements is both variable and visible. Domestic authorities can use the exchange rate premium to provide information about the magnitude of the distortions imposed by the system. In contrast, a dual-exchange regime may be unfeasible for countries with very thin capital markets. In these countries, the financial exchange rate would tend to be very volatile and perhaps unstable. Capital controls would be the sensible alternative for regulating the impact of speculative capital movements.

Dual exchange rates can also be useful as short-term policies. Countries that have decided to adjust their exchange rate often have difficulty in deciding how large the adjustment should be. A temporary dual-rate system is sometimes used to attain information about the appropriate adjustment size. Policymakers should be careful about their interpretation of the floating rate in a dual rate system, however—there is no particular reason for it to bound the appropriate unified rate.[10] Dual rates can also be used in the transition from a fixed rate to a more flexible exchange regime. Authorities can gradually shift items from a pegged commercial exchange rate to a flexible rate, for example, while continuing to subsidize particular commodities.

6. Conclusions

This chapter has examined the main exchange and commercial policy tools, excluding devaluation, that can be used to improve the balance of payments. Although these tools differ from each other considerably, they show some important similarities. The major lessons to be drawn from the discussion are summarized below.

The chapter has focused on policies that have a differentiated impact on domestic activities. Multiple exchange rates and import quotas, for example, concentrate on relative price changes, in particular for traded goods. These policies can have critical microeconomic effects (on resource allocation, sectoral growth rates, and the distribution of income) in addition to macroeconomic effects. An assessment of the likely effects of the policies can therefore be quite complex.

On the one hand, there are no costless and reliable policies that will allow a country to maintain a substantially overvalued exchange rate indefinitely. Import quotas, multiple exchange rates, tax and subsidy schemes, or other commercial policies may improve the trade balance, at least in the short run. But these can also result in large changes in domestic relative prices, reallocation of resources, the emergence of black markets, illegal transactions, and a redistribution of domestic income toward those groups with access to restricted commodities. The imposition of capital controls and dual exchange rates to reduce net capital outflows can also lead to black markets and illegal activities that can siphon foreign exchange away from official markets. Regulations and restrictions become increasingly difficult to enforce in an environment where the current set of policies is perceived to be unsustainable.

On the other hand, the policies can be very useful tools for balance of payments management. Capital controls or dual exchange rates are sensible policies for limiting speculative capital inflows and outflows that may disrupt the domestic economy. Multiple exchange rates, or tariff schemes, can be used to improve the trade balance while helping to mitigate the impact of the adjustment on particular sectors or socioeconomic groups. If the policy is transitional or the implicit taxes and subsidies are not excessive, the costs of the distortions will tend to be small.

An important issue in selecting policies to improve the balance of payments is the cause and the nature of the imbalance. In particular, policymakers should distinguish between temporary and long-run or structural payments problems. Unfortunately, the distinction is easier to make in theory than in practice, but it can critically influence the appropriate policy choice. We have seen, for example, that a system of import quotas can effectively target a desired trade balance improvement in the short run. Over a longer horizon, it is possible for such a policy to shift domestic resources away from export production and actually to exacerbate the trade imbalance. Policies that achieve a trade balance improvement in the short run are often not appropriate for longer-run structural adjustment.

One conclusion emerges clearly: special exchange arrangements and trade and capital restrictions are not substitutes for the more fundamental policy changes required to reverse large and persistent balance of payments deficits. At best, they will simply postpone the inevitable adjustments, but they may exacerbate the problems and make adjustment more difficult. Appropriate policies to address large and persistent imbalances include adjustments in the real exchange rate, in the fiscal position, and in monetary growth.

Appendix 1. Jamaica in the 1970s

The Jamaica experience during the 1970s provides a clear example of potential problems associated with addressing balance of payments difficulties through increased exchange controls. Jamaica began to experience external difficulties in the early 1970s. The current account was in chronic deficit, with exports highly concentrated among a few key sectors (bauxite/aluminum, agricultural exports—primarily sugar and bananas—and tourism). These problems were exacerbated by capital flight in anticipation of a devaluation of the Jamaican dollar and by reduced foreign investment as construction projects in the bauxite/aluminum sectors were completed.

The policy response to the deteriorating foreign exchange position included a substantial rise in trade restrictions. Quantitative restrictions on imports (including food) were sharply increased, and exchange controls were tightened as the government tried to defend an overvalued exchange rate. One outcome was a rise in domestic prices, concentrated in particular on commodities in short supply because of import restrictions.

At the same time, domestic and commercial policies resulted in heavy taxes on agricultural exports. During 1970–78, the farmgate prices offered to farmers selling their crops for export remained substantially lower than domestic currency values of world market prices. The free-on-board (f.o.b.) prices for sugar and bananas increased by 4.13 percent and 7.77 percent a year during 1970–78; farmgate prices increased by only 5.06 percent a year for bananas and actually declined by an average of 1.25 percent for sugar. In 1975, for example, the pricing policies were equivalent to a system of multiple exchange rates in which foreign exchange earnings were taxed by 20 percent and 50 percent for sugar and bananas, respectively.

The outcome was a substantial decline in agricultural exports and in foreign exchange earnings. Total output of sugar declined annually by 2.9 percent from 1970 to 1978 (see table 7-7). Output of bananas supplied to the marketing boards declined at an annual average rate of 7.4 percent, whereas coconuts declined by 21 percent. The causes of this decline are clear. Import restrictions resulting in shortages of traditional food imports, particularly starches, led to an expansion of the domestic market for bananas and coconuts. Although farmgate prices were kept below world market prices, prices in these local markets were rising dramatically. In particular, the domestic prices of starchy foods and cereals grew at an average rate of 16.4 percent during 1970–78.

Overall, agricultural exports declined by approximately 33 percent between 1972 and 1979. In contrast, most Latin American countries

Table 7-7. Growth Rates of Jamaican Agricultural Prices and Output, 1970–78

(percent)

Item	Farmgate prices	F.o.b. prices	Output
Sugar	−1.25	4.13	−2.90
Bananas	5.60	7.77	−7.43
Coconuts	5.06	4.67	−21.00

Source: Stephen K. Pollard and Douglas H. Graham, "Price Policy and Agricultural Export Performance in Jamaica," *World Development,* vol. 13 (September 1985), pp. 1067–75, table 2, p. 1069.

experienced positive growth in agricultural exports, exploiting strong world demand to increase their foreign exchange earnings.

The pricing policies also had implications for the distribution of income. Marketing boards generated revenues by selling exports at higher prices than they paid to domestic farmers. In the case of sugar, consumers benefited, as domestic prices were controlled below the world market prices. (The 1977 subsidy was estimated to be $10.6 million.) The beneficiaries of implicit taxes on other exports, however, were often owners of processing plants who purchased the commodities at low domestic prices. These people had strong incentives to influence decisions or to obtain seats on the marketing boards.

The long-run balance of payments situation was exacerbated through policy choices in the early 1970s. Restrictions to limit imports and improve the balance of payments initially allowed the country to postpone adjustment but significantly reduced foreign exchange earnings from agricultural exports. The country has recently embarked on a program of structural adjustment designed in part to provide incentives for export promotion and to undo the shift in production.

The decline in Jamaica's agricultural exports is largely attributable to a combination of import restrictions that raised domestic food prices and to export pricing policies that taxed agricultural exports.

Appendix 2. Capital Flight

Capital flight, or speculative capital outflows, arise when domestic investments are expected to be unsafe or to yield low returns relative to returns available abroad. These outflows can severely exacerbate domestic balance of payments difficulties and increase pressure for a devaluation.

There are at least five potential causes of capital flight.

- Exchange rate overvaluation and expected devaluation
- Political instabilities and social unrest
- High and volatile inflation
- Low domestic interest rates (because of interest rate ceilings)
- Rapid monetary expansion, large fiscal deficits, or other domestic policies that are perceived to be unsustainable

Capital outflows occur through a variety of channels. Domestic importers, for example, attempt to obtain foreign exchange before its price rises in domestic currency, while exporters postpone surrender of foreign exchange earnings to the central bank. These leads and lags in international payments can significantly reduce short-run foreign exchange inflows. Illegal channels are often important. These include smuggling, overinvoicing imports, and underinvoicing exports.

Because of the illegal component, capital flight is difficult to measure. Estimates can be obtained by exploiting the balance of payments accounting identity. The identity states that any capital flight must be offset by accumulation of external debt (public and private), by net capital inflows from foreign direct investment (FDI), by a current account (CA) surplus, or by reserve losses.

Capital flight = Debt (public + private) + FDI + CA surplus − Reserves

Estimates obtained from this formula are not, however, ideal, because our measures of the components on the right-hand side are often inaccurate. Underinvoicing and overinvoicing, for example, imply differences between actual and reported trade flows. (Sometimes these figures can be improved by comparing reported imports with data from the countries of origin, by comparing reported exports with data from the countries of destination, or by examining domestic data on savings, investment, and flow-of-funds accounts.)

Despite these measurement difficulties, capital flight estimates are quite informative. They show that capital flight is widespread and that some countries, notably Argentina, Mexico, and Venezuela, have experienced massive outflows. Estimated capital flight for these and five other countries during 1979–82 appear below.[11]

Country	Billions of U.S. dollars
Mexico	26.5
Venezuela	22.0
Argentina	19.2
Brazil	3.5
Portugal	1.8
Korea, Rep. of	0.9
Uruguay	0.6
Turkey	0.4

Appendix 3. Black Markets for Foreign Exchange

Unofficial, or black, markets for foreign exchange exist in nearly all countries that are subject to foreign exchange controls. The *World Currency Yearbook* (1985, p. 36) cites functioning black markets for 115 currencies as of December 30, 1983. The U.S. dollar is the most frequently traded currency in these markets. Black market prices for dollars exceed prices in official markets in virtually all of these cases, with black market premiums ranging from 3 percent in Peru to 11 percent in Turkey, 66 percent in Egypt, 223 percent in Turkey, and 300 percent in

Bolivia. In many countries, black markets are small and have little impact on the economy. In some countries, however, black market transactions account for a large share of economic activity and divert scarce foreign exchange and other resources away from official markets.

In economies with exchange controls, black markets satisfy foreign exchange demands that are not met through official channels. There are three general categories of demand. First, residents may seek foreign exchange to circumvent import restrictions, to avoid very high tariffs, or to purchase smuggled commodities. Second, residents may hold dollars for precautionary reasons to avoid interruption of import consumption in the future. Uncertainties about the future availability of foreign exchange through official channels, for example, and long delays between authorization and acquisition increased incentives to hoard dollars in both Jamaica and Venezuela. Third, residents who wish to hold foreign assets for speculative reasons will turn to the black market when capital controls restrict their ability to do so officially.

The supply of foreign exchange to the black market comes from a variety of sources. Four important sources are tourism, workers' remittances from abroad, over- and underinvoicing, and proceeds of smuggled exports.

Widespread black markets can cause a number of problems. They tend to drain official reserves by diverting foreign exchange away from official markets. Recorded remittances of Turkish workers living abroad, for example, are highly sensitive to movements in the black market premium. Similarly, in Sri Lanka, exports of gems shift in and out of official markets. After a 20 percent devaluation of the official exchange rate in November 1977, recorded gem exports jumped by 684 percent. The black market premium had stood at 177 percent prior to the devaluation.

Black markets may also influence domestic inflation and resource allocation. To the extent that domestic consumption goods or intermediates are imported through the black market, depreciation of the black market exchange rate will increase domestic prices just as if the country had imposed a multiple-exchange regime. In fact, a country that imposes exchange controls as an alternative to devaluation to avoid inflation may end up with higher rates of inflation than would have resulted from devaluation. Like multiple-exchange regimes, black markets will alter relative prices and will influence the allocation of resources. Black markets emerge as a result of exchange controls, however, and it is difficult to assess the net result without reference to a particular system of controls. Additional costs from black markets arise through increased corruption and through resources devoted to monitoring activities and to law enforcement.

Finally, let us turn to the available policies for dealing with widespread black markets. Increasing the range of transactions permitted on official markets will reduce the size of the black market and will shrink the black market premium. This process could involve a relaxation of exchange controls and exchange rate adjustment—either a devaluation or a shift to a more flexible exchange arrangement, such as an exchange auction system. It is important for the new exchange regime to be perceived as credible and sustainable.

A second option pursued by a number of countries has been to legalize the parallel market. Although this scheme may be effective in channeling foreign exchange back to the official markets in the short run, experience suggests that its success will be short-lived if strict exchange controls remain. Typically, a third black market emerges and diverts foreign exchange once again as the exchange rate depreciates.

Selected Bibliography

Adams, Charles, and Jeremy Greenwood. "Dual Exchange Rate Systems and Capital Controls: An Investigation." *Journal of International Economics,* vol. 18 (February 1985), pp. 43–64.

Aizenman, Joshua. "Adjustment to Monetary Policy and Devaluation under Two-Tier and Fixed Exchange Rate Regimes." NBER Working Paper 1107. Cambridge, Mass.: National Bureau of Economic Research, 1983.

Arida, Persio. "Macroeconomic Issues for Latin America." *Journal of Development Economics,* vol. 22 (June 1986), pp. 171–208.

Baer, Warner, and Michel E. A. Hervé. "Multiple Exchange Rates and the Attainment of Multiple Objectives." *Economica,* vol. 29, no. 114 (May 1962), pp. 176–84.

Balassa, Bela, and others. *The Structure of Protection in Developing Countries.* Baltimore, Md.: Johns Hopkins University Press, 1971.

Barbone, Luca. "Essays on Trade and Macro Policy in Developing Countries." Ph.D. diss. Massachusetts Institute of Technology, 1985.

Berstein, E. M. "Some Economic Aspects of Multiple Exchange Rates." *IMF Staff Papers,* vol. 1, no. 2 (September 1950), pp. 224–37.

Bhagwati, Jagdish N. *The Anatomy and Consequences of Exchange Control Regimes.* Cambridge, Mass.: Ballinger, 1978.

Buffie, Edward F. "Price-Output Dynamics, Capital Inflows, and Real Appreciation." Philadelphia: University of Pennsylvania, January 1983; processed.

————. "The Macroeconomics of Trade Liberalization." *Journal of International Economics,* vol. 17 (August 1984), pp. 121–37.

Cardoso, E. "Stabilization in Latin America: Popular Models and Unhappy Experiences." Boston University Center for Latin American Studies, Discussion Paper 56. Boston, Mass., January 1983.

Collins, S. M. "Fixed Exchange Rates: Devaluations and Credibility Crises." Ph.D. diss. Massachusetts Institute of Technology, 1984; processed.

Corbo, Vittorio, Jaime de Melo, and James R. Tybout. "What Went Wrong with the Financial Reforms in the Southern Cone?" *Economic Development and Cultural Change,* vol. 34, no. 3 (April 1986), pp. 607–40.

Corden, W. M. "Structure of a Tariff System and the Effective Protective Rate." In Jagdish N. Bhagwati, ed., *International Trade: Selected Readings.* Cambridge, Mass.: MIT Press, 1981.

——— . "Protection, the Exchange Rate, and Macroeconomic Policy." *Finance & Development,* vol. 22 (June 1985), pp. 17–19.

Cumby, Robert E. "Monetary Policy under Dual Exchange Rates." NBER Working Paper 1424. Cambridge, Mass.: National Bureau of Economic Research, 1984.

Decaluwe, B., and A. Steinherr. "A Portfolio Balance Model for a Two-Tier Exchange Market." *Economica,* vol. 43, no. 170 (May 1976), pp. 111–25.

de Macedo, Jorge Braga. "Exchange Rate Behavior with Currency Inconvertibility." *Journal of International Economics,* vol. 12 (February 1982), pp. 65–81.

De Melo, Jaime, and Sherman Robinson. *Trade Adjustment Policies and Distribution in Three Archetype Developing Economies.* World Bank Staff Working Paper 442. Washington, D.C., 1982.

Dervis, Kemal. "Analysis of the Resource Pull Effects of Devaluation under Exchange Control." *Journal of Developing Economies,* vol. 7, no. 1 (March 1980), pp. 23–47.

de Vries, Margaret. "Multiple Exchange Rates: Expectations and Experiences." *IMF Staff Papers,* vol. 12, no. 2 (July 1965), pp. 282–311.

Diaz Alejandro, Carlos F. "Southern Cone Stabilization Plans." In William R. Cline and Sidney Weintraub, eds., *Economic Stabilization in Developing Countries.* Washington, D.C.: Brookings Institution, 1981.

——— . "Latin American Debt: I Don't Think We Are in Kansas Anymore." *Brookings Papers on Economic Activity,* vol. 2 (1984), pp. 335–405.

Dickie, Paul M., and David B. Noursi. "Dual Exchange Markets: The Case of the Syrian Arab Republic." *IMF Staff Papers,* vol. 22, no. 2 (July 1975), pp. 456–68.

Dornbusch, Rudiger. "Argentina since Martinez de Hoz." Cambridge, Mass.: Massachusetts Institute of Technology, 1984; processed.

——— . "External Debt, Budget Deficits, and Disequilibrium Exchange Rates." NBER Working Paper 1336. Cambridge, Mass.: National Bureau of Economic Research, 1984; processed.

——— . "Special Exchange Rates for Capital Account Transactions," *World Bank Economic Review,* vol. 1, no. 1 (1985), pp. 3–33.

——— . "Multiple Exchange Rates for Commercial Transactions." Cambridge, Mass.: Massachusetts Institute of Technology, 1985; processed.

Dornbusch, Rudiger, and Daniel Valente Dantas. "The Black Market for Dollars in Brazil," *Quarterly Journal of Economics,* vol. 98 (February 1983), pp. 25–40.

Easterly, William. "Devaluation in a Dollarized Economy: Theoretical Models in the Mexican Context." Colegio de México, Centro de Estudios Economicos, Documentos de Trabajo 1984-4. Mexico City, 1984.

Ethier, Wilfred. "The Theory of Effective Protection in General Equilibrium:

Effective-Rate Analogues of Nominal Rates." *Canadian Journal of Economics*, vol. 10, no. 2 (May 1977), pp. 233–45.

Fleming, Marcus J. "Dual Exchange Markets and Other Remedies for Disruptive Capital Flows." *IMF Staff Papers*, vol. 18, no. 1 (March 1971), pp. 25–47.

Flood, Robert P. "Exchange Rate Expectations in Dual Exchange Markets." *Journal of International Economics*, vol. 8, no. 1 (February 1978), pp. 65–77.

———. "Capital Mobility and the Choice of Exchange Rate System." *International Economic Review*, vol. 20, no. 2 (June 1979), pp. 405–16.

Flood, Robert P., and Nancy Peregrim Marion. "The Transmission of Disturbances under Alternative Exchange Rate Regimes with Optimal Indexing." *Quarterly Journal of Economics*, vol. 97 (February 1982), pp. 43–68.

Kaldor, Nicholas. "The Role of Devaluation in the Adjustment of Balance of Payments Deficits." Report to the Group of Twenty-four. New York and Geneva: United Nations Development Programme and United Nations Conference on Trade and Development, April 1982.

Krueger, Anne O. *Foreign Trade Regimes and Economic Development: Liberalization Attempts and Consequences.* Cambridge, Mass.: Ballinger, 1978.

Krugman, Paul, and Lance Taylor. "Contractionary Effects of Devaluation." *Journal of International Economics*, vol. 8, no. 3 (August 1978), pp. 445–56.

Lanyi, Anthony. "Separate Exchange Markets for Capital and Current Transactions." *IMF Staff Papers*, vol. 22, no. 3 (November 1975), pp. 714–49.

Lizondo, J. S. "Unifying Multiple Exchange Rates." *Finance & Development*, vol. 22 (December 1985), pp. 23–24.

McCarthy, F. Desmond, Lance Taylor, and Iradj Alikhani. *Trade Patterns in Developing Countries, 1970–81.* World Bank Staff Working Paper 642. Washington, D.C., 1984.

Marquez, Jaime. "Currency Substitution, Duality, and Exchange Rate Indeterminacy: An Empirical Analysis of the Venezuelan Experience." Federal Reserve Board, *International Finance Discussion Papers*, no. 242 (May 1984), pp. 1–26.

Marshal, Jorge. "Advance Deposits on Imports." *IMF Staff Papers*, vol. 6, no. 2 (April 1958), pp. 239–57.

Nowak, Michael. "Quantitative Controls and Unofficial Markets in Foreign Exchange: A Theoretical Framework." *IMF Staff Papers*, no. 2 (June 1984), pp. 404–31.

Obstfeld, Maurice. "Capital Controls, the Dual Exchange Rate, and Devaluation." NBER Working Paper 1324. Cambridge, Mass.: National Bureau of Economic Research, April 1984.

———. "The Capital Inflows Problem Revisited: A Stylized Model of Southern Cone Disinflation." *Review of Economic Studies*, vol. 52 (1985), pp. 605–25.

Olgun, Hasan. "An Analysis of the Black Market Exchange Rate in a Developing Country: The Case of Turkey." *Weltwirtschaftliches Archiv*, vol. 2 (1984), pp. 329–47.

O'Neill, Helen. "HICs, MICs, NICs, and LICs: Some Elements in the Political Economy of Graduation and Differentiation." *World Development*, vol. 12, no. 7 (July 1984), pp. 693–712.

Ortiz, Guillermo. "Dollarization in Mexico: Causes and Consequences." In Pedro Aspe-Armella, Rudiger Dornbusch, and Maurice Obstfeld, eds.,

Financial Policies and the World Capital Market: The Problem of Latin American Countries. Chicago, Ill.: University of Chicago Press, 1983.

Peregrim, Marion N. "Insulation Properties of a Two-Tier Exchange Market in a Portfolio Balance Model." *Economica,* vol. 48, no. 149 (February 1981), pp. 61–70.

Pollard, Stephen K., and Douglas H. Graham. "Price Policy and Agricultural Export Performance in Jamaica." *World Development,* vol. 13 (September 1985), pp. 1067–75.

Schlesinger, Eugene. *Multiple Exchange Rates and Economic Development.* Princeton Studies in International Finance 2. Princeton, N.J.: Princeton University Press, 1952.

Sheik, M. A. "Black Markets for Foreign Exchange, Capital Flows, and Smuggling." *Journal of Development Economics,* vol. 3, no. 1 (March 1976), pp. 9–26.

Sherwood, Joyce. "Revenue Features of Multiple Exchange Rate Systems: Some Case Studies." *IMF Staff Papers,* vol. 5, no. 1 (February 1956), pp. 74–107.

Stockman, A. C. "Exchange Controls, Capital Controls, and International Financial Markets." NBER Working Paper 1755. Cambridge, Mass.: National Bureau of Economic Research, 1985.

Swoboda, Alexander K. "The Dual Exchange Rate System and Monetary Interdependence." In R. Z. Aliber, ed., *National Monetary Policies and the International System.* Chicago, Ill.: University of Chicago Press, 1974.

Taylor, Lance. *Structuralist Macroeconomics.* New York: Basic Books, 1983.

_____ . "Stabilization and Growth in Developing Countries: How Sensible People Stand." Cambridge, Mass.: Massachusetts Institute of Technology, 1986; processed.

Tyler, W. G. "Effective Incentives for Domestic Market Sales and Exports: A View of Anti-Export Biases and Commercial Policy in Brazil, 1980–81." *Journal of Development Economics,* vol. 18 (August 1985), pp. 219–42.

Williamson, John. *The Open Economy and the World Economy.* New York: Basic Books, 1983.

World Bank. *World Development Report.* New York: Oxford University Press, various issues.

Notes

1. See International Monetary Fund, *Exchange Arrangements and Exchange Restrictions* (Washington, D.C., 1984), pp. 512–17, for details.

2. The infant industry can be protected by raising its domestic relative price, perhaps through a tariff. A small country, which cannot influence world prices, could accomplish the same thing through a tax on other exports (for example, on traditional exports). The export tax reduces the domestic relative price of the other exports and shifts resources toward the infant industry. This is one rationale for the trade regimes that implicitly tax traditional exports.

3. There may be long lags in the domestic expansion, especially if additional capital must be installed. The expansion may never materialize if the protection is expected to be short-lived or if there is uncertainty about future policies and conditions.

4. It is possible for a quota to result in less domestic production if the domestic industry is imperfectly competitive. By restricting supply from abroad, quotas increase the market power of domestic producers.

5. Jagdish N. Bhagwati and T. N. Srinivasan, *Foreign Trade Regimes and Economic Development: India* (New York: National Bureau of Economic Research, 1975), table 11, pp. 160–61.

6. See Paul Krugman, *Strategic Trade Policy and the New Economics* (Cambridge, Mass.: MIT Press, 1986), for further discussion of strategic issues for protection.

7. For an assessment of the Argentinian and other Southern Cone stabilization plans, see Vittorio Corbo, Jaime de Melo, and James R. Tybout, "What Went Wrong with the Financial Reforms in the Southern Cone?" *Economic Development and Cultural Change,* vol. 34, no. 3 (April 1986), pp. 607–40.

8. In Uruguay, where a similar program was implemented, inflation rates actually increased during the initial period of capital inflows.

9. From February to December 1982, the controlled rate was devalued by 250 percent in nominal terms, whereas the free rate was devalued by 450 percent. See International Monetary Fund, *Exchange Arrangements and Exchange Restrictions,* for a detailed description of the Mexican exchange rate regime.

10. See J. S. Lizondo, "Unifying Multiple Exchange Rates," *Finance & Development,* vol. 22, no. 37 (December 1985), pp. 23–24, for a discussion of the issues involved in choosing the appropriate magnitude of exchange rate adjustment.

11. World Bank, *World Development Report 1985* (New York: Oxford University Press, 1985), p. 64.

8

Exchange Reserves as Shock Absorbers

John Williamson

THE CENTRAL BANKS of most countries hold stocks of international reserves, primarily in the form of liquid holdings of U.S. dollars, to smooth out imbalances between foreign receipts and payments. These stocks permit the central banks to keep the exchange rate stable even though the balance of payments may be in surplus or deficit. More fundamentally, such stocks can enable the authorities to stabilize the domestic economy when it is buffeted by balance of payments shocks.

The differing experiences of Colombia and Mexico during 1975–84 vividly illustrate the role of exchange reserves. Both countries experienced strong, favorable external shocks during part of the decade: Colombia from high coffee prices in 1977–79 (reinforced by the narcotics boom), Mexico from high prices and demand for oil just as its expanded supply was coming on stream in 1979–81. Both countries were forced to confront the Latin American debt crisis that broke in 1982. The diametrically opposed policies that they had adopted in response to their earlier good fortune meant, however, that Colombia was able to avoid debt rescheduling and negative growth, whereas Mexico ran out of cash, was forced to declare a moratorium on debt service, and was thus obliged to seek peremptory adjustment, which resulted in negative growth in 1982–83.

The critical difference in policy reactions to the balance of payments luck of the late 1970s was Colombia's decision to maintain steady growth and save most of the increase in its foreign exchange earnings. In contrast, Mexico spent all—and more—of the increase in its receipts to grow more rapidly. As table 8-1 shows, Colombia built up its foreign exchange reserves to peak in 1980—reserves were ten times their 1975 level and greater than twelve months' worth of imports. Moreover, Colombia refused to borrow extensively from the banks and let the dollar fall to a discount on the black market rather than allow its nontraditional export industries to be bankrupted by the country's tem-

Table 8-1. Aspects of the Economic Performance of Colombia and Mexico, 1975–1984

Year	Colombia				Mexico			
	Reserves (millions of dollars)	Imports (millions of dollars)	Growth (percent)	Debt (billions of dollars)	Reserves (millions of dollars)	Imports (millions of dollars)	Growth (percent)	Debt (billions of dollars)
1975	475	1,424	2.4	3.4	1,383	6,278	5.6	16.9
1976	1,101	1,665	4.7	3.6	1,188	5,771	4.2	21.8
1977	1,747	1,979	4.2	4.0	1,649	5,625	3.4	27.1
1978	2,366	2,552	8.5	4.3	1,842	7,992	8.3	33.6
1979	3,844	2,978	5.3	5.7	2,072	12,131	9.2	40.8
1980	4,831	4,283	4.1	6.8	2,960	18,896	8.3	53.8
1981	4,801	4,730	2.3	8.3	4,074	24,037	7.9	67.0
1982	3,861	5,358	0.9	n.a.	834	14,435	-0.6	82.0
1983	1,901	4,464	0.8	n.a.	3,913	7,721	-5.3	n.a.
1984	1,364	3,980	3.0	n.a.	7,272	n.a.	3.5	n.a.

Source: IMF, International Financial Statistics, and William R. Cline, International Debt: Systemic Risk and Policy Response (Cambridge, Mass.: MIT Press, 1984), table E1.

porary affluence. (Export industries nonetheless suffered a severe loss of competitiveness.)

In contrast, Mexico allowed imports to quadruple, never built up reserves to more than two months' worth of imports, used its export boom as the basis for a borrowing spree to increase absorption even more than income, and allowed its non-oil exports to atrophy. The results were a spectacular short-run boom in 1978–81, followed by a financial crisis and deep recession. During the whole decade 1974–84, Mexico's per capita growth was 16.0 percent, marginally less than Colombia's 16.3 percent, despite oil resources that came on stream, raising petroleum exports from 0.2 percent of GDP in 1974 to 6.2 percent of GDP in 1984, and despite Mexico's having incurred almost four times as much external bank debt per head by 1984.

Many countries (though not in Latin America) had a better decade-long performance than Colombia. The contrast between Colombia and Mexico is interesting because Colombia's only obvious advantage was its more prudent macroeconomic policies and, in particular, its use of exchange reserves (and foreign borrowing) as shock absorbers.

1. Reserve Composition

The standard definition of reserves is "those assets of a country's monetary authorities that can be used, directly or through assured convertibility into other assets, to support its rate of exchange when its external payments are in deficit."[1] Because the U.S. dollar is now the currency that is overwhelmingly, indeed almost exclusively, used for intervention in the exchange markets, the preeminent reserve assets are holdings of dollar-denominated liquid assets—notably U.S. Treasury bills and bank deposits. These may be demand deposits or time deposits with a term measured in days, held either with the Federal Reserve or at commercial banks. In the latter case, deposits may be held either in New York or in the Eurodollar market. About 28 percent of foreign exchange holdings are in the currencies of other industrial countries, principally in deutsche mark, yen, sterling, Swiss francs, French francs, and Dutch guilders.[2]

The other category of assets that fit the definition of reserves is claims created by the International Monetary Fund (IMF), namely, special drawing rights (SDRs), and reserve positions in the Fund. The SDR is a reserve asset introduced in 1970 following lengthy international negotiations to create a synthetic reserve asset to supplement gold, which was the basic reserve asset at that time. In concept, the SDR scheme is simple. From time to time, the IMF "allocates" SDRs to its members in proportion to their quotas. Countries can then sell their SDRs to acquire a currency, either from a country that agrees to accept the SDRs from them or from a (surplus) country that the Fund "designates" to accept SDRs for use in intervention in the exchange market. Thus deficit countries tend to run down their holdings of SDRs, whereas surplus countries build up theirs. The SDR mechanism thus provides a method of financing payments imbalances.

The SDR provides unconditional liquidity. That is, the IMF cannot refuse to facilitate a member's use of its SDR holdings because it disapproves of the country's policies, whether these involve reckless monetary expansion, armed aggression, or both. As long as the country has a payments deficit that it wishes to finance and wants to use its SDR holdings for this purpose, the Fund is obliged either to designate another member to receive the SDRs or to accept the SDRs itself in exchange for currency held in its portfolio.

In exchange for the privilege of receiving SDRs, a country accepts two duties (apart from the obligation to repay in the event of the scheme's termination or a decision to cancel SDRs). One duty is to pay interest on the SDRs it has received by allocation. Currently this interest rate is equal to the weighted-average interest rate on the five major currencies in the "basket" whose value determines the value of the SDR. The other duty is to accept SDRs and supply currency in return when designated to do so by the Fund. Countries are designated to receive SDRs only when they have a reasonably strong external position, in terms of their balance of payments and their gross reserves, and they cannot be designated if their existing SDR holdings exceed 300 percent of their net cumulative allocations. Most countries satisfy a request to accept SDRs by transferring dollars from their reserves to the country that is using its SDRs, which means that the transaction simply changes the composition of their reserves, giving them more SDRs and fewer dollars.

In most respects except the manner of their creation, reserve positions in the Fund are very similar to SDRs. They arise for two reasons. The most important is that, when the Fund lends to country A, it does so by providing it with the currency of country B. Unless country B happens to be the United States, A will ask B (say, Belgium) to exchange Belgian francs for dollars that A can use in intervention. Thus once again, the surplus country B ends up exchanging part of its dollar holdings for a claim on the IMF, whereas the deficit country A obtains dollars in exchange for a liability to the IMF (rather than, as in the case of the SDRs, a rundown in its assets). Country B's claim on the IMF can, like SDRs acquired from other members, be used unconditionally to finance a payments deficit. All that a country wishing to use its reserves position need do is to ask the Fund for currency, which the Fund provides by supplying the currency of another country (which thus either enhances that country's reserve position in the Fund or, if it was a net borrower, reduces its net debtor position).

The other source of reserve positions in the Fund is the "reserve tranche." This is a claim on the Fund that members establish by paying 25 percent of their quota subscription in the form of reserves assets (SDRs, dollars, or, in the past, gold) rather than in their own currency. Countries can also withdraw this reserve tranche to finance a payments deficit, and it therefore constitutes a part of the reserve position in the Fund.

Gold is still customarily counted as a part of reserves, although it no longer satisfies the accepted definition of a reserve asset because it can be neither used directly to support exchange rates not converted at any assured rate into an asset that can be used for that purpose. Most central banks still hold gold, however, and include it in their reserves (although the accounting price used to value gold varies, from the old official price of SDR35 per ounce to a price based on that quoted in the London market—which of course leads to erratic fluctuations in the statistical value placed on gold reserves).

Data on the actual composition of the reserves of developing countries are shown in table 8-2. Perhaps a more interesting question concerns the principles that should determine the choice among alternative reserve assets.

The first principle is that countries should hold a sufficient volume of funds to meet regular needs for intervention in a form such that they can be mobilized for that purpose immediately, that is, in highly liquid balances of the country's intervention currency. Once this "transactions" need has been satisfied, the country can invest its remaining assets

Table 8-2. Composition of Reserves of Developing Countries, 1979–85

(billions of SDRs, except where indicated)

Item	End of 1979	1980	1981	1982	1983	1984	March 1985
Foreign exchange	113.6	128.2	133.1	131.0	139.5	161.1	152.5
Reserve positions in the Fund	4.0	6.1	7.8	8.4	13.6	14.3	14.3
SDRs	3.2	2.9	4.5	3.7	2.9	3.1	2.8
Total reserves excluding gold	120.8	137.2	145.3	143.1	155.9	178.5	169.7
Gold							
Quantity (millions of ounces)	155.4	165.1	165.6	161.4	160.8	160.3	160.1
Value at London market price	60.4	76.3	56.6	66.8	58.6	50.4	53.5

Source: IMF *Annual Report*, 1985, table 13.

according to the standard principles of portfolio management, with the goal of securing the highest possible expected rate of return consistent with a given degree of risk exposure.

Expected rates of return consist of the nominal interest rate plus the expected rate of appreciation of the asset in question. Nominal interest rates on the various reserve currencies are easily ascertainable with the aid of contemporary electronic gadgets. Nominal interest rates on Fund-related assets are only calculated in arrears, but because they are based on an average of the interest rates in the major currencies, they are approximately forecastable. The nominal interest rate on gold is zero (or negative, if one includes storage costs).

By far the most important part of the return, however, consists of the appreciation of one asset in terms of another. This part of the return is also, of course, less predictable. Some monetary authorities are prepared to guess how assets are likely to move relative to one another and are likely to make essentially speculative investments on that basis. Most monetary authorities, however, pride themselves on being conservative rather than speculative investors, primarily concerned with minimizing risk (although how they reconcile this approach with their continued large holdings of gold, that most speculative of all assets, is something of a mystery).

An interesting intellectual question is the meaning of a monetary authority that minimizes exposure to risk. Under any normal circumstances, for example, one will minimize risk as measured in dollars by holding reserves in dollars, but for a country that trades primarily with, for example, Europe, the purchasing power of its reserves will fluctuate as the dollar goes up and down against the European currencies. The implication is that countries might consider holding "precautionary" reserves (the balance above "transactions needs") in a set of currencies that match the pattern of trade. Broadly speaking, this thinking makes sense; however, it leaves three murky areas.

First, should a country take into account imports, exports, or both? Because the purpose of holding reserves is to cover excesses of imports over exports, imports are surely relevant. Indeed, a country's exposure to exchange risk lies in those currencies where the country has more imports than exports, and hence the country should concentrate its reserve holdings so as to reduce risk.

Second, is the currency composition of a country's debt relevant as well as the currency composition of its trade? The answer is surely yes. When calculating the currency composition of trade deficits, imports should be interpreted to include projected debt service payments in the various currencies. If the currency composition of debt has itself been chosen on risk-minimizing principles, the debt will tend to be concentrated on those currencies in which the country runs a trade surplus. A country such as Singapore, for example, that sells primarily to the United States but buys primarily from Japan can hedge its debt by borrowing in dollars. In so doing it will tend to reduce the dominance of the bilateral current account deficit with the yen area and therefore, on the rule given above, the extent to which precautionary reserves should be concentrated in yen.

Third, what exactly is meant by the currencies that "match the pattern of trade"? Are these the currencies of the countries from which imports originate and to which exports are destined or those in which trade is denominated? What about trade with other developing countries? Remember that reserves are held for the purpose of financing deficits. If the dollar appreciates, then all imports denominated in dollars will tend to increase in price in the short run, but only those that actually come from the United States should be expected to sustain most of their price increase for as long as the dollar stays high. Even other countries in the dollar area can be expected to devalue against the dollar to restore their competitiveness in the medium term. Thus there is little reason to suppose that the price of imports from other developing countries will be systematically associated with exchange rates of the reserve currencies—though the price of oil, which has for some years been an administered dollar-dominated price, is a possible important exception. Hence a tentative answer is that countries should concentrate on the reserve currency areas from which imports originate and to which exports are destined. The main qualification is that, in the case of exports of homogeneous primary products, the relevant destination areas are those for total world production of the commodity in question rather than those to which national production happens to be exported.

The fact that the SDR is defined as equal to a basket of the five major international currencies with weights that roughly reflect the importance of those currencies in international trade and finance raises the question of whether the SDR can provide a natural hedge. Given the argument developed above that hedging involves a country's holding reserves in those currencies against which it is in bilateral deficit, this possibility seems unlikely: bilateral deficits are typically concentrated in particular areas, not scattered around in proportion to total trade.[3]

The development of financial markets may be making the above analysis irrelevant from the standpoint of choosing reserve composition, although at the same time it may be increasing the relevance for financial management. Until recently, essentially the only way to manage risks through financial markets, apart from covering specific transactions in the forward markets, involved choosing the asset and liability composition of asset portfolios and debt, respectively. The development of extensive options markets, however, is providing the possibility of divorcing risk exposure from asset composition. If and when the maturities offered in options markets lengthen, hedging risks arising from the currency composition of trade by better means than choice of the currency composition of reserves may become possible and rational.

Risk reduction is only one of the two criteria relevant to selecting reserve composition: the expected rate of return matters, too. As the market probably equates expected rates of return on different currencies better than monetary authorities can speculate, however, it is prudent to make hedging the dominant determinant in the choice of reserves.

2. Purpose of Holding Reserves

The contemporary view of reserves is that they function as inventories to absorb shocks. That is, the central bank accumulates reserves when receipts of foreign exchange exceed payments and draws down its stocks in the reverse situation to try to stabilize the domestic economy. Thus the fluctuation of reserves permits at least partial insulation of the domestic economy from shocks to the balance of payments

This view contrasts with an older one that arose during the years of the gold standard, namely that the purpose of reserves is to provide backing for the domestic money supply so as to prevent the overissue of money and to establish confidence in the integrity of the monetary unit. The currency boards that Britain established to provide money for its colonies operated in this way and issued local currency only against the receipt of sterling (foreign exchange) when the colony had a balance of payments surplus.

Such a system has both advantages and disadvantages in comparison with the alternative system of having money controlled by a central bank empowered to buy domestic as well as foreign assets. One advantage is that it ensures balance of payments adjustment and precludes balance of payments crises because any payments deficit leads to a fall in the money supply, which curbs the demand for imports and thus reduces the deficit. Another advantage is that sustained, domestically generated inflation cannot occur. A currency board system, however, makes it necessary to tie up valuable foreign exchange that could be used to buy imports to promote development in the sterile task of backing the money supply. The other disadvantage is that a currency board system rules out any attempt to stabilize the economy in the face of external shocks; for example, a rise in export prices automatically increases the income of exporters and the domestic money supply, thus exerting a double expansionary impetus, and no attempt is made to offset this effect.

Most independent countries have chosen to wield monetary sovereignty by establishing central banks. If this tactic is to help stabilize rather than destabilize income, the authorities must have realistic estimates of the normal (or sustainable) path of the economy. In particular, they should try to quantify the following two key concepts:

- The potential level of output (sometimes also called "full employment output" or "internal balance"). This is the maximum level of output that the economy is capable of producing on a sustained basis, in view of the fact that an overheated economy will accelerate inflation and will sooner or later require a deflationary policy, with attendant loss of output, to bring inflation under control.[4]
- The normal balance of payments position. Estimating this position requires a view on the normal levels of a series of variables that influence the payments outcome, including prices of the country's primary product exports and the other determinants of its terms of trade, the world business cycle, the sustainable level of capital inflow, and the normal level of domestic output.

Successful stabilization would imply that normal output is the same as potential output. But this situation immediately poses a conundrum: what if the normal balance of payments situation that would prevail with domestic output at full capacity, and all other key variables at their expected long-run values, were to involve a significant deficit (or, for that matter, a surplus)? The answer is that the economy is not in a long-run equilibrium situation—it needs to adjust its balance of payments. Specifically, it needs to adjust its payments position through what are known as expenditure-switching policies, which redirect sales from the home to the export market or redirect production from nontradables to tradables. Such a policy typically means a real devaluation of the domestic currency. When a country has successfully adjusted its payments position so that its payments will balance on average over the business cycle while it produces at full potential output, it is said to be in fundamental equilibrium or in long-run external balance.

Reserves have two potential shock-absorbing roles. One arises in an economy where the balance of payments is in long-run equilibrium but is being bombarded by a series of temporary shocks that threaten to buffet the domestic economy. A classic case is a temporary decline in the prices of major commodity exports. Under a currency board system, the resulting payments deficit would lead to a decline in the money supply that would reinforce the exporters' loss of income and would magnify domestic recession. Monetary independence provides the opportunity to stabilize income. The decline in export receipts is countered by a temporary fiscal deficit, and the central bank replaces its foreign assets by government paper, thus preventing or at least mitigating the recessionary effect of the temporary weakening in commodity exports. When exports start to boom again, the operation goes into reverse, with the government running a fiscal surplus (relative to normal) and the central bank rebuilding its reserves and reducing the proportion of government paper in its portfolio. With luck, the level of domestic income and absorption will remain relatively stable, and thus both the waste of idle capacity in recession and the inflationary pressures of the boom will be avoided. Such a stabilizing strategy demands that the central bank hold sufficient reserves before the export shortfall occurs and that it allows its reserves to fluctuate. (It also requires the government to exercise a significant measure of skill, sophistication, and flexibility in the implementation of fiscal policy.)

The second shock-absorbing role of reserves is to permit a measured pace of adjustment. Suppose that the value of the country's commodity exports declines with no expectation of a subsequent rebound, as in the case above, perhaps because of substitution of synthetic materials. Then the country is no longer in a long-run sustainable position; it has to undertake a program of balance of payments adjustment. If it had no reserves or other way of financing a temporary current account deficit, for example, by foreign borrowing, the country would have to deflate output enough to cut the demand for imports by an amount equal to the fall in exports because there are far longer lags in expenditure-switching methods of adjustment than in expenditure reduction. If, however, it can draw on its reserves to finance a temporary deficit, then it can devalue and cut back demand by no more than is needed to make room for the additional production of exports, thus minimizing the recession. Once again, adequate initial reserves and a willingness to use them when the occasion demands can help to stabilize income.

In practice, governments can never be certain whether payments shock will be reversible or permanent or how long a reversible shock will last. Even if they do know with certainty how long a shock is going to last, they still face the need to rebuild reserves (assuming that reserves were initially at their ideal level). For these reasons, prudence demands that under most circumstances a shock to the balance of payments be countered by at least a measure of adjustment. The optimal mix of financing and adjustment will depend on assessment of the probability that the shock will be reversed, how quickly such reversal will occur, and whether it will suffice to replenish reserves to their target level.

Although the optimal response to any single shock will depend on assessments of its likely duration, the general strategy will depend upon the expected properties of the whole series of future shocks. This general strategy can be characterized in the two interdependent dimensions of a target or norm for the reserve stock (which determines how much scope there is, on average, for financing a shock) and the speed of adjustment. The two are inversely related: a greater willingness to adjust rapidly reduces the need for reserves.

3. The Norm for the Reserve Stock

A country's norm or target for the reserve stock should depend upon four factors:

- The vulnerability of its balance of payments to shocks—greater vulnerability requires a bigger norm.
- The consequences of running out of reserves (reserve depletion)—worse consequences require a bigger norm.
- The (opportunity) cost of holding reserves—higher costs call for a lower norm.
- The speed and reliability of adjustment—faster adjustment permits economizing on reserves.

Because of its importance, the last factor is discussed in the next section. The other factors are dealt with below.

Payments Shocks

Shocks to the balance of payments may arise from either internal or external sources. Internal shocks may in turn be divided into those that arise from the side of demand and those that arise from the side of supply. Each of these may in turn be subdivided. Shocks to demand may involve changes in either income or prices (or in some cases both; for example, excess demand may increase first income and then prices). Shocks to supply may be temporary (the classic example is a bad harvest) or permanent (such as the coming on stream of a new oil field). Permanent supply shocks may also be called structural changes.

Appropriate policy reactions depend upon the source of the shock to the balance of payments. Determining the appropriate reactions requires that in every case a key question be asked: is the shock creating a deviation from internal balance or long-run external balance or both? If the shock consists of a domestic boom that causes inflationary pressures, pulls in more imports, and hence causes a payments deficit, then the country is no longer in internal balance. But unless domestic inflation is allowed to undermine competitiveness because of a commitment to a fixed nominal exchange rate, there is no reason to suppose that long-run external balance is threatened. The appropriate policy response is therefore to cool the domestic boom by fiscal or monetary tightening (and to restore competitiveness, if that has been threatened, by a nominal devaluation), which will suffice both to reestablish internal balance and to end the reserve loss. A domestic price shock independent of an income shock can be countered by an offsetting exchange rate change.[5]

A temporary supply shock, such as a bad harvest, is the classic case in which a country should draw on reserves and undertake a contracyclical expansionary policy to limit the loss in real income. The magnitude of past shocks indicates what might be expected in the future, although a country can never be sure that a future drought will not be even longer or worse than a past one.

A permanent supply shock, such as the coming on stream of a new resource or the exhaustion of an old resource, will usually change long-run external balance and will therefore require the adoption of an adjustment policy. Because countries can usually foresee such changes, however, they create little need for drawing on reserves.

It is not as easy to provide a neat taxonomy of external shocks. Empirically the most important shocks are probably still those to the terms of trade that involve changes in the prices of imports or of primary product exports. Many developing countries now have heavy debts contracted at floating interest rates, however, so changes in world interest rates can also have a major impact on the balance of payments. Indeed, changes in the availability of external loans, such as the cutoff experienced by most developing countries in the wake of the Mexican moratorium in August 1982, provide a separate and newly important form of external shock. Nowadays many developing countries export manufactures or other goods or services that do not fit the stereotype of homogeneous primary products sold on a competitive market, which have relatively constant prices but quantities that are sensitive to the state of the world business cycle. Finally, changes in the exchange rates among the developed countries can affect the balance of payments of developing countries, notably by depressing the dollar value of exports receipts relative to the value of debt service obligations (most of which are dollar denominated) when the dollar appreciates.

Appropriate policy reactions to an external shock from any of these sources demand an evaluation of whether the shock is likely to be transitory or permanent. If it is likely to be transitory, then the key questions are whether it is pushing the economy away from internal balance and whether reserves are adequate to permit a policy of attempting to stabilize income. If it is likely to be permanent, then the key questions are the magnitude and form of the adjustment measures needed to restore long-run external balance, and the extent of reserves—do they suffice to permit a measured pace of adjustment, or is output depressed below internal balance by more than may be needed to provide incentives for the necessary reallocation of resources? Adjustment tends to be particularly time consuming in the least developed countries because of their inelastic production structures, which means that expenditure switching requires structural change rather than just a redirection of existing facilities toward external markets.

Experience may again be able to provide some guide as to the level of reserves needed to cope with external shocks. Because most external shocks have economic rather than climatic causes, however, the danger that the past will prove a poor guide to the future is even greater than with domestic shocks. The prices of primary commodities, for example, increased far less during the 1983–85 recovery than would have been expected on the basis of experience.

Reserve Depletion

On August 13, 1982, Mexico ran out of reserves. The central bank had no more liquid assets at its disposal with which to pay for imports or to service its debt. The Mexicans therefore had to declare a moratorium on debt service payments and had to look for bridge loans. The condition on which they got these loans was that they negotiate a large drawing from the IMF, which involved severe deflationary conditionality (which produced the 1983 drop in total output of some 5 percent shown in table 8-1), so as to secure a rapid turnaround in the balance of payments (which it did).

Other reactions to reserve depletion are possible. It may be possible, for example, to allow the exchange rate to float. The domestic currency will certainly depreciate and almost certainly overshoot, producing inflationary pressures, a fall in living standards, and probably a recession.[6] If the public sector has debt service obligations in foreign currency that exceed its foreign currency earnings, however, the government will probably be reluctant to resort to floating because it would then have to pay a high price to buy the extra foreign exchange it needs from the private sector. In that case the official exchange rate is more likely to remain pegged (probably after devaluation) while a black market rate with a large premium on the value of foreign exchange emerges.

A third reaction is to try to muddle through without taking any decisive action. Arrears are allowed to accumulate, imports eligible for purchase at the official exchange rate are cut to the bone, and more and more imports are bought illegally at the black market rate (or parallel rate). The costs of such inaction are typically very high indeed. Trade credit evaporates, so that imports have to be bought on a cash basis at much higher prices than creditworthy customers pay. The distortions produced by massive discrepancies between the official and parallel rates are severe: with a premium of 1,000 percent on the parallel rate, exports fail to occur even though exports could buy imports that are worth ten times as much at the parallel rate as their cost of production to the domestic economy.

Although a country that runs out of reserves does not find itself arraigned in a bankruptcy court and threatened with liquidation, like a company that exhausts its cash, the consequences are nevertheless unpleasant. Most countries are prepared to take fairly severe measures to avoid having things ever reach such a state.

The Cost of Reserve Holding

The cost of holding reserves is an opportunity cost; that is, the cost is measured in terms of what could be done with the cash involved if it were not being held as reserves.

One thing that could be done with the cash is to buy more imports. At the very least, the buying of additional imports would permit investment to be stepped up by the amount of the extra imports. The opportunity cost of reserves is then the rate of return on investment minus the rate of return earned by the reserves. The extra imports could also be used to reduce savings (and increase consumption) while investment was held constant. In that case, the opportunity cost of reserve holding is the marginal rate of time preference of consumers (less the yield on reserves), which in a perfect neoclassical world would be equal to the marginal rate of return on investment.

When a country is constrained by a shortage of foreign exchange to hold output below its potential level, the opportunity cost of holding reserves is even higher because the use of reserves to buy more imports would allow output to be increased and not just absorption.[7] Indeed, in extreme cases of foreign exchange stringency, the shadow price of foreign exchange, which is the same thing as opportunity cost of reserves, is several times its official price, the exchange rate.[8]

For countries with access to the international capital market, an alternative use of reserves is to run down foreign borrowing. The cost of reserve holding is then the difference between what the country has to pay when it borrows and what it receives when it places those funds back in the international market. This difference is typically quite substantial, a matter of 2–4 percent, because reserves are placed at short term, whereas they need to be borrowed at long term.[9]

4. Speed of Adjustment

The fourth determinant of the optimal norm for the stock of reserves is the speed with which a country is prepared to adjust its balance of payments when the need arises. Unlike the size of payments shocks, the costs of reserve depletion, and the opportunity cost of reserve holding, however, the speed of adjustment is a policy variable that the authorities can influence. When they select a norm for the reserve stock, they should choose the speed of adjustment rather than view it as an exogenous variable that they have to accept.

Four factors determine the cost of rapid adjustment.

The Composition of an Import Cutback

Rapid adjustment almost inevitably involves a cutback in imports because it normally requires considerable time (and often investment) to redeploy resources into the expansion of exports. In a country that imports a substantial volume of consumer goods for which domestic substitutes exist, an import cutback will be much less painful than in a country that imports almost exclusively intermediate goods essential for the maintenance of domestic production and capital goods essential for future growth, and that lacks domestic substitutes. Such a country should therefore aim to avoid being forced into rapid adjustment, even at the cost of holding a higher level of reserves.

Export Elasticities

A country with little capacity to curb its imports at reasonable cost will tend to have a low price elasticity of demand for imports. In the same way, a country with low short-run price elasticities on the export side will find it difficult to expand exports rapidly. For a single country, at least, the price elasticity of demand for exports is normally high,[10] whereas, the typical problem is that the short-run elasticity of supply of exports is low.[11] In other words, even with a high elasticity of demand for exports, there can be little supply response in the short run. Once again, rapid adjustment is bound to be costly.

The Exchange Rate Regime

A general presumption is that a more flexible exchange rate regime is more conducive to rapid adjustment for two reasons. The first is that the improvement in competitiveness owing to a devaluation provides an opportunity to curb imports and promote exports (assuming that there is any elasticity at all in the demand for imports and the supply of exports). But the country is denied this opportunity if it keeps its exchange rate unchanged. The second reason is that, under favorable conditions, a depreciation will tend to induce a capital inflow. The nec-

essary favorable conditions are that speculators interpret the depreciation as essentially once and for all, rather than as the start of a trend, so
that they anticipate a subsequent appreciation (or at least accept that the
needed depreciation has now occurred).[12] Provided that the depreciation reduces their expectation of further depreciation in the future,
speculators will be more inclined to repatriate funds and less inclined to
continue sending capital abroad. This change in speculation relieves the
payments deficit and perhaps even secures a net inflow of foreign
exchange on capital account with which to finance the current account
deficit.

A sufficiently large depreciation will normally convince the market
that a rebound of the rate (at least in real terms and relative to the interest differential) is to be expected. The problem is that, when confidence
in economic policy is lacking, the depreciation needed to reverse capital
flight may be so large as to wreak havoc with macroeconomic policy.
Such major overshooting of the exchange rate can confront the authorities with a choice between accommodating the inflationary pressures
induced by the depreciation and allowing a severe recession to develop.
For this reason, only when there is a fair measure of confidence in economic policy do countries generally feel able to take the risk of allowing
their exchange rates to float. Without this confidence, countries cannot
safely rely on exchange rate movements to provide rapid adjustment,
or—perhaps more accurately—rapid financing of current account
deficits.

Foreign Borrowing

One way to finance current account deficits pending their adjustment
is, as noted above, to allow the exchange rate to move to a level that will
induce a private capital inflow. Another way is to borrow abroad, either
from the international capital market or from official sources, notably
the IMF.

A country that could rely on perfect and instantaneous access to the
international capital market would have no need for reserves. It could
derive all the liquidity it needed from the liability side of the balance
sheet. A country that could rely on perfect but noninstantaneous access
would need to hold reserves only to cover any deficits that might arise
until it could replenish its reserves by borrowing more. In reality, of
course, countries do not have perfect access in the sense of unlimited
ability to borrow at the going interest rate, let alone guaranteed access
on which they can rely when things go wrong. On the contrary, it is in
general most difficult to borrow precisely when reserves are most
needed. Nevertheless, to the extent that a country can prudently rely on
being able to borrow more when the need arises, it will be in a position to

economize on its holdings of reserves and to adjust its (overall) balance of payments more rapidly.

The only source from which developing countries can normally borrow reserves is the IMF. They can borrow relatively modest sums with low conditionality, the requirement being only that the country "demonstrate reasonable efforts to overcome its difficulties," under the following three facilities:

- The first credit tranche permits countries to draw up to 25 percent of their quota.
- The compensatory financing facility allows drawings of up to 50 percent of the quota to (a) countries that export primary commodities and encounter payments difficulties caused by temporary shortfalls in export proceeds largely attributable to circumstances beyond their control or (b) countries that import cereals and encounter reversible increases in the cost of cereal imports.
- Buffer stock financing permits drawings of up to 45 percent of the quota to help countries finance contributions to approved international buffer stocks of primary commodities.

Substantially larger sums, which can accumulate to more than 400 percent of quota, are available under the Fund's high-conditionality facilities. Drawings under these facilities require that the country commit itself to an adjustment program approved by the Fund. The facilities consist of the higher-credit tranches (75 percent of quota), the enlarged access policy (270 percent of quota, or 330 percent in exceptional circumstances), compensatory finance (an additional 33 percent of quota for either export shortfalls or cereal excesses or 60 percent for both together), and the extended facility (140 percent of quota).

The Fund requires that the measures adopted under the high-conditionality facilities achieve a recovery in the balance of payments within the program period (typically twelve to eighteen months, although it can be as long as three years). The adjustment programs normally comprise some mix of expenditure-reducing (austerity) policies, involving the reduction of fiscal deficits and restraints on monetary expansion, and expenditure-switching policies, typically devaluation, as well as prohibition of the intensification of import restrictions. Depending on circumstances, programs may also include price- and exchange-control liberalization, limits on short-term foreign borrowing, incomes policies and wage controls, and increases in interest rates. Most high-conditionality programs involve phased disbursement, which is conditioned on the country's meeting key targets designated as "performance criteria." These typically specify maximum rates of domestic credit expansion and the maximum fiscal deficit and prohibit any intensification of import restrictions.

IMF conditionality has proved controversial in many countries. Sensitive issues of national sovereignty are involved, especially when the authorities of a country do not fully share the IMF's view of economic causality. Because adjustment actions to eliminate a payments deficit are almost invariably unpleasant, countries sometimes blame the Fund for imposing austerity that is inevitable if budget restraints are to be respected. Nonetheless, few would assert confidently that the adjustment programs supported by the IMF have always been well designed, let alone well executed. In part, the reason may be that the Fund must treat all its members equally and therefore cannot take the initiative in proposing imaginative solutions that might exploit special possibilities in individual countries. The Fund could, for example, never have pressed on Argentina the sort of bold program to tackle inflation that President Alfonsin announced in June 1985. Initiatives of this sort must originate with the national authorities, not with the IMF.

5. Conclusions

Reserves, provided they are large enough and are allowed to vary appropriately, can help to insulate a country from a variety of shocks to the balance of payments of both internal and external origin. To fulfill this function best, a country needs to hold an adequate volume of transactions balances in its intervention currency, whereas the remainder of its reserves (its precautionary balances) are most usefully deployed in a manner calculated to hedge against an appreciation of the currencies with which it can expect a bilateral payments deficit.

In addition to the choice of reserve composition, reserve policy has two dimensions. One involves the choice of a norm or target for the reserve stock, the other the choice of a (typical) speed of adjustment. The chapter has identified a number of factors that should contribute to a large norm for the reserve stock (the size of payments shocks, the costs of reserve depletion, and a low opportunity cost of holding reserves) and to the normal speed of adjustment (which is decreased by a concentration of imports on essential goods without domestic substitutes, inelasticity in the demand or supply of exports, inflexibility in the exchange rate regime, and lack of opportunities for foreign borrowing). A country with a large reserve stock will be able to afford relatively leisurely adjustment, whereas a country that enjoys few opportunities for rapid adjustment needs to hold relatively large reserves. Countries must thus decide simultaneously on the normal level of reserves to aim for and on the normal speed of adjustment.

Unfortunately, the economic literature provides few guides as to how to translate the above qualitative considerations into concrete numbers.

Perhaps the best guide is still an old rule of thumb that holds that a country should aim to prevent its reserves from falling below three months' worth of imports, a reserves-imports ratio of 25 percent.[13]

Reserves-imports ratios in the range of 30–40 percent were traditionally regarded as comfortable, and this would, perhaps, be a reasonable norm for most countries. Ratios below 20 percent were regarded as dangerously low, posing a constant threat that speculative capital flight would denude the country of the remainder of its reserves and allow a quite inadequate margin to absorb any further shocks.

In recent years, many countries have allowed their reserves to fall to levels lower than those traditionally considered prudent. Most of these countries fall into one or two categories, however. First, most of those with reserves-imports ratios below 20 percent that have not encountered problems are industrial countries, many with floating exchange rates and most enjoying good access to the international capital market. The earlier analysis identified these factors as accelerating the speed of adjustment and deminishing the need for reserves. In theory, indeed, a country with a freely floating exchange rate or instantaneous ability to borrow does not need any reserves at all. The second major category consists of countries—many in Sub-Saharan Africa and others that have had to reschedule debts—that have most certainly been under severe external pressures. Most other countries with low ratios seem to be characterized by some statistical freak; for example, they can effectively call on some part of the assets held by their commercial banks or on a line of credit provided by a continuing or former colonial power.

Quantitative guidance on the appropriate speed of adjustment is even harder to come by. One recent empirical estimate is that, on average, countries have "completely" adjusted (to within about 5 percent of their targets) within five years.[14] This is in fact the traditional planning horizon, and the five-year time frame seems quite a sensible rule of thumb. It is neither so soon as to negate the very purpose of holding reserves (as would occur if any deviation of reserves from target were to prompt peremptory adjustment) nor so distant as to provide no spur to policies that can in due course be expected to restore reserves toward their norm.

Hence the reserve strategy suggested by this analysis is as follows. First, select simultaneously a target for the reserve stock as some fraction of imports (of goods and services) and the anticipated normal speed of adjustment. The target for the reserves-imports ratio should probably lie within the range of 30–40 percent (though perhaps lower for a country with a flexible exchange rate policy and reliable access to the international capital market). Appropriate place within the range should be determined by the expected size of payments shocks, the costs of reserve depletion, the opportunity cost of holding reserves, and the expected speed of adjustment.

Second, when some macroeconomic shock hits the balance of payments, pose the following questions:

- Is the economy deviating from internal balance?
- Has the shock caused a deviation from long-run external balance?
- Are reserves adequate to permit the restoration of long-run external balance (should this be necessary) while preserving or restoring internal balance?
- Is the expected path of the balance of payments such as to restore reserves to their target within five years?

If the macroeconomic policymakers of developing countries constantly pose those questions to themselves in the future, fewer tragedies, such as the waste of Mexico's oil bonanza during the last decade, will occur.

Glossary

Adjustment. The process of altering balance of payments flows to conform to objectives.

Conditionality. The requirements that countries must satisfy to borrow reserves (in contrast to using owned reserves, which are unconditionally available), usually from the IMF. May be subdivided into low conditionality, involving an affirmation that the country is taking appropriate actions to resolve its payments problems, and high conditionality, involving agreement on an adjustment program with the IMF and continued observance of that program as monitored by performance criteria.

Expenditure switching. Adjustment policies, such as a real devaluation, that switch production from domestic to foreign markets or redirect output from nontradables to tradables.

Internal balance. Otherwise known as potential output or full employment output; the maximum sustainable level (or path) of output.

Long-run external balance. Fundamental equilibrium of the balance of payments; a situation in which payments would be in balance if output were at internal balance and all other variables were at their long-run equilibrium values.

Opportunity cost of reserve holding. The rate of return that could be earned by spending reserves.

Precautionary balances. Reserve holdings above those needed for regular intervention in the exchange market.

Reserve depletion. A situation in which reserves are exhausted.

Reserve norm. A target for the stock of reserves.

Reserve position in the Fund. A country's reserve tranche plus its creditor position in the IMF, which can be drawn down unconditionally to finance a payments deficit.

Reserve tranche. The 25 percent of a country's IMF quota that it paid in reserve assets.

Reserves. Liquid assets held by monetary authorities for the purpose of being able to finance payments imbalances unconditionally.

Special drawing rights (SDRs). Reserve assets created by fiat by the IMF, which can circulate among Fund members as a method of financing payments imbalances.

Transactions balances. Reserve holdings needed for regular intervention in the exchange markets.

Selected Bibliography

The analysis of optimal reserve-holding policy was developed largely in the 1960s. The main body of this literature is surveyed in John Williamson, "International Liquidity: A Survey," *Economic Journal*, vol. 83, no. 331 (September 1973), pp. 685–746, and Benjamin J. Cohen, "International Reserves and Liquidity," in Peter B. Kenen, ed., *International Trade and Finance: Frontiers for Research* (Cambridge, Eng.: Cambridge University Press, 1975). Subsequent updatings include Jacob A. Frenkel, "International Liquidity and Monetary Control," in George M. von Furstenberg, ed., *International Money and Credit: The Policy Roles* (Washington, D.C.: International Monetary Fund, 1983), and Sebastian Edwards, "The Demand for International Reserves and Exchange Rate Adjustments: The Case of LDCs, 1946–1972," *Economica*, vol. 199, no. 50 (August 1983), pp. 269–80.

Anand G. Chandavarkar, in *The International Monetary Fund: Its Financial Organization and Activities* (Washington, D.C.:International Monetary Fund, 1984), describes the Fund's operations. Extensive discussion of the present reserve system, with particular attention to the rule of the SDR, can be found in Furstenberg, ed., *International Money and Credit: The Policy Roles*. IMF conditionality is analyzed in both John Williamson, ed., *IMF Conditionality* (Washington, D.C.: Institute for International Economics, 1983), and Tony Killick, ed., *The Quest for Economic Stabilization* (London: Heinemann Educational Books, 1984). A concise description of the SDR scheme appears in John Williamson, *A New SDR Allocation?* (Washington, D.C.: Institute for International Economics, 1984).

Notes

1. Group of Ten, Report of the Study Group on the Creative Reserve Assets (the Ossola Report), 1965, p. 21.

2. The figure of 28 percent assumes that unidentified holdings were distributed between the dollar and other currencies in the same proportion as the identified holdings. The figure relates to the end of 1984 and comes from the IMF *Annual Report*, 1985, table 14.

3. The SDR basket, however, appears much better suited to another role: providing a peg that countries with reasonably diversified trade can use to maintain the exchange rate.

4. In a dynamic economy, of course, potential output grows through time.

5. The prescription in the text neglects the problem of inflation, which can complicate the interpretation of internal balance but does not fundamentally alter the proposed policy assignment.

6. A currency depreciation has both a contractionary monetary effect and an expansionary effect stemming from the redirection of demand to domestic sources as a result of relative price changes. The statement in the text assumes that the monetary effect typically prevails in developing countries in the short run.

7. This analysis is known as the two-gap model.

8. According to the two-gap model, the shadow price of foreign exchange in the exchange-constrained economy is the inverse of the marginal propensity to import. Thus if the marginal propensity to import is 0.2, an extra dollar of foreign exchange permits output to be increased by five dollars.

9. An old adage says that borrowed reserves are no reserves because they disappear just when they are needed. This statement really refers to reserves borrowed short term, which is why the relevant borrowing rate is the long-term rate.

10. It is a different matter if many of the producers of a primary product devalue simultaneously, because overall market demand typically is inelastic. Export revenue measured in foreign exchange may well decline under such circumstances.

11. If the demand for exports were inelastic, which it normally is not, at least for a single country, a high supply elasticity would magnify the loss of export revenue resulting from devaluation.

12. In the case of a high-inflation country with an interest rate sufficiently high to neutralize its regular nominal depreciation intended to keep the real exchange rate constant, the unusual event that must be accepted as once and for all is a real depreciation.

13. Obviously, one must deflate the reserves of individual countries by some appropriate scale variable to obtain internationally comparable measures of the size of a country's reserves. The traditional deflator has been the value of imports of goods and services.

14. Sebastian Edwards, "The Demand for International Reserves and Exchange Rate Adjustments: The Case of LDCs, 1964–1972, "*Economica*, vol. 199, no. 50 (August 1983), pp. 269–80.

9

External Borrowing and Debt Management

Albert Fishlow

AS MUCH AS ANY single factor, the reliance upon external borrowing and the subsequent reaction color the entire process of developing countries' economic performance in the 1970s and the 1980s. At first capital flows of seeming unlimited magnitude and at low cost provided a valuable buffer to these countries against the more variable world economy resulting from the sudden quadrupling of oil prices in 1973. Then, in the 1980s, an abrupt halt to capital flows served the final blow in a succession of new external economic shocks that bared the vulnerability of the indebtedness strategy. How countries have fared in the past several years is almost the direct consequence of the extent of their debt burdens.

In this chapter, the complex problems of debt management are discussed by drawing lessons from practical experience rather than by presenting abstract rules and simple formulas. Formalism is left to an annex that contains an algebraic discussion of debt dynamics and the determinants of stability.

First I deal with the historical experience of capital movements. Recent reliance on external borrowing is novel only in the restricted context of the post–World War II period when public resources became the principal source of finance for developing countries. Earlier, in both the nineteenth century and the interwar period, organized international capital markets flourished and sometimes also failed. The history of that period, with its transition to greater governmental responsibility after 1945, is briefly recapitulated to illustrate the theoretical considerations underlying the demand for and supply of foreign capital.

I then move to the reaction to the first oil shock in 1973 by oil-importing developing countries and their options of finance or immediate adjustment. The use of external borrowing was a rational response, especially because the market supply of finance was favorable and interest costs were low. In virtually accidental fashion, private capital markets assumed new responsibilities in underwriting the economic growth of developing countries.

During the debt crisis of the early 1980s, several external factors contributed to the deterioration of the balance of payments of developing countries; these included the second round of oil price increases, rising interest rates, and recession in industrial countries. I examine the differential impact of this crisis on different groups of countries.

The form and adequacy of the restructuring of international economic policy that took place in the aftermath of the Mexican de facto default in 1982 are next addressed. The International Monetary Fund emerged from the crisis with a new central role. Private banks reorganized their ways of doing business. On the other side, developing countries have experienced the most dramatic decline of living standards since the Great Depression; for some countries the decline has been even lower. The need for these countries to substitute positive adjustment is becoming an increasing political reality.

The prospects for new capital flows and institutional reform necessary to bring about such a restoration of sustainable economic development are also examined. A central issue is whether voluntary lending from banks will resume and under what conditions. The reluctance of banks to increase their exposure in developing countries creates a large shortfall in the resources needed by these countries for appropriate adjustment. The shortfall is not easily counterbalanced by other sources of finance. Limited prospects for capital flows have increasingly encouraged countries to search for more radical solutions to the debt problem.

In the final section the lessons from the rich and varied experience with external borrowing are brought together. The right level of indebtedness must take into account the uses to which it will be put and must reflect realistic assessments of the future. Debt rescheduling, past or present, typically provides modest relief and places an asymmetric responsibility for conservatism upon borrowers. Although it is possible to improve many technical dimensions of debt management, and to hedge more effectively against some exchange and price risks, the onus of an excessive exposure is reflected disproportionately in debtor incomes and economic performance. In the final analysis, developing countries need a better balanced integration into the international economy that insulates against rather than magnifies external shocks and intensifies rather than cancels external opportunities. The right level of indebtedness is embedded in the right development strategy.

1. History of Capital Movements

Three periods may be distinguished in the history of capital movements: the time before World War I, the years between the two world wars, and the decades since World War II.

The Pre–World War I Period

From 1870 to 1914, a global economy was forged, which increased the exchange of manufactured products for the raw materials of the periphery.[1] Underlying this extension of trade was a system of expanding finance that girded the globe with railways and opened new areas for primary production. Large infusions of capital augmented domestic saving and provided foreign exchange to import the equipment required for massive investment in infrastructure. The scale of such finance was extraordinary. On the eve of World War I, outstanding non-European debt stood at about $270 billion in 1984 dollars, about three times the value of the primary trade it was intended to stimulate. By comparison, developing country debt now, for all capital-importing countries, is about one and a half times the value of exports of goods and services.

The capital flowed primarily from Great Britian and to lesser degrees from France and Germany. Britain accounted for about half of all foreign investment, most of it after 1885; France more than 20 percent; and Germany about 15 percent. The United States began to make small commitments in the 1890s but remained a net debtor until World War I. The claim of foreign capital outflows on domestic resources was parallel: Britain invested 5 percent of its GNP abroad, reaching a peak of 10 percent just before World War I; French and German capital exports averaged a mere 2–3 percent.

The principal recipients of capital were the richer, resource-abundant countries of North America, Latin America, and Oceania. They accounted for about half of total investment and about 70 percent of British assets. In second place, commitment to Eastern Europe (principally Russia) and to Scandinavia accounted for perhaps 25 percent of gross investment. France and Germany were the principal sources. The third group consisted of other peripheral countries in which investment had strong political motivations; these included China, Egypt, India, Turkey, and some African colonies.

Two overlapping processes were at work in the redistribution of capital from the industrial countries. One, centered in London, was motivated by private economic opportunity and the differential returns to be had from investing in resource-rich countries. The growing exports of these countries would service a debt the physical counterpart of which was found in an expanded infrastructure of railways, ports, urban facilities, and so on. The returns realized on such investment, adjusted for its greater risk, exceeded the gains one would make on domestic securities by margins of two to four percentage points. The capital market favored not the poorer countries, but the high-income peripheral ones where returns to both investment and labor were attractive because of abundant resources. Immigration and capital flow went together. Capital-scarce and overpopulated tropical countries received little investment because peripheral primary export potential in the nineteenth century was not significantly dependent on cheap wages. Economically motivated foreign investment in the era was thus far from income equalizing.

For most borrowers, external capital was central to the development process. During 1870–1910, capital inflows in Canada averaged 7.5 percent of GNP and accounted for as much as a third to a half of annual investment. Similar ratios prevailed for Australia. For Argentina, capital flows for the first two decades of the twentieth century accounted for 12–15 percent of GNP and 40 percent of investment. The United States was a prominent exception: throughout the nineteenth century foreign capital inflows did not much exceed 1 percent of GNP.

A second factor determining capital flows was political advantage. The Paris and Berlin capital markets, in which governmental preferences played a large role, were especially sensitive to such considerations. Large commitments to Eastern European countries and strategic peripheral countries followed. Investments frequently went to finance public current expenditures rather than to underwrite productive public works. Consequently, there was a greater incidence of default and write-downs. Although nominal returns were attractive—usually because bonds were sold well below par, and publicity made them seem even more so—the realized results were not always attractive. Such politically motivated investments, however, were smaller in volume during the period than those with economic basis, and not all of them proved to be failures. In the final analysis, private investors had to be persuaded to accept the risks of investments abroad and would do so only under favorable prospects.

The new foreign investment did not manage to keep up with the reflow of income from interest and dividends. Return income, growing at an annual rate of some 5 percent a year, outstripped the expansion of debt at a rate of 4.6 percent between 1870 and 1914. Capital inflows during shorter intervals of peak investment exceeded income obligations. Likewise, individual recipients experienced large import surpluses over brief periods, but there was soon need to generate export surpluses. The very profitability that led to increasing foreign investment translated into limited real resource transfers to debtor countries as a group.

Britain's role as a free trade advocate and practitioner was important. Britain's acceptance of increasing imports was central to the maintenance of financial flows. Its political and economic preeminence also contributed to the enforceability of the private debt instruments. Peripheral countries had every incentive to remain integrated to a rapidly expanding world economy. Denial of access to the new capital required for investment and imports was sufficient to produce rapid accommodation of differences. And when external conditions were adverse, there were opportunities for short-term assistance and long-term rescheduling conditional upon policy changes in developing countries.

The Interwar Period

After 1914, the international capital market underwent profound change. The United States not only became a net creditor but rapidly supplanted Britain as the principal source of lending. Europe, especially Germany, became a large borrower. Official bond issues were much more important than they had been earlier. So was official lending emanating from the war years and immediately thereafter, not to mention the presence of the Allied reparations claims on Germany. Above all, the amount of net foreign investment in long-term assets declined, even in the 1920s, relative to earlier levels; during the Depression, the decline was even greater. Throughout the interwar period, the return of investment income exceeded the application of the proceeds.

Capital flows in the 1920s were no longer an integral part of an expanding world economy. Borrowers had little prospect of rapid export growth with which to service their debts. It did not matter whether the borrowers were peripheral or European countries. Several development countries had completed building their infrastructure and were now confronted by increasing commodity surpluses and declining prices. European governments had not used the resources fully for productive investment, with the result that their revenue growth did not match the higher interest rates paid during the 1920s. Debt was frequently used to pay the interest due on past debt, so that there was an inevitable deterioration in its quality. In the aggregate, however, debtor countries could not borrow enough to meet their service payments fully, and many were therefore required to achieve export surpluses. This trade was not so readily absorbed as it had been earlier. The United States, now at the center of the world economy, was not committed to free trade as Britain had been; its external trade was no more than a small percentage of its GNP. Because the pound was overvalued, much of the import pressure was felt by Britain.

The fundamental problem with lending in the 1920s was its systemic deficiency. Capital flows responded to financial needs for short-term adjustment to the dislocations created by the war and not to considerations of longer-term sustainability. The United States was happy to export capital and to achieve export surpluses. European borrowers sustained their import surpluses by borrowing. Older peripheral debtors ran export surpluses to service part of their obligations; they borrowed the rest. Underlying this equilibrium was the need for continuing net capital flow. In this period, however, unlike the prewar period, there was no natural expansion of trade to validate the increasing debt. Instead, stability depended upon an unlimited supply of finance.

Even before the Depression, as American investors turned away from foreign bonds to speculate on domestic equity, the shakiness of the financial arrangements was evident. After the 1929 crash, the wreckage was everywhere in sight. Germany was the first large country to encounter problems, principally because of its short-term exposure. These problems set the stage for a moratorium on reparations in 1931 and for later formal default. The peripheral countries in Latin America, with the example of disarray at the center, also reduced their debt service unilaterally. The drastic decline of commodity prices left them with few alternatives. Countries that discovered domestic expansion policies and extensive government regulation of the balance of payments tended to fare better than those that were less innovative and less interventionist. Trade shrank and capital markets disappeared except for short-term movements in search of a haven in the United States as war clouds thickened over Europe.

The Postwar Period

The Bretton Woods system consciously sought to remedy the failures of international economic adjustment made transparent by the interwar breakdown. The International Monetary Fund (IMF) was established to monitor short-term adjustment and to satisfy the attendant needs of liquidity. The World Bank was created to provide a reliable supply of long-term capital. The International Trade Organization was conceived to ensure free trade; because it was never ratified, the General Agreement on Tariffs and Trade (GATT), originally organized as a temporary arrangement, took its place.

The Bretton Woods institutions found themselves to be inadequate in the face of the large postwar international economic disequilibrium. There were simply not enough multilateral resources to finance the immediate import surpluses Europe and Japan required for reconstruction. The U.S. Marshall Plan came to the rescue, providing Western Europe with some $11 billion between 1948 and 1951. That capital flow, much in the form of grants, helped to underwrite an improved balance of payments and to initiate rapid growth. Such generosity was in marked contrast to the treatment of reparations and the inter-Allied war loans in the 1920s.

During the 1950s, the United States also began a program of loans and grants to developing countries. Other industrialized countries joined as their own income levels increased. At the same time, the World Bank began to shift its emphasis from reconstruction to economic development. The progressive decolonization of the developing countries elicited many new demands from Asia and Africa. These were added to the needs of Latin American countries eager to sustain their industrialization strategies undertaken during the Depression and the war. Some developing countries, especially those with resource bases or attractive internal markets, were also able to attract direct foreign investment. There was already a tension between the appropriate mix of official borrowing and the use of equity finance: the United States favored a policy climate that relied most heavily on the latter. But as table 9-1 shows, however, loans dominated.

Until the end of the 1960s, capital flows to developing countries were derived from two sources: official lending and direct investment. Bonds and, to a much lesser extent, equity, characteristic of the portfolio investment of the pre-1945 period, were nonexistent. Partly for that reason, developing countries sought increased access to official resources. In 1960, governments created the International Development Association (IDA) as an affiliate of the World Bank to provide concessional finance for low-income countries. Regional development banks were also established for Latin America (1959), Africa (1964), and Asia (1966). The United States undertook a special bilateral program for Latin America with the establishment of the Alliance for Progress in 1961. Despite such efforts, the sum of all flows from industrial countries to developing countries declined from 1 percent of industrial country GNP in 1961 to 0.8 percent in 1970. Official assistance fell even more. External finance, therefore, did not exceed 3 percent of developing country income.

Table 9-1. Financial Flows to Developing Countries
(billions of 1980 dollars)

			Private			
Year	Total	Official development assistance	Total	Direct private investment	Portfolio	Export credits
1956–60	21.9	13.2	8.7	—	—	—
1961–70	29.0	16.2	11.5	6.0	2.6	2.9
1971–80	76.6	28.1[a]	38.1	10.7	19.9	7.4

Note: Data between periods are not strictly comparable because of redefinition. Dollars have been deflated by GDP deflator for industrial countries.

a. $19.8 billion excluding assistance from the Council for Mutual Economic Assistance and the Organization of Petroleum Exporting Countries.

Sources: 1956–60: OECD, Development Assistance and Efforts in 1961 of the Members of the Development Assistance Committee (September 1962); 1961–70: OECD, Development Assistance, 1971 Review (1971); 1971–80: OECD, Development Cooperation, 1981 Review (1983).

Because of the limited levels of capital inflow, some of the middle-income developing countries began to tap the expanding Eurodollar market at the end of the 1960s. These included Brazil, Republic of Korea, Mexico, and other newly industrializing countries whose income and export growth made them attractive risks for private bank finance. After the first oil shock, the intensity of demand and the size of the eligible list of borrowing countries expanded greatly. This expansion ushered in a decade of the largest borrowing since the beginning of the century.

Determinants of Demand and Supply

The demand for capital by developing countries depended on the potential returns' exceeding their cost. For private borrowers, it depended on private gains' exceeding the borrowing cost. For official borrowers—and they dominated from the beginning—it depended on additional social returns on top of actual enterprise receipts. The externalities from public infrastructure investment yielded a socal rate of return in excess of the net revenues that might be obtained from user charges. The social return, after all, was the justification for direct provision of public works and subsidies, such as land and grants or interest guarantees, to assist private infrastructure ventures. Such investment contributed more to total growth than is indicated by direct profits.

What made returns high in developing countries in the pre-1945 period was the scarcity of capital—not merely relative to labor, but especially relative to natural resources. Exports were resource intensive. Domestic saving was inadequate to exploit all profitable opportunities. There was also an important foreign contribution of technological and managerial skill, whether in directly productive or infrastructure projects.

In the post-1945 period, a new source of higher social returns to external capital emerged: it was the premium of foreign exchange earnings over market value. Development economists recognized that noncompetitive imports were of special importance to developing countries' investment and, hence, their capacity for sustained growth. Because export demand was limited to primary products, and supply flexibility at the early stages of development was inadequate, domestic resources could not simply be switched to the export sector to permit the purchase of needed foreign inputs. In addition, because trade and capital flows were controlled, foreign exchange markets were typically overvalued. The overvaluation left a margin between the market value and the shadow price of foreign exchange, which enhanced the value of borrowing beyond its addition to capital accumulation. External debt complemented domestic saving. Increased imports made it possible to use the domestic saving potential that would otherwise have gone to naught. The contribution to total product by foreign capital exceeded the direct return on domestic investment. There was thus an additional reason for developing countries to seek direct foreign investment and loans.

On their side, private suppliers of capital always looked to a return higher than could be earned on domestic applications—one that was commensurate with what was viewed as a greater risk. The risk had two components. One was the differntial information about individual projects in countries that were distant. Glowing prospectuses and investment plans frequently differed from reality. The other was the risk that private returns might not translate into foreign exchange because of payments problems.

External debt is also characterized by sovereign risk, and hence by both national capacity and willingness to pay, above and beyond the returns of the spcific project. All foreign lending, whether to private firms or government agencies, depends upon macroeconomic policies for continuous servicing. The only effective claim a lender has is upon domestic currency. If it is true that an underlying guarantee to official debt is that countries do not go bankrupt, it is equally true that project lending is, in the end, balance of payments finance. Even carefully designed investments may suffer because of balance of payments problems. This phenomenon is regarded as the external transfer problem.

For official debt, there is also an internal transfer problem. Productive official undertakings may not be able to pay off automatically through proportionally larger tax receipts. The greater the externalities, the more necessary are overt measures to recapture the benefits from private beneficiaries. How to accomplish the transfer is a domestic political decision because distributional issues are involved.

These risks, which have become so familiar lately, are not recent artifacts. Widespread debt servicing difficulties arose in the crises of the 1870s, 1890s, and the 1930s as a result of deteriorating internal and external domestic conditions. Official debt could sometimes not be serviced, although private obligations were frequently met. Some countries occasionally refused to resume payments on debts they deemed exaggerated and partially fraudulent.

Yet on the whole, high returns on foreign capital have been not only anticipated but realized except during periods of war and high inflation. Defaults by developing countries have not been significant. Rescheduling that preserves the value of obligations, rather than significant writedowns, has been the rule. Even the settlements after the Depression became favorable to developing countries as a result of intervening inflation and the reduced service payments that were eventually negotiated.

The restraint shown by lenders is partially responsible for this record. Because of the risks, borrowers face a rising supply curve for credit: the larger the exposure, the greater the cost.[2] Hence borrowers are, or should be, dissuaded from excessive reliance on external capital. In addition, however, individual debtors, left to themselves, overborrow by ignoring the repercussions on cost for potential borrowers later. Government intervention after the fact is important; it need not take a political form. It suffices to condition additional resources upon changes in policy and performance. In addition to receiving immediate liquidity the prospect of continuing access to capital markets has discouraged countries from opting for default.

Rules for debt management thus become more complicated in application than the straightforward, and correct, theoretical principle that marginal returns should exceed marginal costs. Three reasons stand out.

First, externalities influence both returns and benefits; one cannot simply trust in private decisions to achieve the right capital inflow. The marginal returns simultaneously depend upon the social profitability of additional units of domestic saving, foreign exchange, and, sometimes, public expenditure. Second, one is dealing with an unknown and, in the case of long maturities, far distant future. Uncertainities abound on the evolution of the economy and the external environment. At least in the past, one could rely on fixed interest rates as a given. In recent years, even that element of cost is subject to recalculation every six months. Third, there is the further complication of systematic cyclical excesses that have been so far left out.[3] New lending begets more lending by stimulating domestic growth; it also furthers worthwhile projects while providing the foreign exchange necessary to service past debt. Projections on both the lending and borrowing sides can become overoptimistic, however, which can lead to curtailed finance and self-fulfilling balance of payments problems. When real returns and costs are being assessed, susceptibility to such fluctuations matters.

The complexity of the problem is not an excuse for policy abdication. On the contrary, reliance on private markets to determine capital inflow leaves much to be desired. This discussion emphasizes the need to qualify simplistic analyses of the benefits of reliance on external capital inflow—in place of greater domestic saving, or exports, or public sector revenues—by important additional considerations.

2. The First Oil Price Shock

The quadrupling in oil price in 1973–74 posed for oil-importing countries the decision of how best to respond. To the extent that the oil price shock was temporary, finance was clearly the appropriate choice for countering the ensuing balance of payments deficit. It did not matter that finance was clearly the appropriate choice for countering the ensuing balance of payments deficit. It did not matter that finance was relatively for a short term; the need was temporary.

If the change in relative prices and external environment were more enduring, then structural adjustment would be necessary. But medium- and long-term finance could permit a gradual, and hence more efficient, reallocation of productive resources away from energy-intensive activities, especially those reliant on oil, and toward exports and import substitutes. Such adaptation would be relatively capital-intensive and would require additional saving as well as foreign exchange to meet the immediate balance of payments disequilibrium.

Whatever the evaluation of the permanence of the oil price rise, countries were inclined to use finance to ease the decline in real income caused by the deterioration in the terms of the trade. The alternative would have been an immediate and full reduction of real income to reduce imports and stimulate exports. The required devaluation presumed that domestic wages and prices would not rise to curtail its effects, that productive structures were flexible, and that international demand was elastic. These conditions were not universally applicable in developing countries. The prospect of a temporary halt in growth rate was certainly not attractive for many countries that had only recently improved their performance as the result of greater integration into the international economy. Finally, spreading recession in the industrial countries made the direct strategy of paying for oil through expanded exports seem highly unfeasible.

In the end, finance and gradual adjustment won over immediate austerity in a broad range of countries, including several small industrial economies. The prominent exceptions were the poorest developing economies. They had access only to limited official resources, modestly enhanced by the creation of a special IMF oil facility to ease the transition. Taiwan, preoccupied with the implications of financial dependence, opted for immediate adjustment rather than increased borrowing. Latin American countries generally found larger capital inflows a welcome alternative to an abrupt change in domestic policies and performance.

The widespread decision in favor of finance was helped by favorable supply conditions. Banks now wanted to lend internationally. Intense competition among them soon drove down the premium over the London interbank offer rate (LIBOR), the cost of funds in the Eurocurrency market. Banks were responding to changes in international market conditions: the sudden increase in the surpluses of the oil-exporting countries—on the order of $60 billion in 1974—added to the global supply of loanable funds as a result of higher propensities to save in those countries. Because of a strong desire for liquidity, the Eurocurrency market was a preferred habitat for such surpluses. Both the premium and the LIBOR declined. Money was cheap because it was in abundant supply. Indeed, measured against the increased prices of exportables that were part of worldwide inflation, interest rates were highly negative.

In following market signals, developing countries helped to contribute to adjustment to the international economic disequilibrium. Their demand for petrodollars and increased imports from the industrial countries compensated for the tax of the oil price increase. Balance of payments surpluses of oil-producing countries would be offset by the deficits of oil-importing developing countries. At this time some people despaired that the international economy might be unable to withstand such a large, sudden transfer of resources from oil importers to oil exporters; these people were therefore calling for much more radical solutions. Financial intermediation made intervention, military or economic, unnecessary. The ensuing rapid recovery of world trade and income contrasts starkly with the vicious circle of decline and protectionist restrictions in the 1930s.

On their side, banks found in their new customers an important source of profits. Banks made more money on attractive commissions and spreads on loans to developing countries than on domestic borrowers. Low, or even negative, real interest rates were no worry: they were even welcome in minimizing the real debt service obligations of developing country borrowers and made them better credit risks. As long as bank depositors were willing to accept negligible returns, and surplus oil exporters had such preferences for liquidity, the recycling arrangements were quite satisfactory.

As table 9-1 shows, private bank loans dominated other sources of developing country finance in the 1970s. Syndication permitted associations of large numbers of banks, regardless of their national origin. The Eurocurrency market was more international than even nineteenth-century arrangements had been. Political distinctions were irrelevant. Eastern European and developing countries of different political persuasions were all eligible; what counted was the ability to pay. Loans could be arranged in a matter of months, without the bother of project detail or policy prescriptions from official lending agencies.

The difficulty with such arrangements was that the need for finance was based not on a small and immediate dose of liquidity but on structural adjustment. Market signals and the maturity of the loans were short term. Countries bore virutally all the risk of the mismatch. Loans typically ranged between six and ten years in length. Interest rates, moreover, were readjustable every six months in accordance with variations in LIBOR (and in later contracts, in the U.S. prime rate at the option of the lender). These applied to all past floating-rate debt. The consequences of variability in exchange rates had to be borne by lenders as well because the dollar—in which some two-thirds of loan contracts were denominated—was no longer fixed. Finally, the majority of loans required government guarantees, which were more likely to be forthcoming for public, rather than private enterprises. Paradoxically, as external capital provided by the private market increased, so did the bias in favor of public borrowers.

The new source and volume of finance, in short, were potentially precarious rather than a secure basis for effective adjustment to a changed international economy. The structure of Eurocurrency lending made it difficult for borrowing countries to plan efficient use of the external resources obtained. Debtors borrowed no longer to meet balance of payments needs but rather to sustain high growth rates. High growth rates in turn could unlock more loans on the basis of good performance. Credit analysis was primitive. Old rules of thumb were no longer applicable. The oil shock resulted in levels of indebtedness that would have been regarded as unprecedented and unwise only a few years before.

Debt (see tables 9-2–9-5) grew so rapidly in the 1970s at a nominal rate in excess of 20 percent a year. That expansion, in conjunction with low real rates of interest and inflation, bloated export growth and concealed the lurking difficulties of debt dynamics. Starting from low levels of debt, capital inflows were able to finance an excess of imports over exports and hence a resource transfer that contributed to higher investment and an increase in domestic income. Over time, the capacity to sustain a continuing transfer requires ever larger absolute capital inflows on the one side and limited counterclaims of interest income on the other. The basic equation is $r_d = (M - X)/D + i$: the rate of growth of debt is equal to the size of the resource transfer relative to debt plus the rate of interest (see the appendix to this chapter). Debt-export and debt-income ratios converge, even with continuing balance of payments deficits and foreign saving, provided that export and product growth rates exceed the interest rate.

Another way to put the matter is that debt grows inertially at the rate of interest, even when there is no longer any transfer of resources. By borrowing to pay interest, the debt is increased, without providing a basis for higher rates of domestic investment. The higher the interest rate, the fewer the opportunities to use finance as an instrument of medium- and long-term adjustment. At the same time, for given rates of export growth, higher interest rates make countries less creditworthy by reducing the coverage of such fixed payments. Larger shares of exports are committed to debt service, impelling creditors to impose quantitative limits on new lending.

Such considerations, however, received limited attention during 1974–78. Instead, the emphasis was placed upon the superior perform-

Table 9-2. Current Account Deficits of Developing Countries
(billions of dollars)

Region	1973[a]	1978	1980	1981	1982	1983	1984	1985
All capital-importing countries	11.3	56.4	77.0	113.0	103.0	60.4	34.4	43.0
Africa	1.9	15.5	5.4	25.6	24.8	15.3	10.3	5.7
Asia	2.6	8.7	21.9	23.7	20.2	17.0	7.6	18.2
Western Hemisphere	4.7	19.4	30.2	43.3	42.0	11.4	4.9	5.9

Note: Current accounts shown are net of official transfers.
a. Non-oil developing countries.
Source: International Monetary Fund.

Table 9-3. External Debt of Developing Countries
(billions of dollars)

Region	1973[a]	1978	1980	1981	1982	1983	1984	1985
All capital-importing countries	130.1	339.1	567.6	662.0	751.6	798.4	840.7	888.3
Short term	18.4	71.8	112.9	135.6	158.0	132.7	132.7	120.4
Long term	111.8	327.3	454.8	526.4	593.6	665.8	707.9	767.9
Africa	14.2	72.4	94.3	103.1	117.1	125.1	129.3	128.5
Asia	30.0	93.2	133.4	151.9	175.3	193.5	206.6	229.7
Western Hemisphere	44.0	155.9	230.7	287.0	328.6	340.6	355.9	368.3

a. Non-oil developing countries.
Source: International Monetary Fund.

Table 9-4. Debt-Export Ratios of Developing Countries
(percent)

Region	1973[a]	1978	1980	1981	1982	1983	1984	1985
All capital-importing countries	115.4	132.4	110.4	122.9	148.6	158.8	152.8	163.0
Africa	71.5	124.2	87.6	112.3	148.6	164.4	167.7	168.6
Asia	92.9	81.0	70.1	71.5	84.0	89.2	84.2	93.5
Western Hemisphere	176.2	217.2	182.8	208.8	267.2	287.5	273.3	295.0

Note: Table includes exports of goods and services.
a. Non-oil developing countries.
Source: International Monetary Fund.

Table 9-5. Debt Service Ratios of Developing Countries
(percent)

Region	1973[a]	1978	1980	1981	1982	1983	1984	1985
All capital-importing countries	15.9	19.0	17.1	20.5	23.6	22.0	22.9	24.1
Africa	8.8	15.3	13.6	15.5	19.6	22.8	24.8	27.0
Asia	9.6	10.3	8.2	9.5	11.2	10.8	11.8	12.3
Western Hemisphere	29.3	37.9	33.3	41.1	49.6	43.0	42.4	44.1

Note: Amortization and interest payments relative to exports of goods and services have been included.
a. Non-oil developing countries.
Source: International Monetary Fund, *World Economic Outlook.*

ance and higher investment ratios of borrowing countries. Debt-export ratios had increased between 1973 and 1978 but at a relatively modest rate. The gamble of finance still seemed very much worth taking. Although some countries had already been forced to reschedule some of their external debt, the need for rescheduling was attributed to inadequate policies rather than to a systemic defect. Debt was considered a solution rather than a problem. In the words of one observer writing in 1980:

In sum, the overall debt situation during the 1970s adapted itself to the sizable strains introduced into the payments system and, in broad terms, maintained its relative position vis-à-vis other relevant variables. Though some countries experienced difficulties, a generalized debt management problem was avoided, and in the aggregate the outlook for the immediate future does not give cause for alarm.[4]

3. The Second Oil Price Shock

A deteriorating global economic environment would prove the optimistic prognosis far off the mark. Oil prices soared again under the impulse of uncertain supplies as war broke out in the fall of 1979 between Iran and Iraq. After considerable volatility in the spot market, the new average 1980 oil price settled at a level almost two and a half times its 1978 value. The immediate aggregate impact of the new price was a surplus of more than $100 billion in 1980 for the member nations of OPEC and a current account deficit for the non-oil developing countries of almost the same amount.

Once again, there was a recession in the industrial countries as contractionary policies sought to contain cost-induced inflation. In 1980, however, unlike 1974–75, the commitment to restraint was more serious. The earlier tolerance for inflation in preference to unemployment had yielded to a frontal attack upon price increases. The ensuing slowdown in the activity of industrial countries had a prolonged and significant effect on the export earnings of countries. An essential element of the new economic strategy was reliance on a tight monetary policy, which induced higher nominal and real interest rates. Where before the capital market provided finance for balance of payments deficits, it now penalized not only the flow but also, because of the large amount of floating-rate debt, the past stock.

Various studies have quantified the consequences of these cumulative adverse developments.[5] They differ largely in the assumptions made about the state of the world. They generally agree, however, on the importance of the crippling oil price shocks and even on their relative magnitudes. Next comes the recession-induced decline in export earnings, and terms of trade effects. This negative influence is felt most strongly in 1982. The impact of higher interest rates is felt in the same year; their balance of payments effects are offset in part by the interest-bearing reserves held by developing countries and by the continuing importance of official fixed-interest lending to the lower-income developing countries. For major borrowers, and for regions such as Latin America, the consequences were more adverse.

Overall, the result of these external shocks was to convert the large realizable 1982 current account deficit of $87 billion to a much more modest $12 billion. In other words, the sometimes drastic efforts of developing countries to expand exports and restrain imports in the early 1980s would have met with resounding success in the absence of the additional shocks. In 1982 alone, the value of imports was cut back by $40 billion. Such actions only managed to prevent the soaring current account deficit from becoming totally unmanageable, however; they did not avoid the need for still more finance.

Debt increased between the beginning of 1980 and the end of 1982 at an annual rate of 16 percent, almost as rapidly as after 1973. But the expensive capital inflows served largely to postpone the imminent day of reckoning rather than to provide meaningful relief. This statement was true for three reasons.

The first reason was the increasing short-term nature of bank lending. Between the beginning of 1980 and the end of 1982, almost 30 percent of increased debt was less than a year's maturity; for countries with mounting debt service difficulties, the ratio was even higher. Loans were made with even shorter maturity just when the second oil shock was presenting new evidence that fundamental adjustment would be required for accommodation to the volatile international economy. The banks responded by seeking to safeguard their large exposure against impending repayment problems. Individual rationality merely increased the aggregate cash flow burden of already hard-pressed debtors and provoked the problem.

The second reason for diluting later indebtedness was the allocation of debt to offset rising interest payments. In 1978, gross interest payments represented about half of the current account deficit of capital-importing developing countries. By 1982, they had increased to 90 percent. New debt went to service old debt at higher rates of interest. The debt dynamics were catching up and were soon to require perverse resource transfers (that is, trade surpluses) to maintain a semblance of order in the external accounts. From a situation in which there was no apparent foreign exchange constraint, a crisis was looming in which the balance of payments dominated all other policy objectives.

The third reason primarily responsible for the deteriorating state of affairs was the changing external conditions. It is difficult to justify the simultaneous policy failure that forced more than thirty countries to reschedule their debts from 1980 onward. Yet the policies of developing countries and the performance of the international capital market, flush with new deposits from oil-surplus countries, are also not blameless. They are another reason why later capital flows must be distinguished from the earlier flows.

The Southern Cone countries accelerated their indebtedness after 1978; until the end of 1981 their debt trebled, and their imports swelled, even as they were paying record interest rates for finance. Capital inflows were encouraged as a way of combating domestic inflation, but their more enduring effect was to encourage speculation and finance military purchases. Oil exporters, and in particular Mexico, relied heavily on borrowing to sustain high rates of growth of product and disproportionate increases of imports. They were attractive clients because they were rich. A bloated public sector absorbed the proceeds.

The countries that voluntarily borrowed large sums at the new, and increasing, real interest rates prevailing in the early 1980s were asking for trouble. Above and beyond the international rate, one had to be concerned with bearing the exchange risk emanating from devaluations that a deteriorating balance of payments might provoke. Overvalued exchange rates were temporary. Productive applications in real assets that would repay borrowing costs were not plentiful. It is not surprising that much of the foreign exchange obtained in the second round of debt expansion was diverted to capital flight by those who understood the situation better than foreign bankers. Large losses, amounting to half and even more of foreign exchange receipts, were experienced by Argentina, Mexico, and Venezuela.

Although economic deterioration was not exclusively a Latin American problem, the brunt after 1979 fell on the region. Oil was an important import for several countries, and the price rise was unanticipated. In addition, Latin America was most heavily indebted, accounting for some 40 percent of the debt of developing countries. The region was more dependent upon commodity exports than the East Asian countries, and hence its terms of trade were subject to greater deterioration as disinflation took hold. Latin American countries possessed the highest proportion of floating-rate debt as well as the highest ratio of debt to exports. Internal policies of continued expansion in 1980, as the external situation worsened, did not help. Even before the denouement of the crisis with Mexico's inability to meet its payments in August 1982, retrenchment had become necessary. It was enforced by external bankers increasingly unwilling to lend the amounts required to sustain continuing income growth.

For the small, open, and resource-poor East Asian countries, the second oil shock was as severe as the first one. The response was immediate recession in Korea and slow growth elsewhere. What made a great difference—for East Asian exports slowed during the recession as well—was a much lower ratio of debt to exports, and a lower average interest rate on the debt. Imports did not have to be cut back to meet large interest outlays, and additional finance was available. The large Asian countries emerged substantially unscathed. The limited integration of these countries into world trade and financial markets provided a natural buffer against the new adverse international climate. The debt crisis went virtually unperceived, as higher rates of agricultural productivity sparked a period of sustained growth.

For the poor countries of Africa, the crisis of the early 1980s prolonged a decline that had already taken on serious proportions. Their problem was not so much a debt crisis as a trade collapse. Between 1978 and 1983, the terms of trade of Sub-Saharan Africa deteriorated by some 28 percent, almost twice as much as for all nonfuel exporters. To maintain minimal imports, larger official borrowing and short-term relief from the IMF was necessary. In conjunction with the export stagnation, debt-export ratios increased sharply. The debt problem of this region was to come later, with the inability to meet the repayments of principal and modest interest outlays due official creditors, who, ironically, could not reschedule easily.

The picture steadily darkened from the fall of 1979, as the debt and balance of payments statistics of table 9-2 make apparent. The apparently successful adjustment to the first oil shock through a liberal dose of private finance—unprecedented in the postwar period—soon transformed itself into a major problem. The financial pages in industrial countries made evident the growing concern with the solvency of creditor banks. But the progress of developing countries was no less at stake. In industrial countries recession accompanied by high oil prices and interest rates translated into widespread depression for the largest debtors.

4. Coping with the Debt Crisis

On a fateful and unlucky Friday, August 13, 1982, the finance minister of Mexico personally visited the IMF, the U.S. Treasury, and the Federal Reserve Board. The visits were more than courtesy calls. His alarming message was everywhere the same: Mexico could no longer service its debt. Thus the debt crisis officially began. The specific response to the Mexican case helped to shape the general approach that was gradually to be put in place for Argentina, Brazil, and other nations.

The International Monetary Fund emerged at the center of the new arrangements. It was to perform three central functions in managing debt crisis. The first function—and it was the most innovative one— was to impose conditionality upon the banks. The size of the private debt kept the Fund from taking independent action in designing a stabilization package as it customarily did. Limited Fund resources would have been immediately dissipated in meeting private obligations. The banks would not only have to forgo return of their principal but would have to ante up additional resources in a way compatible with an overall adjustment strategy. By treating banks as a group—and indeed taking decisions out of their hands—the IMF averted the free-rider problem already evident in the shortening maturity of bank lending. Each individual bank, in a market context, would be reluctant to take the right action in the hope that the others would, leaving it to benefit; in the aggregate, all would desist and would be worse off than through collective action. The Fund collectivized bank involuntary lending.

Banks would be willing to put up more credit only if they believed they were safeguarding their initial exposure rather than throwing good money after bad. The second function of IMF intervention was to provide that guarantee by enforcing a stabilization package designed to return debtor nations to creditworthiness. This IMF seal of approval had always been important but after the fact rather than before. Banks had previously had the luxury of waiting and seeing. They could do so no longer. Central authority thus assured against the moral hazard of reckless debtor borrowing with no intention to repay. Never before had the Fund taken on such a generalized responsibility for the adjustment of developing countries.

The third and the more traditional function of the Fund was to be the principal source of official liquidity to help finance the balance of payments deficits to countries as they embarked upon adjustment. Although bridge loans from the Bank for International Settlements, from central banks, and even from governments were to be necessary on occasion, the Fund was the focal point. In eventual recognition of the gravity of the crisis, additional resources were made available through an IMF quota increase to meet the multiplying needs.

In a matter of months, conditions of access to private capital markets were dramatically changed. For their part, banks have changed their ways of doing business. Representative groups from the largest banks have been set up to negotiate with the principal debtor countries and bring to bear a broader collective interest. Under official pressure, an emphasis upon immediate profitability, which led to rising spreads and commissions for involuntary rescheduling, has been replaced by easier terms to reward good behavior. This new flexibility also manifested itself in 1984 in acceptance of multiyear rescheduling, consolidation of public debt due in the near term, and its extension over a much longer period (fourteen years in the Mexican case). Appropriately, spreads were actually lower at the beginning of the period, and no fees were collected.

The stance of the banks—and syndication means that there are many of them (more than 500 in the case of Mexico)—is not, however, uniform. Large international banks have reasons to stay in because many enjoy earnings from subsidiaries in the developing countries, and others have profitable private clients. Smaller banks—and the problem tends to be most acute in the United States, where the money center banks have been selling off participations to regional banks for several years—have no such commitment. They prefer not to extend new loans involuntarily and have succeeded in placing more of the burden on the money center banks.

Because of the disparity of national regulations that affect banks, similar differences in taste extend to European and American banks. The former have accumulated loan loss reserves at a faster rate, in part because of more favorable tax treatment. Hence the European banks are more amenable to write-downs than to new infusions of lending and increased debt. American banks have concentrated on capital increases that have significantly reduced their sensitivity to deterioration of their assets.

These arrangements, like petrodollar recycling in 1974, have worked better than many expected. Countries have not defaulted. The international financial system has not come unglued; it has in fact been strengthened. Institutional innovation has worked best, however, to safeguard the solvency of creditors rather than to restore the economic health of debtors. Stabilization has succeeded primarily in achieving trade surpluses of unprecedented levels that have permitted the uninterrupted payment of interest without significant entry of new capital. The consequence is a large negative cash flow on debt account. The outflow of interest from capital-importing countries in 1985 was $83 billion; net borrowing was about $30 billion.

Internal equilibrium has been sacrificed in many cases to meet the single objective of improved external performance. Debtor countries have been plagued by low rates of capital formation as the crisis has evolved into a longer-term problem. For countries with debt servicing problems, the ratio of debt to GDP has declined from 25.6 percent in 1979 to 18 percent in 1985. High real domestic interest rates, which have accompanied austerity programs, have neither attracted capital inflows from abroad nor significantly increased domestic saving. Rather, these rates have crowded out private investment as the public sector gained command over the resources required to service internal and external debt. Conventional monetary and fiscal policies have failed to restrain inflation, despite a significant decline in real wages in most countries with adjustment policies. That is the reason for the bolder initiatives in recent years in Argentina, Brazil, and Peru. Despite aggressive exchange rate devaluations in debtor countries, adjustment has led to reductions in demand and employment and has not led to sustained, compensating expansion of output in the export- and import-competing sectors.

Debtor developing countries have experienced lower growth as the bottom line. The average increase in GDP for those with debt servicing problems was less than 1 percent a year from 1981 to 1985, which was a decline in per capita terms. These results are unprecedented in the post-war period. From 1968 to 1977, the average growth was 5.6 percent. Successive annual IMF forecasts have progressively lowered expected performance, and even these have usually been overoptimistic.

Debtor countries have nonetheless continued to pay rather than to default. They have done so, in part, because the present arrangements have always promised more than they delivered. Economic recovery of industrial countries was supposed to resolve the liquidity problem by offering better prospects for export volume and for terms of trade. The depreciation of the dollar was supposed to boost prices of commodities. Current lower oil prices were supposed to underwrite more rapid, and noninflationary, growth in the industrial countries and to bring in their wake interest rate relief. Above all, normal capital flows were expected to resume to countries that had demonstrated commitment to the adjustment strategy.

Debtor countries have, thus far, consistently experienced fewer benefits that have been predicted. Debt-to-export ratios have not dramatically declined. Banks have retreated even from the modest expectation of nominal lending equal to the rate of inflation. As the balance sheets of banks improved, they have taken a harder line on extending new credit. Improvement in the balance of payments has been achieved in the face of continuing adverse terms of trade that make export growth costly in welfare terms. Even after a surge in the exports of developing countries in 1984, expansion in 1985 and 1986 was limited. The bulk of the gains continue to emanate from continuing import restraint. Real commodity prices have not accompanied dollar depreciation. Growth prospects for industrial countries in 1986 have been revised downward.

The response of debtor countries has been to intensify their efforts to elevate the debt problem from a technocratic one to be resolved by the IMF to one for which the industrial countries had a direct political responsibility. This objective, in existence from the very beginning, was evident in the appeal for direct U.S. participation in the first stage of the

Mexican negotiations. Subsequently, however, as definitive improvement continued to be postponed, the Latin American countries created a formal, high level consultative mechanism, the Cartagena Group. Although the achievements of this group appear to be modest—it has not functioned as a coordinated debtors' cartel, to the disappointment of some—Cartagena's existence has not gone unnoticed. Greater flexibility and sensitivity on the part of the banks as well as the IMF have not been entirely spontaneous.

Debtor countries see the elevation of the debt problem to an international political level as the logical counterpart of the domestic political pressures they themselves encounter for improved performance. After several years of austerity, patience is wearing thin. Internal failures are increasingly seen as the direct consequence of external interest payments that continue to drain large sums (5 percent, and even more, of GDP) for the largest debtors.

More countries, in addition to the isolated example of Peru, may soon turn out to be unwilling to continue to service their debt under present conditions. The distinction between capacity and willingness blurs in the case of sovereign debt. Insolvency is not clear-cut; there are no assets to be valued and foreclosed. Even the frequently cited rule "export growth must exceed the rate of interest for countries to be able to pay" depends on the presumption that countries are unwilling to accept continuing export surpluses. As long as surpluses are achieved, interest can be paid, and the growth of debt can be held in check. The capacity to pay is defined by standards of acceptable national sacrifice.

A new element influencing those standards is the pattern of recent political change. There has been a strong tide against authoritarianism in developing countries and especially in the problem debtors. Some of the blame for excessive debt accumulation can be attributed to the policy errors of earlier governments, and this point has not been lost on the populace. New leaders have almost invariably been committed to solutions to the debt problem within a framework of continuing international economic integration and cooperation. They have not failed to couch appeals for a broader perspective on the debt problem in terms of its contribution to the democratic values espoused by industrial countries that are members of the Organisation for Economic Co-operation and Development (OECD).

Despite occasional involvement, however, the industrial countries have been largely absent players in the present policy framework. They have entered only to extend temporary bridging loans to debtors and to renegotiate bilateral loans, including export credits, in the Paris Club. Their limited role, as much as any other factor, explains the lack of enthusiasm for more radical plans for debt relief that have come forward at various times since 1982. Central to almost all such schemes is a need for official resources, frequently in modest proportions, to back up more generous rescheduling of debt to limit private bank losses.

Until recently, there was little evidence of a willingness by industrial countries to contribute. Indeed, even the quota increase for the IMF encountered considerable resistance in the U.S. Congress. At the Seoul meeting of the Bank and Fund in 1985, U.S. Secretary of the Treasury James Baker finally unveiled a new initiative on the debt problem. It was motivated by the demonstrated reluctance of banks to sustain lending, involuntary or voluntary, at even a modest pace; by the increasing frustration of developing countries at the prospect of continuing austerity; and by the general fatigue and accumulating resentment of all the actors in the crisis: the banks, the countries, and even the IMF.

The Baker Plan has three components: structural change by the debtors, which emphasizes increased reliance on the private sector; tax, labor market, and financial reforms; and trade liberalization.[6] Conditional upon such efforts, multilateral development banks will increase their net lending modestly ($9 billion over three years), and private banks will lend an additional $20 billion over the same period. The plan differs in two ways from the policies put in place in 1982. One is the greater emphasis upon fundamental, structural change in developing countries and a prescription of growth, rather than adjustment, strategy. The other is the direct involvement of the U.S. government, rather than the IMF, in inducing greater finance.

The package is a clear recognition that the debt problem is no mere matter of a temporary shortage of liquidity, with rapid restoration of voluntary private finance. It also makes a tentative step in the direction of greater responsibility by industrial countries for the debt problem. More controversial is its attribution to developing country policies of a larger share of blame for the debt problem, with a correspondingly lesser share to external shocks. And doubts persist on whether the finance proposed is, in fact, adequate.

5. Prospects for New Capital Flows

The current account deficits of developing countries have sharply diminished in recent years.[7] The reduction is more a matter of supply than demand: the means to finance them is no longer available. Projections by the IMF and the World Bank have progressively reduced feasible future deficits, not because they imply excessive increases in debt, but because there is no likelihood of financing them. The residual variables in such calculations become the rate of growth of imports and of developing country output. Recent calculations, starting from minimal growth targets, suggest that countries could absorb $20 billion–$25 billion of funds; this is about double the targets under the Baker Plan.

Limited finance and poor performance by developing countries threaten to stretch into the 1990s. It is the logical aftermath of the disruption of capital flows stemming from the debt crises. This emerging medium-term problem is irrelevant for those who continue to characterize the present danger as a short-term liquidity shortfall. According to them, modest additional finance will suffice to encourage developing countries to undertake the necessary internal and external adjustment. Declining debt-export ratios will restore creditworthiness, and voluntary lending will resume on a sounder basis than before. The burden of responsibility is on the developing countries to demonstrate their capacity to reform and manage their economies more effectively. Even the Baker Plan's calculations of needed resources rest on immediate balance of payments needs, not on growth targets.

Such an optimistic conclusion rests on a series of interlinked assumptions. The first is that the OECD motor will support the export expansion needed by developing countries to maintain improved external accounts. The second is that the selective additional lending will be forthcoming in response to improved indexes of creditworthiness once banks have improved their capital-loan ratios. The third is that continuing trade surpluses and negative resource flows do not create economic impediments to the growth of output or set up internal political opposition.

Despite an accumulating array of statistical evidence on the responsiveness of developing countries' export volume and terms of trade to industrial countries' economic performance, the only certain conclusion seems to be that the results vary widely, depending on the country and the time period. The engine of OECD growth is not unfailingly reliable, nor is it immune to cyclical swings. At the heart of the favorable projections is a constant external impulse, permitting a large cumulative gain. The results do not bear out a benign prognosis. A 10 percent recovery in the income of industrial countries since 1982 has translated into only an 11 percent increase in the value of exports of debtor countries. This figure does not take into account the impact of possible protectionist impulses in the industrial world.

Equally questionable is the effect of balance of payments improvement on access to new finance. One cannot simply take the 1970s as a standard against which to measure the likely future commitments of commercial banks. That period was an aberration because it was fueled by the rapid expansion of Euromarket deposits and by unduly favorable expectations. Banks then did not contemplate providing large amounts of funds to finance the current account deficits of developing countries into an indefinite future. They are even less likely to do so now. Recent history has been chastening. Banks, as well as debtor countries, have been reminded of their limitations as development institutions. To presume or even propose that voluntary bank lending of significant magnitude will resume is imprudent. On the supply side, it goes against the record of the past, when lenders typically failed to return to the international market for a long time after a crisis, and it goes against the ongoing transformation of financial markets.

The banking industry is undergoing profound change. Syndicated loans have fallen into disfavor as banks have preferred roles as intermediaries in the issuance of securities and other marketable papers.

Financial instruments have multiplied, sharing in common a limited bank balance sheet exposure. Banks have taken their profits in the form of commissions and fees rather than in interest income. This "securitization" internationally has gone hand in hand with financial deregulation in domestic markets and extension of banks into new activities. Both have gone against resumption of high levels of lending to developing countries on a traditional basis.

By way of confirmation, note that the improved capital-loan ratios of U.S. banks in recent years have not prompted a new supply of lending. Similarly, the larger loan-loss reserves of the European banks have not elicited any willingness to make large, new loan commitments. On the contrary, despite reductions in interest rates that are favorable to creditworthiness, credit flows even to nonproblem debtor nations have slowed. This trend corresponds with the view of many bankers who foresee little likelihood of even a modest recuperation in voluntary lending.

Increased bank finance, moreover, would not automatically relieve the plight of the problem debtors. Projections by the World Bank and the IMF assume resumption of flows, at least to maintain the real value of outstanding credit. Virtually all of the loans, however, go to finance balance of payments deficits of the Asian countries. The large low-income countries in that region have been growing much more rapidly in recent years, with little private debt. The small, open economies have also sustained relatively high export growth and hence are also deemed creditworthy. Finance remains constrained for the large debtors who need it most; their current accounts deficits do not increase.

The right policy objective is to keep banks engaged in the short term through involuntary lending to permit a gradual transition to other sources of finance in the longer term. One cannot have a sudden change in the volume of current capital flows while maintaining the integrity of the stock of past obligations—at least not so long as interest payments remain a large debit item. Such was the logic of involuntary lending in the first instance. More explicit and coordinated governmental inter-

vention, rather than IMF suasion, may be necessary to sustain capital flows as banks tire. Involuntary lending is not a one-time or immediate expediency but a process that is likely to continue for several years.

Banks, at the same time, should also be encouraged to expand short-term lending to meet the legitimate needs of expanding trade. A more aggressive export guaranty authority would undoubtedly help. Developing countries will also have to borrow to meet the bulk of their growing reserve needs in the future. That is another secure and appropriate application of bank loanable funds. Both uses offer a basis for limited expansion of voluntary credit but not an expansion large enough to meet financing requirements.

Bank willingness to lend again to developing countries is partially inhibited by the proven illiquidity of earlier commitments. Recently, a limited secondary market in loans for developing countries has begun to develop. It has depended upon swaps to suit the different asset preferences of individual banks, as well as sales at discount to buyers able to convert the debt at face value in domestic currency. Such transactions promise gradually to reduce the burden of past indebtedness as markdowns are passed along and foreign obligations are converted into domestic equity. Reduction of this burden will improve the real prospects for economic recovery in debtor countries but is unlikely to be reflected in near-term enhancement of creditworthiness. There will also have to be some controlled pace at which assets are marked down to prevent immediate effects on the balance sheets of banks. Such market responses go in the right direction of allocating losses from past mistakes without continuing penalty. Benefits of these responses, however, will be reflected more in reduced outflows from developing countries than in new inflows to them.

Foreign direct investment will not take up much of the shortfall in finance for two reasons. The first is quantitative. Current and past levels of direct investment are small relative to needs. A discrete leap in new foreign commitments would mean much larger participation in the economies of developing countries than most countries and investors would find comfortable or profitable. The second reason is that such flows are highly sensitive to domestic economic performance. They are procyclical rather that countercyclical. Limited foreign investment is now reinforcing the effect of inadequate bank lending rather than off-setting it. Altering legislation in developing countries can help in conditioning a larger upturn, but it is unlikely to advance a recovery.

Equity participation also frequently appears in the guise of proposals for wide-ranging privatizations that would exchange loans in state enterprises for private shares. Apart from internal political resistance, a central problem with resolving the debt burden in this fashion—or, as some have even suggested, exchanging debt for direct claims in oil or

other natural resources—is the price at which the transaction occurs. If the enterprises are profitable and well run, there is little reason to spin them off except at a premium to reflect their quasi-monopoly advantages in developing economies. If they are not profitable, then buyers will want the state to bear the full loss while securing important advantages and converting depreciated loans at par value and above. In the final analysis, the virtues of privatization would depend on their own merit and would not be predetermined solely by the convenience of easing the burden of past debt.

Another potential source of finance receiving much attention in the past year is the repatriation of previous capital flight. Indirect evidence suggests that public borrowing in some developing countries may have been substantially diverted into private assets held abroad. The estimates derive principally from comparison of outstanding debt with cumulative balance of payments deficits and secondarily from information on the size of private deposits held abroad by nationals of developing countries. Among the largest disparities are those for Argentina, Mexico, the Philippines, and Venezuela. Total sums exceed $100 billion.

This capital flight is increasingly held up as a measure of lack of private confidence and allows the commercial banks to rationalize their unwillingness to make new loan commitments. It is not new, of course; much of the outflow occurred during the period of extravagant lending after the second oil shock at interest rates that were incompatible with productive application and occurred frequently from oil-exporting economies that had just realized windfall benefits. Banks sometimes shortened their maturities as a measure of their concern, but they continued to lend. Local citizens did even better in assessing the high degree of uncertainty and likely negative outcome.

This stock of external resources is relevant to the financing problem but more for its longer-term potential than for its short-term promise. This stock of capital, by definition, is owned by those who are either risk averse or pessimistic or both. It will take a long period of good economic and political performance before repatriation of capital from abroad will find domestic appeal. High domestic rates of interest and promising beginnings will not do. Schemes that create new dollar assets abroad to attract fleeing capital run the risk of rewarding, and hence motivating, future flight. One must be careful, moreover, with generous amnesty schemes in the midst of domestic austerity.

The long-term good that can come from these resources is that further asset diversification looks less attractive. At the margin, particularly with some prospect of durable recovery, domestic assets should compete more effectively and keep savings in the country. On occasion, some of the capital held abroad may be brought back to finance promis-

ing investment projects. If domestic policy proves sound, past capital flight can be a modest source of finance, but like foreign investment it cannot be counted on to initiate economic recovery.

That is the heart of the matter. In the absence of minimal guaranteed finance, realized economic performance is likely to fall short of what is necessary to attract supplementary sources of capital inflow, whether conventional or in the form of the variety of new instruments explored by Lessard and Williamson.[8] Efficient adjustment will not take place with external finance tightly constrained. The future will be sacrificed to immediate needs to satisfy the balance of payments. Poor performance will beget lack of creditworthiness and continued inadequate finance. The self-fulfilling prophecy yields a low-growth trap.

To close the financing gap requires three complementary actions. The first is an increase in official flows to restore an appropriate public-private balance in development finance that was discarded in the 1970s. The second is a reduction in the disproportion between outflows to service private sector debt and voluntary inflows. The third is a domestic development strategy that emphasizes not only export growth but also efficient import substitution as a means of conserving foreign exchange.

After seeing rapid growth in the 1970s, net official lending has stagnated and has even declined in the 1980s. Public resources have played no large part in adjustment to the second oil shock except after the fact through injections of liquidity in the conjunction with stabilization. The IMF, not the World Bank, has been at center stage. Even so, multilateral development institutions are rapidly using up their lending authority and will need new increases in capital in the future to sustain even present levels. Yet such levels must be substantially increased if there is to be adequate finance. Nowhere is this more apparent than in the Sub-Saharan case, in which payments to official lenders accompanied by slowed new commitments are producing a significant debt problem. The additional lending must be in the context of an articulated medium-term development strategy, rather than being project oriented, if it is to be fully effective. Virtually all informed opinion is of the same mind, but the problem is that the prospects for achievement of the political consensus for increases in official lending continue to be bleak.[9]

Various efforts have been made to increase the leverage of official lending by tying it more closely to private credits through cofinancing, sometimes through different maturities for private and official institutions and sometimes by extending guarantees. These efforts are welcome, but the scope of private participation remains quantitatively modest, on the order of about $4 billion as compared with a World Bank and IDA contribution of $6 billion. Although welcome, these arrangements do not much ease the concern about inadequate financial flows. Rather, the public contribution should be seen as complementary in a larger sense, whether or not it is directly associated with cofinancing of specific projects. More limited official lending will make other private flows much less probable and efficient. One important advantage of adequate public flows is the corresponding opportunity for policy discussion and consultation.

Even an expansion of official lending, which is far from assured, would have to be accompanied by other efforts to stanch the private cash outflow that is hampering the efforts of debtor countries to recover. Radical proposals to ameliorate the debt problem start here. They range from outright write-down of debt to capitalization of interest to be repaid in the future, a form of guaranteed relending that leaves the debt burden intact.

Enthusiasm for doing something waxes and wanes with each minicrisis and miniresolution. In the final analysis, the banks have limited incentive to take initiative as long as they continue to be paid and are able to avoid large new commitments of resources while doing so. The myopia is part of the failure of capital markets to clear away the mistakes of the past. It is the reason for public leadership. To some degree, the Baker Plan is a recognition of that vacuum. Although it is welcome, it needs amendment in three important respects.

First, the resources the Baker Plan proposes to make available to the fifteen debtor countries in greatest trouble are limited. They are simply not large enough, especially after the oil price fall in the beginning of the year, to meet financial needs for adjustment through growth. By conservative calculations, they are too small by a factor of two. Also, the plan does not place enough emphasis upon increases in public lending in the future and upon the continuing means for accomplishing these increases.

Second, the focus is upon a narrow balance of payments approach to finance. Calculations exclude the possibility that the high-debt countries, because of the diversion of domestic saving to interest payments, need external resources despite a temporary capacity to generate trade surpluses. By the criterion of balance of payments Brazil has no problem. But this is a short-term view. Brazil's trade surpluses are too large and are being achieved because finance is available.

Third, the Baker Plan starts from the assumption that the principal source of the debt problem is the inadequate macroeconomic policies of developing countries: the balance of payments deficits were caused by excessive public sector expansion and corresponding internal expenditure. As a result, the plan's conditionality threatens to be unnecessarily intrusive and contentious in insisting upon private market signals and a radically diminished public presence. Although there is broad agreement in developing countries on the need to move in this direction, many find objectionable the uniformity of the development strategy suggested. Experience in the past few years confirms that conditionality works best when it conforms to an internal diagnosis of economic problems rather than an external one. Correct policies require implementation if they are to be successful.

Moreover, the plan's focus on trade liberalization misses an essential substantive component of future policy. Even with projections of continuing export growth and lower interest rates, countries will have to reduce their import requirements progressively in the medium term for appropriate adjustment. More limited finance in the future than in the past requires more attention not only to domestic saving but also to efficient import substitution. In this way every projection shows that future debt growth stays within reasonable bounds. Export performance by itself cannot bear the burden of external equilibrium. Domestic policy therefore has a central role, but it must be a balanced one.

6. Policy Lessons

The difficulties of the past several years highlight three types of policy lessons. The first relates to the appropriate size of the debt; the second to its management; and the third to the need for development strategies that better integrate financial openness.

Debt capacity has been figured in different ways and has been measured by different indicators. Where all foundered was in the inability to take into account the large changes in interest rates and trade growth that were in store. These rendered almost all initial calculations overoptimistic. Consequently a first conclusion is that uncertainties play a large role in determining outcomes. Ordinary uncertainties are compounded by the reliance on bank loans. The structure of the capital market and the more variable external environment impose a margin of caution and conservatism in figuring the gains that derive from undertaking fixed obligations. Consequences are asymmetric. The costs of downside error and reductions in economic activity are likely to be greater than the upside benefits from better economic performance.

Calculations of debt capacity cannot be called irrelevant, however; rather, more attention must be paid to the possibility of more adverse scenarios when they are interpreted. These debt capacity magnitudes are conventionally figured with regard to two different but simultaneous needs that capital inflow satisfies. Borrowing increases saving to finance domestic investment and borrowing permits an excess of imports over exports. There is also a third need that is relevant when governments lack command over resources: public borrowing finances a public sector deficit. Debt capacity is determined by the ability to generate the return flow through debt service by continuing growth of saving, exports, and governmental receipts on the one side and the costs represented by the interest rate on the other. The higher the interest rate is, the greater the offset is against the real resource availability of given inflows. This fact creates a paradox: the higher the interest rate, the larger the debt-to-income, debt-to-export, or debt-to-public-revenues ratios must be to satisfy a needed transfer of resources while debt capacity, in the sense of comfortable coverage of outflows, declines. The appendix to this chapter explores some of these considerations in more detail.

Various rules—such as what current account deficit ratios or what debt service ratios should not be exceeded—are sensitive to particular environments. The higher rates of inflation of the 1970s, for example, meant that debt service ratios were given an upward shift for the same transfer of resources. Higher nominal interest rates were equivalent to paying large amounts of amortization to offset the erosion of principal by inflation. Had historical standards been applied, borrowing would have been excessively curtailed.

Continuing the availability of external capital is another crucial element. Perfectly elastic supplies of finance, as long as domestic applications yield increments to income that exceed the costs, imply that debt should continue to grow. In reality, costs do rise with greater exposure and set a more appropriate limit. But the dramatic reevaluation of developing countries' prospects by lenders made earlier levels of debt excessive. The consequences upon the debtor also enter. If there are limited penalties for default, then a more aggressive strategy is indicated; if default is impossible, and the costs are borne largely by the borrower, that is an additional argument for caution.

If the rules for appropriate debt must be approximate and conditional, those for debt management can be more precise. First, it is clear that many developing country debtors themselves knew too little about their total exposure. Private debt frequently went unrecorded. Even debt of public agencies was not always known. Interbank obligations were not counted as part of external indebtedness even when they became a source of balance of payments relief. Correspondingly, debt service commitments were inexact. It follows that better information systems are required and, to facilitate broader public discussion of appropriate policy, information needs to be more widely disseminated.

Second, to reduce the uncertainty inherent in exchange rate variability, borrowing in different currencies should correspond more closely to the flows of foreign exchange earnings. Such borrowing provides a direct hedge against the impact of exchange rate fluctuations. It cannot preclude the more complicated indirect effects that may show up in commodity prices and terms of trade from variations in the value of the dollar, but it can make debt service more stable.

Third, maturity mismatches should be reduced as much as possible. Short-term resources should not be used for projects whose return will not be realized for many years. Longer-term investments will have to be geared more closely to the availability of official lending, to cofinancing arrangements, and of course to domestic saving.

Fourth, interest rates for bank borrowing should be specified in terms of the bank cost of resources—that is, the LIBOR rate rather than the U.S. prime rate. Contracts specified in the latter terms became progressively more expensive as rates diverged in the early 1980s. As an indicator of the terms on which international bank credit is available, LIBOR is likely to be more reliable than a national lending rate that is itself no longer a benchmark for loan transactions.

Fifth, more information exchange among debtor countries is desirable, with regard not merely to terms of restructuring past debt but also to terms of future commitments. This knowledge will be especially useful the greater the potential reliance upon new and more individualized debt instruments.

There is a final lesson. An effective debt strategy is part of an overall development strategy. The developing countries that fared best in the successive shocks to the international economy were those with balanced rather than asymmetric integration and those that made a conscious allocation of external saving to productive projects. Large debts became a burden in Latin America in large measure because that region substituted financial openness for more adequate adjustment. Inflows of external resources resolved the balance of payments disequilibrium in lieu of more aggressive exchange rate policy and realignment of consumption and production.

More is involved than just the question of whether borrowing was done by the private or public sector. The belief, advocated by some in the 1970s, that the appropriate level of debt could not be exceeded so long as private lenders and borrowers were the actors was not upheld by experience. Private profit maximization did not lead to extra care by lenders; they correctly understood that, guaranteed or not, governments would have to stand behind the loans. Also, private borrowers were no better than public borrowers at calculating their correct exposure under the threat of failure. The calculus of the private sector was not more precise than that of the public sector.

Furthermore, the issue is simply not one of the correct ordering of liberalization, with free capital flows awaiting reduced protectionism against imports. The lesson has been learned that it is dangerous to ignore the adverse impact on the current account of allowing the capital account to respond to immediate market signals. The international capital market is highly mobile but imperfect. It is not clear that developing countries, even after focusing on goods markets, will ever want to follow a completely open financial strategy. A major task in the next decade is to increase reliance on national saving. Doing so will mean giving first priority to making internal capital markets work better; complete openness may serve as a hindrance in capturing domestic resources.

The key requirement for most developing countries is better balance. More debt is needed to avoid the counterproductive restriction on imports that is now characteristic of many debtors. Access to finance and liberalization must go together. More exports are also needed so that the burden of sustaining imports does not fall exclusively upon finance. More import substitution is needed for the same reason and as a logical and efficient part of a resumed growth of industrial and agricultural production. Such policies would exploit the opportunities of the international economy rather than reap the consequences of vulnerability.

In the aftermath of the trying experience of the past several years, these lessons seem to have been learned, but to put them into practice will require developing countries to do more than demonstrate their own commitment. Whether the debt problem of the 1980s turns out to be a watershed for more productive development in the 1990s or a decisive impulse toward a less productive, inward-oriented rejection of international integration depends also upon the lessons learned by the industrial countries.

Appendix. Debt Dynamics

The basic equations determining the rate of change of debt over time relate it to the gap it finances:

(9-1) $D = M - X + iD$ Foreign exchange gap

(9-2) $D = I - S + iD$ Savings gap

(9-3) $D = G - T + iD$ Public sector gap

In all cases, the change in debt is inertially determined by the interest rate plus the real resource gap.

Debt-to-export, debt-to-product, and debt-to-tax ratios converge to limits, in accordance with a constant proportional financing gap, provided that the interest rate is less than the export growth rate, the growth of income, and the growth of government revenue. Initial growth rates of the debt decelerate as limiting ratios are approached.

These limits are:

(9-1a)
$$\text{LIM}_{t\to\infty}\ \frac{D}{X}\ =\ \frac{\alpha}{r_x - i};$$

where α is the ratio of the gap to exports

(9-2a)
$$\text{LIM}_{t\to\infty}\ \frac{D}{X}\ =\ \frac{\beta}{r_y - i};$$

where β is the ratio of the gap to income

(9-3a)
$$\text{LIM}_{t\to\infty}\ \frac{D}{X}\ =\ \frac{\gamma}{r_t - i};$$

where γ is the ratio of the gap to taxes

Even if the rates of growth of activity are not greater than the interest rate, a stable relationship may hold. But then the mathematical sign of the gap must change: surpluses must be produced to finance the excess interest requirements from past due debt. That, of course, is exactly what has been happening in the case of many debtors. The issue is whether such an arrangement is possible or desirable, permanently or even for a long period.

Note that creditworthiness is inversely related to the interest rate because higher interest rates imply that larger shares of earnings must be allocated to debt service. This reduces the coverage of interest payments. Higher interest rates also, of course, for a given growth rate of debt trigger a reduced degree of real finance, with possible indirect consequences on economic performance.

Selected Bibliography

Cline, William R. *International Debt: Systemic Risk and Policy Response.* Cambridge, Mass.: MIT Press, 1984.

Dornbusch, Rudiger. "Policy and Performance Links between LDC Debtors and Industrial Nations." In William C. Brainard and George L. Perry, eds., *Brookings Papers on Economic Activity 2.* Washington, D.C.: Brookings Institution, 1985.

Dornbusch, Rudiger, and Stanley Fischer. "The World Debt Problem: Origins and Prospects." *Journal of Development Planning,* no. 16 (1985), pp. 57–82.

Fishlow, Albert. "The Debt Crisis: Round Two Ahead?" In Richard Feinberg and Valerian Kallab, eds., *Adjustment Crisis in the Third World.* Washington, D.C.: Overseas Development Council, 1984.

_____ . "The Debt Crisis: A Longer Perspective." *Journal of Development Planning.* no. 16 (1985), pp. 83–104.

_____ . "Lessons from the Past: Capital Markets during the Nineteenth Century and the Interwar Period." *International Organization,* vol. 39, no. 3, (Summer 1985), pp. 383–439.

Kindleberger, Charles P. *Manias, Panics, and Crashes.* New York: Basic Books, 1978.

Lessard, Donald, and John Williamson. *Financial Intermediation beyond the Debt Crisis.* Washington, D.C.: Institute for International Economics 1985.

McDonald, Donough C. "Debt Capacity and Developing Country Borrowing: A Survey of the Literature." *International Monetary Fund Staff Papers,* vol. 29, no. 4 (December 1982), pp. 603–46.

Sachs, Jeffrey. *Theoretical Issues in International Borrowing.* National Bureau of Economic Research Working Paper 1189. Cambridge, Mass., August 1983.

Smith, Gordon W., and John T. Cuddington, eds. *International Debt and the Developing Countries.* Washington, D.C.: World Bank, 1985.

Taylor, Lance. "The Theory and Practice of Developing Country Debt: An Informal Guide for the Perplexed." *Journal of Development Planning,* no. 16 (1985), pp. 195–228.

Wionczek, Miguel, ed. *Politics and Economics of External Debt Crisis: The Latin American Experience.* Boulder, Colo.: Westview Press, 1985.

Notes

1. For this section, I have drawn extensively on my article "Lessons from the Past: Capital Markets during the Nineteenth Century and the Interwar Period," *International Organization,* vol. 39, no. 3 (Summer 1985), pp. 383–439.

2. For a recent useful discussion, see Jeffrey Sachs, *Theoretical Issues in International Borrowing,* National Bureau of Economic Research Discussion Paper 1189 (Cambridge, Mass., August 1983).

3. Charles Kindleberger has especially emphasized the cyclical quality of capital markets. See *Manias, Panics, and Crashes* (New York: Basic Books, 1978).

4. Bahram Nowzad and Richard C. Williams, eds., *External Indebtedness of Developing Countries,* Occasional Paper no. 3 (Washington, D.C.: International Monetary Fund, 1981), p. 11.

5. These numerical estimates come from my "The Debt Crisis: Round Two Ahead?" in Richard Feinberg and Valerian Kallab, eds., *Adjustment Crisis in the Third World* (Washington, D.C.: Overseas Development Council, 1984).

6. This description follows Secretary Baker's initial presentation in Seoul.

7. This section condenses a much more detailed treatment in my "Capital Requirements for Developing Countries in the Next Decade," *Journal of Development Planning,* no. 17 (forthcoming).

8. Donald Lessard and John Williamson, *Financial Intermediation beyond the Debt Crisis* (Washington, D.C.: Institute for International Economics, 1985).

9. In more receptive times, this would be an opportune moment, with interest rates being low, to establish an interest rate compensatory fund at the IMF analogous to that for export prices. It would impart a stabilizing presence in the event of an unanticipated reversal in the recent trend. A new oil facility would also be indicated but this time financed by industrial country consumers for the benefit of debtor oil exporters. The drop in price is temporary and should be cushioned by finance. We are now erring in assigning too low a present value to the oil reserves of debtor nations.

10

Opening Up: Liberalization with Stabilization

Michael Bruno

A STYLIZED ECONOMY at the highly protected stage would have quantitative restrictions or would face high tariffs on its imports. It would have exchange controls on capital flows. Its domestic financial markets would be segmented and "repressed" (to use the terminology of McKinnon 1973), with credit being rationed by a primitive, government-dominated banking system and with a highly risky curb market supplying funds at excessively high interest rates. Its labor market might be segmented or "dualistic," with an urban, relatively organized, industrial labor force (whose union structure, practices, and rigidities would often resemble those of industrial economies) coexisting with a large, primarily informal rural work force that is more flexible.

The extent of control or inflexibility in different markets of course differs among countries, but it helps to regard a very high initial degree of inflexibility and "closedness" as the starting point for reform. Krueger (1978) and Bhagwati (1978) have classified the various stages of reform as an economy moves from a closely protected system to one that is substantially open to free trade in goods and financial flows.[1] How would one stylize the final target stage of "openness" (Phase IV or V in the Bhagwati-Krueger study)? Few observers would argue against the complete removal of restrictions on the free flow of goods and services. An efficiently functioning domestic financial market would also be an essential feature of a "liberalized" economy. One should bear in mind, however, that even industrial countries control the flows of foreign capital to some extent. And some imperfections in the labor market are quite common in many advanced countries.

The objective of this chapter is not to evaluate the pros and cons of a particular target choice of a liberalized economy but rather to focus on the difficulties that arise in the process of transition. One particular problem that has afflicted many attempts at reform in the past relates to the fact that the reform, in most cases, starts when the economy is in serious macroeconomic disequilibrium—that is to say, when it faces severe foreign exchange shortages and high inflation as a result of devaluations and large government deficits. Thus reform packages often contain both a long-term market liberalization strategy to promote more efficient resource allocation and short-run stabilization policies to reduce inflation and balance of payments difficulties. Reform packages, which seem to be successful for a time, may collapse if the macroeconomic policy environment is inconsistent, and the economy would then cycle back to an earlier, less liberalized phase.

A closely related problem relates to the general equilibrium (or disequilibrium) nature of economic interdependence and the fact that speeds of adjustment in various markets differ. For this reason in particular the transition strategy from a prereform regime to a postreform open economy is more important than the choice of the end product. Two points need to be made. First, a very rapid trade liberalization process in the product market may be preferable to a gradual process for reasons of credibility and long-term efficiency. The costs of labor unemployment in the transition period, however, could be sizable. Such costs were less of a problem in Chile during the authoritarian period in the 1970s but were one of the reasons for the choice of a gradualist (and yet very successful) tariff reform in Israel in the 1960s and 1970s. Second, it is unwise to ignore the fact that the speed of adjustment in the financial markets (and thus the response of the nominal exchange rate to capital flows in a financially opened-up economy) may be very fast, sometimes instantaneous, whereas the response of exports and import substitutes to changes in the real exchange rate (if the trade account is opened up) may be sluggish.[2]

1. Sequence of Liberalization Measures

The removal of quantitative restrictions on imports, the unification of import tariffs and export subsidies, and the gradual or speedy elimination of tariffs constitute the opening up of the "real" side of the economy. The opening up raises the efficiency with which labor and physical capital are allocated among productive sectors.

In the process of trade liberalization, increasing importance is attached to the real cost of foreign exchange or the real exchange rate. The real exchange rate is measured as the nominal exchange rate (pesos or liras per dollar) divided by some measure of the domestic costs (for example, wages) or prices (for example, consumer prices), with some correction for world inflation. The key relative price determines the relative profitability and the allocation of production and investment between tradable and nontradable goods. Other things being equal, a real depreciation will eventually draw more resources into the production of exports and import substitutes, which will improve the current account of the balance of payments. A real appreciation of the exchange rate will make exports less profitable and imports more profitable than domestic production, thus increasing the deficit on current account. An increased surplus on the capital account will be required to finance this deficit.

If private capital flows are prohibited or are nonexistent, it may be advantageous for the government to borrow abroad to finance a large deficit in the early stages of industrialization. The funds collected could be used to develop the export industry, provided the internal rate of return in the production of exports exceeds the marginal cost of foreign borrowing. The government may pay back these loans as the economy develops. During the growth process, the real exchange rate will also need to grow. It should do so at a rate that equals the difference between the internal and external real rate of return to capital.[3] This statement must be modified when technical progress is made in exports or import substitution, or when a country's export prices in world markets are high, because then growth in the real exchange rate may be unnecessary.[4] Even in these cases, however, the real exchange rate will need to be maintained at a certain level over time.

During the 1950s and 1960s, most developing countries pegged their currencies to those of other countries and sometimes maintained crawling exchange rates together with exchange controls. There was not much of a private capital market in the world anyway, and one could say that countries opened up on the real side long before it became relevant to open up the economy for capital flows. Successful trade liberalization with export-led growth was carried out by Korea, Taiwan, Singapore, Hong Kong, and Israel.

In the 1970s, the recycling of petrodollars for the first time made possible financial opening up along with, or even before, the real opening up of trade flows. This recycling sent conflicting signals on the real exchange rate, especially in some Latin American countries.

Problems arise with the promotion of production and investment in tradable goods when short-term market prices do not give the "correct" long-run allocation signals to producers or consumers. Consider, for instance, a country that permits short-term capital inflows. The real interest rates for short- and medium-term loans may be low or even negative in the world capital market. (Such indeed was the case during much of the 1970s.) Countries would thus have an incentive to borrow for investment in the production of goods at levels of profitability that are lower than the long-run real interest rates at which the loans would eventually have to be repaid.

Such an imbalance in interest rates can be further aggravated if domestic stabilization policy, with its associated restrictive monetary policy, causes the real marginal cost of domestic credit to rise considerably above the long-run world interest rate. This gap between the foreign and domestic interest rates will—in the absence of intervention (such as a tax on capital imports) and under free capital mobility—cause substantial capital inflows and will result in a surplus in the capital account. The surplus in the capital account, of course, will eventually be matched by a deficit in the current account along with a real appreciation of the domestic currency. This deficit will, in turn, depress exports and profits in tradable goods production and will encourage the importation of a variety of temporarily cheapened goods, particularly consumer goods or capital goods used in the production of nontradable home goods.

The mechanism for the real appreciation of the domestic currency will depend on the nature of the exchange rate regime. Under a pegged nominal exchange rate, domestic monetary expansion (as a result of the rise in exchange reserves) will raise prices and will erode the real value of the currency. Under floating rates, a nominal appreciation is likely and would not be a problem if the capital inflow and the underlying reduction in world interest rates were permanent. Because they are bound to be temporary, however, the situation will sooner or later be reversed (as it has been in the early 1980s for many of the countries).

The different speed with which asset markets and product (as well as factor) markets adjust therefore becomes crucial. Financial assets may be switched from domestic to foreign holdings very quickly if signals change. (A telephone conversation to a financial agent may be all that is needed.) It will take years, however, to switch resources into an export industry (or into a domestic industry producing an imported consumable). Uncontrolled opening up of financial markets before or together with the real opening up of the economy has generally ended in failure, has created a foreign exchange crisis, has increased unemployment, and has often generated runaway inflation.

Why would a country want to adopt financial liberalization before a full liberalization of the trade account has taken place? First, in contrast to the situation in which there is opening up of the real product side, governments face less opposition in the financial field from powerful vested interests whose rents will be cut following exposure to foreign competition. Second, the availability of additional foreign funds eases the investment-financial problem and enables governments to keep domestic interest rates high while some domestic sectors avail themselves of seemingly cheap foreign finance. Third, in many cases governments use the funds to increase their own expenditure without having to resort to taxes and without having to run the printing press.

The destabilizing effect of capital flows that may accompany the opening up of the financial market need not be in one direction. If the capital account is opened when the domestic capital market is still repressed, and if interest rates are kept at artificially low levels, massive capital outflows may take place. Such outflows may also occur if the economy is opened up and inflation and foreign exchange difficulties increase in the wake of a large government deficit, signifying a loss of confidence in the government's ability to control the situation, as happened in Argentina in 1978–82 and in Israel in 1984–85.

Some attempts at far-reaching reform in the 1970s took place in Latin America.[5] Argentina, Chile, and Uruguay originally followed protectionist development strategies with a high degree of government intervention in almost all fields of economic activity. By the mid-1970s, they had liberalized external trade, had permitted capital to flow freely, and had removed restraints over financial markets. Domestic commodity markets were also decontrolled; only labor markets were partly liberalized.

The timing and sequencing of these liberalization measures differed from country to country. Argentina and Uruguay first opened up financially and only later began to reduce tariffs. Chile liberalized trade first and only then permitted capital to flow freely. All three countries moved toward liberalization after periods of severe inflation and high fiscal and foreign exchange deficits.

In its initial stages, stabilization and liberalization achieved considerable success though sometimes at great adjustment cost (for example, in Chile). The conventional contractionary monetary and fiscal policies that were implemented reduced internal imbalances and inflation but also resulted in a sharp drop in real wages, employment, or both (in Chile and Uruguay, for instance). During the second phase, an exchange-rate-based antiinflation policy was initiated by a planned slowdown in the rate of nominal devaluation. A central feature of the measure was a substantial real appreciation of the exchange rate following massive capital inflows in response to sustained interest rate differentials. The result was a severe crisis in the export sector. This phenomenon has become known as the "Southern Cone syndrome," though several other countries, including Mexico and Israel, had similar experiences during the 1970s. By the 1980s, Argentina, Chile, and Uruguay were in a severe foreign exchange crisis and a deep recession (see table 10-1).

The reasons for failure varied. In Argentina and Uruguay, the wrong order of liberalization was partly to blame. Trade liberalization should have preceded capital flows; the current account should have been kept ahead of the capital account. An economy that liberalizes its foreign trade should avoid unnecessary and destabilizing movements of short-term capital.

Even in Chile, where the sequencing of reforms was in the "right" order, the sudden increase in capital flows during 1979–81 was a major

Table 10-1. Macroeconomic Performance in the Southern Cone, 1965–83
(percent)

Item	Import substitution 1965-73	Prereform crisis 1973-75	Phase 1 1976-78	Reforms Phase 1	Reforms Phase 2 1978-80	Postreform recession 1981-83
			Argentina			
Average annual growth rate						
Gross domestic product	4.2	2.9	0.8	—	3.7	−3.0
Expenditure	4.2	3.3	−1.6	—	8.6	−6.1
Gross fixed investment	6.6	0.1	4.9	—	4.0	−15.1
Consumer price index	23.5	77.6	245.6	—	128.3	188.5
Average						
Fiscal deficit/GDP	3.0	12.0	7.7	—	7.9	17.8
Unemployment rate	5.7	2.4	3.4	—	2.2	4.7
Real wage index (1976 = 100)	125	154	100	—	118	111

Chile

	1965-70	1971-73	1974-76	1977-78	1979-81	1982-83
Average annual growth rate						
Gross domestic product	4.3	0.5	3.1	9.0	7.3	−7.8
Expenditure	5.1	1.3	−8.2	11.9	10.2	−14.4
Gross fixed investment	5.3	−9.8	−7.8	16.7	17.8	−26.6
Consumer price index	23.3	149.7	358.0	79.0	30.2	11.7
Average						
Fiscal deficit/GDP	2.1	16.1	5.1	1.3	−2.1	3.1
Unemployment rate	6.0	4.6	14.2	13.6	12.2	22.2
Real wage index (1969 = 100)	98	98	69	82	100	82

Uruguay

	1965-70	1971-73	1974-76	1977-78	1979-81	1982-83
Average annual growth rate						
Gross domestic product	1.9	−0.4	4.3	3.2	4.7	−7.2
Expenditure	2.9	−0.2	1.9	3.6	5.6	−11.2
Gross fixed investment	7.3	−10.8	25.0	10.5	6.9	−24.8
Consumer price index	49.8	62.7	69.2	51.3	54.0	33.3
Average						
Fiscal deficit/GDP	1.9	3.2	3.8	1.9	0.0	6.4
Unemployment rate	8.2	8.1	9.7	12.4	8.4	13.7
Real wage index (1968 = 100)	104	102	86	70	64	54

Source: Corbo, de Melo, and Tybout (1986), table 1.

cause of the subsequent crisis. Harberger (1982) attributed the peso's real appreciation of up to 25 percent to the increase in capital flows during this period. A wrong wage policy—real wages rose even when inflation slowed because wages were indexed to past inflation—accentuated the crisis. Chile's experience highlights the need to consider the interdependence of markets in the transition process.

2. Liberalization of Trade

In the early stages, trade liberalization usually involves the removal of quantitative restrictions and their substitution by tariffs of uneven rates across sectors. In the second stage and sometimes in the third, gradual (or quick) unification of effective rates of protection takes place across sectors. The long-run benefits of such processes lie in the efficiency gains derived on the production side (there is an overall increase in the foreign exchange revenue earned in export industries, or saved in import substitutes, per unit of labor and capital) and on the consumption side (the same basket of products can be obtained at lower prices).

The liberalization process involves two kinds of costs to the economy. One is distributional. Laborers, managers, and investors in the protected industry stand to lose, at least temporarily, from the removal of a protective wall in a sector in which they have a vested interest. These groups may oppose the liberalization process through the political system. Unemployment of labor in particular is socially undesirable. The other class of problems has to do with the balance of payments. Other things being equal, there will be a rise in imports that will not immediately be matched by a rise in exports (even if their relative remuneration rises in the process). In the absence of free private capital inflow (which, I have argued, could be undesirable for other reasons), controlled external assistance would be of great help.

The more rapid the liberalization process, the less flexibility there is in factor mobility between sectors; the less assistance from abroad, the more costly (or even prohibitive) the reform can be. In contrast, the more protracted and prolonged the reform process, the more danger there is that the reform will not be credible, that the "right" investment and employment decisions will not be made, and that the reform will gradually peter out.

The choice of adjustment speed will depend on the aversion that countries have to high temporary unemployment. In Chile, the problem of credibility did not arise because the drastic liberalization program was carried out very rapidly. The efficiency gains were very high, but so were the unemployment costs, especially in industry. In Israel, fear of unemployment slowed the pace of successful liberalization programs over a period of twenty years.

One way of overcoming the credibility problem (in countries such as Israel) is to preannounce the whole program of tariff removal. Such preannouncement of a tariff-reduction schedule helps minimize uncertainty. Furthermore, gradualism helps to minimize the unemployment consequences by indicating where displaced labor can profitably be employed.

The longer the time allowed for adjustment, the easier it is to smooth the process of transition to a new structure of industrial activity. The transition could also be smoothed by providing for some compensation to alleviate the distributional consequences of a rapid shift. Before the reforms can be credible, the "right" signals will need to be sent on the profitability of capital. Even though producers in the protected industry that is subject to tariff removal expect an eventual policy reversal because of balance of payments or political pressures, investment for a time will continue to take place in the "wrong" industries. (Such was the case in Argentina during the 1970s; see Rodriguez 1983). Factor adjustment will thus be slow and may also be in the wrong direction. When there is free capital inflow, the result may be overborrowing, especially when borrowers expect to be bailed out by the government once the times turn bad.

Liberalization needs to be accompanied by appropriate macroeconomic policies that take into account both the internal and external imbalance in economy during the transition. If we assume that the reform starts from a position of balance of payments equilibrium, import liberalization in itself will increase the total import bill. If adjustment assistance from abroad is not forthcoming or is insufficient to tide the country over the external imbalance, macroeconomic policy must be geared to redress the balance through suitable instruments. These could involve a fiscal tightening (which might be needed anyway to compensate for the loss of tariff revenue because of a second-stage tariff unification), combined with exchange rate devaluation to promote exports, and measures to keep domestic wages and prices from reversing the real devaluation. In principle, when there is exchange control, a devaluation could also be replaced by a uniform tariff on imports and a subsidy on exports. If exports alone are to be promoted (on the assumption that there is a built-in antiexport bias), a subsidy on exports would have to be based on value added. If the domestic capital market is segmented (or "repressed"), the proexport bias can also be supported by investment grants and subsidized credit.

Two country examples are given below. One is the very drastic and seemingly successful, though costly in terms of unemployment, trade liberalization policy pursued by Chile. The other is the gradualist, sometimes erratic, yet employment-sensitive reform carried out by Israel.

Chile

Reform of the commodity market usually calls for a deregulation of domestic prices and a reduction of tariff and nontariff barriers to trade. Chile introduced a far-reaching commodity market reform in both of these areas during 1973–79.[6] In the early stages, prices were deregulated and subsidies eliminated in the domestic market. More than 500 enterprises were privatized. The multiple-exchange-rate system was unified, beginning with a large devaluation. All nontariff restrictions were lifted, and the tariff structure was unified in a relatively short time. During 1974–79, the average tariff was brought down from 90 percent to a uniform 10 percent. The authorities had to contend with an open inflation of 1,000 percent after the price liberalization. They responded by sharply reducing the large government deficit, through a drastic cut in public expenditures and a substantial tax reform, and by selling public enterprises.

Good copper prices in 1973 and a rollover of outstanding debt service for 1973–74 eased the adjustment to the oil shock. The subsequent plummenting of copper prices forced a large devaluation and a severe austerity program in 1975. Here, then, is a clear example of simultaneous liberalization and stabilization by means of devaluation.

The government deficit was virtually eliminated by 1977, and inflation was gradually brought down to below 10 percent by 1981, but only temporarily (see table 10-1). The GDP growth rate showed enormous fluctuations, first falling steeply in per capita terms during 1973–75, then rising very substantially during 1976–80 (more than regaining the previous drop) before falling again as a result of recession in 1981–82. The social cost of a steep rise in unemployment and a sharp change in income distribution away from wage income was high, however. Open unemployment (excluding the Minimum Employment Program), which had never dropped below 10 percent, rose dramatically to more than 20 percent by 1982. The unemployment may be traced to a number of causes, including the negative effect of the stabilization program on the demand for labor, the elimination of 100,000 jobs in the public sector, and the trade liberalization that generated a major readjustment in the manufacturing sector. Despite the persistence of high unemployment, real wages and salaries increased during 1976–80; by 1981 they had surpassed the 1970 levels.

An increase in minimum wages and backward wage indexation during the period of disinflation accounted in part for the subsequent worsening of the employment situation and the loss of competitive power of Chile's industry during the last stage of the disinflation strategy. The eventual failure of the stabilization policy should be attributed not to the trade liberalization program as such but rather to the opening up of the capital account and to the adoption in 1978 of the exchange rate as the main tool for combating inflation.

Israel

Table 10-2 presents some salient macroeconomic data. Trade liberalization in Israel during 1952–77 underwent changing stresses, but there were no major reversals in policy.[7] A rigid system of controls gave way to a much more open market economy. Government intervention in foreign trade and other economic activities decreased. Even after twenty-five years, however, trade liberalization has not been completed. It is expected that all measures of protection will be removed only by the end of the 1980s. The liberalization has been gradual and has been undertaken in three phases. The first, in 1952, relied on the exchange rate; the second, in 1962, shifted the form of protection; and the third, starting in 1968, introduced preannounced unification of tariffs and removed the antiexport bias in trade policy.

With the establishment of the state in 1948 and the exclusion of Israel from the sterling area, the economy for the first time confronted a serious shortage of foreign currency. Foreign exchange control was introduced to attain a number of objectives. These included support for the government's policy of containing inflation despite accumulating demand pressures, preventing the import of luxuries at a time when low-income groups had to forgo necessities, and encouraging large-scale import substitution to achieve substantial self-sufficiency in a politically difficult environment.

As the disequilibrium of the system became pronounced, rationing became stringent, black markets spread rapidly, and production was hampered by shortages of raw materials. A major devaluation in February 1952 marked the first departure from previous policies. From then on, government policy began to move away from direct control and relied more on the price mechanism.

In 1962, the new economic policy was announced, and the export orientation of the economy became firmly established (even though an antiexport bias in terms of effective protection persisted). Most quantitative controls on imports were abolished and replaced by tariffs, which were gradually lowered. Foreign trade became more export oriented. The share of export production in total output increased. There was also a shift away from traditional exports (citrus in agriculture and textiles in manufacturing). A large part of the increase in industrial exports came from a small number of export enterprises. The export bias of the exchange rate policy combined with the export subsidy policy was supported by investment grants and subsidized loans and credits.

During 1952–77, the increasing balance of payments deficit was

Table 10-2. Selected Variables, Israel, 1960–86

Phase[a]	Number of quarters	Inflation (consumer price index)	GDP growth rate	Unemployment[b]	Current account deficit/GDP[c]	Real export price[d]
1. Normal growth, 60:1–65:1	20	7	9.6	3.6	20	9.3
2. Recession, 65:1–67:2	9	6	-1.5	10.4	15	-1.1
3. Recovery, 67:2–70:1	11	2	14.6	4.5	19	4.7
4. Boom, 70:1–73.3	14	14	9.1	2.6	22	2.2
5. War and oil shock, 73:3–77:2	15	36	2.6	3.6	31	-0.7
6. Traverse, 77:2–79:4	10	71	3.0	2.9	24	5.3
7. High inflation plateau, 79:4–83:3	15	123	1.6	4.2	20	-5.3
8. Runaway inflation, 83:3–85:2	8	382	1.3	6.6	16	8.2
9. Stabilization, 85:2–86:1	3	25	—	6.6	15	6.0

Note: The figures are annual percentage rates based on quarterly compounding.

a. The year is listed first, followed by the quarter. Thus "60:1" means the first quarter of the year 1960.

b. End-of-period unemployment rate as a percentage of labor force.

c. Total deficit (including defense imports) divided by GDP (this is a *level* ratio) times 100.

d. Rate of change of export prices, at effective exchange rate, deflated by consumer price index (in the last three periods the measure is the real effective exchange rate against a basket of five currencies as shown in figure 10-2).

Source: Bruno and Fischer (1984), table 1, updated.

financed only in part by unilateral transfers. These had to be supplemented by loans, which raised foreign debt and debt servicing to exceptionally high levels. Concern about a possible shortage of foreign exchange in an economy relying heavily on imports of raw materials and investment goods led the government to take measures to contain and eventually to reduce the balance of payments deficit. Three types of measures were taken:

- Restrictive fiscal and monetary policy to reduce the demand for imports of raw materials and investment goods, create capacity for the expansion of exports, and restrain domestic costs. These measures were implemented most forcefully in 1952–53, 1966–67, and 1974–77. They slowed down economic activity in these periods and increased unemployment, fortunately only temporarily (there was a peak of 12 percent in 1967, compared with an average of only 3–4 percent during the other periods). The objective was achieved, however: the measures did improve the balance of payments.
- Investment grants, loans, tax concessions, and protective tariff incentives to foster foreign exchange earnings or savings. Eligibility for these incentives was governed by the minimization of domestic resource cost per unit of net foreign exchange earned or saved.
- Systematic devaluations of the exchange rate every few years. When the devaluations were accompanied by highly restrictive fiscal and monetary measures (as in 1952 and 1971), they were quite successful. When restraining measures were lacking (as in 1962 and 1974), the real exchange rate went back to what it had been prior to the devaluation. The infrequent and fairly large changes in the official exchange rate were supplemented by continuous changes in export subsidies, import controls, and protective tariffs. The changes resulted in a fairly continuous crawling effective rate on major exports and import substitutes. At the same time, the effective exchange rate on noncompeting imports, services, and capital imports, whose supply was considered inelastic, was kept constant (that is, usually low relative to the inflation rate) between one major devaluation and the next. Between 1955 and 1962, the official rate was held constant (at 1.8 Israeli pounds, I£, per U.S. dollar) even though domestic prices rose by more than 50 percent. The result was a fairly complex system of multiple exchange rates even though the average real effective rate on exports and import substitutes was kept high to meet long-term balance of payments targets.

In 1962, the government undertook further reforms by abolishing the multiple-exchange-rate system and by devaluing the exchange rate from I£1.80 to I£3.00 per U.S. dollar in the official rate (though only from I£2.65 to I£3.00 per U.S. dollar in the effective rate on exports). Export subsidies were abolished, tariffs were lowered, and the remaining quantitative import controls were gradually replaced by tariffs. However, the massive influx of capital in the wake of a large devaluation (a natural concomitant of a fixed-exchange-rate system) increased the domestic money supply. The absence of a sufficiently strong restrictive monetary policy and the reluctance to abandon the formal fixed-exchange-rate system accelerated domestic inflation and made the reintroduction of multiple exchange rates unavoidable. The extent to which domestic production was protected can be gauged from an estimate of effective protection rates. In 1968, the effective protection was 85 percent for import substitutes, compared with 28 percent for exports, six years after the extensive program of import liberalization had begun.

In 1968, at a time of relative low unemployment and a relatively comfortable balance of payments situation, a small devaluation of 3–3.5 percent was combined with a 15-percent across-the-board cut in all tariffs. This measure was followed the next year by a preannounced tariff unification scheme for the period 1970–75 consisting of six annual cuts in tariff rates. By October 1973, when war broke out and an oil crisis began, a substantial part of the tariff reduction had been accomplished. The overall effective rate of protection had fallen from about 80 percent in 1968 to 42 percent in 1972. This process continued during 1972–77 at a somewhat slower pace; a proexport bias started to develop after 1973. In 1975, Israel moved to a crawling peg—pegging first to the U.S. dollar and later to a basket of currencies. But a variety of measures protected the production of import substitutes and promoted the production of export goods. By 1977 the relative protection rate on import substitutes stood at 18 percent, whereas that on exports remained at 35 percent.

The trade liberalization process in Israel was extremely gradual, systematic, and in one direction. Overall economic performance, at least until the oil crisis, was impressive. Real growth rates averaged 9–10 percent a year, whereas exports grew at 12–18 percent. Imports, in comparison, increased at moderate rates that brought about a substantial improvement in the current account. Inflation averaged 7 percent a year during 1960–72—quite a moderate rate in view of the high growth rate in real product. Well-developed indexation arrangements kept the real economy and the functional income distribution immune to the distorted cost of inflation. The unemployment rate, in sharp contrast to the situation in Chile, exceeded the 3–4 percent average only once in twenty-five years—in 1966–67—and did so as a result of a fairly conventional cyclical recession that had nothing to do with the liberalization process as such.

For both investors and workers, the structural change in the economy was sufficiently gradual (and credible) to make the transition toward liberalization relatively smooth. The accompanying macroeconomic and exchange-rate policies, though often erratic and sometimes mistaken, were reasonably supportive. Still other countries must be warned before they rush to follow Israel's example. Israel has had the benefit of substantial foreign aid and relatively easy loans, so that the transition has been relatively slow and painless. The real per capita foreign debt during 1962–72 grew at 14 percent a year almost double the rate of GDP per capita growth, but it was a very comfortable debt in terms of interest costs and repayment scheduling.

3. Liberalization of Financial Markets

In a typical preliberalization economy, financial intermediation is relatively underdeveloped. The public holds money in a few primary securities. Investment will be financed mainly from companies' retained earnings and government loans. Short-term credit is usually rationed at official interest rates that are below the inflation rate. The unorganized financial curb market plays an important role, but being segmented and highly imperfect, the marginal cost of borrowing becomes quite high in real interest rates. The main source of money supply is government deficit and positive changes in the private sector's external trade balance that feed into foreign exchange reserves and thus into the money supply. Raising the official credit ceiling or bank reserve requirements— important instruments of monetary policy in such an economy—will increase the cost of working capital for many companies. Monetary restraint may thus have a direct cost-increasing and output-reducing effect on the aggregate supply long before its more traditional demand-contracting role makes itself felt.

Governments generally cannot raise enough revenue from regular taxes to meet the desired levels of expenditure on both their current and capital budgets. The absence of open markets in primary securities implies that the government cannot market its debt outside the banking system. Forced sales of government debt to the banking system through a system of reserve requirements (sometimes reaching 50 percent or more on bank deposits) is a major form of public finance. Restrictions on bank lending allow authorities to provide implicit or explicit subsidies on loans to preferred customers without making budgetary allocations. Usually the resources that can be mobilized are insufficient; the government obtains the rest to finance its deficit by running the printing press.

Because real yields on domestic currency and demand deposits are low or negative, people will prefer to hold foreign money or foreign assets with higher returns. To prevent such asset substitution, tight exchange controls are usually enforced, together with controls on domestic financial markets. Because of the foreign exchange shortage, however, governments may permit private firms to borrow abroad. Even though foreign interest rates are relatively high, they will still be lower than the rates on the domestic curb market. At pegged (or crawling) exchange rates, exchange reserves will be augmented and the money supply increased, with accompanying inflationary consequences.

Various problems connected with the opening up of financial markets have to do with the imperfections of the market and the nature of government fiscal dependence on the inflation tax. First, if the domestic financial market were liberalized, then the inflation tax would be lost as a major source of government finance. The government deficit must be reduced along with, or before, the relaxation of controls on domestic financial markets. Otherwise the liberalization attempt will be thwarted by inflation. Failure to satisfy this condition was one reason for the failure of the Argentinian financial liberalization attempt in 1980–81 (McKinnon 1982). The liberalization of the domestic deficit, is in turn necessary for the successful opening up of the capital account. Because the inflation tax is levied on transactions in domestic money, similar restrictions must be imposed on foreign borrowing and lending. Otherwise households and firms will tend to avoid the domestic banking system (and thus the inflation tax) by borrowing and lending in foreign exchange. This tendency in turn will erode the domestic currency base and can easily lead to an acceleration of the inflation rate.

Second, a similar negative effect will be produced if the values of domestic liquid assets are indexed to the exchange rate. Some countries that introduced this type of financial innovation (Argentina, Israel, Mexico, Peru, and Uruguay) found that in real terms it narrowed the domestic currency part of the financial system. As long as the government deficit is not reduced, the contraction in demand in real terms for domestic money can only lead to an inflationary explosion.

One of the most dramatic failures associated with capital account liberalization, without accompanying fiscal measures, occurred in Israel in 1977. While the country was still in the process of gradual liberalization of the current account and was operating a fairly flexible crawling-peg exchange rate, a newly elected government began to liberalize the capital account and to introduce a floating exchange rate after a large initial devaluation. The liberalization package consisted mainly of an almost complete decontrol of foreign exchange flows and decontrol of the holding of foreign assets by domestic residents. The package also included a new liquid bank deposit that was denominated in domestic currency but was indexed to the exchange rate (the so-called PATAM account).

As table 10-2 shows, within two years the inflation rate had jumped from an annual rate of about 20 percent to more than 120 percent.[8] It stayed at that level during 1979–83 before jumping to 300 percent in 1984 and 500 percent at the beginning of 1985. Explanations for these discrete jumps in the inflation rate vary. One explanation attributes the jumps to the results of the large initial devaluation, the big increases in real wages during 1978 and 1979, and the attempt to return to an effective crawling peg after a brief real appreciation of the currency in the wake of an interest rate gap. An alternative explanation for the inflation is that the real demand for domestic money fell in the wake of the introduction of the PATAM accounts and that the very large inflow of short-term capital was monetized at constantly rising exchange rates. Whatever the explanation, the capital account liberalization coupled with the introduction of a liquid foreign-exchange-linked money substitute was bound to fail miserably in the absence of domestic fiscal, capital, and labor market reforms.

The lesson to be learned from Argentina, Israel, Uruguay, and some other Latin American countries is that capital accounts should be opened up at the very end of the liberalization process. Domestic fiscal and monetary reforms and trade liberalization should be allowed to run their course first. It remains an open question whether completely free transactions in foreign deposits or currency can be justified even in a most open economy. Even some of the most liberal industrial countries tend to keep varying degrees of restrictions on their capital accounts. The restrictions depend on the choice of exchange rate regime, which in turn is closely linked with the choice of nominal anchors for the domestic price system.

4. Stabilization from High Inflation

Many economies, in the process of opening up, find themselves in serious internal or external macroeconomic imbalance. Double-digit inflation, often even triple-digit inflation, is one indication of this imbalance. Crises in balance of payments and a run on foreign exchange reserves are other indicators. Policies adopted to tackle one set of problems frequently exacerbate another set. A devaluation, for example, may worsen inflation, at least in the short run, whereas a temporary price freeze may lead to a foreign exchange crisis. The opening-up process often begins at a time of simultaneous internal and external disequilibrium, and even if it does not, this problem may arise at a later stage. One is thus invariably led to ponder the necessary links between the choice of stabilization policies and the maintenance of the liberalization process.

When an economy, in the course of opening up, encounters prolonged periods of inflation and persistent balance of payments crises,
the problem in most cases lies in the government budget deficit. Lack of
a sufficiently broad tax base leads governments to rely on the inflation
tax. But even where a broad tax base exists, high inflation tends to erode
it. Inflation leads people to find ways of avoiding and evading the payment of regular taxes. The mere deferral of tax payments by, say, one
month, when the monthly inflation rate is 10 percent, results in a one-
time 10 percent loss of revenue. Such deferral or avoidance explains
why high inflation rates increase the budget deficit. High inflation rates
are, of course, caused by a resort to the printing press (that is, the budget
deficit is financed by a loan from the central bank). In addition, if
the capital account is opened up prematurely, inflation is accelerated
because of the enhanced availability of foreign exchange.

The destabilizing effect of the budget deficit in an open economy is
not confined to inflation, however. The budget deficit constitutes negative public savings, which in turn increase the current account deficit of
the balance of payments (when it is viewed as the difference between
domestic savings and investments). Spurts of high inflation and crises in
balance of payments go hand in hand with budget deficits. Moreover,
the government deficit, when it depletes foreign exchange reserves,
may indirectly accelerate inflation as a result of price-increasing coun-
termeasures such as devaluations. It is thus a prerequisite for both stabilization and an orderly conduct of the liberalization process to close the
government budget deficit through a cut in expenditure, a tax reform,
or both.

Is the elimination of budget deficits also a sufficient condition for
rapid stabilization from an initially high-inflation starting point? The
answer is a qualified negative. Although the source of prolonged inflationary pressures is in most cases a large budget deficit, elements of inertia in the dynamics of inflation may give inflation a life of its own after a
time. Inflation may accelerate in response to external price shocks, for
example, even when the government deficit is small or has not risen.

The dynamics of a high-inflation process usually manifest stepwise
jumps in the inflation rate. This rate may persist at a more or less stable
level for periods extending from a few months to several years until a
new price shock results in another stepwise jump in the inflation rate.
The inflationary processes in Argentina, Brazil, and Israel in the 1970s
and early 1980s offer good examples. Such inflation-rate jumps are
often not correlated with the size of the government deficit, but they
are related indirectly through the balance of payments repercussions on
exchange rate policy.

The essence of the high-inflation process is the degree of accommodation to the price level of the various nominal (domestic-currency-

dominated) magnitudes, such as the monetary aggregates, the exchange rate, and the wage rate. Such accommodation is built in either endogenously or through policy design, because a lack of synchronization between any two magnitudes is bound to lead to sharp changes in their relative size and is thus bound to affect the real economy. If money (or credit) does not adjust with inflation, the resulting credit squeeze will lead to a drop in output and employment. If the exchange rate is not made to "crawl" with inflation, the resulting real appreciation will harm the current account and will cause a loss of exchange reserves. If wages do not adjust with prices, real wages will erode and require a cost-of-living allowance (COLA).

As inflation accelerates, the length of the lag in adjustment of wages to inflation will fall from annual adjustments to semiannual, to quarterly, and finally to monthly adjustments. In the absence of formal arrangements of this kind, the adjustments will take place in leaps and bounds, always with the same end product: the economy will lose its nominal anchor. There will be nothing left to hold down prices. Costs of production, which are primarily determined by labor costs (wages) and import prices (the exchange rate) will rise with prices of final goods. The automatic rise in money and credit will help to validate the rise in prices on the demand side. Yet the process may appear to show temporary stability as long as there is no external shock to the price system. Once such a shock takes place (for example, an increase in oil prices or a devaluation), it will lead to a permanent increase in the rate of inflation, because only in this way can a permanent real devaluation or reduction in the real wage take place.

Because the link between the budget deficit and the inflationary process is indirect, some think the inflationary process is nothing but a bubble and believe that it is the expectations of inflation and the various indexation mechanisms that make the system go on expanding like a bubble. According to this view, a temporary freeze on wages, exchange rates, and prices is enough to make the bubble disappear. If the source of internal and external disequilibrium coming from the budget deficit is not eliminated, however, the temporary freeze is bound to end up in a renewed inflationary explosion.

Another mistaken belief is that a gradual reduction in the rate of devaluation would gradually reduce the rate of inflation. This strategy could take the form of a preannounced "tablita," a common practice in a number of Latin American countries in the 1970s. Attempts at gradualism failed not only because they were not accompanied by contractionary fiscal measures but also because the various nominal magnitudes were not synchronized in the process of disinflation. Even when a slowdown in the rate of devaluation slows the rate of inflation of producer and consumer prices, as long as there is a lag in such adjustment there will be a real appreciation, with negative consequences. Likewise, if prices come down faster than wages (because of lagged COLA indexation), real wages will increase, with corresponding negative effects on economic activity and international competitiveness.

The implications of the inflationary process for a stabilization reform are several.

- Any serious stabilization program must tackle the primary sources of imbalance in the economy: the budget and the current account deficits.
- Rapid stabilization can be brought about only by simultaneously treating the synchronized disinflation of all nominal magnitudes; in particular, the indexation of wages to past prices must be suspended at least temporarily. Forward indexation, however—obtaining workers' support for a temporary wage freeze in return for future compensation if prices are not stabilized as a result of the program—need not be excluded.
- The stabilization program must include steps to ensure that the newly established low (or, with luck, zero) inflation equilibrium will be stable. Thus if the program includes a system of price controls (these may be needed both to guarantee a wage freeze and to support an early break in the public's inflationary expectations), it must also incorporate a clearly defined method of gradual price decontrol once relative stability has been achieved. In addition, a credible new nominal anchor (or series of anchors) must be established.

In an economy with a strong and independent central bank (if it does not exist it can be established as part of the stabilization program), some key monetary aggregates (such as the quantity of money or total nominal credit) could serve as a suitable target variable. In this case, greater flexibility could be allowed on nominal-exchange-rate adjustments. Typically, in a small, open economy that is inflation prone, exchange rate targeting may be more effective if it is accompanied by a clearly defined wage policy (to prevent erosion of international competitiveness). Immediate 100 percent adjustment of wages to external shocks needs to be prevented.

Sharp disinflation may in fact be preferable to a gradualist strategy. Although the potential for an increase in unemployment has been used to justify a gradualist approach to trade liberalization, the same argument can be turned around in favor of a rapid disinflation. The sharper and more comprehensive the stabilization package, the more credible the government's intentions will be and the sharper the turnaround in inflationary expectations. Sharp disinflation will require a shorter period of restraint on credit and economic activity. A prolonged and gradualist disinflation strategy will require a prolonged contractionary monetary and fiscal policy. Because such a policy usually entails substantial unemployment, both political and social considerations make it a less advisable course to follow.

Disinflation strategies were followed successfully in some European countries after the first and second world wars. The most quoted historical example is the stabilization of the German economy in 1923. In the very recent past, a number of semiindustrialized economies in the process of opening up have found themselves running into stepwise three-digit inflation rates. Stabilization packages of the kind mentioned here were recently adopted in Argentina, Brazil, and Israel.

A brief description of Israel's July 1985 program appears below.[9] Figures 10-1–10-3 show the behavior of the key factor prices for recent periods.

After the ill-conceived opening up of the capital account in 1977, Israel's inflation rate quickly rose to, and stayed at, the annual rate of more than 120 percent for about four years (1979–83). An attempted gradual disinflation based on an announced slowdown in the rate of devaluation brought about a sharp real appreciation and ended in a

Figure 10-1. Gross and Net Real Wage Movements in Israel, 1980–86
(1980 = 100)

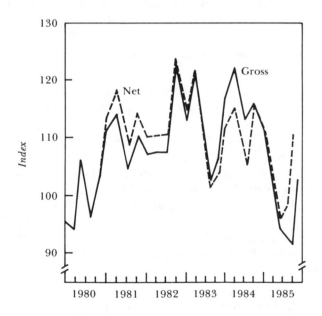

Source: Bank of Israel, *Recent Economic Developments.*

Figure 10-2. Real Effective Exchange Rates on Israeli Exports, 1978–86

(1984 = 100)

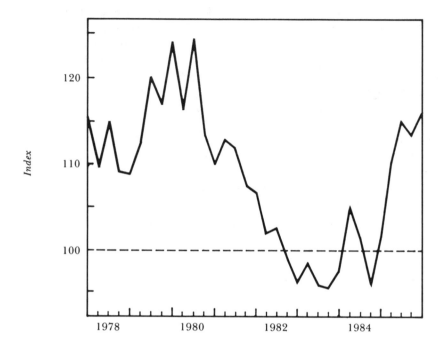

Source: Bank of Israel, *Recent Economic Developments.*

large devaluation in October 1983. The inflation rate accelerated first to 300 percent and later, in the first half of 1985, to 500 percent annually. Although a series of government measures helped to improve the current account during 1984 and the first half of 1985, the economy was losing foreign exchange reserves in capital flight quite rapidly because of a loss of confidence in the ability of the government to honor its obligations. Partial attempts to tackle the stabilization problem, which included an incomes policy at the end of 1984 and early 1985, failed miserably because they were not backed by a supporting fiscal policy and an exchange rate freeze. A comprehensive stabilization program was eventually adopted in July 1985 with the following main ingredients:

- The budget deficit was cut from about 15 percent to 5 percent of GDP by removing subsidies on basic goods and exports. This

Figure 10-3. Nominal Interest Rate, Inflationary Expectations, and the Inflation Rate, April 1985–March 1986

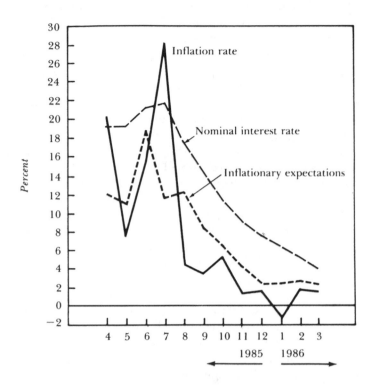

Source: Bank of Israel, *Recent Economic Developments.*

removal was incomplete in order to limit price-shock repercussions.

- After an initial step devaluation of about 20 percent, the government announced a freeze on the exchange rate, credit, and prices, on condition that the trade unions agree to a temporary wage freeze. The eventual result was a wage bargain in which the COLA indexation agreement was temporarily suspended and some preannounced wage increases were granted.

- A series of supplementary measures were taken in the financial and capital markets. The abolition of the foreign-exchange-linked liquid bank accounts (PATAM), a major ingredient of the capital account liberalization of 1977–78, was the main one. The change of currency to a new shekel (corresponding to 1,000 old shekels) was adopted only about six weeks after initiation of the program and was a purely formal act (unlike the Argentinian austral and Brazilian cruzado, which were an integral part of the respective parallel programs.)[10]

The effects of the program were dramatic. After a sharp initial rise in the price level because of the devaluation, inflation dropped from an average monthly rate of 12–15 percent, first to 3–4 percent and then to 1–1.5 percent a month. The balance of payments and exchange reserves showed a substantial improvement (helped, no doubt, by special aid from the United States and an earlier trend of improvement in the trade balance). The fiscal target was overachieved by the large tax dividend coming from sharp disinflation itself. Real wages first fell sharply and then recovered. (In April 1986, the time of this writing, there is some danger of overshooting the target on wages in the private sector.) The real exchange rate continued to rise in the first stage of the program and stayed high (helped by the appreciation of European currencies against the dollar and the maintenance of a fixed shekel-dollar rate). Finally, a reduction of nominal interest rates by the Bank of Israel, at a time when inflationary expectations declined rapidly, raised real interest rates to a very high level. Experience in other countries (for instance, Argentina) has shown that this problem is common in the early stabilization phase.

It is too early to say whether the July 1985 program is the last major step to be taken toward stabilization and whether Israel's efforts can from now on be confined to completion of liberalization in both the real trade and domestic capital markets. One will also need to await more balanced judgement on the stabilization programs of Argentina and Brazil as time and future developments evolve.

Selected Bibliography

Bhagwati, Jagdish N., ed. 1978. *Anatomy and Consequences of Exchange Control Regimes*. Cambridge, Mass.: Ballinger.

Bruno, Michael. 1986. "Sharp Disinflation Strategy: Israel 1985." *Economic Policy*, April.

Bruno, Michael, and Stanley Fischer. 1984. *Inflationary Process in Israel: Shocks and Accommodation*. National Bureau of Economic Research Working Paper 1483 (Cambridge, Mass., October 1984).

Bruno, Michael, and Zvi Sussman. 1979. "Exchange-Rate Flexibility, Inflation, and Structural Change: Israel under Alternative Regimes." *Journal of Development Economics*, vol. 6, pp. 483–514.

———. 1981. "Floating versus Crawling: Israel 1977–79 by Hindsight." In John Williamson, ed., *Exchange Rate Rules: The Theory, Performance, and Prospects of the Crawling Peg*. London: Macmillan.

Corbo, Vittorio. 1985. "Reforms and Macroeconomic Adjustments in Chile during 1974–1984." *World Development*, vol. 13. no. 3 (August), pp. 893–916.

Corbo, Vittorio, Jaime de Melo, and James R. Tybout. 1986."What Went Wrong with the Financial Reforms in the Southern Cone?" *Economic Development and Cultural Change,* vol. 34, no. 3 (April), pp. 607–40.

Dornbusch, Rudiger. 1982. "Stabilization Policy in Developing Countries: What Lessons Have We Learned?" *World Development,* vol. 10 (September), pp. 701–08.

Dornbusch, Rudiger, and Stanley Fischer. 1985. "Stopping Hyperinflations Past and Present." Cambridge, Mass.: Massachusetts Institute of Technology, November; processed.

Edwards, Sebastian. 1984. "The Order of Liberalization of the External Sector in Developing Countries." *Essays in International Finance,* no. 156 (December), pp. 20–24.

———. 1985. "Stabilization with Liberalization: An Evaluation of Ten Years of Chile's Experience with Free Market Policies, 1973–1983." *Economic Development and Cultural Change,* no. 32 (January), pp. 223–54.

Halevi, Nadav, and Joseph Baruh. Forthcoming. "The Timing and Sequencing of Trade Liberalization: Israel, 1952–77." Unpublished manuscript, World Bank research project no. 673–31, Washington,D.C.

Harberger, Arnold. 1982. "The Chilean Economy in the 1970s: Crisis, Stabilization, Liberalization, Reform." In Karl Brunner and Allan H. Meltzer, eds., *Economic Policy in a World of Change.* Carnegie-Rochester Conference Series on Public Policy, vol. 17. New York: Elsevier North-Holland.

Krueger, Anne O. 1978. *Foreign Trade Regimes and Economic Development: Liberalization Attempts and Consequences.* Cambridge, Mass.: Ballinger.

McKinnon, Ronald I. 1973. *Money and Capital in Economic Development.* Washington, D.C.: Brookings Institution.

———. 1982. *The Order of Economic Liberalization: Lessons from Chile and Argentina.* Carnegie-Rochester Conference Series on Public Policy, vol. 17. New York: Elsevier North-Holland.

Michaely, Michael. 1982."The Sequencing of a Liberalization Policy: A Preliminary Statement of Issues." World Bank, Country Policy Department, Trade and Adjustment Policy Division; processed.

Rodriguez, Carlos A. 1983. "Politicas de Establizacion en la Economia Argentina, 1978–1982." *Cuadernos de Economia,* vol. 19 (April), pp. 322–40.

Sargent, Thomas J. 1982. "The Ends of Four Big Inflations." In R. E. Hall, ed., *Inflation: Causes and Effects.* Chicago, Ill.: University of Chicago Press.

Yeager, Leland B., and others. 1981. *Experiences with Stopping Inflation.* Washington, D.C.: American Enterprise Institute.

Notes

1. These stages reflect a comparative study of ten countries conducted by the National Bureau of Economic Research in the mid-1970s. Of the ten, Brazil, Israel, and the Republic of Korea were at that time considered the most successful cases.

2. The nominal exchange rate is the price ratio of domestic monies to foreign monies and as such depends heavily on relative asset positions and financial flows in response to interest rate differentials across national borders. The real exchange rate is the nominal exchange rate divided by some measure of

the domestic cost (wages, for example) or prices (wholesale prices) corrected for world inflation. The real exchange rate is a key relative price in the real commodity and factor markets. It is of significance as a long-run allocation device between the production of tradables (exports and import substitutes) and nontradables.

3. The argument hinges on the equilization of rates of return on two assets whose relative price changes—the rate of return on the domestic real asset—should in equilibrium be equal to the rate of return on a foreign real asset (or liability), corrected for the change in their relative price, which is the real exchange rate.

4. During the process of import liberalization, relative efficiency in the production of tradables may in fact rise over time in a manner that may reduce the need for real depreciation. A substantial improvement took place in Israel's current account during the years of import liberalization in the 1960s, for example, when real exchange rates were stable. For details, see Bruno and Sussman (1979).

5. For more details, see Corbo, de Melo, and Tybout (1985) and the special August 1985 issue of *World Development*.

6. This analysis is based on Corbo (1985) and Edwards (1985).

7. For an early analysis of this episode and its aftermath, see Bruno and Sussman (1981).

8. This discussion is based on Bruno and Sussman (1979) and Halevi and Baruh (forthcoming).

9. Comparative surveys are given in Sargent (1982), Yeager and others (1981), and Dornbusch and Fischer (1985). Detailed descriptions of the 1985 Israeli stabilization plan and its aftermath appear in Bruno (1986), on which the present discussion is based.

10. Whether or not a change of currency is announced as an integral part of a monetary reform is more a question of psychology and credibility than of direct economic consequence. The Israeli monetary reform was originally conceived in terms of an immediate change in currency, but this conception was dropped from the July plan for fear that another corrective devaluation might sooner or later be required, thus suggesting that this step should be postponed until after stabilization had been assured. The actual date chosen was dictated by technical considerations of note issue by the Bank.

11

Policymaking and Economic Policy in Small Developing Countries

Arnold C. Harberger

ECONOMIC DISCUSSION of small developing countries is typically based on the so-called small country assumption that such nations have no influence on the world prices of their imports and exports and must accordingly take these prices as given. The present chapter departs from tradition in focusing on another attribute of small developing countries, namely their small endowment of people able to do a good job of setting government policy and staffing the agencies that carry it out. The criterion that I use for smallness is a 1983 population of fewer than 20 million.

The countries listed as low-income economies in the 1985 *World Development Report* included the two population giants, China and India, plus another half dozen—Zaire, Burma, Ethiopia, Vietnam, Pakistan, and Bangledesh—with populations, in ascending order, of between 30 million and 100 million. The rest of the low-income economies listed have populations ranging from fewer than 3 million (Bhutan, Central African Republic, and Togo) to about 20 million (Kenya, Sudan, and Tanzania), with the remaining twenty low-income countries for which population estimates are given lying mainly in the range of from 4 million to 15 million. Ten of these have between 4.5 million and 7.5 million inhabitants.

The lower-middle-income economies have a similar concentration by population size. Nine have fewer than 3 million people, and seven have more than 25 million (Colombia, Egypt, Indonesia, Nigeria, Philippines, Thailand, and Turkey). Between these limits lie twenty-one countries, of which thirteen have between 6 million and 10 million inhabitants. In the two groups taken together, thirty-two countries had estimated 1983 populations of between 3 million and 10 million.

1. Some Simple Demographic Facts

Demographic considerations weigh heavily in all these countries. By and large, they have experienced relatively rapid population growth, with the result that less than a fifth of their populations are over the age of forty. This is the first key demographic fact. The age cohorts that one would expect to provide the top leadership are, simply put, small.

The second key fact has to do with the education of the potential leadership cohorts. They would mostly have been at the age to receive higher education in 1960 or earlier. Yet the data for 1960 show hardly any small developing countries in which more than 1 percent of the population aged twenty to twenty-four was enrolled in higher education. On the whole, it is the larger countries (Colombia, Egypt, India, the Philippines, and Turkey) that were providing higher education to significantly more than 1 percent of their relevant age cohorts in 1960. Of the thirty-two low-and lower-middle-income countries with 1983 populations of between 3 million and 10 million, none in the low category had reached the 1 percent ratio by 1960, and only seven of the lower-middle-income group had attained 2 percent or more by that year. Of the latter, the highest percentage enrollment in higher education was attained in Costa Rica (5 percent) and Bolivia (4 percent). The Dominican Republic, El Salvador, Honduras, the People's Republic of the Congo, Senegal, and Tunisia barely reached 1 percent. The percentage enrollment in the rest of the thirty-two countries was negligible.

A country of 6 million people, as of 1983, would thus normally have fewer than 1.2 million over the age of forty. Of these, fewer than 1 percent would typically have received any higher education. This educated elite would have the task of leadership—not just in making economic policy and not just in carrying on the many functions of government but in all areas of the economy. Of this educated elite encompassing about 12,000 people over the age of forty would come the ministers of state, the ambassadors, the generals and the colonels, the judges and the lawyers, the accountants and the auditors, and the tax collectors and the teachers plus, of course, the engineers, agronomists, technicians, and business people needed to help lead the country into the modern age. Viewed in this light, the responsibilities facing so small a band of people seem truly awesome.[1]

The implications of this second demographic fact are both sobering and enlightening. Perhaps the first thing that occurs to outside observers when they contemplate all the tasks confronting so small a group is the urgency of keeping the processes of government—the laws, the regulations, and the procedures and indeed the very scope of the public sector—as simple as possible. Taxes should be simple and easy to collect. Budget processes should be straightforward and clear. Legislation should be drawn so that exceptions and special cases are very rare. Most of the tasks of detailed administrations should be defined so that they can be managed by someone whose education has not gone beyond high school (or even a primary school)—for such a person will probably end up doing the job.

These considerations tend to reinforce the technical conclusions of good policy economics, which argues in favor of relatively "neutral" taxes such as moderate and uniform import duties (where they exist at all) and uniform or moderately progressive value added taxes on grounds of economic efficiency. These are good taxes for a small developing country because, in addition to their relative neutrality and efficiency, they are simpler to administer than are taxes that are more specialized and differentiated in their coverage or more complicated in their underlying concept. These taxes might plausibly be managed by the personnel at hand.

Small developing countries should especially avoid the all too common trap of endowing regulators, administrators, and other government officials with wide discretionary powers. Such powers are dangerous even in economies well supplied with trained talent, and with an informed and vigilant public. They can be utterly noxious in countries with a fragile bureaucracy of relatively low administrative competence and a public that does not and probably cannot subject public decisions to careful scrutiny.

2. Demography's Hidden Curse

The logic of the case is clear: faced with a dearth of trained talent, small developing countries should organize their governments so as to use talent as frugally as possible. Policies should take the form of simple, robust rules that are easy to apply and easy to implement. The hand of government, as it impinges on people's affairs, should be even, just, and impersonal.

Therein lies the rub, however—the inherent vulnerability that stems from the demography of small developing countries. It is easy enough for large developed countries to have an impersonal government, blindly (for better or worse) applying the rules and regulations in force, but how can relations between the government and its clientele be impersonal when the entire educated elite numbers only a few thousand people? When many of the leadership class are related by blood and marriage? When most of them have gone to the same schools and have shared with each other the experiences of childhood and youth?

The officials in charge of the customs office will often have to rule on the customs category (determining the rate of tariff) and the valuation (determining the base to which that rate is applied) of goods being imported by firms owned by their uncles, or by entities (perhaps public ones) in which their cousins are responsible for clearing goods through customs. Not just on rare occasions (as in most larger and more advanced economies) but virtually every day or every week tax inspectors will be called upon to question the tax status of their own families, of their friends and former classmates, and of relatives of their friends and classmates. And what about the pressures and tugs of loyalty felt by those officials who must decide the location of a new port facility or must determine the route of a new road or assign licenses that can mean the difference between misery and prosperity for the recipient firms?

The curse of demography in these small developing countries is that, although in one sense the objective circumstances cry for government policy to be executed through an evenhanded, impersonal application of simple rules, in another just as real sense these very circumstances (the small size of the educated elite) conspire against the cries' being met.

It is all too easy for outsiders to react, as many have, with revulsion at what they see as nepotism, cronyism, and corruption. Serious thinking about the problem begins when one realizes that even the most selfless, honorable, and public-spirited of government leaders will have to draw their collaborators from the same pool of educated elite. Reformers and traditionalists alike have nowhere else to turn. By and large, the people they appoint will have something in common with them—ties of family, religion, school, club, and ethnicity and very often all of the above. Not only will these ties exist between the government leaders and their appointees, but the same ties will also exist between the appointees and the clientele over which their authority is mainly exercised.

Thus the age-old issue of rules versus authorities poses more powerful personal and moral dilemmas in small developing countries than it does in more advanced and larger ones. Ties of kinship, background, and friendship, which are if anything deeper than in advanced economies, impinge with insistent regularity on government functionaries in the small developing country. Bureaucrats cannot avoid these pressures. Not only must they be faced, but they must be dealt with, for practical purposes, nearly every day.

In such an environment true and dedicated reformers can easily end up isolating themselves from just about everybody. They can offend their families and their peer groups and can easily turn themselves into objects of ridicule and scorn. They are likely to lose their jobs as well as their friends.

Thus life is difficult for government functionaries in small developing countries. The choices are intrinsically more painful to the individual, and painful choices are at the same time more common. How do people react to such problems? How does human nature help them maintain their sanity, their dignity, and their self-respect? What strategy do dedicated reformers find it best to follow?

The key to these questions lies in the tendency of human beings everywhere to justify (to themselves at least) what they are doing. The world is not full of people with evil motives. Quite the contrary; most acts that turn out to be bad are done, not only without evil intent, but typically with a sincere conviction that the acts are genuinely good. Manufacturers the world over who plead for special protection do so convinced that such protection is good not just for them but also for society at large. The same is true when farmers plead for price supports, commuters for low bus and train fares, union workers for minimum wages (usually not for themselves but to help prevent union wages from being undercut by other groups). It is said that a good salesman believes in his product even when that product is inferior. Salesmen who believe their products are inferior will likely be replaced by people who do not have to fight their conscience to present a convincing case.

Government functionaries in small developing countries naturally adapt to a view of the world as a complicated place. Those who accept at face value the economist's simplified approach to problems may by that very act nullify their potential power and influence. Functionaries more readily survive, however, who truly and sincerely believe that the world is too complicated to permit direct application of the economist's simple principles.

My point is that those who take fully to heart the razor-sharp logic of economics will be at an inherent disadvantage relative to those who feel comfortable with a world view that is at once fuzzier but more flexible, softer but more malleable. One cannot help but admire the artful eloquence of civil servants in developing countries—not just within their own bureaucracies but in international councils as well. The successful bureaucrat in a developing country has a subtler perception of nuances, a more practiced capacity to avoid giving offense, a supreme gift, some might say, for walking and talking around an issue without quite meeting it head-on.

I believe that the characteristic traits of administrators in developing countries are no accident but result from a process of natural selection. The facile mind, the easy and ready tongue, the quick perception of subtle distinctions—even the capacity to invent distinctions on the spot—help to determine survival and advancement in many bureaucracies and probably nowhere more so than in the small developing countries.

It is important to realize that the naturally selected cast of mind of officials in the developing country does not mean that they cannot mold policy in accordance with the dictates of economic professionalism. The mindset does make it harder to accept economic principles as a package of precepts according to which policies will be mainly judged, but it does not prevent or even particularly inhibit the adoption of policies that are good from an economic point of view.

The most straightforward way to consider the way of thinking of the official in a developing country is simply as a fact of life. It is neither good nor bad; it is simply present as an integral part of the scene. The way of thinking will likely be present among supporters of good economic policies and among their opponents. More than being a determinant of how economic policy turns out, it conditions the process of how decisions are reached.

3. Professionalism

As a long-time believer in the power of economic policy to affect, for good or ill, the lives and the welfare of people, I have emphasized the need for us to cultivate what I call "professionalism" within those branches of the profession of economics that deal with policy issues. I distinguish the profession from the science of economics by analogy to medicine. The profession of medicine is what is taught in medical school, what doctors use in their actual practice. In contrast, the science of medicine has its cutting edge in the work of medical researchers extending the frontiers of knowledge. The work of the scientist is on the frontier; the work of the professional embodies the fruits of decades, even centuries, of scientific advance. The work of the professional is also enhanced by experience; a good medical practitioner knows from experience, for example, that certain deviations from an ideal diet or from some other health regime are not too serious, whereas others are more worrisome.

The situation is similar in the practice of professional economics. Where economic scientists extend the frontiers, practitioners ideally embody the corpus of knowledge and experience inherited from the past. The scientist's interest lies in what was not known even five or ten years ago, whereas the bread and butter of the professional's work lies in applying what has for the most part been known for decades.

Professional economists concerned with policy also have a lot in common with medical practitioners in the way in which they use their experience. Just as medical practitioners can advise against smoking but still treat smokers for their various ailments (whether related to their habit or not), so economists can advise against restrictive trade regimes and in favor of rationalizing the tax system even though they will probably continue to treat their "patients" after many elements of the good advice have passed unheeded. Moreover—and this is in a sense one of the important tests of professionalism—they should realize, even as they dole out advice, not only that most of their prescriptions will not be followed but that the patient will probably survive anyway.

Only rarely is it fatal when medical patients deviate from the advice of their doctors. Fatalities are even rarer when countries fail to implement the best judgment of economic policy professionals. Although the theory of economic policy is often quite clear in saying that on economic grounds one policy is much better (or less costly) than another, one does not pay an infinite price by failing to follow it. The price—the economic cost that one incurs when one deviates from good policy prescriptions—is typically finite and often not of portentous magnitude.

Thus although the structure of an ideal economic policy that emerges from economic theory is quite rigid, the actual structures of policy in the real world are, like the world view of policymakers in developing countries, softer and more malleable. The rigidities of real-world structures come not from theories and concepts but from the forces and pressures to which all governments are subject and, overwhelmingly, from the heavy hand of inertia that almost always and almost everywhere works to perpetuate what is already there.

The art of good policymaking consists of perceiving at any given moment the forces and pressures working to change the policy structure; in sensing at what points the existing structure is more plastic, more amenable to change; and finally in channeling the pressures (enlisting their aid, as it were) so as not just to modify the structure but also to improve it (among other things, by reducing the aggregate price that is paid by the economy, day in and day out, for its policy weaknesses).

Nations differ greatly in the quality of their policy structures and in the cost to the economy of the burden caused by the cumulation through time of policy mistakes or misjudgments. Perhaps the most important task of professional economists in developing countries is to help countries reduce this cost when it is large and at the very least to keep it from growing when it is small. (Here, as in most of life's arenas, it is much easier to tear down something of quality than it is to build or restore it.)

The special attributes of small developing countries are not grounds for modifying the above diagnosis. Rather they condition the reality with which professional economists deal. The smaller the economy, the more unique the pressures and forces working to influence the policy structure are likely to be and the less applicable the "standard" interest-group categories of agriculture, manufacturing, organized labor, commerce, and so on will be. The smaller the leadership elite, the more characteristics peculiar to it—including its own cliques, factions, and rivalries—are likely to play a dominant role in defining pressures and points of resistance. These elements challenge the perception and the sensitivity of those striving to improve economic policy, but they do not change the fundamental nature of either the process of policy reform or the contribution that the economics profession can make to it.

4. The Lessons of Experience

A country's economic policy has so many facets, so many different instruments, and so many objectives and avenues of intervention that it is clearly impossible to summarize them simply. The lessons of experience are, however, easier to summarize. They counsel prudence and restraint; they argue against yielding to the temptations of quick fixes of any kind. On the whole, what appear to be quick fixes or easy solutions have proven instead to be traps for the gullible and the unwary.

Inflation is an area in which temptation has proven hardest to resist. The reason may be that first doses of inflationary credit expansion are almost always popular and may indeed bring an initial benefit to the economy. Over the long haul, however, the ill effects of inflation come to predominate.

Experience suggests, too, that inflation usually comes packaged with many other policy mistakes, the cumulation of which contributes to a poor economic preformance generally. In table 11-1, I have taken a reduction of exports as a percentage of GDP to connote the likelihood of an inward-looking, protectionist policy. We know that policies of artificial import substitution have the effect of reducing the economic incentives facing exporters. By now we have accumulated vast experience with countries whose actual efforts at import substitution had precisely this effect. Nonetheless, we must recognize that other forces (especially the movements of world market prices for its principal export products) also influence a country's exports. Hence the movement of the exports/GDP ratio only suggests the possibility of protectionist policies and does not imply with certainty that they will come into being.

These introductory remarks facilitate the interpretation of table 11-1. The listed countries were selected because their inflation rates had increased significantly and the GDP growth rate of each had fallen significantly. I interpret this fall not as a direct reflection of inflation but as suggesting that other policy mistakes may have combined with inflationary finance to reduce the countries' growth possibilities. In addition, in every one of the listed low-income countries, the exports/GDP ratio fell substantially. Inward-looking policies almost certainly played a significant role in several of these cases.

The lower-middle-income countries that are listed in table 11-1 share with the low-income countries the experience of a sharp decline in the growth rate (actually a plunge into negative growth in all but one case). Additional evidence suggests significant policy deterioration in several of the cases, although factors extraneous to policy were of course also at work. Notably, the lower-middle-income countries (mainly in Latin America) did not exhibit the same uniform fall in export ratios that the low-income countries displayed.

At the bottom of each panel, the median value of each variable for the listed countries is juxtaposed with the median value for the other small countries in the income category. For the low-income category these other countries are Afghanistan, Benin, Burkina Faso, Burundi, Guinea, Haiti, Kenya, Malawi, Mali, Nepal, Niger, Rwanda, Sri Lanka, and Togo. For the lower-middle-income category they include Cameroon, Côte d'Ivoire, the Dominican Republic, Guatemala, Honduras, Lesotho, Liberia, Mauritania, Papua New Guinea, Paraguay, People's Democratic Republic of the Congo, People's Democratic Republic of Yemen, Senegal, Tunisia, Yemen Arab Republic, Zambia, and Zimbabwe. The criterion of smallness was a 1983 population of fewer than 20 million. Apart from size, the only grounds for exclusion of a country was lack of the relevant information in the 1985 *World Development Report.*

The list of the other small countries presented in the foregoing paragraph quite decisively indicates that they constitute very heterogeneous groups with respect to culture, ethnicity, economic specialization, physical characteristics, region, and so on. In no sense can they be considered to be specially suited to produce a superior economic performance. Nonetheless, table 11-1 gives the impression that they are. These other small countries have lower inflation (mainly because of the selection criterion), but they also reflect a superior growth performance as well as a marked increase in export ratios. The table suggests that the listed countries fell upon bad times at least in part because of policy mistakes. Other countries of similar size seem to have been able to avoid such a quick acceleration of inflation, such a deep fall in growth rates, and such a sharp cut in the export ratio. This contrasting behavior between countries falling prey to the inflation virus, as against their less susceptible counterparts, mirrors quite faithfully the earlier experience of larger countries.[2]

Table 11-2 presents somewhat different evidence and from a somewhat different perspective. Whereas table 11-1 implies that the inflation disease tends in small countries to reflect a more general policy malaise (just as seems to be the case for larger countries), table 11-2 focuses on inflationary outbreaks in countries regardless of size. Perhaps as a consequence of the manner in which the criterion of selection worked in table 11-1, the countries in table 11-2 are divided into an African group and a Latin American group. The precise selection criterion for this table was that the country should have an average inflation rate of more than 20 percent in the three years 1981–83. This criterion was applied to all the countries in each group, with the result that three countries with more than 20 million population (Sudan, Tanzania, and Zaire) entered the list for Africa, whereas four (Argentina, Brazil, Colombia, and Mexico) entered that for Latin America.[3]

Table 11-1. "Inflationary" Low-Income and Lower-Middle-Income Countries

Country	Population, 1983 (1)	Rate of inflation 1965–73 (2)	Rate of inflation 1973–83 (3)	Per capita GDP growth rate 1965–73 (4)	Per capita GDP growth rate 1973–83 (5)	Exports as percentage of GDP 1965–73 (6)	Exports as percentage of GDP 1973–83 (7)
Low-income countries							
Central African Republic	2.5	3.8	20.1	n.a.	−1.3	27	23
Ghana	12.8	8.1	51.6	1.2	−4.4	17	5
Sierra Leone	3.6	1.9	14.7	2.0	−0.2	30	12
Somalia	5.1	3.8	20.1	n.a.	0.0	17	10
Uganda	13.9	5.6	62.7	0.2	−4.9	26	5
Median	5.1	3.8	20.1	1.2	−1.3	26	10
Other small, low-income countries (median)	6.0	4.0	10.8	1.2	1.4	13	22

Lower-middle-income countries

Bolivia	6.0	7.5	35.2	2.0	−1.1	17	19
Costa Rica	2.4	4.7	23.2	4.1	0.3	23	35
El Salvador	5.2	1.6	11.7	1.0	−3.1	27	21
Jamaica	2.3	5.9	16.0	3.9	−3.0	33	40
Nicaragua	3.0	3.4	16.5	1.0	−5.2	29	21
Peru	17.9	10.1	52.3	0.7	−0.6	16	21
Median	4.1	5.3	19.8	1.5	−2.0	25	21
Other lower-middle-income countries (median)	6.1	3.6	9.7	2.6	0.5	25	31

n.a. Not available.

Note: Countries shown are those whose average rate of inflation in 1973–83 exceeded their average rate in 1965–73 by more than ten percentage points. All data are from World Bank, *World Development Report 1985* (New York: Oxford University Press, 1985). Columns (1), (2), and (3) are from *World Development Report*, table 1. Columns (4) and (5) are constructed by subtracting from the GDP growth rates of *World Development Report*, table 2, the corresponding population growth rates of *World Development Report*, table 19. Columns (6) and (7) are from *World Development Report*, table 5.

Table 11-2. Inflation, Growth, and Other Economic Indicators, Selected African Countries, 1965–67 and 1981–83

Country	Annual inflation rate (π)[a]		Annual GDP growth (g)[b]		Private credit ratio (p)[c]		Exports / GDP ratio (x)[d]		Inflationary finance ratio (β)[e]	
	1965–67	1981–83	1965–67	1981–83	1965–67	1981–83	1965–67	1981–83	1965–67	1981–83
Low-income countries										
Ghana	11 <	87	−0.05 >	−2.8	0.31 >	0.09	0.07 >	0.03	0.040 <	0.059
Madagascar	3 <	27	2.4 >	−4.0	1.37 >	0.42	0.16* >	0.13*	0.004 <	0.061
Sierra Leone	5 <	41	5.2 >	3.5	0.67 >	0.16	0.28 >	0.18	0.013 <	0.099
Somalia	4 <	34	n.a.		0.75 >	0.30	0.17* >	0.10*	n.a.	
Sudan	3 <	27	0.2* <	6.3*	0.53 >	0.39	15* >	11*	0.022 <	0.041
Tanzania	0 <	27	8.4 >	−2.5	1.09 >	0.06	0.27 >	0.10	0.015 <	0.142
Uganda	5 <	23	3.6* >	−2.1*	0.75 >	0.30	0.26* >	0.05*	n.a.	
Zaire	17 <	49	6.0 <	0.5	0.15 >	0.20	0.45 >	0.36	0.034 <	0.089
Median	5 <	30	3.6 >	−2.1	0.71 >	0.25			0.019 <	0.094
Lower-middle-income countries										
Argentina	30 <	204	7.5 >	−2.7	0.53 <	0.66	0.08 <	0.12	0.043 <	0.161

	π[a]		g[b]		p[c]		x[d]		β[e]	
Bolivia	7	< 144	6.1	> −5.7	0.24	< 0.41	0.22	< 0.24	0.018	< 0.114
Brazil	46	< 115	10.6	> −1.3	0.06	< 0.70	0.08	< 0.09	0.006	> 0.054
Colombia	11	< 24	4.4	> 1.4	0.56	< 0.79	0.12	> 0.11	0.004	< 0.015
Costa Rica	1	< 53	7.8	> −3.6	0.73	> 0.47	0.24	< 0.42	0.019	> 0.003
Ecuador	4	< 26	7.3	> 0.6	0.79	< 0.90	0.17	< 0.23	0.005	> −0.005
Mexico	4	< 63	6.6	> 0.7	0.47	> 0.36	0.10	< 0.16	0.006	< 0.118
Nicaragua	n.a.		6.6	> 3.1	0.99	> 0.66	0.26	> 0.16	0.005	< 0.148
Peru	12	< 84	5.2	> −2.6	0.57	> 0.51	0.17	< 0.22	0.009	< 0.057
Uruguay	73	> 34	0.2	> −4.2	0.77	> 0.90	0.16	< 0.18	0.030	< 0.064
Median	11	< 58	6.6	> −1.9	0.56	< 0.66	0.17	0.17	0.007	0.060

n.a. Not available.

a. π = Annual inflation rate; average of the three-year period. From *International Financial Statistics*.

b. g = Annual real GDP growth rate; average of the three-year period. An asterisk signifies that data from *World Development Report 1985*, table 2, on GDP growth rates for 1965–73 and 1978–83 were used in lieu of (unavailable) *International Financial Statistics* data for 1965–67 and 1981–84.

c. p = Private credit ratio represents consolidated monetary system credit to the private sector divided by total credit of the monetary system. Data, from *International Financial Statistics*, are averages of the above ratios (end-of-year figures) for the three years in question.

d. x = Ratio of exports to GDP. Data are from national accounts figures given in *International Financial Statistics* for the three years in question. Where *International Financial Statistics* data were unavailable (denoted by an asterisk), figures from *World Development Report 1985*, table 5, on export ratios for 1965 and 1983 were used instead.

e. β = "Inflationary" finance ratio, defined as the increase over the year in monetary system (consolidated banking system) credit to the public sector, expressed as a fraction of the year's GDP. Data are averages of these ratios for the three years in question.

The periods covered in table 11-2 are three years (1965–67) from the relatively stable 1960s together with three (1981–83) from the comparatively tumultuous 1980s. The countries are compared on five different measures: inflation rate (π), GDP growth rate (g), private sector credit ratio (p), exports/GDP ratio (X) , and "inflationary" finance ratio (β). Rather surprisingly, only one of the countries (Uruguay) whose 1980s inflation rate was more than 20 percent had a higher rate of inflation in the mid-1960s. Apart from this one case, all the countries listed in table 11-2 experienced a major upward shift of inflation between the mid-1960s and the early 1980s.

The syndrome depicted in table 11-2 includes a rise in the rate of inflation, a major decline in the growth rate of real GDP, a reduction in the share of total bank credit going to the private sector, a reduction in the export ratio, and the government's increasing reliance on borrowing from the banking system. These tendencies are initially true for all the African countries listed. In Latin America, the picture is mixed with respect to the private credit ratio and the exports/GDP ratio. A crude interpretation is that the Latin American countries had already to a degree learned that it does not pay to squeeze private sector credit or to indulge in exaggerated import substitution. These were indeed two of the important messages to be drawn from the Latin American experience of the 1950s and early 1960s.

Although these lessons had been learned at least to a degree, the inflationary countries in Latin America, like those in Africa, exhibited a very poor growth performance in the early 1980s—poor both in absolute terms and in relation to the preformance of their neighbors. In Latin America, the median growth rate of the listed countries fell from 6.6 percent a year in 1965–67 to −1.9 percent in 1981–83. At the same time, the developing countries of the Western Hemisphere that are not on the list and that have annual growth rates recorded in the 1985 yearbook of *International Financial Statistics*, had growth rates that fell from a median of 5.4 percent in 1965–67 to 0.9 percent in 1981–83. Although the listed African countries had median growth of 2.4 percent in 1965–67 and − 2.1 percent in 1981–83, the developing countries of Africa that do not appear in table 11-2 (because they averaged less than 20 percent inflation in 1981–83) had median growth of 5.4 percent in the earlier period and 2.0 percent in the later one.

To sum up, I have suggested that small countries when they have significant policy weaknesses display symptoms similar to those revealed by somewhat larger countries. This assertion cannot be proved, for in the final analysis there is no substitute for the detailed study of each county's experience that leads to a careful diagnosis based on direct evidence. The study of just a few key variables for many countries at a time cannot do justice to each case, but it can be suggestive.

Small countries selected by a criterion of inflation (taken as suggesting the absence of a full and disciplined control over the instruments of policy) have growth performances that are inferior to those of their less inflationary counterparts. At the same time, the former countries reveal other signs (reduced exports and private sector credit, increased financing of government through the banking system) of policy weakness. On the whole, when the behavior of small and not so small developing countries is measured by the same crude yardstick, remarkably similar syndromes are associated with less than successful cases, regardless of size.

It is important to call attention to the peculiarities of small countries to help outsiders appreciate the societal backdrop against which the dramas of policy are worked out. Such an appreciation may help outside experts more readily to understand the evolution of policies in a small-country setting. This greater understanding in turn could conceivably help make outside advice more pertinent to the problems and more sensitively conditioned to the setting in which they must be confronted. But it does not change the fundamental nature of major policy weaknesses or the main ways in which those weaknesses can be surmounted. Thus in spite of all that may be special or peculiar about how policy is influenced and formed in small developing countries, when all is said and done, the lessons of experience nonetheless remain the same.

Notes

1. The tasks seem even more formidable when one considers the support capabilities of the same economies. Although the typical small developing economy was providing higher education to less than 1 percent of the relevant age cohorts, the corresponding figure for secondary education was typically about 2 percent in the low-income countries and about 5 percent for most of the small lower-middle-income countries. Bolivia, Costa Rica, Cuba, Ecuador, El Salvador, and Jamaica are the notable exceptions among lower-middle-income countries with populations of 3 million to 10 million.

2. See, for example, Arnold C. Harberger and Sebastian Edwards, "Causes of Inflation in Developing Countries: Some New Evidence," paper presented at the annual meeting of the American Economic Association, New York, December 1982.

3. A number of observers share my opinion that the characteristics of smallness that I have emphasized in the preceding sections of this paper in fact apply to a number of countries with quite large populations. In mixing larger and smaller countries, however, I make no claim to that effect. I merely note a general similarity in the symptoms that appear along with inflation.

Part II

Country Studies

12

Argentina

Domingo F. Cavallo

DURING THE FIRST three decades of the twentieth century, Argentina achieved growth in GDP of 4.6 percent—higher than that of Australia, Brazil, Canada, or the United States (see table 12-1). Even though the average growth rate dropped to 1.8 percent during the 1930s on account of the Great Depression, Argentina's economic performance was better than that of most other countries. Beginning with World War II, it was a different story. Argentina's GDP grew at a lower rate than that of other nations. In per capita terms, Argentina's average growth of 1.3 percent a year fell behind 2.6 percent of Australia, 3.4 percent of Brazil, 3.2 percent of Canada, and 2.3 percent of the United States. In fact, Argentina's growth performance deteriorated while the performance of other countries improved. A number of factors can explain the contrast in economic performance during these periods; external balance policies followed by the country are perhaps the most important.[1]

The structural changes experienced by the Argentinian economy are illustrated in figure 12-1. Until the 1940s, long-term growth rates were similar for the different components of GDP. Between 1940 and the early 1950s, agriculture stagnated, exports experienced a sharp decline, and government services expanded very rapidly. Starting in the early 1950s, agriculture grew again, although at a somewhat slower pace than in preceding decades; government services went back to a lower rate of growth (more in line with that of agricultural GDP); and exports (a reversal of the trend) began to grow at a rate similar to that of total GDP.

Was the stagnation in agricultural output during the 1940s and the early 1950s the result of unfavorable economic incentives or institutional and nonprice factors such as the system of land tenure, lack of entrepreneurship in the agricultural sector, and the like? Even without reference to the extensive empirical evidence that agriculture has a strong supply response to prices, the indexes plotted in figure 12-2

Table 12-1. Population and GDP Growth in Selected Countries, 1900–84

(percent)

Period	Argentina	Australia	Brazil	Canada	United States
	Annual rate of growth of population				
1900–1904 to 1925–29	2.8	1.8	2.1	2.2	1.6
1925–29 to 1935–39	2.1	1.1	2.0	1.3	0.8
1935–39 to 1980–84	1.7	1.8	2.6	1.5	1.4
	Annual rate of growth of GDP				
1900–1904 to 1925–29	4.6	2.6	3.3	3.4	2.9
1925–29 to 1935–39	1.8	1.4	3.0	0.4	0.6
1935–39 to 1980–84	3.0	4.4	6.0	4.7	3.7

Sources: Argentina Instituto Nacional de Estadísticas y Censos, *Censo Nacional de Población y Vivienda* (Buenos Aires), various annual issues; Domingo Cavallo and Yair Mundlak, *Agriculture and Economic Growth in an Open Economy: The Case of Argentina* (Washington, D.C.: International Food Policy Research Institute, 1982), p. 19; O. J. Firestone, "Canada's Economic Development, 1867–1953," in *Income and Wealth*, vol. 7 (London: Bowes and Bowes, 1958), pp. 240–76; *Historical Statistics of U.S. Colonial Times to 1957: A Statistical Abstract Supplement* (Washington, D.C.: U.S. Department of Commerce, 1960); International Monetary Fund, *International Financial Statistics* (Washington, D.C.: IMF), various annual issues; Arthur Smithies, "Economic Growth: International Comparisons: Argentina and Australia," in *American Economic Review: Proceedings*, vol. 55, pt. 1 (1965), p. 30; *Statistical Abstract of Latin America*, vol. 23, edited by James W. Wilkie and Peter Reich (Los Angeles: University of California Press, 1982); and United Nations, Economic Commission for Latin America, *Statistical Yearbook for Latin America, 1978* (New York: ECLA, 1979).

strongly suggest that the structural changes were induced by changes in relative prices.[2]

Figure 12-2 shows two key relative prices in the Argentinian economy. One is wholesale prices of nonagricultural goods divided by the consumer price index, and the other is producer prices of agricultural goods divided by the consumer price index. The agricultural producer price index has been computed in two ways: by using the agricultural component of the wholesale price index and by means of an index of producer prices computed from f.o.b. export prices in dollars multiplied by the nominal exchange rate for agricultural exports and adjusted for taxes on exports. The indexes in the numerators represent prices of tradable goods, and the indexes in the denominators represent prices of predominantly home goods. Thus these indexes may also be

Figure 12-1. Indexes of GDP and Value Added by Agriculture, Government Services, and Exports in Argentina, 1913–84

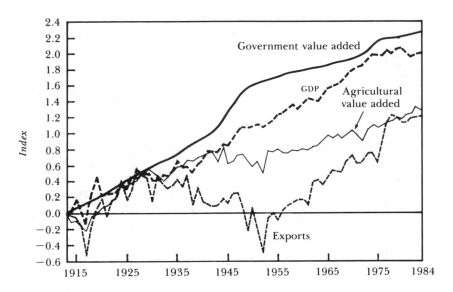

Note: Indexes are in logarithmic scale, with 1913 = 0.

Source: Argentina Instituto Nacional de Estadísticos y Censos, *Censo Nacional de Población y Vivienda*, Buenos Aires, various annual issues.

denominated real effective exchange rates for nonagricultural and agricultural goods ("real" to make clear that they refer to deflated prices and "effective" to indicate that the effects of commercial policies in creating differential exchange rates have been taken into account).

Figure 12-2 clearly shows that during the 1930s and the 1940s the relative prices of agricultural goods were low when compared with the level that had prevailed in previous decades and the relative prices for nonagricultural tradable goods. Consequently, agricultural growth in the 1940s was also low, as would be expected in an economy with price-responsive sectoral supplies. In addition, the sharp decline in exports in the 1940s (see figure 12-1) is the outcome of reduced incentives to produce exportable goods. Furthermore, domestic consumption increased because consumer prices were lower and real income of urban wage earners higher as a result of the expansion of government services and the production of import substitutes.

The gap between agriculture and nonagriculture prices relative to the price of home goods increased at the beginning of the 1930s and

Figure 12-2. Prices of Agricultural and Nonagricultural Tradable Goods Relative to the Price of Home Goods in Argentina, 1913–84

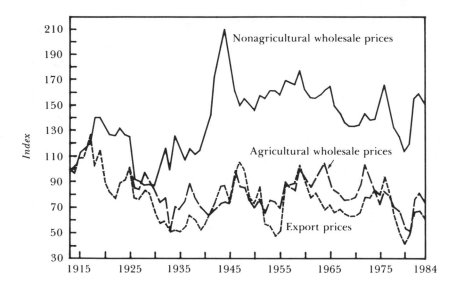

Source: Argentina Instituto Nacional de Estadísticos y Censos, *Censo Nacional de Población y Vivienda*, Buenos Aires, various annual issues.

continued to do so until the early 1950s and has been only partially reversed since then. The gap may reflect deteriorating foreign terms of trade, protectionist commercial policies, or both.

The formulas below permit the computation of agriculture and nonagriculture prices relative to the price of home goods:

$$\frac{P_a}{P_h} = \frac{P_x^f E_x}{P_h}$$

and

$$\frac{P_{na}}{P_h} = \frac{P_m^f E_m}{P_h}$$

where P_a and P_{na} are the price indexes of agricultural and nonagricultural goods, P_h is the price index of home goods, P_x^f and P_m^f are border dollar prices of exports and imports, and E_x and E_m are indexes of effective nominal rates of exports and imports.

The increasing gap between P_{na}/P_h and P_a/P_h may result from an increase in the foreign prices of imports relative to the foreign prices of exports, or from an increase in the effective exchange rate for imports relative to the effective exchange rate of exports. This difference in effective exchange rates may be created by any of the instruments commonly classified as commercial policies. These include taxes on exports, tariffs on imports, and quantitative restrictions, such as bans, quotas, and licenses. The difference may also be caused simply by different official exchange rates during periods of exchange controls when foreign exchange is purchased and sold only by the monetary authorities.

1. Foreign Terms of Trade and Commercial Policies

It has been argued that the foreign terms of trade tend to deteriorate in the long run and that this trend is responsible for the poor export and growth performance of Argentina. Consider figure 12-3. It shows the longest available series on Argentinian foreign terms of trade, which was constructed precisely by the institution that first hypothesized the deterioration in the terms of trade: the Economic Commission for Latin America of the United Nations. It covers the period 1913–84, and it quite clearly indicates that there is no such long-term trend. The terms of trade do fluctuate a lot, but the overall trend is fairly stable. Furthermore, this conclusion is reinforced if we take into account the changes in

Figure 12-3. Foreign Terms of Trade in Argentina, 1913–84
(1960 = 0)

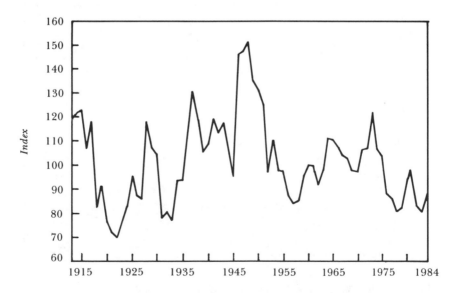

Source: Central Bank of the Argentinian Republic, *Statistical Bulletin.*

quality of the goods exported and imported. Manufactured goods predominate on the import side, whereas exports are mainly agricultural products. It is known that quality improvements over the period 1913–84 were more important in manufactures than in agricultural commodities. The argument regarding the trend toward the deterioration in the terms of trade was made by analyzing the behavior of export and import prices from the immediate post–World War II period when there was a boom in agricultural commodities. That starting point, however, is simply a peak in the fluctuating series of foreign terms of trade. Consequently when the picture is considered in a long-term perspective, the deterioration hypothesis with respect to foreign terms of trade is not supported by the data.

Therefore, the divergent behavior of agriculture and nonagriculture prices from the Great Depression until the early 1950s must have resulted from policies applied by Argentine governments. This point is evident from the collection of real effective exchange rates presented in figure 12-4, which also reveals several important characteristics of the external balance policies applied by Argentina.

Figure 12-4 shows the plot of four real-exchange-rate indexes.

Figure 12-4. Real Effective Exchange Rates in Argentina, 1913–84

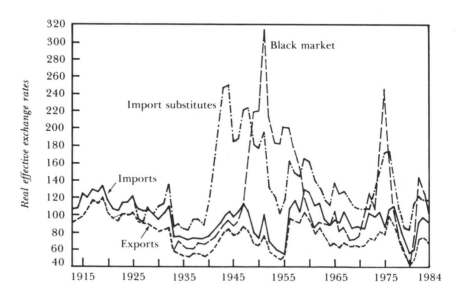

Source: Central Bank of the Argentinian Republic, *Statistical Bulletin.*

- The real effective exchange rate of exports (REER_x):

$$\text{REER}_x = \frac{P^f\,\text{NER}_x\,(1-t_x)}{P_h}$$

where P^f is an index of foreign prices, NER_x is an index of the nominal exchange rate of exports, t_x is the tax rate on exports, and P_h is the consumer price index used as indicator of home good prices.

- The real effective exchange rate for imported goods (REER_m):

$$\text{REER}_m = \frac{P^f\,\text{NER}_m\,(1+t_m)}{P_h}$$

where the symbols represent the same concepts in the previous formula except that imports (m) have replaced exports (x).

- The real effective exchange rate for import substitutes (REER_{ms}):

$$\text{REER}_{ms} = \frac{P_{na}\,(1+t_m^{i,69})}{P_h}$$

where P_{na} is the wholesale price index for nonagricultural goods (and in this case is taken to be equal to one in 1969) and $t_m^{i,69}$ is an implicit rate of nominal protection for import substitutes computed for 1969.[3]

- The real exchange rate in the free market (RER_b):

$$\text{RER}_b = \frac{P^f\,\text{NER}_b}{P_h}$$

where NER_b is the nominal-exchange-rate quotation in the free market (legal or black, depending on the period).

To compute the different real exchange rates, whenever an index of foreign prices is needed, the same price index P^f was used. This was done to show only the differences in effective exchange rates resulting from commercial and other domestic policies and not those that stem from changes in foreign terms of trade. P^f was obtained as a geometric average of P_x^f and P_m^f with equal weights.

The main conclusions that can be drawn from figure 12-4 are the following.

First, real effective exchange rates varied considerably over time. They fluctuated much more than the foreign terms of trade. The real effective exchange rate for exports varied from a minimum of 43 (in 1980) to a maximum of 117 (in 1916). The real effective exchange rate for actual imports ranged between 54 (in 1955) and 135 (in 1919). The real effective exchange rate for import substitutes showed still wider variations, ranging from 82 (in 1980) to 250 (in 1944). In the black market, the variation observed in the real exchange rate ranged from a low of 44 (in 1980) to a high of 316 (in 1952). Note that the foreign terms of trade ranged only between 72 (in 1921) and 151 (in 1948).

Second, real effective exchange rates for exports were much lower in the 1930s, in the 1940s, and in the first half of the 1950s than in the decades preceding the Great Depression. For this reason the relative price of agricultural goods declined from the 1930s to the early 1950s compared with those prevailing in the previous decades (see figure 12-2). Although $REER_x$ has recovered since the mid-1950s, it has never returned to the level of the early decades. New sharp drops are observed from 1978 to 1980.

Third, real effective exchange rates for imports and exports moved relatively close together for most of the period. The implication is that the variation in explicit taxes on exports and imports was not very large. Until 1929 the explicit taxes were used to create differential incentives to produce export goods and import substitutes, but such was not the case after 1930. Since that year, import prohibitions, import quotas, and special import licenses have been used with varying intensity to restrict imports and to promote the domestic production of import substitutes. For most of the period, therefore, $REER_m$ represents only the import price of commodities that are not produced in the domestic economy, whereas the incentive to produce import substitutes is better represented by $REER_{ms}$. In 1930, $REER_{ms}$ began to diverge from both $REER_m$ and $REER_x$. The increase in $REER_{ms}$ was especially large during World War II, the natural outcome of the import restrictions resulting from the conflict itself, but $REER_{ms}$ remained very high after the war until the early 1950s. Furthermore, even though it dropped to lower levels afterward, it stayed much higher than $REER_m$ and $REER_x$ for the rest of the period.

The behavior of $REER_{ms}$ (compared with $REER_x$) shows the large antiexport bias introduced in the economy, especially during and immediately after World War II. This bias has remained a permanent characteristic of the Argentinian economy. No doubt the antiexport bias has affected growth much more than the long-term trend of the foreign terms of trade.

Fourth, the real exchange rate in the free market (RER_b), which is the relevant exchange for tourism, hoarding, and smuggling, began to differ from the $REER_x$ in 1933 when exchange controls were instituted, but it did not diverge significantly until 1946. In that year the real exchange rate in the free market jumped, and it stayed very high throughout the Peronist regime. In the early 1960s, when exchange controls were eliminated, the free-market exchange rate again very closely approached that of exports, the only difference between the two rates being export taxes. During the rest of the 1960s, the black market rate was in between

REER$_x$ and REER$_{ms}$, as in the 1930s. It reached very high levels during the second Peronist period (1974–75). The gap between the black market and the export exchange rate was eliminated between 1978 and 1980 when exchange controls and export taxes were removed. Since 1981, black market exchange rates have increased again as exchange controls have been reimposed.

Figure 12-5 plots foreign and domestic terms of trade for tradable commodities together. The multiple-exchange-rate regime causes the difference between the two curves. The incentives to produce exportable goods as compared with the incentives to produce import substitutes were clearly far apart. It may be concluded that the downward trend of domestic terms of trade from the 1930s until the mid-1950s resulted from policies pursued by the country and not from the trend in the foreign terms of trade.

2. Short-Term Cycles and the External Sector

External balance policies affected not only long-term growth but also the cyclical behavior of the economy in the short run. This can be

Figure 12-5. Foreign and Domestic Terms of Trade in Argentina, 1913–84

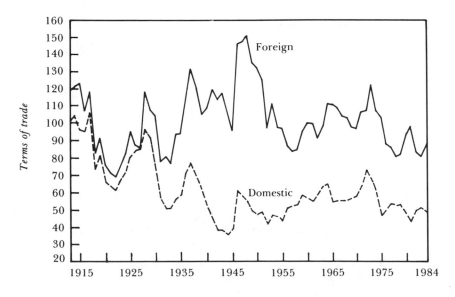

Source: Central Bank of the Argentinian Republic, *Statistical Bulletin.*

noticed by comparing the characteristics of recessions before and after the mid-1950s.

Between 1913 and 1984, there were thirteen "recession periods": 1914, 1916–17, 1925, 1930–32, 1940, 1945, 1949, 1952, 1959, 1962–63, 1975–76, 1978, and 1981–82. Until the mid-1950s, the recession years were accompanied by sharp reductions in agricultural output and in the volume of exports. The only exception was 1930–32, when agricultural output showed reduction only in the first year. Export prices declined substantially during the recessions of 1930–32, 1945, 1952, and 1974–75.

During the earlier recessions, inflation sometimes increased and sometimes declined. Figure 12-6 shows that during the recession periods of 1916–17, 1945, 1949, and 1952, inflation increased, and during those of 1925, 1930–32, and 1940, it either decreased or did not change. In any case, the rate of inflation was generally low, especially when compared with that of later years.

The periods of recession after the mid-1950s appear quite different. They were not particularly related to declines in agricultural output and export volume. On the contrary, in most of these periods exports went up. Large declines in foreign terms of trade were observed only during 1974–75. Consequently, neither agricultural supply shocks nor

Figure 12-6. Rate of Inflation in Argentina, 1913–84

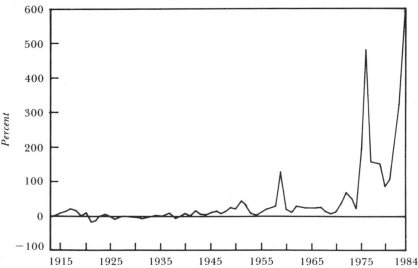

Source: Central Bank of the Argentinian Republic, *Statistical Bulletin.*

deterioration in foreign terms of trade seems to have been as crucial in explaining recessions after the mid-1950s as it was for the recessions of previous decades. Another big difference between the two sets of recession periods related to inflation. Figure 12-6 shows that, after the mid-1950s, the inflation rate accelerated during the recession years. The only exception was 1978, when the inflation rate remained unchanged. These years were therefore typically years of stagflation crisis.

3. The Real Exchange Rate for Exports

The changes over time in the real exchange rate for exports to a large extent determine fluctuations in an economy's trade balance. But what factors affect the real exchange rate? Theory suggests that, in an economy opened to foreign trade and foreign financial flows, which does not use quantitative restriction on imports, the real exchange rate may depend on foreign terms of trade, on taxes on exports and imports, and on the net flow of foreign capital. Increased taxes on exports and imports will result in the deterioration of the real effective exchange rate for exports. Higher inflows of foreign capital will lower the trade balance but will also result in the deterioration of the real exchange rate. The sign of the foreign terms of trade effect cannot be determined from the theory because substitution and income effects move in opposite directions.

The events in Argentina until 1939 are in accord with the theory of the free-market open economy. In figures 12-7 and 12-8, there is a positive correlation between the real exchange rate and the trade balance and a negative correlation between the real exchange rate for exports and taxes on foreign trade.

A very simple regression shows that taxes on foreign trade and the trade balance explain a large proportion of the variation in the real exchange rate for exports between 1913 and 1939:

(12-1)
$$\log \text{REER}_x = \underset{(1.80)}{19.89} - \underset{(14.0)}{3.24} \log \frac{1+t_m}{1-t_x} + \underset{(3.6)}{1.39} \frac{\text{TB}}{\text{PGDP}}$$

$$\bar{R}^2 = 0.89$$

Durbin-Watson statistic (DW) = 1.88

where TB is the trade balance and PGDP is the gross domestic product (both at current prices).

During this period, neither the foreign terms of trade nor any of the macropolicy indicators provided significant additional explanation for the behavior of the real exchange rate.

The situation was very different, however, during 1940–55. All the imports were quantitatively controlled by the government; the economy was completely closed; and there were extensive wage, price, and

**Figure 12-7. Real Effective Exchange Rate for Exports
and the Trade Balance in Argentina, 1913–84**

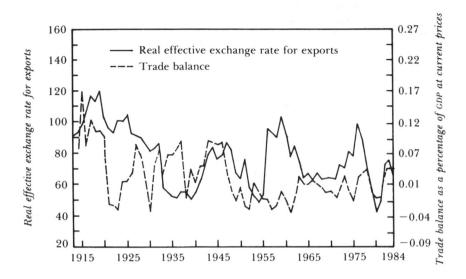

Source: Central Bank of the Argentinian Republic, *Statistical Bulletin.*

**Figure 12-8. Real Effective Exchange Rate for Exports
and Taxes on Foreign Trade in Argentina, 1913–84**

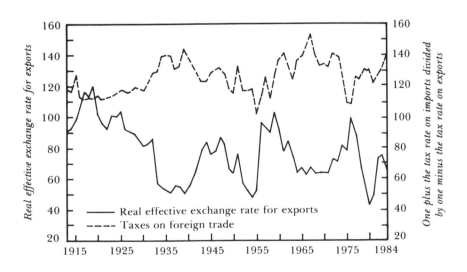

Source: Central Bank of the Argentinian Republic, *Statistical Bulletin.*

exchange controls. In such an economic policy setting, one should not expect the real exchange rate to depend on the same factors as in the free-market open economy of the previous period. Indeed, the taxes on foreign trade were not significant variables in explaining the real exchange rate. Three variables presented significant coefficients in the large trials of alternative regressions: (a) agricultural output as a ratio of nonagricultural output (GDP_{agr}/GDP_{na}), (b) the proportion of government expenditures (PG) over GDP (both at current prices) and (c) the proportion of the trade balance over GDP. The equation for the period 1940–55 is:

(12-2)
$$\log REER_x = 6.10 - 0.03 \frac{GDP_{agr}}{GDP_{na}} + 0.03 \frac{TB}{PGDP} - 0.34 \log \frac{PG}{GDP}$$
$$\quad\quad\quad (5.0) \quad (2.0) \quad\quad\quad\quad (2.0) \quad\quad\quad (1.3)$$
$$\bar{R}^2 = 0.45$$
$$DW = 1.38$$

In the equation, agricultural output as a proportion of nonagricultural output captures much of the large supply shocks that affect the production of exportable goods.

Finally, expansive fiscal policies, represented by the proportion of government expenditures in total output, had a dampening effect on the real exchange rate because government has a high propensity to purchase home goods. Furthermore, under a fixed nominal-exchange-rate regime, expansionary domestic policies lead to a deterioration in the real exchange rate for exports. The behavior curve of government expenditures as a proportion of GDP is shown in figure 12-9. Another important factor that helps explain variations in the real exchange rate for exports is the difference between the rate of nominal devaluation of the currency and the rate of monetary expansion. This relationship is shown in figure 12-10.

Equation 12-2 supports the view that the sources of exchange rate overvaluation during 1940–55 were expansionary fiscal policies, absolute protection to nonagricultural sectors, and restricted imports of basic inputs and capital goods not produced domestically. In addition, variations in the real effective exchange rate for exports were induced by large supply shocks that affected agricultural production. Because of extensive wage and price controls, however, taxes on foreign trade did not affect the value of the real exchange rate.

During 1956–84, the determinants of the real exchange rate for exports changed again. Quantitative import restrictions were reduced but not eliminated. Therefore, protection for nonagricultural production was somehow in between that of the 1940–55 period and that of the previous decades. Exchange rate policy became more important as large devaluations, "dirty" floating, fixed exchange rates, and adminis-

Figure 12-9. Real Effective Exchange Rate for Exports and Government Expenditures in Argentina, 1913–84

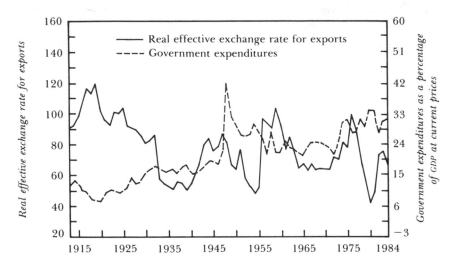

Source: Central Bank of the Argentinian Republic, *Statistical Bulletin.*

Figure 12-10. Real Effective Exchange Rates for Exports, Nominal-Exchange-Rate Management, and Monetary Policy in Argentina, 1913–84

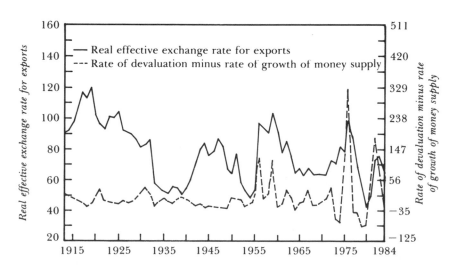

Source: Central Bank of the Argentinian Republic, *Statistical Bulletin.*

tered minidevaluations alternated over the period. These institutional changes are reflected in the real exchange equation estimated for 1956–84:

$$
\begin{aligned}
\text{(12-3)} \quad \log \text{REER}_x = \ &11.53 - 0.96 \ \log \frac{1+t_m}{1-t_x} + 0.83 \ \log \frac{M}{\text{GDP}} \\
&\ (5.9) \quad (3.0) \qquad\qquad\quad (3.3)
\end{aligned}
$$

$$
\begin{aligned}
&-0.85 \ \log \frac{\text{PG}}{\text{PGDP}} + 0.09 \ (\hat{E}-\hat{M}_1) \\
&\ (4.7) \qquad\qquad\quad (3.3)
\end{aligned}
$$

$$
\begin{aligned}
&+ \ 0.15 \ (\hat{E}-\hat{M}_1)_{-1} + 0.05 \ (\hat{E}-\hat{M}_1)_{-2} \\
&\ (6.1) \qquad\qquad\qquad (2.2)
\end{aligned}
$$

$$\bar{R}^2 = 0.80$$
$$\text{DW} = 1.33$$

where E is the rate of devaluation of the domestic currency and M_1 is the rate of growth of money supply. The difference between these two variables, that is, $E - M_1$, summarizes the effect of exchange rate management and monetary policy on the real effective exchange rate for exports.

Note that for the period 1956–84, as in 1913–39, taxes on foreign trade again help explain the changes in the real exchange rate for exports. The volume of imports was also significant, as expected in a situation in which the quantities imported were partly under the control of the government. Nevertheless, M/GDP indicates the intensity of the protection coming from quantitative restrictions on imports. Accordingly, M/GDP has a positive coefficient, showing that larger imports increase the real exchange rates for exports.

Equation 12-3 also shows that fiscal policy, as represented by the ratio of government expenditures PG to GDP, does affect the real exchange rate. Finally, nominal-exchange-rate devaluations exceeding the rate of growth in the money supply also have strong effects on the real exchange rate, as is captured by the three lags of the $E-M_1$ variable. Longer lags did not have significant coefficients.

The strong effects of fiscal, monetary, and exchange rate policies during 1956–84, compared with the 1913–39 period, clearly relate to the presence of quantitative restrictions on imports in the more recent period, which enlarges the size of the nontradable sectors of the economy.

Equation 12-3 suggests that the big fluctuations experienced by the real exchange rate since 1956 resulted from economic policies rather than from external shocks. Periods of overvaluation were experienced as a result of expansionary fiscal and monetary policies, especially when these policies were accompanied by fixed nominal exchange rates or by a rate of devaluation not in line with the rate of expansion of aggregate demand. Overvaluation was eliminated through large nominal devaluations. The characteristic stagflation crises of the 1956–84 period were closely related to the policy-induced cyclical variations in the real exchange rate. These played a crucial role in creating the recurrent balance of payment crises observed in the Argentinian economy.

4. Speculation and Hyperinflation

Each big devaluation in Argentina induced sharp reductions in M_1/Y and M_3/Y, the money and time deposits as proportions of income (see figure 12-11). These reductions in the demand for domestic money accompanied increased speculation by economic agents in the exchange rate markets. When tight exchange controls existed, black market premiums increased tremendously. When exchange controls were eliminated during 1979–81 and economic policies overvalued the domestic currency, the natural outcome was capital flight and large tourism expenditure abroad. This period was known in Argentina as the "Plata Dulce" (sweet money) years. The recurrence of big devaluations not only increased the risk of hyperinflation because of widespread wage indexation to inflation but also reduced the demand for domestic money.

Figure 12-11. M_1 and M_3 as Percentages of GDP in Argentina, 1913–84

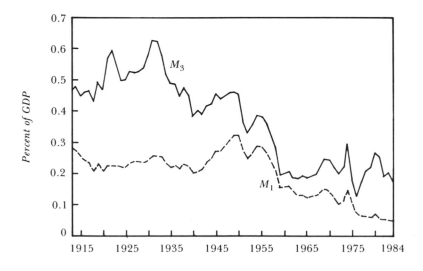

Source: Central Bank of the Argentinian Republic, *Statistical Bulletin.*

Figure 12-12 shows the fiscal deficit as a proportion of GDP for the years 1913–84. The fiscal deficits of the period 1973–84 were only slightly larger than those in the years following World War II. Inflation rates never exceeded 50 percent a year in the late 1940s, however, whereas they ranged between 80 percent and 600 percent a year during 1973–84. No doubt wage indexation, low demand for domestic money, and a long history of widespread foreign exchange speculation have created a big contrast between the Argentinian economy of the 1980s and that of the 1940s. The achievement of price stability is thus a difficult task for present-day policymakers.

Figure 12-12. Fiscal Deficit as a Percentage of GDP in Argentina, 1913–84

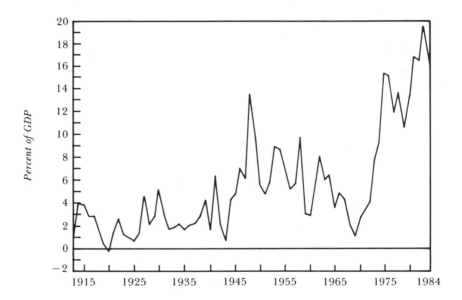

Source: Central Bank of the Argentinian Republic, *Statistical Bulletin.*

Notes

1. Diaz Alejandro has emphasized the importance of external balance policies in explaining Argentina's long-term performance since World War II. See Carlos Diaz Alejandro, *Essays on the Economic History of the Argentine Republic* (New Haven, Conn.: Yale University Press, 1970). Cavallo and Mundlak's econometric study on Argentinian growth performance supports most of Diaz

Alejandro's early conjectures on the effect of trade distortions and exchange rate overvaluation on growth; see Domingo Cavallo and Yair Mundlak, *Agriculture and Economic Growth in an Open Economy: The Case of Argentina*, Research Report 36 (Washington, D.C.: International Food Policy Research Institute, 1982). For a different explanation of Argentina's poor growth performance, see Guido Di Tella and Manuel Zymelman, *Las etapas del desarrollo económico argentino* (Buenos Aires: European Development Bank, 1967), and Aldo Ferrer, *La economía argentina: Las etapas de su desarrollo y problemas actuales* (Mexico City: Fondo de Cultura Economica, 1963). For an interpretation emphasizing linkages between economics and politics, see Richard Mallon and Juan Sourrouille, *Economic Policymaking in a Conflict Society* (Cambridge, Mass.: Harvard University Press, 1975).

2. For empirical evidence, see Cavallo and Mundlak, *Agriculture and Economic Growth in an Open Economy,* and Susana Gluck, "Resena de estimaciones de oferta agricola pampeana," *Ensayos Económicos* (Buenos Aires, Central Bank of the Argentinian Republic), no. 10 (June 1979), pp. 35–84.

3. This analysis is based on a careful comparison of nominal protection and domestic prices as well as border prices for a large number of goods. For details see Julio Berlinsky and Daniel Schidlowsky, "Incentives for Industrialization in Argentina," in Bela Balassa and associates, *Development Strategies in Semi-Industrialized Economies* (Baltimore, Md.: John Hopkins University Press, 1982). Berlinsky and Schidlowsky's estimates of the average implicit rate of protection in 1969 are very similar to the rate obtained for the same year when similar procedures are employed to compute the REER$_{ms}$ using the actual average rate of import tax reported by Carlos Diaz Alejandro for 1929 as benchmark for t_m^i. It is very reasonable to apply average rate of import tax for t_m^i in 1929 because quantitative import restrictions were not employed in that year.

13

Brazil

Mario Henrique Simonsen

A CONTROVERSIAL case study is the highly unorthodox economic policies that Brazil followed from 1950 through 1980 to promote growth and trade. The result was impressive growth rates, but despite this success some analysts believe that the policies were never appropriate for the country. Others argue that Brazil had such a dynamic economy that it could afford to make any grandiose policy mistake.

1. From Coffee Valorization to External Debt

Until the late 1920s, Brazil was, despite its geographic size, a typical example of a small, open economy, with imports and exports together averaging 23 percent of GNP. The country specialized in a few agricultural exports (mainly coffee) and imported most of the raw materials and industrial goods. Infant industries were heavily protected, not as a matter of economy strategy but to raise revenues through import duties. To improve the country's terms of trade, particularly for its coffee, exports were restricted to increase external prices by what came to be known as the valorization policies.

The improvement achieved in the terms of trade (from an index of 100 in 1920 to 186 in 1929) helped push Brazil toward an outward-looking growth policy. Real GNP grew at an average annual rate of 5.3 percent in the 1920s. The government made the mistake, however, of transferring the monopoly profits to domestic procedures instead of absorbing them through export taxes. Excess profits led to excess supply, which weakened the country's monopoly over coffee production. Understanding of the problem was delayed by the fact that coffee is a perennial crop whose current supply depends, with a long lag, on past prices.

For these mistakes Brazil had to pay a high price. The country became too dependent on coffee, which was the source of 73 percent of total export revenues between 1924 and 1929. A powerful coffee lobby obtained credit, fiscal, and exchange rate preferences to guarantee high profits for coffee producers. Export profits (then the major source of domestic savings), rather than being used for economic diversification, were invested in new coffee plantations by risk-averse enterpreneurs.

Coffee prices ultimately collapsed because of the downward shift in external demand, because of domestic overproduction, and because of the lagged response to price incentives in the previous decade. The government tried to minimize the losses of coffee producers by devaluing the exchange rate, and by burning a sizable part of the excess production it created an international scandal at the time. Export earnings nevertheless declined by 60 percent between 1929 and 1932, so that the government was forced to implement tough import controls. These controls marked the beginning of a thirty-five-year period of inward-looking growth policy.

In the initial stages, import substitution was encouraged as an ad hoc response to balance of payment problems caused by trade disruption during the Great Depression and by external supply shortages during World War II. Even so, the policy helped Brazil to escape the impact of the Great Depression. Real GNP fell 5 percent between 1929 and 1932 but recovered quickly thereafter. The overall growth rate of GNP was 4.5 percent. These rates were better than those in the industrial countries. Between 1939 and 1945, the growth rates again declined as a result of supply shortages (see table 13-1).

In 1946, import controls were abolished because trade surpluses during World War II had accumulated $800 million in reserves. Import liberalization was successfully used to dampen inflation, but because the exchange rate was overvalued, reserves were depleted within eighteen

Table 13-1. Average Annual Rates of Growth of Real GNP
(percent)

Period	Agriculture	Industry	Total GNP
1920–29	4.0	5.3	5.2
1930–39	2.0	7.6	4.5
1940–45	1.6	4.6	3.1
1946–55	4.6	9.5	7.5
1956–61	4.6	10.0	8.0
1962–67	2.4	4.1	3.7
1968–73	3.9	13.1	11.1
1974–80	4.8	7.2	7.1
1981–86[a]	1.6	1.6	2.8

a. 1986: Provisional data.
Source: Getulio Vargas Foundation.

months. Controls were eventually reintroduced, and import substitution was officially made the core of a new growth strategy. The main argument made was that Brazil's comparative advantages lay in a few products that faced an inelastic external demand and that outward-looking growth policies would burden the country with heavy losses in external terms of trade. Emerging local industries were heavily protected by a mix of import controls, multiple exchange rates, and high import duties. New financial institutions, funded by additional taxes and forced savings, channeled large amounts of money into highway construction and into investments in steel, cement, capital goods, oil, and electric power. Moreover, the special incentives offered by the Kubitschek administration (1959–60) also helped broaden industrial diversification, transforming Brazil into a manufacturer of automobiles, trucks, consumer durables, and capital goods.

Although inward-looking policies were based on controversial theories, the results were spectacular. Between 1929 and 1964, real GNP grew at average annual rates of 5.6 percent and industrial output at 7.8 percent. For 1946–64, the figures were 7 percent and 8.9 percent, respectively. Real exports and imports, however, stagnated during the thirty-five-year period of import substitution. For instance, the share of imports as a percentage of GNP fell from 23.8 percent in 1929 to 5.6 percent in 1964. The implication is that the new policy failed to keep a proper balance between infant-industry protection and comparative advantages in international trade. The cruzeiro remained overvalued. The economy grew at an impressive rate, however, because savings, investment, and economic diversification were encouraged.

In 1964, policymakers decided to examine whether export stagnation was the outcome of external demand inelasticities or of poor exchange rate incentives. The outcome of the debate was that the multiple-exchange-rate system was abolished and the currency was devalued. Import duties were reduced in 1966, exchange rates were indexed through a crawling-peg mechanism in 1968, and subsidies were provided for the export of manufactures in 1969.

The market response was tremendous: exports increased from $1.6 billion in 1965 to $6.2 billion in 1973. For the first time, industrial products, such as textiles and footwear, became important export items that reduced the country's vulnerability to changes in coffee prices. From 1968 through 1973, Brazil's growth rates exceeded 10 percent a year and inflation declined. These were the golden years of the so-called Brazilian miracle, which apparently displayed the virtues of outward-looking growth policies.

The miracle ended with a $4.7 billion trade deficit in 1974, partly the result of the quadrupling of oil prices and partly the effect of the overheating of demand in 1973. A new administration decided to keep the country growing at 7 percent a year. To promote external adjustment, import substitution and export promotion investment programs were initiated. The trade gap was to be filled by a controlled increase in external debt. This adjustment strategy (subsequently reinforced by a number of protectionist actions) would have worked if real interest rates had remained low and if the economy had not had to absorb further adverse external shocks. The second oil shock in 1979 and 1980, however, and high dollar interest rates changed everything. Brazil's external debt went out of control in 1980, and the country was trapped by the collapse of commercial bank recycling in 1982.

Because of credit rationing, the external accounts had to be adjusted immediately. The cruzeiro was devalued 30 percent in real terms in 1983. The initial results were disappointing: an escalation of inflation rates combined with unprecedented recession. Then, in 1984, with a vigorous export-led recovery effort, real GNP increased 4.5 percent, and a trade surplus of $13 billion was recorded. The trade surplus was substantially higher than the target under the adjustment program supported by the International Monetary Fund (IMF). The structural adjustment policies initiated by Brazil in 1974 finally paid off. In spite of the annual inflation rate, which had been 220 percent since 1983, the country is now growing at 6–7 percent a year and is maintaining a sound balance in its payments position.

Any judgment regarding Brazil's trade and exchange rate policies would be controversial. A $100 billion external debt combined with a 220 percent inflation rate hardly allows the country to be described as a success story. Yet the 7 percent growth rate recovery since 1984 cannot be cited as evidence of failure.

A balanced view may be that since World War I Brazilian economic policies have moved from naive orthodoxy to overregulation. On the positive side, the government's intervention in most instances encouraged savings and investments. On the negative side, excessive intervention reduced wage-price flexibility and the ability to respond to external shocks.

2. Indexation Issues

Inflation is part of the Brazilian way of life. Since the early 1950s, annual inflation rates have ranged from 11 percent in 1952 to 223 percent in 1984. Price increases were moderately stable until 1958, averaging 17 percent a year, but they quickly escalated thereafter to 92 percent in 1964, first as a consequence of the expansionary policies of the Kubitschek administration, then as a result of the populist engagements of the Goulart administration. After the military took over the government in 1964, the inflation rate was brought down to 15–20 percent until the early 1970s. After the first oil shock in 1974, annual price increases leaped to 37 percent on average. Expansive monetary, fiscal, and incomes policies pushed the average inflation rate to 100 percent a year in 1982 and to more than 200 percent a year after early 1983.

Until 1964, escalator clauses were illegal in Brazil. Usury laws established a nominal interest ceiling of 12 percent a year. With soaring inflation rates, bond markets were doomed. Government deficits were therefore fully financed by money creation. The expansion of the money supply did not run completely out of control, however, partly because of credit rationing and partly because in the late 1950s a number of escapes were found in the usury ceilings. In order to dampen price shocks the government often tried to impose money illusion by law. Tenancy laws virtually froze nominal rents by indefinitely extending rent contracts after their maturity at the option of the tenant. Public utility profits and depreciation allowances were limited by law to fixed percentages of the historical cruzeiro net asset values. A proliferation of supply limitations was the natural outcome of this set of regulations. A collapse was avoided only because the government invested heavily in public utilities and because subsidized loans were massively extended to the privately owned public utility companies.

From the end of World War II until 1964, the government experimented with four different exchange rate policies. First, until August 1953, the Bretton Woods dollar/cruzeiro parity was kept unchanged. With domestic inflation rates exceeding 10 percent a year, the exchange rate became progressively more overvalued. An unprecedented rise in coffee prices and tough import controls, however, sustained the overvalued cruzeiro.

Second, the fixed exchange rate was replaced by a complicated multiple-rate system with no fewer than twelve different dollar/cruzeiro rates: four different fixed rates for exports (the least attractive was for coffee and the most favorable for manufactured products); fixed rates for privileged imports (such as oil and wheat); five different rates for other imports determined by foreign exchange auctions; and a floating rate for financial transactions. The fixed rates were often realigned to cope with the domestic inflation rate of 20 percent a year.

Third, in early 1961, the short-lived Quadros administration established a unique floating exchange rate that resulted in a big cruzeiro devaluation. Because of monetary accommodation, the result was 45 percent inflation when price increases should have been only temporary.

Fourth, to dampen the price increases, the Goulart administration turned back to the multiple-exchange-rate system (though it was less complicated than the preceding one) and to quantitative import controls. Inflation continued to escalate because of increased budget deficits and generous increases in nominal wages.

The new military government in 1964 introduced a radical program to fight inflation, promote external adjustment, and encourage savings and growth. Under the program, budget deficits were to be eliminated by fiscal reform; bonds and taxes were to be indexed to encourage private savings; money supply was to be regulated by an independent central bank; rents and public utility rates were to be corrected for past inflation and then indexed for future general price increases; income policies were to break the wage-price spiral; realistic exchange rates were to be pursued to promote balance of payments equilibrium; import duties were to be lowered, and capital and imports were to flow unhindered.

The fiscal reform achieved considerable success. The budget deficit was brought down from 4 percent to 1 percent of gross domestic product. The indexation of capital market instruments encouraged savings and restored the mortgage market. Tax indexation reduced tax evasion. (In 1963, when the inflation rate was running at 80 percent a year, the penalty on tax arrears was only 32 percent a year.) New rent policies led to the recovery in housing construction. The proposal for an independent central bank still remains to be fulfilled. Although the central bank has been created, it shares some of the traditional functions of the long-established Banco do Brasil. Both banks are supervised by a monetary council chaired by the minister of finance.

The income policy was implemented in July 1965 and deindexed wages from inflation rates. It played a major role in fighting inflation. Nominal wages were fixed for a twelve-month period, then adjusted for the expected inflation rate, so that the average purchasing power remained equal to the average real wage of the past twenty-four months and showed some productivity gain.

The rationale for the wage rule of July 1965 is described in figure 13-1. In an inflationary economy, where nominal wages are adjusted at constant time intervals (for example, one year), two concepts must be distinguished: the average real wage (W_m) and the wage peak (W_0). The average real wage is what the economy can afford to pay labor and is the level that should be maintained by incomes policies except for small productivity adjustments. The real wage peak is attained immediately after a nominal increase. Because the average/peak ratio decreases with inflation, peaks should be lowered whenever the inflation rate is expected to decline. With decreasing inflation rates, nominal wages should be adjusted less than proportionally to past cost-of-living increases.

Figure 13-1. The Average Wage and the Wage Peak

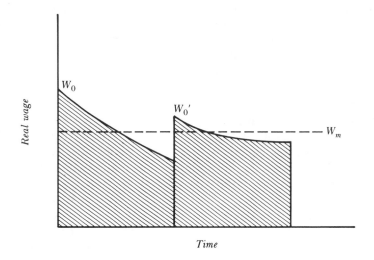

From a technical standpoint the July 1965 wage formula consisted of staggered-wage determination based on rational expectations. It became an incomes policy device because both the productivity gain and the expected rate of inflation for the following twelve months were decreed by the government, so that no room remained for collective bargaining or strikes.

In cases where individuals negotiated with their employers, wages could be adjusted. Individual negotiations were never prohibited by the government. In other cases, real wages were squeezed if the authorities underestimated future inflation rates. In 1965, for instance, the cost of living increased 45 percent, although the inflation rate forecast was 25 percent; in 1966 the figures were 41 percent and 10 percent, respectively, and, in 1967, 24 percent and 15 percent. In fact, the average wage in the manufacturing industry declined 25 percent between 1964 and 1968, less because of the weakened position of labor unions after the 1964 revolution than because of the new policy that increased indirect taxes, real rents, and public utility rates; cut subsidies; and promoted a strong real-exchange-rate devaluation. The real wage decrease was accompanied by declines in inflation rates from 92 percent in 1964 to 24 percent in 1967. Industrial output dropped by 4.7 percent in 1965 but then increased by 9.8 percent in 1966. The July 1965 wage policy paved the way for a seven-year period of accelerated growth and declining inflation.

Exchange rate policies actually brought the balance of payments into equilibrium without the need for capital and import controls and even resulted in a significant accumulation of reserves in 1965. In 1966, import duties were substantially reduced, but the current account remained close to equilibrium. The only criticism to which exchange rate policies were vulnerable in that period was that they took the Bretton Woods regime too seriously. Although inflation rates were reduced considerably, they were not brought down to the one-digit figures of the United States. Hence devaluations could not be avoided for long, and this was quickly perceived by economic agents. The result was a huge drawdown of reserves, which (among other inconveniences) complicated the management of monetary policy. Reserves increased swiftly after each devaluation and then gradually declined until a new devaluation became a self-fulfilling prophecy.

Imaginative as they might have been, the economic policies of the Castello Branco administration (1964–67) could not last for long. Most incomes and financial assets were indexed but not wages and exchange rates (not to mention money, because a government should never give up the possibility of collecting some inflation tax).

Wages and exchange rates were indexed in 1968. The new wage law retained the 1965 formula, but the wages in the previous twelve months entered the formula not by their actual values but by those that would have prevailed if inflation rates had been properly foreseen. In practice, the implication was that nominal wages were to be adjusted every twelve months in proportion to the increase in the cost of living plus a productivity gain. This backward-looking indexation, instead of stabilizing the average purchasing power W_m, simply restored every twelve months the real wage peak W_0 adjusted for productivity increases (see figure 13-2).

Because the average/peak ratio decreases with the inflation rate, the new wage rule implied that inflation could decline only as long as average real wages grew faster than the officially determined productivity gain. Moreover, because the law gave a floor rather than a ceiling to changes in labor compensation, it introduced an asymmetry between inflation acceleration and inflation deceleration. In fact, markets were free to increase the peak W_0 but not to reduce it except through labor turnover, which was the only way to escape the law. Yet this device was highly costly for skilled workers and virtually useless for nonskilled ones, because minimum wages were adjusted by the same indexation rule. In short, backward-looking wage indexation introduced adverse short-run inflation-output tradeoffs, which discouraged quick antiinflationary policies and favored monetary accommodation. The problem was not perceived until 1973 because, during the golden years of the Brazilian miracle, average real wages rose faster than the officially determined productivity increases. In fact, inflation rates declined

Figure 13-2. Restoration of Wage Peaks

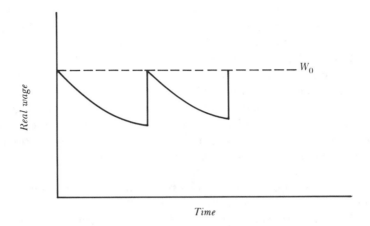

steadily from about 25 percent a year in 1967 to about 16 percent in 1973. Thereafter the expansive monetary policies of 1972 and 1973, combined with the first oil shock, increased the annual inflation rate to 35 percent in 1974. Tight monetary policies were then tried but soon abandoned because wage indexation was considered to be encouraging the wage-price spiral. Eventually the government chose monetary accommodation, which kept the annual inflation rates in the range of 35–40 percent a year until 1978.

Two imprudent policy steps taken in late 1979 increased inflation rates further. First, the government decided to control interest rates, which expanded the money supply by 75 percent. Second, a new wage law reduced the nominal wage adjustment interval from twelve months to six. Then the previously annual inflation rate became the six-month inflation rate. Tight monetary policies were implemented in 1981 and again in 1982 but encountered the adverse tradeoffs created by backward-looking indexation. As a result, the country had to experience the first major industrial recession since 1965 with an unimpressive antiinflationary package. Inflation rates declined from 110 percent in 1980 to only 95 percent in 1981 and 100 percent in 1982. This picture sharply contrasted with the much milder recession of 1965, when the annual inflation rate dropped from 92 percent to 34 percent.

Under external credit rationing, the country was forced to adjust its balance of payments in 1983. Key policy changes included a 30 percent real-exchange-rate devaluation and substantial indirect tax increases and subsidy cuts. Because of the prevailing wage indexation rules, however, there was an acceleration of the inflation rate. In fact, inflation leaped to 210 percent a year, notwithstanding tight monetary policies.

In mid-1984, the government decided once again to turn to monetary accommodation.

Exchange rate indexation had been introduced in August 1968 to reduce the swings in external reserves caused by discontinuous devaluations since 1964. As a basic guideline, the cruzeiro/dollar rate was changed by small percentages and at irregular intervals of time (ten to fifty days until 1978), depending on the inflation rate differential between Brazil and the United States. Slight adjustments were made to this basic rule by taking into account fluctuations of the dollar against other major currencies; differentials in the inflation rate among the major countries of the Organisation for Economic Co-operation and Development (OECD); changes in terms of trade; and problems with the balance of payments.

The collapse of the Bretton Woods system provided an excuse for a real 9 percent appreciation in the cruzeiro/dollar rate between 1970 and 1973; the real-exchange-rate index appears below in constant cruzeiros per constant dollars.

1968	108.4	1976	98.2
1969	108.7	1977	98.0
1970	109.4	1978	99.2
1971	107.4	1979	128.7
1972	106.1	1980	106.0
1973	100.0	1981	115.6
1974	99.6	1982	118.7
1975	100.5	1983	157.5
		1984	163.5

For the next six years the real parity was kept virtually unchanged. On December 7, 1979, the tradition was broken by a 30 percent devaluation of the cruzeiro. The currency realignment that followed was only temporary because the increase in the cruzeiro/dollar rate was predetermined at 50 percent for 1980, substantially below the 110 percent inflation rate. A return to the traditional crawling-peg rules was announced in early 1981, with a change that allowed for some exchange rate depreciation until 1982. Exchange rates were to follow domestic inflation rates, without discounting the price increases in the United States. Then, in February 1983, the central bank declared a maxidevaluation of the cruzeiro by 30 percent.

Compared with other Latin American countries that have used exchange rate overvaluation as an instrument to delay price increases, Brazil with its crawling peg may appear to have achieved some success since 1968. Brazil at least managed to index not only wages but also the exchange rate, and at short intervals. After the fact one may argue that a real-exchange-rate devaluation should have been decreed after the first oil shock or at least immediately after the second. (The 30 percent maxidevaluation in December 1979 was actually a step in this direction but was virtually neutralized by the 1980 predetermined increase in the cruzeiro/dollar rate.) In any case, it should not be forgotten that the collapse of the Bretton Woods system blurred the notion that the equilibrium exchange rate could be used as an instrument for current account performance, as shown by the performance of the U.S. economy in 1984 and 1985.

Brazil must be criticized for choosing the complicated strategy of substituting widespread indexation for price stability. One may argue that price stability as a goal could never have been reconciled with the country's expansive monetary and fiscal policies and that informal indexation arrangements were eventually to emerge. Informal indexation systems, however, seldom introduce as much inflationary rigidity as the backward-looking wage/price links of the Brazilian economic legislation. In nonindexed economies relative price changes often impose once-and-for-all price increases. The equivalent effect, under the Brazilian indexation regime, is a permanent leap in the inflation rate. A professional mathematician might accept the notion that in an indexed economy what matters is not the inflation rate but inflation acceleration, provided all incomes and financial assets are homogeneously adjusted for inflation with the same lags. Most economic agents, however, regard high inflation rates as a symptom of economic mismanagement, partly because agents are not adequately trained in abstract reasoning. Moreover, even the professional mathematician would immediately conclude that homogeneous indexation is nothing but a useless exercise in complication.

For policymakers, high inflation is the worst of all worlds. They rarely succeed in fighting it except in periods of favorable supply shocks. Moreover, realizing that their rating will be highly damaged if inflation accelerates, they try to postpone any adverse relative price change as long as possible. This concern largely explains the proliferation of export subsidies and selective import restrictions after 1968, when the Brazilian economy became almost fully indexed. It also explains why, in the same year, capital controls were reintroduced, which led to a black market (but officially condoned) exchange rate. In fact, widespread indexation is a lively example of overregulation that has impaired relative price flexibility and prevented quick domestic responses to external challenges.

3. Balance of Payments Policies

Table 13-2 prevents Brazil's balance of payments data for 1961 through 1984. In the early 1960s, as a consequence of inward-looking growth

Table 13-2. Brazil's Balance of Payments, 1961–84

(millions of U.S. dollars)

Year	Exports[a] (1)	Imports[a] (2)	Trade balance (1) − (2) (3)	Services and transfers (4)	Current account (3) + (4) (5)	Autonomous capital flows (6)	Errors and omissions (7)	Surplus or deficit (−) (5) + (6) + (7) (8)
1961	1,403	1,292	111	−327	−261	327	49	115
1962	1,214	1,304	−90	−362	−452	244	−138	−346
1963	1,406	1,294	112	−283	−171	3	−76	−244
1964	1,430	1,086	344	−263	81	140	−217	4
1965	1,596	941	655	−372	283	79	−31	331
1966	1,741	1,303	438	−471	−33	205	−19	153
1967	1,654	1,441	213	−490	−277	66	−34	−245
1968	1,881	1,855	26	−534	−508	541	−1	32
1969	2,311	1,993	318	−599	−281	850	−20	549
1970	2,739	2,526	213	−835	−622	1,060	107	545

1971	2,878	3,250	−372	−915	−1,287	1,566	257	536
1972	3,991	4,235	−244	−1,245	−1,489	3,492	436	2,479
1973	6,199	6,192	7	−1,695	−1,688	3,512	355	2,179
1974	7,951	12,641	−4,690	−2,432	−7,122	6,254	−68	−936
1975	8,670	12,210	−3,540	−3,160	−6,700	6,189	−439	−950
1976	10,128	12,383	−2,255	−3,762	−6,017	6,595	615	1,192
1977	12,120	12,023	97	−4,134	−4,037	5,278	−611	630
1978	12,659	13,683	−1,024	−5,966	−6,990	11,891	−639	4,262
1979	15,244	18,084	−2,840	−7,902	−10,742	7,657	−130	−3,215
1980	20,132	22,955	−2,823	−9,984	−12,807	9,679	−344	−3,472
1981	23,293	22,091	1,202	−13,217	−11,728	12,917	−578	611
1982	20,175	19,395	700	−17,710	−16,310	7,851	−368	−8,828
1983	21,899	15,428	6,740	−13,308	−6,837	1,538	−670	−5,969
1984	27,004	13,937	13,068	−12,902	166	−1,822	215	−1,441

a. f.o.b.

Source: Central Bank of Brazil.

policies, Brazil's exports stagnated at about $1.4 billion. Coffee accounted for 50 percent of total export revenues. Services and transfers, including interest on the $3 billion external debt, cost about $300 million a year. As a result, changes in the current account largely reflected import fluctuations. Access to external capital was strongly restricted. Autonomous capital inflows adjusted for errors and omissions were limited to an average of $76 million a year between 1961 and 1965. Reserves being scarce, the balance of payment deficits of 1962 and 1963 were partly financed by a buildup of $300 million in commercial arrears. Adjustment policies in 1964 and 1965, based on strong exchange rate devaluations and tight controls on aggregate demand, helped increase reserves and improve the country's international credit standing. What increased the reserves, however, was not growth in exports but decline in imports.

As a consequence of the policy changes in the mid-1960s, exports and imports increased swiftly between 1965 and 1973. The export boom was a response to the crawling-peg exchange rate, to the world economic growth, and to the special incentives for export diversification (which included export subsidies for manufactured products). Imports increased because of more liberal trade policies and a high rate of domestic economic growth (10 percent a year). Deficit in the service account also increased swiftly, from an average of $300 million in the early 1960s to $1.7 billion in 1973. Because the trade balance remained close to equilibrium, net service payments virtually equaled the current account deficits. Because of access to external capital (Brazil benefited greatly from the development of the Eurodollar markets), autonomous capital inflows largely exceeded current account deficits. As a result of successive external surpluses, foreign reserves had increased to an unprecedented $6.4 billion by the end of 1973.

Accumulated current account deficits increased the country's net external debt (that is, total debt minus reserves) from $3 billion in the mid-1960s to $7.2 billion in December 1973. Yet this debt did not arouse concern for several reasons: Brazil had avoided short-term borrowing; the central bank held sizable reserves; the country had a good international credit standing; and the increase in indebtedness was accompanied by an export boom. In fact, net external debt as a percentage of annual exports fell from 200 percent in the mid-1960s to less than 120 percent in 1973.

In 1974, however, the new Geisel administration faced an unprecedented trade deficit of $4.7 billion and a current account deficit of $7.1 billion partly because oil prices were quadrupled but also because of the lagged response to the expansive monetary policies in 1972 and 1973. Although the additional cost of oil import was matched by export growth (from $6.2 billion in 1973 to $8 billion in 1974), the 104 percent increase in dollar imports (from $6.2 billion to $12.6 billion) proved to be burdensome. Average import prices increased 50 percent, and the quantities imported also increased 36 percent. The implication was that Brazil was trying to grow beyond its means.

Adjustment policies were considered necessary, but opinions differed as to the manner and the speed of achieving adjustment. The minister of finance wanted to control aggregate demand to keep savings rates high in order to finance export promotion and import substitution. The minister of planning wanted the economy to keep growing at 10 percent a year; such growth was a central assumption of the second national development plan. The president of the central bank was less concerned with debt growth than with managing the maturity profile of debt. He wanted additional borrowing to be encouraged, provided that short-term indebtedness was avoided and reserves kept at safe levels.

The compromise reached was that Brazil should grow at 7 percent (rather than 10 percent) a year between 1974 and 1978. An ambitious investment program financed by both domestic and external savings was implemented to foster export growth and encourage import substitution. This strategy, however, could yield only long-term results; immediate actions were considered necessary to reduce the current account deficit. The most natural choice would have been a real-exchange-rate devaluation. This option was discarded for two reasons. First, considering the backward-looking wage-indexation regime, a real-exchange-rate devaluation would have increased the inflation rate permanently. Second, it would have imposed heavy losses on externally indebted firms, undermined confidence in the exchange rate, and discouraged further borrowing abroad. Consequently Brazil once again chose to complicate matters: it increased subsidies to manufactured exports, imposed higher import duties, increased taxes on oil products, and required advance deposits (with zero nominal interest rate) on a large list of import items. Some nonessential imports, such as automobiles, were simply prohibited.

The export incentives and import surcharges yielded some impressive results until 1977. A simulation made by the Ministry of Finance in early 1975 showed that these measures would result in an annual increase of $1.3 billion in the noninterest current account balance. Net foreign debt would escalate to $35.5 billion in 1981 and would then begin to decline gradually. The $1.3 billion increase per year corresponded to one-fifth of the noninterest current account deficit in 1974. The simulation, reproduced in table 13-3, shows how balance of payments projections were made in Brazil in the mid-1970s; it is based on the following hypotheses:

- Foreign direct investment would average $800 million a year; the annual increase in net external debt would therefore equal the current account deficit minus $800 million.

Table 13-3. Cumulative Debt Projection, 1975–82
(billions of U.S. dollars)

Year	Net initial debt (1)	Noninterest current account deficit (2)	Net interest payments (1) × 0.1 (3)	Net final debt (1) + (2) + (3) − 0.8 (4)	Exports (5)	Debt-to-export ratio (4)/(5)
1975	13.4	5.2	1.3	19.1	9.2	2.1
1976	19.1	3.9	1.9	24.1	10.6	2.3
1977	24.1	2.6	2.4	28.3	12.2	2.3
1978	28.3	1.3	2.8	31.7	14.0	2.3
1979	31.7	0	3.2	34.1	16.1	2.1
1980	34.1	−1.3	3.4	35.4	18.5	1.9
1981	35.4	−2.6	3.5	35.5	21.3	1.6
1982	35.5	−3.9	3.6	34.4	24.5	1.4

Source: Simulation results by the author.

- Noninterest current account deficits would decline according to a predetermined formula.
- Annual interest payments would correspond to 10 percent of the net external debt at the beginning of the year.
- Dollar exports would grow at 15 percent a year.

The simulation now appears to be an exercise in naive optimism, because Brazil's net external debt increased to about $100 billion in 1983. In a growing economy with a fixed real exchange rate, a steady improvement in the noninterest current account can be attributed only to structural adjustment or to anticipated gains in the terms of trade. In 1975, there was no reason to anticipate such gains or to overestimate the speed of response to structural adjustment.

What actually happened is shown in table 13-4. The annual current account deficit decreased from $7.1 billion in 1974 to $4 billion in 1977. The result was better than had been forecast by the 1975 debt simulation: a drop in the current account deficit from $7.1 billion to $5 billion during the same period. The decline of the noninterest current account deficit to $1.9 billion was partly in response to monetary and trade policies and partly the result of improved terms of trade. Because the current account deficit, as a proportion of GNP, was reduced to the level that had prevailed before oil prices quintupled, a number of analysts wrongly concluded that Brazil had completed its external adjustment program. Then, in 1978, because of unusually bad crops that cost substantial export losses, worsened terms of trade, and a fall in government savings from 4 percent to 2.3 percent of GNP, the noninterest current account deficit again increased to $4.3 billion.

Table 13-4. Brazil's Current Account Deficit, 1971–84
(billions of U.S. dollars)

Year	Noninterest current account deficit	Net interest payments	Current account deficit
1971	1.0	0.3	1.3
1972	1.1	0.4	1.5
1973	1.2	0.5	1.7
1974	6.5	0.6	7.1
1975	5.2	1.5	6.7
1976	4.3	1.8	6.1
1977	1.9	2.1	4.0
1978	4.3	2.7	7.0
1979	6.5	4.2	10.7
1980	6.5	6.3	12.8
1981	2.6	9.1	11.7
1982	5.0	11.3	16.3
1983	−2.7	9.5	6.8
1984	−10.2	10.0	−0.2

Source: Central Bank of Brazil.

These adverse conditions, combined with expected increases in oil prices and in dollar interest rates, required much stronger adjustment policies in 1979. In January a five-year program was announced to phase out subsidies to manufactured exports gradually, to advance deposits on imports, and to progressively devalue the real exchange rate. By the second half of the year, the need for even more radical changes had become evident: the current account deficit had deteriorated sharply, and reserves, which had peaked at $11.9 billion in December 1978, had begun to decline.

Once more policymakers were divided, and once again they compromised to keep the country growing at accelerated rates. Their choice was critical because noninterest current account deficits and dollar interest rates were pushing Brazil's external debt to unprecedented levels. Growth policies were no longer supported by high domestic savings. Domestic savings, which had averaged 24.4 percent of GNP between 1970 and 1973 and 24.2 percent between 1974 and 1978, fell to 18.1 percent in 1979 and to 16.4 percent in 1982 (see table 13-5). External savings, which in the past financed additional investment, were now being used to promote increased consumption.

Even the 30 percent devaluation announced on December 7, 1979, failed to adjust the external accounts for two reasons. First, subsidies to manufactured exports and advance deposits on imports, which were being phased out slowly under the five-year program, were eliminated immediately. Second, the exchange rate predetermination introduced in 1980 offset any impact the devaluation might have had in real terms.

Table 13-5. Savings and Investment as a Percentage of GDP

Year	Gross domestic savings Private (1)	Government (2)	Total (3)	External savings (4)	Gross capital formation (3) + (4)
1970	13.76	5.46	19.22	1.32	20.54
1971	12.60	5.85	18.45	2.64	21.09
1972	12.81	5.76	18.57	2.52	21.09
1973	14.75	6.30	21.05	2.11	23.16
1974	14.16	4.49	18.65	6.74	25.39
1975	17.58	3.87	21.45	5.39	26.84
1976	14.87	4.31	19.18	3.92	23.10
1977	15.79	3.93	19.72	2.28	22.00
1978	16.71	2.37	19.08	3.47	22.55
1979	15.48	2.32	17.80	4.74	22.54
1980	16.02	1.09	17.11	5.33	22.44
1981	16.82	1.09	17.91	4.41	22.32
1982	14.53	−0.39	14.14	6.08	20.22
1983	13.68	−1.36	12.32	3.34	15.66
1984	19.38	−2.82	16.56	−0.02	16.54
1985	25.96	−8.02	17.94	0.10	18.04

Source: Getulio Vargas Foundation.

Because reserves were almost depleted, the government made a 180 degree turn in economic policy in January 1981. Interest rate controls were abolished, monetary policies were lightened, minidevaluations in the exchange rate accelerated, and export subsidies and import surcharges were restored. The immediate impact of these measures was a sharp drop in the noninterest current account deficit from $6.5 billion in 1980 to $2.6 billion in 1981, but the success cost Brazil a 1.6 percent real decline in its gross domestic product. The effect on the current account was also diluted by the $2.8 billion increase in interest payments. Breaking its past tradition of prudent debt management, the country resorted to heavy short-term borrowing to delay an external liquidity crisis. Even overseas branches of Brazilian banks used their access to money markets to extend balance of payment loans to the government. These measures did not help. By late 1982, the current account deficit had increased to $16.3 billion. Two other factors complicated Brazil's recovery: the Mexican moratorium on loan repayment ended the rollover of loans by commercial banks, and Brazil's export credits to a number of developing countries became illiquid. As a result, external reserves were quickly depleted, and Brazil had to apply for an IMF-supported adjustment program.

The initial program, drawn up by the Brazilian government and approved by the IMF in February 1983, experienced some technical difficulties. First, it presupposed that tight monetary and fiscal policies, combined with a 1 percent a month real-exchange-rate devaluation, could increase Brazil's trade surplus from $700 million in 1982 to $6 billion in 1983. It failed to distinguish between nominal deficits in the public sector and real deficits—an important distinction in a largely indexed economy. Second, it assumed that inflation rates could easily recede from 100 percent in 1982 to 70 percent in 1983, in spite of widespread backward-looking income indexation and substantial indirect tax increases and subsidy cuts. It appears, in retrospect, that the hastily prepared program was intended to convince commercial banks to roll over the principal, to maintain commercial credit and interbank facilities, and to increase their Brazilian exposure by a projected $4 billion.

In February 1983, the Brazilian authorities concluded that a 30 percent real-exchange-rate devaluation was absolutely necessary to improve the country's external performance. A second letter of intent was sent to the IMF in which the inflation target was revised from 100 percent to 90 percent. Inflation rates escalated to 200 percent a year, however, and the public sector deficit increased swiftly in nominal values (although not in real terms). Because the performance criteria to which Brazil and the IMF had agreed were determined in current cruzeiros, Brazil was considered out of compliance with the terms of the second letter of intent. In May, the IMF decided to suspend the disbursement of the second installment of the extended credit facility. Commercial banks subsequently reduced Brazil's access to the money market and to commercial credits.

As a result Brazil faced an unprecedented credit crunch, which forced adjustment to the external budget constraint. Exports grew from $20.2 billion in 1982 to $21.9 billion in 1983 and could have grown further had they been supported by adequate commercial credit facilities. Imports fell from $19.4 billion to $15.4 billion, partly because of an increase in domestic oil production and a decline of 3.2 percent in real GNP but especially because imports were rationed strictly.

The trade surplus increased to $6.7 billion, and the noninterest current account balance showed a $2.7 billion surplus. Foreign exchange controls became inevitable, and as a consequence, the black market rate premium increased from 25 percent to 90 percent.

A new agreement was reached with the IMF in December 1983. Fiscal policies were to address the real public sector deficit, not the nominal one. Backward-looking wage indexation, it was recognized, made reductions in inflation difficult. Proposals for adjusting rents, wages, and mortgage installments for 80 percent of past inflation were rejected by Brazil's Congress. An unfortunate compromise was to keep the 80 percent dampening coefficient for rents and to use a regressive rule to adjust wages. This wage rule fully compensated wages at lowest levels for past inflation while squeezing middle-class incomes. The proposal was accepted by the IMF.

Under the new adjustment program, commercial banks organized a $6.5 billion new money facility in early 1984 to clear interest arrears and restore the country's reserve position. In fact, that year Brazil did not take in any additional external capital because it was able to obtain a small current account surplus. The $13 billion trade surplus exceeded the IMF-supported targets.

Brazil's trade balance improved in 1984 partly because of economic growth in OECD countries, especially the United States. The improvement, however, resulted more from the structural adjustment policies initiated in the mid-1970s. The country now exported what is had previously imported, such as steel products, paper and pulp, capital goods, petrochemical products, aluminum, and so forth. Imports fell from $15.4 billion to $13.9 billion in spite of import liberalization. The economy grew at 4.5 percent a year. The trade balance largely reflects the effectiveness of import substitution policies, especially the increase in domestic oil production.

In spite of a good performance in the balance of payments in 1984, Brazil's adjustment policies were not endorsed by the IMF because the country had not complied with the inflation rate targets. As a result, Brazil was not able to sign a multiyear loan-rescheduling agreement with commercial banks, although it was able to obtain postponement in the payment of principal and to preserve the country's access to commercial credit and money market facilities. Because the current account is expected to approach equilibrium, Brazil has no difficulty in meeting its interest obligations and in holding external reserves at between $8 billion and $9 billion. Nonetheless, the failure to reach an agreement suggests differences in perception. Brazilian policymakers may be reluctant to adopt antiinflationary policies that would require a budget cut as well as a radical reform of the indexation system. The IMF, because of its statutory function, may tend to focus on external adjustment rather than on domestic price stability.

4. Conclusions

Since the end of World War II, Brazil's policymakers have chosen high growth rates as the basic goal of economic management. Whether this policy has made optimal use of the country's resources is debatable. There is no way to quantify the welfare gains that would have resulted if alternative economic policies had been adopted.

Brazil managed to dodge the old economic dictum that chronic inflation cannot be reconciled with sustained growth by resorting to economywide indexation. An inflation rate of 200 percent a year, of course, hardly adds to the country's welfare or to its growth potential. Brazil's emphasis on infant-industry protection in the twenty years following World War II is accepted by some as well justified. Indeed, many of the infant industries of the 1950s and the 1960s became internationally competitive in the 1970s and the 1980s. Yet there was no plausible reason to combine protection with exchange rate overvaluation. The structural adjustment policies that were adopted helped the country weather the first oil shock. One can argue that shorter-term adjustment policies were necessary. This point is debatable, however, because the external current account improved substantially between 1974 and 1977. That gradualism should have been abandoned in 1979 is less debatable; at that time, one could foresee that Brazil's external debt was becoming a big problem.

A net external debt that has an annual interest bill of $10 billion is a heavy burden on the country. In the absence of additional external loans and foreign direct investment, it forces Brazil to transfer abroad 4.3 percent of its current GDP. Yet a number of empirical studies show that the contribution of external loans to the increase in the domestic production of tradable goods will largely exceed the interest bill. This conclusion does not imply, however, that the foreign debt did not exceed its optimum level.

The structural adjustment policies initiated in the mid-1970s yielded impressive results. Between 1974 and 1984, real GDP increased 47 percent. Exports in constant dollars increased 59 percent, and imports fell 48 percent. The exports were well diversified. The share of coffee in total exports dropped from more than 50 percent until the mid-1960s to 9 percent in the early 1980s. Oil production increased from 180,000 to 550,000 barrels a day. Nearly 60 percent of Brazil's oil needs come now from domestic production. Net oil imports fell from $8.7 billion in 1982 to $5.1 billion in 1984. Massive investments have transformed Brazil from a net importer to a net exporter of a number of items, such as steel, aluminum, pulp and paper, petrochemical products, and capital goods. From this point of view, Brazil's external debt accumulation was much healthier than that of most other Latin American countries. The latter used their access to foreign credit markets to finance exchange rate overvaluation, which contributed to excess consumption and capital flight.

Brazil's present challenge is to sustain the growth rate. The growth policies should be outward looking for at least two reasons. First, export expansion is the only way to reconcile additional borrowing abroad with declining debt-to-export ratios. Second, import substitution policies cannot be relied upon forever to reduce the import-to-GNP ratio. The crucial issue for Brazil is restoration of the domestic savings rate, currently only 14 percent of GNP, to the 24 percent average that prevailed between 1970 and 1978. An increased propensity to save, in the good Brazilian tradition, appears to be the only possible way of accelerating economic growth.

Selected Bibliography

Pechman, Clarice. *O dolar paralelo no Brasil.* Rio de Janeiro: Paz e Terra, 1984.

Setubal Filho, L. *A experiencia cambial Brasileira.* São Paulo: Unipress Editorial, 1871.

Simonsen, Mario H. *Brasil 2002.* Rio de Janeiro: APEC-BLOCH, 1972.

———. "Indexation: Current Theory and the Brazilian Experience." In Rudiger Dornbusch and Mario H. Simonsen, eds., *Inflation, Debt, and Indexation.* Cambridge, Mass.: MIT Press, 1983.

———. *Desindexação e reforma monetaria.* Rio de Janeiro: Conjuntura Economica, 1984.

———. "The Developing-Country Debt Problem." In Gordon W. Smith and John T. Cuddington, eds., *International Debt and Developing Countries.* Washington, D.C.: World Bank, 1985.

Villela, A. V., and W. Suzigan. *Politico do governo e crescimento da economia Brasileira, 1889–1945.* Serie Monografica no. 10. Rio de Janeiro: Instituto de Planejamento Econômico e Social, 1973.

14

Indonesia

Malcolm Gillis and David Dapice

ECONOMIC PERFORMANCE in Indonesia during the past two decades has been widely regarded as successful. External adjustment policies played a significant role in the success. Some lessons may be learned from Indonesia's adjustment process. The lessons may not be as clear-cut as economists and policymakers might wish, however, because cross-currents underlying economic policymaking in Indonesia are no less complex than in other countries. At different times, these currents have crisscrossed one another; on occasion, they have combined to create turbulence. This pattern has been found in particular in the area of external adjustment policy. Two enduring but not necessarily compatible constants may be discerned during the period 1965–85.

1. Historical Overview

First, policymakers have consistently viewed the exchange rate as a primary policy instrument for nearly two decades, and by most standards it has been employed with some success. This approach sharply contrasts with policies prevailing in eastern and southern Africa.[1] Second, other elements of trade policy, infused with autarkic influences since Indonesia's independence, have slowly moved in the direction of greater protection, beginning with tariffs and later including quantitative restrictions.

As a result, there has been an uneasy coexistence between an exchange rate policy that exemplifies one aspect of outward-looking development policies and other trade policies that seem to display signs of inward-looking strategies. This bifurcated policy focus is not the result of any confusion among policymakers. Rather, the agencies responsible for exchange rate and tariff policy are not the same as those exercising authority over nontariff restrictions on imports, and different philosophies prevail among them.

Some observers may interpret the evidence from Indonesia as an illustration of how a sensible exchange rate policy (together with supportive fiscal and monetary policy) can be vitiated by protectionistic excesses. Others may find in the recent Indonesian experience proof of compatibility between import protectionism and long-term growth, at least in nations with relatively large populations. The lessons of that experience, however, are not so easily distilled.

Evolution of the Economy

INDEPENDENCE THROUGH 1965.   By 1952, the year of independence, the economy was nearing the end of recovery from a dozen years of wartime occupation and a bitterly contested struggle for independence from the Netherlands. Even so, real GDP per capita grew by only about 1 percent a year until 1960. The subsequent five years were disastrous for the economy: the standard of living for the population was lower in 1965 than in 1959. Real per capita income in 1965 was $230 in 1983 dollars; inflation exceeded 600 percent in both 1965 and 1966; and the transport, power, irrigation, and water supply infrastructure lay in ruins.[2]

THE PERIOD 1965–85.   The two decades since 1965 present an entirely different picture. By the end of 1984, the 159 million inhabitants of the archipelago enjoyed real per capita income of $585 in 1983 dollars. Over the period 1965–85, only Hong Kong, the Republic of Korea, Singapore, and Taiwan experienced more rapid improvement in per capita GNP. Among countries with more than 25 million inhabitants only Brazil matched Indonesia's performance.

The marked increase in living standards was made possible by rapid growth in GDP after 1967. In the eight years prior to the first oil boom (1965–73), including the low-growth years 1965–66, GDP grew at an average of 6.3 percent (see table 14-1). Although oil production in Indonesia never exceeded four barrels per person a year (about one-half of the output of Nigeria and one-tenth of that of Venezuela), the inflow and utilization of oil revenues after 1973 had a major impact on economic performance. GDP growth after 1973 was only marginally higher than in the previous seven years and below the pace of growth in the three years prior to the first oil boom.

Structural transformation proceeded swiftly. The share of agriculture in GDP fell sharply from 52 percent in 1965 to 30 percent in 1983 (see table 14-2). At the same time, the share of manufacturing grew from 8 percent in 1965 to 15 percent in 1983, whereas the share of services increased from 36 percent to 48 percent, respectively.

Table 14-1. Average Annual Growth of Real GDP, Population, and Real per Capita GDP, 1952–84
(percent)

Year	Real GDP	Population	Real GDP
1952–59	3.2	2.0	1.2
1961–65	1.8	2.6	−0.8
1966–71	6.0	2.1	3.9
1972	9.4	2.4	6.9
1973	11.3	2.4	8.7
1974	7.6	2.4	5.1
1975	5.0	2.4	2.5
1976	6.9	2.4	4.4
1977	8.8	2.4	6.2
1978	7.8	2.4	5.3
1979	6.3	2.4	3.8
1980	9.9	2.4	7.3
1981	7.9	2.0	5.8
1982	2.2	1.8	0.4
1983	5.0	1.8	3.2
1984	6.5	1.8	4.6
	Average growth		
1965–73	6.3	2.1	4.1
1973–84	7.1	2.2	4.8
1965–84	6.5	2.2	4.3

Note: From 1961 to 1984, real GDP is in 1980 prices.

Sources: International Monetary Fund, *International Financial Statistics Yearbook 1984* (Washington, D.C., 1985); and World Bank data.

Indonesia made the transition in 1967 from hyperinflation to sustained growth perhaps as rapidly as any country in the postwar era. After the triple-digit inflationary years of 1965–68, inflation slowed to 9 percent in 1970 and 4 percent in 1971 (see table 14-3). For the subsequent period 1973–83, the inflation rate, averaging 18.8 percent annually, matched precisely that of lower-middle-income developing countries and was only marginally higher than the 14.1 percent experienced by Hong Kong, Korea, Singapore, and Taiwan.[3]

EXTERNAL TRADE. As in most other rapidly growing economies, the structure of Indonesia's imports changed radically over the past two decades. During 1966–69, the period of economic rehabilitation and recovery, imports of consumer goods averaged 42 percent of total imports; intermediate goods constituted another 36 percent; and capital goods made up the rest of imports.[4] By 1984, the share of consumer

Table 14-2. Sectoral Composition of GDP and Real Growth Rates, 1965–83, in 1973 Constant Prices
(percent)

Sector	Real growth rate, 1972–83	Sectoral share in GDP			
		1965	1974	1980	1983
Agriculture	4.1	52	39	31	30
Food	4.5				
Smallholder and estate crops	5.7				
Forestry	−1.0				
Livestock	3.7				
Fisheries	4.3				
Mining	5.2	4	12	9	8
Manufacturing	12.3	8	10	14	15
Services	9.5	36	39	46	48
Utilities	13.5				
Construction	14.0				
Trade	7.7				
Transport and communications	11.4				
Banking	13.1				
Ownership of dwellings	13.2				
Public administration	11.5				
Other services	2.4				
Total GDP growth	7.3				
Growth in nonmining GDP	7.6				

Source: World Bank data.

goods in total imports (excluding imports by the oil sector) had dropped to 12 percent in response to two decades of concerted import substitution in consumer goods. Intermediate goods still maintained their level at 36 percent, and capital goods accounted for more than 50 percent of the total.[5]

The exports, of course, had been dominated by hydrocarbons since 1973, first by oil exclusively and more recently by oil and liquified natural gas (LNG). Even as late as 1971, however, rubber was the leading source of export earnings, followed closely by timber (see table 14-4). Timber became the leading export for a brief period (1972–73). Thereafter, oil and LNG revenues never accounted for less than 50 percent of all export earnings; oil's share exceeded two-thirds of total export earnings in 1980–81. Manufactured exports were relatively insignificant throughout the 1960s and 1970s at about 3 percent of the total in 1977–78. Although this figure has increased to nearly 12 percent in 1983, on a per capita basis Indonesia's manufactured exports are minuscule when compared with those of neighboring Malaysia, Thailand, and the Philippines.[6]

External Policies

The responsibility for the design and execution of policies concerning exchange rate, exchange control, foreign savings (including commercial borrowing), and other complementary fiscal and monetary policies lies with the "economic agencies" headed and staffed by economists. These include the State Coordinating Ministry for Economy, the Ministries of Finance and Industry, the central bank, and the planning board. Policies governing quantitative restrictions on imports and nontax policies concerning direct foreign investment are the responsibility of the so-called sectoral agencies, which include the ministries of Industry and Agriculture, the State Ministry for Promotion of Domestic Content, and the Foreign Investment Board. The sectoral ministries are generally associated with more inward-looking industrialization policies, whereas the economic ministries tend to be identified with policies that are relatively more outward oriented.

EXCHANGE RATES AND EXCHANGE CONTROLS.   The Indonesian rupiah was persistently overvalued in the decade after 1955.[7] As the degree of overvaluation progressively worsened after 1959, administrative allocation of foreign exchange grew more pervasive. By 1961, a bewildering system of exchange controls involving virtually complete licensing of imports had been set in place; this system coexisted with a complex network of multiple exchange rates and prior deposits on imports. After 1959, Indonesia resorted to devaluation only under extreme circumstances—for example, when negative net foreign exchange reserves appeared in 1963.

Exchange controls were slowly loosened after the collapse of the economy in 1966. The rupiah was devalued sharply that year, but multiple exchange rates remained until 1970, when exchange controls and multiple rates were abolished.[8] Since 1970, Indonesia has placed no administrative controls on foreign exchange. Indonesians can freely hold any currency they desire, foreign exchange can be freely transferred without prior approval, and no records are kept on inward or outward private flows of foreign exchange.

After the unification of all exchange rates in 1970, the rupiah was pegged to the U.S. dollar for the subsequent eight years, beginning with

Table 14-3. Selected Economic Indicators, 1953–83

Year	Annual inflation (percent)	Net official gold and foreign exchange reserves (millions of U.S. dollars)	Reserves (months of non-oil imports)	Percentage of GDP Total central government taxes	Oil taxes	Liquid assets
1953–59	25	n.a.	n.a.	n.a.	n.a.	n.a.
1960	19	301	n.a.	13.8	n.a.	n.a.
1961	72	122	0	13.2	n.a.	n.a.
1962	160	94	0	5.4	n.a.	n.a.
1963	128	−16	0	5.1	n.a.	n.a.
1964	135	−49	0	4.2	n.a.	n.a.
1965	596	−73	0	3.9	n.a.	n.a.
1966	636	−77	0	4.0	n.a.	n.a.
1967	111	−78	0	7.1	0.9	6.1
1968	84	−93	0	7.2	1.2	5.4
1969	10	−86	0	9.0	1.7	5.5
1970	9	−52	0	10.3	2.0	9.4

Year						
1971	4	−106	0	11.7	3.0	11.8
1972	26	422	3	13.0	4.3	15.1
1973	27	649	3.5	14.3	5.1	14.6
1974	33	1203	2.4	16.4	9.1	13.6
1975	20	490	1.2	17.7	9.9	15.8
1976	14	1226	2.8	18.8	10.5	17.5
1977	12	2423	3.4	18.6	10.2	16.5
1978	7	2580	4.3	18.8	10.1	17.0
1979	22	4145	5.8	20.9	13.3	16.8
1980	12	6480	6.8	22.5	15.4	17.6
1981	6	6085	5.1	22.6	16.0	17.8
1982	9	4154	3.3	20.8	13.7	18.0
1983	11	4808	4.2	20.3	13.4	16.4

n.a. Not available.

Note: The annual inflation rate is measured by the consumer price index for Jakarta, which was revised in 1979. The new price index contains a larger number of goods and services, and the proportion of their composition has been changed.

Source: For 1953–81, Malcolm Gillis, "Episodes in Indonesian Economic Growth," in A. C. Harberger, ed., *World Economic Growth* (San Francisco, Calif.: Institute for Contemporary Studies, 1984). For 1982–83, Bank Indonesia, *Indonesian Financial Statistics*, various issues.

Table 14-4. Indonesian Exports, 1968–83
(amounts in millions of U.S. dollars)

Year	Total exports	Net oil and LNG		Rubber		Timber		Manufactures	
		Amount	Percent	Amount	Percent	Amount	Percent	Amount	Percent
1968	647	78	12.0	232	35.8	15	2.3	20	3.0
1969	660	112	17.0	307	46.5	34	5.1	n.a.	n.a.
1970	761	152	20.0	259	34.0	130	17.1	n.a.	n.a.
1971	896	135	15.0	223	25.0	170	19.0	n.a.	n.a.
1972	982	192	19.5	211	21.5	275	28.0	n.a.	n.a.
1973	2,546	641	25.2	483	19.0	720	28.3	77	3.0
1974	4,671	2,638	56.5	425	9.1	615	13.2	114	2.4
1975	5,011	3,138	62.6	381	7.6	527	10.5	144	2.9
1976	6,573	3,710	56.4	577	8.8	885	13.5	196	3.0
1977	7,951	4,445	55.9	608	7.6	943	11.9	245	3.1
1978	8,006	4,010	50.1	774	9.7	1,130	14.1	360	4.5
1979	13,146	6,975	53.1	1,101	8.4	2,166	16.5	447	3.4
1980	16,095	10,610	65.9	1,078	6.7	1,672	10.4	540	3.4
1981	13,795	9,761	70.8	770	5.6	952	6.9	865	6.3
1982	11,094	7,166	64.6	614	5.5	899	8.1	853	7.7
1983	12,606	7,371	58.5	692	7.6	1,123	8.9	1,484	11.8

n.a. Not available.

Note: Total exports are the sum of total non-oil exports, net oil exports, and net gas exports in millions of U.S. dollars.

Source: For 1968–76, Malcolm Gillis, "Episodes in Indonesian Economic Growth," in A. C. Harberger, ed., *World Economic Growth* (San Francisco, Calif.: Institute for Contemporary Studies, 1984), table 4. For 1977-83, World Bank data.

Rp373 and ending with Rp415 in 1978. Following a 33 percent devaluation in November 1978, the exchange rate was again devalued to Rp625 and was ostensibly pegged to a basket of currencies. In practice, however, the rupiah remained linked to the U.S. dollar until 1982, when the rupiah-dollar rate depreciated by nearly 8 percent. Following another 28 percent devaluation in March 1983, the rupiah-dollar rate was allowed to depreciate slowly, and in small steps, from Rp970 in April 1983 to Rp1,121 in September 1985.

The exchange rate system prevailing in 1985 bears little resemblance to that of two decades earlier. In 1965, all foreign exchange was administratively allocated, little was dispensed by 1968, and none by 1970 when multiple exchange rates were abolished. As more active use has been made of exchange rate policy since 1970, fears of the alleged destabilizing effects of exchange rate adjustments have receded. Even as late as the mid-1970s, maintenance of a fixed exchange rate was widely viewed as both a prerequisite for national economic stability and the prime symbol of it. It was argued that the private sector was unable (or not ready) to cope with the uncertainties of crawling pegs, managed floats, or the wider band systems. This argument has rarely been heard in the 1980s. Indonesian businessmen have in a few short years proven no less adept in adjusting to a crawling-peg system than their counterparts in Brazil and elsewhere. Movements in exchange rates are no longer regarded as precursors of national calamity.

POLICIES TOWARD FOREIGN SAVINGS.   Prior to 1966, inflows of foreign savings were either prohibited or tightly regulated. Since that time, Indonesia has made liberal use of all forms of foreign savings—foreign aid, foreign direct investment, and, since 1973, foreign commercial borrowing. Indeed, foreign savings, principally in the form of foreign aid, financed nearly one-third of gross investment in the four years of economic rehabilitation after 1965. In recent years, the share of investment financed by foreign savings has varied considerably from zero to as much as 50 percent (see table 14-5). The composition of foreign savings, however, has changed from an almost exclusive reliance upon foreign aid to a mix of direct investment and debt finance, both official debt and private commercial debt, virtually all of which is government debt. Still, Indonesia's external public debt by 1983 was $21.7 billion, which, at about 29 percent of GNP, was below the average for middle-income nations. Debt service was 13 percent of total exports, well below the ratio for such countries as Brazil (29 percent) or Mexico (36 percent).[9] The Indonesian government prefers to express its debt service ratio as a percentage of net exports (total exports minus imports of goods and services by the oil sector). Viewed in this way, the ratio of debt service to total exports was about 21 percent.[10]

Table 14-5. Gross Investment and Sources of Finance, 1967–83
(percentage of GDP)

Year	Gross domestic investment	Foreign savings — Oil company investment[a]	Other foreign investment	Recorded commercial borrowing inflows	Foreign aid inflows	Total foreign inflows	Domestic savings — Government savings	Private domestic savings[b]	Total domestic savings	As percentage of gross investment
1967	8.0	n.a.	0.0	0.0	3.0	3.0	−1.2	6.2	6.2	77.5
1968	8.8	n.a.	0.0	0.0	2.8	2.8	0.0	6.0	6.0	68.2
1969	11.7	1.1	0.1	0.0	3.3	4.5	1.0	6.2	7.2	61.5
1970	13.6	1.3	1.4	0.0	3.6	6.3	1.7	5.6	7.3	53.7
1971	15.8	2.3	2.5	0.0	3.7	8.5	2.2	5.1	7.3	50.8
1972	18.8	2.2	3.1	0.0	3.5	8.8	3.4	6.6	10.0	53.2
1973	17.9	2.5	2.0	1.3	3.0	8.8	3.8	5.0	8.8	50.8
1974	16.7	3.1	0.8	0.9	2.2	7.0	6.9	2.8	9.7	58.0
1975	20.3	3.5	1.8	4.0	3.9	13.2	7.2	0.0	7.2	35.5
1976	20.7	3.0	1.1	2.4	5.1	11.6	8.3	0.8	9.1	44.0
1977	20.1	1.9	0.6	1.7	4.1	8.3	7.3	4.5	11.8	58.7
1978	20.5	1.9	0.9	1.2	4.6	8.6	6.8	5.4	12.2	58.6
1979	20.9	2.2	0.6	2.0	4.5	9.3	8.5	3.1	11.6	55.5
1980	20.9	3.0	0.5	1.2	3.4	8.1	10.1	2.7	12.8	61.2
1981	21.4	2.4	0.4	4.0	2.0	8.8	11.3	1.3	12.6	58.8
1982	22.6	1.9	0.5	4.6	2.2	9.2	8.6	4.8	13.4	59.3
1983	24.1	2.1	0.3	2.8	5.0	10.2	8.6	5.3	13.9	57.7

n.a. Not available.

a. The sum of exploration and development investment.

b. Includes savings of public enterprises.

Source: Malcolm Gillis, "Episodes in Indonesian Economic Growth," in A. C. Harberger, ed., *World Economic Growth* (San Francisco, Calif.: Institute for Contemporary Studies, 1984), updated by figures supplied by the Ministry of Finance for 1982 and 1983.

TAXES AND OTHER RESTRICTIONS ON INTERNATIONAL TRADE. During the first three years of Indonesia's economic recovery program (1968–71), taxes on international trade accounted for 36 percent of total tax revenue: by 1984, according to World Bank data, they had dropped to 6 percent as revenue from oil began to increase.

In 1966, the import tariff structure, along with the rest of the tax structure, had been profoundly warped as a result of the government's desperate search for tax revenues during the period of hyperinflation. Nominal rates of tariff in excess of 200 percent were not uncommon; smuggling was of course rampant.[11] In 1968, as part of a broader program of trade liberalization, duties were progressively lowered in eight separate steps, ending in 1973. Even by 1971, the highest rate of nominal protection (duty rates applicable to import value) for any industry was 89 percent (for bread and bakery products). Nominal protection for the textile goods and wearing apparel industries had been reduced by almost half to 70 percent.[12] Some 250 items, or 30 percent of the total, were still subject to rates in excess of 60 percent. Collection rates on total imports declined steadily until 1972 because of successive reduction in tariff rates and the growth of duty-free imports by foreign and domestic investors: the overall collection rate (duties as a share of total imports) was only 11 percent in 1972, half as high as in 1969.[13]

In 1973, duties were further reduced, but from that year onward, Indonesian trade policy turned progressively more protectionist. Trade restrictions were increasingly put into effect through a variety of quantitative restrictions on the importation of consumer and intermediate goods.

Export taxes, once as much as 8 percent of revenue, have steadily declined in importance in recent years. In 1970, for instance, export taxes were levied on virtually all traditional commodities, including copra, rubber, pepper, timber, and minerals. By 1976, export taxes on many agricultural commodities had been abolished, and that on rubber had been halved to 5 percent. By 1984, the only significant export tax in force was a 20 percent levy on logs (the export of which was banned in 1985) and 10 percent on mineral products (including tin and nickel).

2. A Tale of Three Devaluations

Indonesia's recent success in managing its debt has frequently been attributed to the manner in which the nation has managed its exchange rate and associated macroeconomic policies. Each devaluation, of course, differed from the others. Outside shocks from the world economy often influenced the postdevaluation course of the economy as much as internal management.

Typically, a devaluation is undertaken when an economy imports more than it exports and cannot borrow on a sustainable basis to finance the deficit. By increasing the amount of local currency needed to buy a dollar (or any other unit of foreign currency), the domestic price of exports, imports, and import substitutes rises. Devaluation is therefore expected to increase the volume of exports and lower the level of imports. In some cases, it is possible to improve the trade balance while increasing total output. Often, however, the economy must also contract, because the short-term responsiveness of many exports and imports to price increases may be limited. In any case, real wages and sometimes other types of income are squeezed as prices of tradable goods rise more than domestic wage rates, rents, and so forth. If the domestic inflation rate rises following a devaluation, local wages and prices will rise too, and the intended benefit of the devaluation—a more competitive cost structure for local producers—will be lost. Effective management of an economy thus calls for low rate of inflation following a devaluation so that the desired adjustment in exports and imports can proceed.

The 1971 Devaluation

In 1971, Indonesia was still recovering from the 1964–68 period of hyperinflation and severe economic dislocations. Although the economy began to grow again after 1967, considerable repairs and reconstruction were needed following nearly a decade of tight foreign exchange and inadequate upkeep of roads, other infrastructure, and factories. A rescheduling of external debts in 1967 had given the economy some breathing space, but net foreign exchange reserves (official short-term assets less official short-term liabilities) were actually negative through 1970 and continued to be so into mid-1971 (see table 14-3). Against this backdrop a decline of 8 percent in exports and an increase of 29 percent in imports, from the last half of 1970 to the first half of 1971, appeared particularly troublesome. This change occurred in spite of low inflation—only 2–3 percent in the previous twelve months. With little room to maneuver and a great deal of uncertainty about future trends, the government decided to devalue by 10 percent from Rp378 to Rp415 to the dollar in August 1971.

The hyperinflation in the 1960s had caused the use of money to fall sharply in real terms. As a result the government was able to increase the money supply in 1971 by 32 percent while holding inflation in check at 4 percent (see table 14-3). In 1972, the money supply was increased by 36 percent. The government budget was balanced, however, without any domestic borrowing. The Jakarta price index rose only 4.5 percent from August 1971 to August 1972, a rate little different from that in Japan and the United States.

Shortly thereafter, however, internal prices began to rise sharply in response to an unusually poor rice harvest in Indonesia and increases in world market prices of rice.[14] Rice carries a large weight in the Jakarta price index; as a result the index rose by 25 percent from August to December 1972. In spite of rising inflation in industrial countries, the cost advantage of the devaluation had been largely dissipated by August of 1973, by which time domestic prices were 50 percent above the predevaluation level. Even so, the period of price stability following the devaluation was marked by lower import growth. Nominal imports in the first three quarters of 1971 were $859 million; although they too rose slightly to $866 million over the next three quarters, they declined in real terms.

Export performance was more varied. Low world prices in 1972 of some major commodities, such as coffee or rubber, offset some of the incentive effects of the devaluation. Although oil and timber exports did increase, it is difficult to argue that the devaluation was the reason. Because the cost of producing oil, timber, and minerals is low compared with world prices, output growth continued even after general Indonesian prices rose. In 1973, however, the volume of rubber production did rise by 13 percent over 1971 and 1972 levels in response to sharp increases in world rubber prices. Manufactured exports nearly doubled in value from 1971 to 1972, albeit from a small base.

The 1978 Devaluation

Indonesia experienced rapid growth in international reserves in the early years after the first oil boom despite the squandering of several billion dollars of revenues by the state oil company, Pertamina. The rapid growth in reserves led to a surge in inflation. Prices more than tripled between the end of 1971 and 1977 but were held down to 3 percent during the first nine months of 1978. Nonetheless, many non-oil sectors, such as rubber and manufacturing, began to experience severe difficulty because of a steady increase in the real exchange rate. (For a discussion of this concept, see the appendix to this chapter.) Although these sectors were competitive in 1971, their rupiah costs had more than tripled, while costs in industrial nations and in other developing countries that exported rubber and other primary commodities had less than doubled, so that the competitiveness of Indonesia was reduced. The export volume of rubber in 1977, for example, was lower than that of 1973, and real earnings from rubber were even more so. Many manufacturers were demanding greater protection from imports made cheap by overvaluation of the rupiah. Yet in spite of rapidly growing imports, the balance of payments was healthy. Growing timber and oil exports allowed foreign exchange reserves to grow by $1 billion in 1977 to the highest levels in Indonesia's history. Thus there was no pressure to devalue because of inadequate foreign exchange or a poor trade balance.

Continued heavy reliance on oil, however, was regarded as a risky proposition. First, the growth in domestic consumption of oil products, which had been twice as fast as real growth in GDP for several years, threatened to reduce significantly the supplies of exportable petroleum. Second, because the prospects for oil prices in the near term as well as in the long term appeared uncertain, it was realized that future growth would have to come from non-oil sectors, especially labor-intensive exportables, which were foundering because of high domestic costs. Third, considerations of regional equity and employment required that attention be paid to the declining rubber industry in Sumatra, where several million jobs were involved, and to the growth of labor-intensive industries in Java, the most populous island in the archipelago. These industries had been most severely damaged by the high inflation rates of the past few years. Finally, a devaluation would increase governmental revenues because the government received its oil revenues in dollars.

In 1978, the government decided that a devaluation would help restructure the economy to rely less on oil and to move toward manufacturing and non-oil exports. In mid-November, the exchange rate was increased from Rp415 to Rp625 to the dollar. The increase came as a considerable surprise to many Indonesians, some of whom had been predicting a revaluation of the rupiah. Because of the need to preserve secrecy, little discussion had been possible within the bureaucracy, so the longer-run purposes of the move were not entirely understood when it was announced. In addition, several events overtook the economic managers. Oil prices began to climb abruptly in January 1979. Oil exports, government revenues, and government spending increased sharply in 1979 and 1980. Growth in money supply rose from 25 percent in 1978 to 36 percent in 1979, a further 48 percent in 1980, and 30 percent in 1981.

Under these conditions, a sharp inflation might have been expected, and indeed one followed. The new national consumer price index rose 22 percent in 1979 and a further 16 percent in 1980. (However, cumulative inflation in industrial countries in these two years was 20 percent.) The relative cost advantage provided by devaluation, though reduced, was therefore by no means eliminated by 1981. Although non-oil imports rose from $6.1 billion in 1978 to $6.4 billion in 1979 in current values, in real terms they constituted a decline, if the inflation is considered in the dollar prices of imports. Perhaps the most spectacular result of the devaluation was a very pronounced rise in manufactured exports. These expanded from $173 million in 1978 to $405 million in 1979 and continued to grow in 1980 and 1981 mainly because many log exports had been replaced by plywood exports as a result of other policies (more later), but the initial jump was due to broadly based growth in exports of many products. Overall, the non-oil balance of trade improved from a negative $2.5 billion in 1978 to a negative $1 billion in 1979.

In spite of the subsequent inflation, the 1978 devaluation is widely regarded as successful.[15] Because of the sharp change in relative prices, the large volume of oil-fired public and private spending led to much higher domestic manufacturing output, which increased by more than 50 percent from 1978 to 1981, after adjustments for inflation. Rapid gains were also made in rural nonfarm output and employment. The harm done to both oil exports and import-substituting industries by overvaluation in 1974–78 was partly reversed by the devaluation, which improved their international competitiveness. Indeed, greater gains would have been possible in exports had administrative controls not been imposed to restrain some commodity exports in January 1979. Government officials were fearful that increased exports would aggravate inflation by reducing domestic supply. This mistake was not repeated in 1983.

The 1983 Devaluation

The worldwide boom between 1979 and 1981, political uncertainties in the Middle East, and the 1978 devaluation raised both oil and non-oil export values to levels never approached earlier in Indonesia. Total exports increased from an all-time high of $8 billion in 1978 to $16 billion in 1980. World prices for Indonesia oil tripled after 1978, to $39 a barrel. The rise in export values, in the petroleum sector, however, was accompanied by sharp declines in non-oil exports and a continuing surge in non-oil imports. From 1979–80 (the fiscal year ends on March 31) to 1982–83, non-oil exports fell from $6.2 billion to $3.9 billion, a decline of 37 percent. Some of the decline can be attributed to the 13 percent drop in the prices of many raw materials induced by world recession, but some can be ascribed to lack of competitiveness. (As shown in the appendix, the index fell to 74 percent of its level in 1970.) Meanwhile, non-oil imports rose from $8 billion to $14.1 billion in the same period. Net exports of oil and LNG peaked at $10.6 billion in 1980–81, a year of current account surplus of more than $2 billion. But as oil prices and export volumes fell after 1981, a steadily diminishing net oil surplus was overtaken by a rapidly growing non-oil trade deficit. The current account was $2.8 billion in deficit in 1981–82 and more than $7 billion in deficit in 1982–83; the latter constituted about 8 percent of GDP.

Because the trade imbalance in 1982 was much higher than could be financed by normal capital inflows, capital flight ensued, which caused foreign exchange reserves to fall at a rate of more than a quarter billion dollars a month. To stem private capital outflow in the short term and to improve the non-oil trade balance in the near term, a combination of outright devaluation and controlled floating was put into effect. Only the briefest consideration was given to imposing controls on foreign exchange movements, largely because of unsatisfactory experiences with such attempts in the 1960s. The exchange rate was moved from less than Rp700 to the dollar at the start of 1983 to nearly Rp1,000 by the end of the year. For the second time in five years, the relative prices of tradables and nontradables had been changed sharply.

The 1983 devaluation was successful beyond expectations, in part because both monetary policy and fiscal policy were supportive. Increases in money supply and prices were contained at 10 percent a year in subsequent years. Non-oil exports increased from a predevaluation level of $3.9 billion in 1982–83 to $5.9 billion in 1984–85; manufactured exports grew from $530 million to $1.2 billion in the same interval. The volume of all non-oil exports rose 30 percent and in dollar value by 15 percent. Non-oil imports fell from $14.1 billion to $12.2 billion in the same period. Because net oil and LNG exports were worth $7 billion, the current account deficit shrank from more than $7 billion in 1982–83 to less than $3 billion in 1984–85. The latter figure equaled the capital inflows recorded in 1984–85. In other words, investors were again confident enough to put their money back in Indonesia; foreign exchange reserves rose to more than $10 billion.

The successful turnaround did not reflect good management of the external sector alone. Implementation of a number of other long-postponed measures supported the devaluation and lent credibility to the overall government program for restructuring the economy. The economic decisionmakers seized the opportunities offered by the trade imbalance to make drastic changes in fiscal and financial policy. In mid-May 1983, more than $10 billion of low-priority, capital-intensive projects of the government, amounting to almost 12 percent of GDP, were "rescheduled"—that is, indefinitely deferred. The result was a sharp reduction in both government spending and government import demand. In addition, within three months of the devaluation, the financial system was liberalized to encourage better lending, more competition, and greater mobilization of domestic savings. Most interest rates were deregulated. A new tax system, in preparation since 1981, was announced in November 1983 and was implemented in steps in 1984 and 1985. The new system relies heavily on a rudimentary form of valued added tax. It is simpler, easier to administer and monitor, and likely to raise tax collections from non-oil sectors.[16] Routine spending growth was held to 16 percent a year largely because subsidies on the domestic consumption of petroleum products were reduced. The overall government budget remained balanced.[17] None of the 1983 policy adjustments was made at the behest of international lending organizations or aid donors. The entire program was homegrown.

General Lessons

It is difficult to determine the extent to which the lessons learned from the three devaluations can be applied elsewhere. The degree of continuity in economic decisionmaking found in Indonesia has few parallels elsewhere: the officials who made the decision to devalue in 1971 were the same ones who made the decision to devalue in 1983. Still, even though the environment in the world market, the contribution of oil, macroeconomic management, and the actual course of inflation and trade were different in each case, certain principles underlay all three devaluation episodes.

First, import demand is responsive to higher rupiah prices. For at least several quarters and for as long as several years (depending on subsequent demand management), the real level of imports fell without the use of any form of exchange controls. Given that non-oil imports in current dollars grew from $1 billion in 1970 to more than $14 billion in 1983, it is clear that the general trend was strongly upward. During this period, non-oil output grew in real terms every year, so that declining income does not explain these observations.

Second, some exports respond to devaluation strongly in the short term, others respond weakly, and still others respond not at all. The strong postdevaluation surges in manufactured exports in each instance testify that relative costs can make a difference. Our analysis of rubber exports shows that a 10 percent rise in prices will increase volume by only 2 percent in the short run and perhaps another 2 percent in the six years it takes a newly planted rubber tree to begin production. Production of oil, LNG, and timber probably responds relatively little to the exchange rate because the world price of these resources is quite high compared with their domestic costs of production. In contrast, if the government devalues the rupiah and increases the domestic price of its petroleum products, as Indonesia has done, these measures have an impact on the domestic demand for these products. Our research indicates that for Indonesia a real price increase of 10 percent will reduce demand for gasoline, kerosene, and diesel oil by 4 percent in a few years and will permit an increase in the export of petroleum if the Organization of Petroleum Exporting Countries (OPEC) and demand conditions allow it.

Third, the management of the economy after devaluation will greatly influence the ultimate impact of the devaluation. Rapid increases in money growth and spending will tend to drive up prices and demand and will reduce the benefits of devaluation. A devaluation may still be worthwhile, however, even if expansionary policies are followed. After the second oil boom, a sharp increase in government spending was expected in any case, owing to the political imperative of greater rural development spending and the bureaucracy's penchant for large-scale capital projects. Although the 1978 devaluation probably worsened inflationary pressures, it also boosted non-oil sectors (agriculture and industry) that would otherwise have been under very severe cost pressures.

Fourth, fiscal, financial, and trade policies that support the general thrust of devaluation can serve as a powerful weapon for improving a poor foreign exchange situation and for encouraging income and employment growth in a wide range of domestic economic activities. If export controls and administrative limitations on investment follow a devaluation, however, its positive impact will be severely reduced, as in 1978. The Indonesian experience suggests that devaluation must be used in conjunction with, and as a part of, other policies rather than as a single policy unsupported by any other steps.

3. Trade Policy

Trade policy before 1973 was characterized by a gradual but nonetheless significant dismantling of restrictions on international trade. Tariff rates were progressively lowered, and by 1971 quantitative restrictions on both imports and exports had been virtually eliminated save for certain automobile tires and batik textiles.[18] By 1985, quantitative restrictions on imports were pervasive. Export restrictions, other than export taxes, have been used to a lesser degree, although numerous restrictions still do apply to some exports.[19] Examples include the ban on the export of copra, quotas on log exports during 1981–84, and a total ban on log exports in 1985.

The Decline and Rise of Protectionism

The pressures to turn toward a protectionist trade policy after 1972 can be attributed to several factors. First, the growing overvaluation of the rupiah from 1973 until late 1978 gave rise to increasingly strident demands for protection of import-substituting industries, particularly in textiles, apparel, footwear, and other consumer goods. In the months prior to the devaluation of 1978, for example, the textile industry reported an excess capacity of nearly 60 percent.

Second, the continuing inadequacies (both real and imagined) in the Indonesian customs service offered another reason for increased reliance on quantitative restrictions. Evasion of customs duties, through underinvoicing and outright smuggling, was at least as pervasive in the early 1980s as in the early 1970s.[20] Investors in import-substituting industries with high nominal tariff protection regularly claimed, not without justification, that ineffective and corrupt customs administration allowed many consumer goods to enter at rates of duty well below those nominally prescribed. In desperation many firms sought quantitative restrictions as substitutes for the ineffective protection provided by poor administration of tariffs. In March 1985, the government stripped the customs service of all responsibility for assessing and collecting customs duties and assigned the job to a Swiss survey firm for the period 1985–87.

Third, there is a widespread acceptance of the view, within part of the government and much of the private sector, that the 160 million people in the nation furnish a market large enough to allow most import-substituting industries to attain significant economies of scale and therefore low-cost production. This argument, it is held, justifies significant protection of infant industries, notwithstanding the fact that the most competitive industries in Indonesia have generally been the least protected.[21] Fourth, autarkic notions have been pervasive among industry officials in several sectors, who take the view that "if it can be produced here, in a technical sense, then it should be produced here."

Protection and Import Substitution

All of these factors weakened the case for continued import liberalization after 1972. The turning point in trade policy came in February 1974, when the government prohibited the import of finished sedan cars to rescue an uncompetitive automobile assembly industry, which by 1984 had assembled twenty-seven makes of automobiles with a total production of only 152,000 units. This measure was the first significant breach of a heretofore solid policy of liberalization. Over the next five years, import quotas and bans were extended to a few other industrial goods, including newsprint, some textiles, and motorcycles.

The quantitative restrictions were not used extensively, however, until after 1980. Between 1980 and mid-1985, hundreds of products were added to the list of imports subject to some form of restrictions, so that by 1984, 22 percent (1,154 items) of imports were subject to some form of registration, regulation, quota, or license. The period also saw great innovation in the design and application of these restrictions. Importation of certain agricultural implements, for example, was virtually halted by a device that came to be known as a zero quota—a total ban by any other name. Imports of fruits were stopped by first restricting import privileges to firms designated by the government and then lifting these privileges. Imports of many types of steel were severely curtailed not by quotas or bans but by appointing the high-cost state-owned steel mill (the monopoly producer) as sole importer of steel products.

As a result, by 1984 the level and the variability of effective protection had increased significantly over the levels seen in the early and middle 1970s. One study made by Pitt in 1971 indicated that the effective protection for all importables was 66 percent; a range of negative 13 percent (rice milling) to 701 percent (soap) included several examples of effective protection well in excess of 100 percent (sugar refining, spinning industries, apparel, and automobiles).[22] Negative effective protection for virtually all exportables, averaging negative 11 percent, resulted in an average level of effective protection well below the 66 percent average for importables.

A subsequent study by Pitt indicates that effective protection was even more highly variable in 1975 than in 1971. Even though the average level of effective protection across all industry was 30 percent, there was now a range from a negative 35 percent (batik apparel) to a positive 4,000 percent (tires). On average, according to preliminary estimates of the government, import-competing industries in 1981 received an implicit subsidy on production of slightly more than 200 percent (the automotive industry received more than 700 percent), whereas industries that did some exporting were effectively taxed at an average rate of 1 percent.

By 1985, import substitution had moved beyond consumer goods and into "upstream" intermediate goods, such as steel, polystyrene, and industrial chemicals. High and uneven protection discriminated sharply in favor of import-competing industries and against exportables. Employment generation in manufacturing proved to be below expectations. Although value added in manufacturing grew by 11 percent a year in 1975–82, employment increased by only 4.9 percent.[23] Much of the employment gain was in the cottage and small-scale segment, which produces only one-fifth of manufacturing output. The employment cost of import substitution in manufacturing was high. For 1971, Pitt found that $1 million in increased value added from manufactured exports would have generated 57 percent more employment than an equivalent reduction in competing imports. For 1975, Pitt found that an investment in the less protected exporting industries would have produced four times as many jobs and saved four times the foreign exchange as the same investment in the highly protected import-substituting industries.[24]

High protection discriminated against exportables and employment in export industries in other ways: by worsening exchange rate overvaluation and by raising the costs of downstream industries (such as garments and plastic products). The downstream industries tended to be more labor-intensive than highly protected upstream industries.[25] Furthermore, protection imposed a cost on consumers, particularly low-income consumers. Protection of the textile and footwear industries, for instance, cost consumers a total of $435 million, or 44 percent of their outlays on these items, in 1978.[26] By 1980, trade policies were estimated to have raised costs to consumers by more than Rp5 trillion (in 1985 prices), or about $150 per household a year, in a country with per capita income of less than $600.[27]

The negative impact of aggressive import substitution on employment, export growth, and living standards began to draw growing criticism from export-oriented industries, market-oriented economists, and other public figures not generally identified with liberal trade policies. Such criticisms in the past have often presaged changes in economic policy.

Export Policies

Natural resources and agricultural commodity exports had, until recently, accounted for more than 95 percent of Indonesia's exports. Not until 1982 did manufactured exports reach 10 percent of total exports.

Recurring episodes of overvaluation were not the only causes of sluggish growth of many non-oil exports in Indonesia. Other economic, foreign, and environmental policies also placed a variety of restrictions on the export of raw materials and manufactured products. As late as 1983, thirteen items, ranging from tropical logs to raw rattan, were subject to export prohibitions; exports to South Africa have been banned for years. The export of eighteen items, ranging from fertilizer to salt, sugar, rice, and automobile tires, was at times restricted to increase the supply to the domestic market. The export of eight commodities, including tin, coffee, rubber, plywood, and crude oil, is restricted under international marketing arrangements. Five items, including tobacco, hides, and cinnamon, can be exported only by government-approved exporters. Seventeen raw materials, ranging from palm kernel products to iron ore, copper, tin, bauxite, and cork, are subject to export taxes. Seven wood and other agricultural products are subject to a sliding-scale export tax that varies directly with international prices.[28]

At the same time, a number of other policies have been initiated to promote exports, particularly of manufactures. An export certificate scheme created in 1978 provides drawbacks of import duties and rebates of internal indirect taxes for a variety of exports, primarily manufactures. The combined drawback and rebate has been as high as 44 percent for some textiles (and attracted sharp criticism from the United States) and as low as 5 percent for some intermediate goods. Export-processing zones have been created to encourage labor-intensive, low-value processing for the export market. Export finance arrangements have been streamlined, and exporters are eligible for a variety of special credit facilities. These include cheaper credit, export credit guarantees, and export insurance.

Until 1982, the net effect of this mix of export policies was probably to retard export activity in virtually all sectors. Substantial deregulation of export procedures has been achieved since then, however, except for those products that are prohibited or restricted by international marketing arrangements. Still, some restrictive measures taken earlier are virtually irreversible, particularly for forest-based industry. Between 1978 and 1985, an export tax of 20 percent was applied to logs; the tax rate was zero for plywood and for most sawn timber. In 1983, this structure of export taxes provided high effective protection to value added in the processing of logs: the rate of effective protection was 120 percent for plywood, whereas domestic value added in sawmilling (measured at world prices) was negative. Very high rates of effective protection to plymills and sawmills became infinitely high in 1985, when all log exports were banned. One result of the lack of competitive pressure furnished by these incentives is that Indonesia, the world's second leading producer of tropical hardwood, had one of the least competitive wood-processing industries in the world in 1985.[29]

4. Conclusions

The Indonesian experience with external adjustment and trade policies permits no easy generalizations. The principles underlying exchange rate and external debt policies have been consistently outward looking and prudent in focus. This is not to say that the policies have always been applied consistently, as witnessed by the long period of growing overvaluation from 1971 to 1978 and the failure to restrain the foreign borrowing of the state oil enterprise, Pertamina, in 1972–75. Other trade policies have passed through a curious metamorphosis over the period 1967–84, from liberalization to a distinct inward-looking stance, with recent indications of a reversion to their 1967–72 focus.[30]

Economic performance, as measured by the real growth rate of GNP, seemed, on the surface, not to vary with the management of external policies. Indonesia grew rapidly with liberalization in 1967–73, the period before the oil booms. It also grew rapidly with the combination of rising oil revenues and a distinct protectionistic drift from 1974 to 1981, when the second oil boom began to recede. Until 1980, however, the actual damage from protectionistic policy (when much greater reliance began to be placed on quantitative restrictions) was far less than that indicated by tariff rates. Inadequacies in customs administration severely undercut protectionist aims from 1965 through 1985. The economic cushion provided by petroleum earning and deft management of exchange rate policy enabled Indonesia to withstand a few protectionistic excesses without suffering the type of economic damages that befell such oil-importing countries as Argentina (which had a long history of aggressively protective policies). Indonesia also escaped the fate of such oil exporters as Nigeria, whose failure to use the exchange rate as an instrument of external adjustment policy partly caused a decline in the level of real output from 1975 to 1983.

After the end of the second oil boom in 1982, virtually all major policy changes in Indonesia returned to the policy mix prevalent before the first oil boom. The single exception has been trade policy, which has been the last and strongest refuge of influential rent seekers. The apparent short-term success of six major liberalizing policy reforms in 1983 may have removed much of the political underpinnings of restrictive policies toward imports and exports, but it is too soon to draw any firm conclusions on this issue.

Appendix. The Real Exchange Rate and the Index of International Competitiveness

The real exchange rate of a nation measures not only nominal changes in its exchange rates but also changes in relative inflation rates. If a nation has a higher inflation rate than its trading partners, its industries will also tend to have higher costs in terms of its local currency. If the currency is devalued relative to the currencies of its trading partners, however, the cost of production to local industries in dollars will not rise as much and it may even fall. Suppose, for example, that the Indonesian price index is 100 and the exchange rate is Rp333 = $1. At this price, it costs just Rp333, or $1, to produce a meter of cloth. This level is competitive with industry in the United States. Now suppose that prices and costs rise six times in Indonesia but only double in the United States. If the exchange rate is unchanged, and if cloth production costs rise in line with Indonesian inflation, then it costs Rp2,000 to produce a meter of cloth, or $6 at the old exchange rate. This figure would compare with a cost of $2 per meter in the United States. Suppose, however, that the Indonesian exchange rate is devalued to a level of Rp1,000 = $1. Then the cost of Rp2,000 expressed in dollars is just $2, a level still competitive with industry in the United States. In this example, the real exchange rate has stayed the same because the extra inflation in Indonesia has been offset by the devaluation of the rupiah.

In general, a correct procedure to calculate the real exchange rate is to take a trade-weighted average of nominal exchange rates and inflation rates in the country being studied and its trading partners. (Even this procedure may not be strictly correct if exports of the nation being studied compete with exports from third countries with which it does not trade. It is also desirable to reflect changes in tariffs and other trade barriers that also influence costs.) The broad trend of costs, however, can be seen from calculations based on major trading partners only. In the list below, an index of cost competitiveness is calculated on the basis of exchange rates of the rupiah, dollar, and yen and the relative inflation rates in Indonesia, the United States, and Japan.

Year	Index	Year	Index
1967	106	1976	58
1968	97	1977	55
1969	94	1978	59
1970	100	1979	77
1971	107	1980	74
1972	112	1981	73
1973	90	1982	74
1974	71	1983	94
1975	65	1984	100

The formula for the index is:

$$\text{Index} = 2/3 \cdot \text{Rp/Yen} \cdot \text{CPI}_J/\text{CPI}_I + 1/3 \cdot \text{Rp/\$} \cdot \text{CPI}_{US}/\text{CPI}_I$$

where CPI is the consumer price index and the subscript indicates the appropriate country. In this index (1970 = 100), an increase in Indonesian inflation relative to Japan or the United States will cause the competitiveness measure to decline, whereas a devaluation of the rupiah will cause the index to increase. A higher index means an easier time competing for Indonesian industry; a decline means a harder time.

The index of cost competitiveness shows that the 10 percent devaluation in 1971 indeed improved competitiveness by about 10 percent in 1972 over 1970. This advantage eroded rapidly, however, and by 1977 and 1978 Indonesia was far less competitive than at any time since 1967. The late 1978 devaluation improved the index considerably, although it failed to restore the cost advantages of the earlier years. Only the third devaluation in 1983 brought relative costs back to their 1970 level. The recovery is most apparent for 1984, the first year entirely under the newly devalued exchange rates.

Manufactured Exports

No single series estimates real and nominal values of manufactured exports over the entire period under study. For the 1970–74 period, we have taken chemicals, machinery, metal manufactures excluding tin and copper (which were exported in ingot form but were not otherwise fabricated), and other goods not classified; the total current values in millions of U.S. dollars are:

1970	1971	1972	1974
$11.1	$18.7	$31.4	$53.8

Excluded from these totals are petroleum products; slightly refined agricultural products, such as palm oil, crumb rubber, and tea; and sawn wood. The Standard International Trade Classification numbers are 5, 6, 7, and 9.

The World Bank has provided a series of fiscal year estimates in both current and constant prices for the years after 1974 (see table 14-6). The exports in table 14-6 are somewhat more inclusive, in part because many new products began to be exported in more recent years. (The fiscal year begins on April 1 and ends on March 31 of the following calendar year.)

Not all changes in manufactured exports can be attributed to changes in real exchange rates. The general world economic climate, the phas-

Table 14-6. Indonesian Manufactured Exports, 1975–85
(millions of U.S. dollars)

Year	Current dollars		Constant 1981–82 dollars
	Total	Plywood[a]	
1975–76	144	0	215
1976–77	196	0	288
1977–78	245	0	331
1978–79	360	0	414
1979–80	447	0	461
1980–81	540	0	514
1981–82	865	199	865
1982–83	853	324	870[b]
1983–84	1,484	579	1,587
1984–85[c]	1,649	660	1,830

a. Before 1980–81, the small level of plywood exports was consolidated with timber exports.

b. The higher constant value for 1982–83 through 1984–85 is not an error. Rather, the figures reflect lower U.S. dollar prices for exports of these products after 1982.

c. Estimated.

Source: World Bank data.

ing in of new industries, and export taxes or bans on log exports all influence the ultimate level. It is noteworthy, however, that in each case where there has been a devaluation, there has also been a sharp jump in manufactured exports. This trend was especially noticeable from 1982–83 to 1983–84, when even nonplywood exports jumped from $530 million to $905 million and total real exports rose 82 percent. Similar results come from analyzing the 1977–78 period with that of 1979–81, the two fiscal years before and after the 1978 devaluation. Real exports jumped 55 percent in the period, even without any significant contribution from plywood. And in 1970–74, the increase from $12 million in 1970 to more than $30 million in 1972 must also reflect the considerable volume gains, not simply higher prices. The subsequent sharp gain in 1973 and fallback in 1974 probably reflect world price fluctuations to a large extent, although they are consistent with investment and production decisions following cost changes with a modest lag.

Imports

The International Monetary Fund (IMF) shows a consistent series of current price non-oil imports for all years, but these are based on unadjusted customs data and do not provide any estimate of real (inflation-adjusted) imports. The World Bank has a series from 1975–76 onward that reflects staff estimates; the figures are deflated. For the first three quarters of 1971, the IMF reports non-oil imports of $859 million, whereas the fourth quarter of 1971 and the first half of 1972 saw imports of only $866 million, a real decline. Imports in later months of 1972 shot up sharply, as however, consumption imports grew in response to the poor harvest and capital goods imports jumped because of government procurements. The record of annual non-oil imports from 1967 to 1974 is shown below in millions of current dollars.

Year	Imports
1967	569
1968	720
1969	921
1970	1,137
1971	1,106
1972	1,453
1973	2,607
1974	3,925

The World Bank series is shown in table 14-7 in both current dollars and constant prices.

Table 14-7. Non-oil Imports of Indonesia, 1975–85
(millions of U.S. dollars)

Year	Imports (current dollars)	Imports (1980–81 constant prices)
1975–76	5,090	8,305
1976–77	6,167	10,161
1977–78	7,241	11,307
1978–79	7,543	9,829
1979–80	9,028	10,823
1980–81	11,837	12,213
1981–82	14,561	14,561
1982–83	15,824	16,479[b]
1983–84	14,246	14,271
1984–85[a]	12,565	14,227

a. Estimated.

b. The higher constant values for 1982–83 and thereafter are not misprints. They reflect lower dollar prices for imports after 1981.

Source: World Bank data.

In this case again, it is apparent that the 1978 and 1983 devaluations had a powerful impact on import demand. From 1977–78 to 1979–81, the real volume of non-oil imports actually dropped by 5 percent in spite of rapid growth in the economy. This situation represented a sharp reversal from previous gains and occurred in spite of some loosening of import controls in 1978 and 1979 after the devaluation. Similarly, in 1982–83 imports peaked in real terms at $16.5 billion and then fell by 14 percent during the next two years in spite of continuing growth in real output. It is evident that the change in relative prices caused by the devaluations discouraged the use of imports and encouraged manufacturing output, both for domestic use and for exports.

Notes

1. Two particularly illuminating studies that examine exchange rate policy experience in Africa are Uma Lele, "Tanzania: Phoenix or Icarus?" and Michael Roemer, "Ghana: Missed Opportunities," both in A. C. Harberger, ed., *World Economic Growth* (San Francisco, Calif.: Institute for Contemporary Studies, 1984), pp. 159–96 and 201–26.

2. Malcolm Gillis, "Episodes in Indonesian Economic Growth," in Harberger, ed., *World Economic Growth*, pp. 231–264.

3. World Bank, *World Development Report 1985* (New York: Oxford University Press, 1985), Indicators, table 1.

4. Phyllis Rosendale, "The Balance of Payments," in Anne Booth and Peter McCawley, eds., *The Indonesian Economy in the Suharto Era* (Kuala Lumpur: Oxford University Press, 1981), p. 1975.

5. World Bank data. Figures on imports exclude those made for the oil sector. These are almost exclusively intermediate and capital goods.

6. Indonesian per capita manufactured exports were $5.57 compared with Thailand's $41.00 and Malaysia's $186.64. See *World Development Report 1985*, Indicators, tables 1 and 13.

7. Gillis, "Episodes in Indonesian Growth," p. 240.

8. For a full description of the multiple-exchange-rate system employed in Indonesia from 1966 to 1970, see Anwas Nasution, *Financial Institutions and Policies in Indonesia* (Singapore: Institute of Southeast Asian Studies, 1983), p. 7.

9. Debt service figures are from the *World Development Report 1985*, Indicators, table 16.

10. The Indonesian authorities take the view that a prudent indicator of debt service ratios requires that imports of goods and services of the oil sector, as well as profit repatriation of foreign oil companies, be subtracted from total oil exports to provide a reasonable picture of the country's command over foreign resources furnished by oil. Viewed in this way, total 1983 debt service of $2.7 billion is best expressed as a percentage of total net exports. The ratio of debt service to total exports thus defined as 21.5 percent.

11. Richard N. Cooper, "Tariffs and Smuggling in Indonesia," in Jagdish Bhagwati, *Illegal Transactions in International Trade* (Amsterdam: North-Holland, 1974), pp. 171–85.

12. Mark Pitt, "Alternative Trade Strategies and Employment in Indonesia," in Ann O. Krueger and others, eds., *Trade and Employment in Developing Countries* (Chicago, Ill.: University of Chicago Press, 1981), p. 225.

13. Directorat Djeneral BEA dan Cukai, *Laporan Mingguan* (Jakarta: Directorat Djeneral BEA dan Cukia, 1973), pp. 3–8.

14. Gillis, "Episodes in Indonesian Growth."

15. For another interpretation of the efficacy of the 1978 devaluation, see Heinz Ardt and R. M. Sundrum, "Devaluation and Inflation: The 1978 Experience," *Bulletin of Indonesian Economic Studies*, vol. 20, no. 1 (April 1984), pp. 83–96.

16. Malcolm Gillis, "Macro and Microeconomics of Tax Reform: Indonesia," Harvard Institute for International Development, Discussion Paper 174 (Cambridge, Mass., July 1984).

17. For a somewhat different perspective on the 1983 devaluation, see Bruce N. Glassburner and Mark Poffenburger, "Survey of Recent Developments," *Bulletin of Indonesian Economic Affairs*, vol. 19, no. 3 (December 1983), pp. 15–19; and Phyllis Rosendale, "Survey of Recent Developments," *Bulletin of Indonesian Economic Affairs*, vol. 20, no. 1 (April 1984).

18. In the early 1970s the only prohibited imports other than tires and certain batik fabrics were so classified for social and foreign policy reasons. Imports of mosquito-repellent coals were banned on health grounds. Imports from Israel and South Africa were prohibited on political grounds.

19. Gillis, "Episodes in Indonesian Growth," p. 259.

20. See Cooper, "Tariffs and Smuggling in Indonesia," for a vivid analysis of the extent of smuggling in the early 1970s.

21. The conventional form of the infant industry argument for protection holds that, if industries are given temporary protection in their early stages, they will eventually become so efficient that protection can be reduced. The pattern of protection in Indonesia indicates otherwise: typically the longer an industry has been established, the higher the protection it receives. One highly

regarded unpublished study has shown that the older industries, such as utensils, received in 1985 effective protection as high as 184 percent, whereas newer industries (foil and rods) established after 1982 received lower effective protection of 15–20 percent.

22. Pitt, "Alternative Trade Strategies and Employment," p. 208.

23. Compiled by Richard Porter from *Biro Pusat Statistik,* various issues, 1975–82.

24. Pitt, "Alternative Trade Strategies and Employment," p. 225, and World Bank data.

25. Gillis, "Episodes in Indonesian Growth," p. 260.

26. These figures are based on estimates as yet unpublished by Richard Porter for thirty-two industries in 1980.

27. Sumitro Djojohadikusmo, "Added Value, Productive Employment, and the Balance of Payments," *Jakarta Post,* August 22, 1985.

28. This compendium of export restrictions was drawn from material prepared by Stephen Parker in 1984 and updated by the authors.

29. Malcolm Gillis, "Indonesia: Public Policy, Resource Management, and the Tropical Forest," paper prepared for the World Resources Institute, Washington, D.C., November 9, 1985, pp. 30–40.

30. Gillis, "Episodes in Indonesian Growth," p. 261.

15

Korea

Yung-Chul Park

AN OUTWARD-LOOKING strategy for the past two decades has led the Republic of Korea to be widely acclaimed as representing one of the most successful cases of industrialization. Between 1964 and 1984, Korea's real GNP more than quintupled, growing at a rate of 8.4 percent a year on the average (see table 15-1). Per capita income, among the lowest in the world in the early 1960s, increased sixfold to about $1,600 (in 1984 U.S. dollars) during the same period.

The rapid growth was accompanied by dramatic changes in the structure of industry and employment. Agriculture, which had been the pre-

Table 15-1. Major Economic Indicators

(percent)

Indicator	1960–65	1966–70	1971–75	1976–80	1981–84
GNP growth rate	5.6	10.4	8.6	7.6	7.2
Export growth rate[a]	44.5	36.8	46.1	28.6	13.9
Export as percentage of GNP	3.2	8.6	19.8	26.2	31.7
Exports of manufactures as percentage of GNP	35.5	71.5	84.5	88.2	90.9
Unemployment rate	7.8	5.5	4.2	4.0	4.2
Rate of increase in real wages in manufacturing	−2.3	12.3	5.8	11.9	5.1
Inflation rate (GNP deflator)	18.2	15.3	19.7	21.0	7.5
Current account deficit as percentage of GNP	1.0	6.4	7.0	3.7	3.6

a. Based on custom clearance.
Source: Bank of Korea, *Economic Statistics Yearbook,* various issues.

dominant industry until the early 1960s, accounted for 15 percent of GNP and 27 percent of employment in 1984, whereas the share of manufacturing improved to 31 percent and 23 percent, respectively (see table 15-2). A number of factors have been responsible for Korea's spectacular economic progress, but the most important has been the outward-looking development strategy, particularly export-led industrialization, a strategy that began around 1964 when the policy shift was made from import substitution to export promotion.

1. Exports as an Engine of Growth

As shown in table 15-3, in 1960 commodity exports amounted to $33 million and consisted mainly of such primary products as metallic ores, animal and vegetable products, and raw silk. Since then, exports have risen at an average annual rate of 34 percent to $29 billion in 1984, more than 90 percent of which was manufactured products, such as ships, automobiles, and electronic products. The share of exports in GNP increased from 3 percent in 1960–65 to 32 percent in 1981–84 (see table 15-1).

The phenomenal increase in export earnings accounted for 36 percent of the increase in output growth between 1955 and 1975 (Kim and Roemer 1979) and for more than 25 percent of the increase in total employment between 1960 and 1975 (Hong 1979).

The export growth also changed the structure of the Korean economy drastically (see table 15-2). The manufacturing sector grew 15 percent a year in constant prices and increased its share in GNP from 10 percent in 1963 to 31 percent in 1984, mostly at the expense of agriculture. According to census figures, employment in agriculture, forestry, and fishery dropped from 63 percent of the labor force in 1963 to 27 percent in 1984, whereas the share of manufacturing increased from 8 percent to 23 percent. Unemployment declined from 9 percent in the early 1960s to 4 percent in 1984. Real wages in manufacturing increased by more than 8 percent a year on the average during the 1966–84 period (see table 15-1).

After the middle of the 1960s, Korea had begun to change from a poor agrarian economy with surplus labor to an export-oriented economy specializing first in labor-intensive manufactures and then in capital- and skill-intensive manufactures.

Many authors have argued that Korea's trade orientation was responsible for its phenomenal industrialization success. Considerable evidence shows that the promotion of manufactured labor-intensive exports helps industrialization. It appears, however, that little is known about why import substitution could not lead to the same results. For details, see Krueger (1980, 1981). Indeed, in terms of conventional

Table 15-2. Share in GNP and Employment by Sector
(percent)

Sector	1963 I	1963 E	1965 I	1965 E	1970 I	1970 E	1975 I	1975 E	1980 I	1980 E	1984 I	1984 E
Agriculture, forestry and fishing	43.5	63.1	42.9	58.6	28.7	50.4	24.2	45.9	14.4	34.0	15.1	27.1
Mining	1.9	0.7	2.0	1.0	2.1	1.1	2.0	0.5	1.4	0.9	1.4	1.0
Manufacturing	9.7	8.0	11.0	9.4	14.2	13.2	21.6	18.6	28.8	21.7	30.9	23.2
Social overhead capital and other services	44.9	28.2	44.0	31.0	54.9	35.2	52.3	35.0	55.4	43.4	52.6	48.7

Note: I = Industrial origin of GNP at constant market prices. E = Persons employed by industry.
Source: Bank of Korea, *Economic Statistics Yearbook,* various issues.

Table 15-3. Exports by Commodity Group and Major Commodities
(percentage of total exports)

SITC group[a]	Commodities	1954	1960	1965	1976	1984
0–2	Food and live animals; beverages and tobacco; crude materials except fuel	88.8	79.1	37.8	10.2	5.4
3–5	Mineral fuels; animal and vegetable oils and fats; chemicals	5.9	5.3	1.3	3.4	5.8
6	Manufactured goods classified chiefly by material	4.6	12.0	37.9	30.3	25.2
	Textile yarn and fabrics	n.a.	n.a.	15.0	12.4	8.9
	Iron and steel	0.0	0.0	7.3	4.8	7.0
7	Machinery and transport	0.3	0.3	3.1	16.6	35.8
	Electrical machinery	0.0	0.0	1.1	10.4	13.4
	Transport equipment	0.0	0.0	0.6	4.4	18.9
8	Miscellaneous manufactures	0.2	0.3	19.7	39.2	27.7
	Clothing	0.0	0.0	11.8	23.9	15.4
	Footwear	0.0	0.0	2.4	5.2	4.6
	Wigs and false beards	0.0	0.0	1.3	0.9	0.2
9	Unclassifiable	0.2	3.0	0.1	0.3	0.1
	Total export (millions of U.S. dollars)	24	33	175	7,715	29,245

n.a. Not available.
Note: Export figures are based on custom clearance.
a. Standard International Trade Classification.
Source: Bank of Korea, *Economic Statistics Yearbook,* 1964, 1968, 1977, and 1985.

trade theory, it is difficult to explain why export promotion produces better results than import substitution, because a bias in favor of exports is as bad as a bias against them from an efficiency point of view (Findlay 1981). At least some of the reasons for the superior performance must therefore be sought by opening the door to a variety of explanations outside the realm of conventional theory.

Other analysts have argued that Korea's industrialization was the result of a free trade regime (Westphal and Kim 1977; Westphal 1978). Theory suggests that in such a regime a country can exploit its comparative advantage and can reap efficiency gains. The difficulty with this argument is that Korea has been operating not in a free trade regime but in a highly interventionist atmosphere in which the government actively promotes exports and intervenes extensively in a number of markets, including financial and foreign exchange markets.

Krueger (1980, 1981) offers three reasons why export promotion is superior to import substitution. First, an incentive system that characterizes export promotion is more efficient than a control system, which is the main feature of import substitution. Second, competition against foreign products makes domestic producers more efficient than does a sheltered domestic market. Third, the efficiency gains from trade are an important source of economic growth.

Although these reasons describe the gains from export promotion, the crucial question remains: what produces successful export-led industrial growth, and what does not? In theory, any developing country with surplus labor can develop its industry and sustain rapid growth if it can profitably sell labor-intensive products abroad. In practice, only a few developing countries have been able to do so. The question that arises, therefore, is why can some countries export, whereas others cannot?

For Korea, the answer lies in cultural, historical, and political explanations. A common language and culture have facilitated geographical and social mobility. The Confucian heritage, which attaches a high value to education, has led to nearly 100 percent literacy among the adult population and a highly educated and disciplined labor force. The land reform and redistribution of Japanese-owned assets after World War II destroyed the feudal classes' hold on society and facilitated the emergence of a dynamic capitalist class, which has played a pivotal role in Korean development.

Futhermore, Japan and the United States, with which Korea has had close ties, provided important markets for Korean exports and substantial inflows of capital and technology. (The latter helped link Korean exporters with the international trade networks.) Massive economic assistance from these two countries paved the way for an economic take-off in the mid-1960s, and successful mobilization of foreign commercial borrowings thereafter enabled Korea to achieve an average gross investment rate of 29 percent. The success in mobilizing foreign savings derives mainly from a very high rate of export growth.

Another factor that is uniquely Korean is the centralized nature of the government, which in the 1970s directly or indirectly controlled almost two-thirds of the investment resources of the economy.[1] The government maintains political and social stability and initiates policy changes in ways that would be difficult to implement in Western democracies. Labor organizations, in particular, are kept weak, so that wages are also kept low. The government exercises overwhelming control over resource allocation. In the 1960s, government savings and foreign savings (both determined by the government) financed about 60 percent of Korea's annual domestic investment (see table 15-4). The share has since then declined, but even in recent years it has been close to 40 per-

Table 15-4. Private, Government, and Foreign Savings
(percent)

Item	1961–65	1966–70	1971–75	1976–80	1981–84
Private	43.9	38.9	55.0	66.4	60.2
Government	−2.6	20.0	14.5	20.0	24.4
Foreign	59.6	38.8	30.2	14.2	15.2
Statistical discrepancy	−0.9	2.3	0.3	−0.6	0.2
Gross domestic investment	100.0	100.0	100.0	100.0	100.0

Note: The gross domestic investment has been calculated at current market prices.
Source: Bank of Korea, *Economic Statistics Yearbook,* various issues.

cent. In addition, the government continues to regulate credit allocation in the organized financial sector. Thus it is reasonable to assume
that throughout the 1970s the government was directly or indirectly in
command of almost two-thirds of the investment resources of the
economy.

The resource allocation by the government has not always been efficient. To judge from the remarkable economic performance, however,
the Korean government has succeeded in mobilizing resources from
abroad and at home and in allocating those resources in support of its
high-growth policies (Cole and Park 1983).

2. Disadvantages of the Strategy

Despite its success, Korea's development strategy has created formidable structural problems for policymakers—at least in the short run.
Three sets of problems are particularly noteworthy.

First, reliance on export growth has exposed the Korean economy to
external shocks—such as the oil price increase and trade protectionism—and has made it more sensitive to secular and cyclical fluctuations in trade. The opening up of the economy and the structural
rigidities of government control have restricted the scope as well as the
effectiveness of stabilization policy. Consequently, the problems of
maintaining the internal and external stability of the economy have
been magnified.

Small, open economies are generally vulnerable to the vagaries of
international markets. Korea is more vulnerable because it depends on
the markets of developed countries for its exports and on the markets of
(mainly) developing countries for imports of oil and other raw materials.[2] Because it is poorly endowed with natural resources, Korea's comparative advantage lies in labor- and skill-intensive products. Korea will

Table 15-5. Profile of Korea's External Debt

Item	1965	1970	1975	1979	1980	1981	1982	1983	1984
Gross debt									
Billions of U.S. dollars	0.2	2.3	8.5	20.4	27.3	32.5	37.1	40.4	43.1
Percentage of GNP	5.9[b]	28.2	40.6	32.7	44.6	48.4	52.4	53.7	53.2
Net debt									
Billions of U.S. dollars[a]	0.1	1.6	6.8	14.1	19.8	24.3	28.3	31.1	32.9
Percentage of GNP	1.7	19.7	32.4	22.6	32.4	36.2	40.0	41.3	40.6
Debt service/GNP	0.5	3.3	4.1	5.2	7.3	8.1	8.2	7.6	8.3

a. Gross debt minus external assets, which include foreign exchange reserves, exports on credit, "A" account loans from the head offices of foreign banks to foreign branches of Korean banks, and other items.

b. As percentage of nominal dollar GNP.

Source: Bank of Korea, *Economic Statistics Yearbook.*

be dealt a severe blow if some of the foreign markets for its exports are abruptly closed because of protectionist measure or if it is unable to import oil and other raw materials. In contrast, few countries will suffer from not trading with Korea.

Business investments have become a function of export prospects. Because export earnings fluctuate, depending on world market conditions, monetary policy has become highly procyclical. The export finance system is a case in point. Since 1965, exports with valid letters of credit have received unlimited, subsidized, short-term export credit. Because export loans are tied to the gross volume of export sales and are granted automatically, changes in export earnings destabilize the monetary control mechanism. Thus there has been a considerable loss of control over credit expansion. This problem was not serious in the 1960s, but with the gradual increase in the ratio of exports to GNP, the destabilizing effect has become more serious.

In addition, the fixed-exchange-rate system, underdeveloped money and capital markets, and the relatively easy access to foreign loans have rendered the traditional instruments of monetary policy inoperative. The instruments of direct credit controls have not been fully utilized either, especially when control over domestic liquidity has clashed with the growth objective.

The second problem of Korea's outward-looking strategy is that the country has been saddled with a large foreign debt (see table 15-5). The Korean debt—53 percent of GNP at the end of 1984—is certainly not of Latin American proportions, and the country has demonstrated an ability to service its obligations in recent years.[3] Nevertheless, the size of the debt has made Korea more vulnerable than before to trade protectionism, instability in international financial markets, higher foreign interest rates, and other external shocks.

Korea's export promotion policy itself has very little to do with the external debt problem. Rather, it is the development philosophy, which places economic growth ahead of other objectives, that has been largely responsible for the accumulation of foreign debt.[4] Whenever conflicts have risen between the growth target and the management of debt, Korean policymakers have not hesitated to sacrifice the objective of balance of payments and price stability to the extent that foreign finance has been available.

By the early 1970s, Korea's exceptional growth performance had helped the nation establish creditworthiness in international financial markets. The availability of foreign commercial funds allowed Korean policymakers to continue with the growth-first policy and to choose an adjustment path to external shocks that required little sacrifice in growth and employment. Rapid growth through the promotion of exports was expected to reduce Korea's dependence on foreign resources. Although the growth of output and exports has been impressive, the expansion of domestic savings has not been sufficient to sustain the rapid growth that Korea has achieved. As a result the current account deficit has persisted and has been the major cause of debt accumulation.

The third problem of Korea's strategy is that the dominant role of the government, which was pivotal in promoting export and employment growth in the 1960s, became counterproductive and resulted in a considerable deterioration in both efficiency and equity in the 1970s. As the economy grew in size and sophistication, active government intervention undermined the efficiency of resource allocation, impeded private initiative, and reduced economic flexibility.

In retrospect it seems that Korean policymakers should perhaps have moved away from planning and intervention and relied more on the market much earlier than when they initiated an economic liberalization program in 1980. The inertia bred over the years, and the rigidities of the political structure hardened by the successful government role, delayed economic liberalization. Consequently, there was a massive misallocation of resources in the latter part of the 1970s, and economic power came to be concentrated in a few enterprises that dominated their industries.

In pursuing the outward-looking strategy, the Koreans made serious mistakes. During the 1970s investment in heavy industries was actively promoted because Korea's comparative advantage in exports was perceived to be in skill- and technology-intensive products (such as ships, machinery, and electronic products).Subsidized credit, organizational support, and domestic market protection were made available to these industries. Neither the static comparative advantage nor any other criteria, however, could have justified the heavy investments made in these industries. Not surprisingly, the investment program encountered a host of financing, engineering, quality, and marketing problems that underutilized the production capacities in many of the selected industries, built up strong inflationary pressure, and caused a sharp deterioration in the current account balance. Such a misallocation of resources, many would argue, could have been avoided had the management of the financial system been left in private hands.

Although there are no reliable statistics, several studies have shown an increasing concentration of economic power in a few industrial conglomerates.[5] The cause of this concentration lies in Korea's export-led industrialization strategy, which has channeled, through the managed financial system, a large share of domestic and foreign resources to a handful of firms—usually with a proven export record—selected for export promotion to realize economies of scale (Jones and Sakong 1980, p. 305; Cole and Park 1983, p. 292). In a recent study, the considerable increase in the inequality of income distribution has been attributed by

some writers to the concentration of economic power in a few industries.

3. Conclusions

There is little doubt that the successful promotion of exports has been
primarily responsible for Korea's transformation from a poor agrarian
economy into a semiindustrialized, middle-income country in just over
two decades. The association of export promotion with rapid industrialization, however, is neither unique nor interesting. The fundamental
question is why and how Korea was able to produce and sell abroad
exportables while other countries could not. There is no clear answer to
this question. Various noneconomic factors and the macroeconomic
policies initiated by the government and developed over time have been
important.

The Korean economy is hardly a model of a free trade regime. The
government has assumed a dominant role in the economy from the
early stage of development. It has used direct and indirect controls, and
all other fiscal and monetary instruments available to it, to achieve high
rates of economic growth.

The Korean experience indicates that an interventionist approach
has a number of advantages. Without the existence of a strong government, Korean policymakers would not have been able to carry out difficult economic policies (keeping wages low, for instance). Indeed, it is
difficult to imagine that Korea would have achieved the economic success and the restructuring it has had if the government had introduced a
noninterventionist, liberal economic system in which prices clear markets and allocate resources.

Apparently, however, the small group of people at the top who make
the important economic decisions has failed to accommodate the growing number of affected interest groups in the decisionmaking process.
The group has perhaps also persisted too long in controlling the economy, the structure of which has become increasingly diversified and
complex. When the advantages and disadvantages are all taken into
account, it would be difficult to agree on whether the existence of a
strong government has exerted a positive effect on Korean development. Such an assessment is bound to be influenced by one's view of the
ideal process of economic and social development.

Since 1980. after realizing the limitations of interventionist policies,
the government has embarked on a course of economic liberalization.
The process of liberalization has been painfully slow, however, and has
so far produced little progress (Park 1985).

The "Korean success" is not likely to be replicated elsewhere in the
future. Korea has been able to exploit large export markets, supported
by the rapid world economic growth in the 1960s, the liquidity creation

by international banks in the 1970s, and the surge in U.S. imports in recent years. Still, it is difficult to imagine that the world economy will grow as rapidly in the next decade as it did in the 1960s and 1970s.

Selected Bibliography

Aghevli, Bijan B., and J. Marques-Ruarte. 1985. *A Case of Successful Adjustment: Korea's Experience during 1980–84*. Occasional Paper 39. Washington D.C.: International Monetary Fund.

Cole, David C., and Y. C. Park. 1983. *Financial Development in Korea, 1945–78*. Harvard East Asian Monograph 106. Cambridge, Mass.: Harvard University Press.

Datta-Chaudhuri, M. D. 1981. "Industrialization and Foreign Trade: The Development Experiences of South Korea and the Philippines." In Eddy Lee, ed., *Export-led Industrialization and Development*. Geneva: International Labour Office.

Findlay, Ronald. 1981. "Comment on Export-led Growth Reconsidered." In W. T. Hong and L. Krause, eds., *Trade and Growth of the Advanced Development Countries in the Pacific Basin*. Seoul: Korean Development Institute.

Franck, C. R., Jr., K. S. Kim, and Larry E. Westphal. 1975. *Foreign Trade Regimes and Economic Development: South Korea*. New York: National Bureau of Economic Research.

Hasan, Parvez. 1979. *Korea: Problems and Issues in a Rapidly Growing Economy*. Baltimore, Md.: Johns Hopkins University Press.

Hasan, Parvez, and D. C. Rao. 1979. *Korea: Policy Issues for Long-Term Development*. Baltimore, Md.: Johns Hopkins University Press.

Hong, W. T. 1976. *Seoul: Factor Supply and Factor Intensity of Trade in Korea*. Seoul: Korea Development Institute.

———. 1979. *Trade, Distortions, and Employment Growth in Korea*. Seoul: Korea Development Institute.

Jones, Leroy, 1981. *Jaebul and the Concentration of Economic Power in Korean Development: Issues, Evidence, and Alternatives*. Consultant Paper 12. Seoul: Korea Development Institute.

Jones, Leroy, and Il Sakong. 1980. *Government, Business, and Entrepreneurship in Economic Development: The Korean Case*. Harvard East Asian Monograph 91. Cambridge, Mass.: Harvard University Press.

Kim, Kwang S., and Michael Roemer. 1979. *Growth and Structural Transformation*. Harvard East Asian Monograph 86. Cambridge Mass.: Harvard University Press.

Krueger, Anne O.. 1979. *The Developmental Role of the Foreign Sector and Aid*. Harvard East Asian Monograph 87. Cambridge Mass.: Harvard University Press.

———. 1980. "Trade Policy as an Input to Development." National Bureau of Economic Research, Reprint 11. Cambridge, Mass.

———. 1981. "Export-led Industrial Growth Reconsidered." In W. T. Hong and L. Krause, eds., *Trade and Growth of the Advanced Developing Countries in the Pacific Basin*. Seoul: Korean Development Institute.

Mason, Edward S., M. J. Kim, D. H. Perkins, K. S. Kim, and D. C. Cole. 1980.

The Economic and Social Modernization of the Republic of Korea. Harvard East Asian Monograph 92. Cambridge, Mass.: Harvard University Press.

Park, Y. C. 1985. "Economic Stabilization and Liberalization in Korea, 1980–1984." In *Monetary Policy in a Changing Financial Environment: Proceedings of the Seminar Commemorating the Thirty-fifth Anniversary of the Bank of Korea*. Seoul: Bank of Korea.

――――. 1985. "Korea's Experience with External Debt Management." In G. W. Smith and J. T. Cuddington, eds., *International Debt and the Developing Countries*. Washington, D.C.: World Bank.

Westphal, Larry E. 1977. *Korea's Experience with Export-led Industrial Development*. World Bank Staff Working Paper 249. Washington D.C.

Westphal, Larry E., and Kwang S. Kim. 1977. *Industrial Policy and Development in Korea*. World Bank Staff Working Paper 263. Washington, D.C.: World Bank.

Notes

1. As one author puts it, "No state, outside of the Socialist bloc, ever came anywhere near this measure of control over the economy's investable resources" (Datta-Chaudhuri 1981).

2. In recent years the share of crude oil in Korea's total imports has been higher than 20 percent and that of capital goods more than 30 percent.

3. Korea ranks fourth among developing countries in outstanding debt and has experienced some deterioration in its debt-servicing capacity, but its debt management has been widely heralded as a success. It has been able to maintain rapid growth and to avoid financial difficulties that other countries have had (Aghevli and Marques-Ruarte 1985).

4. This point is evident from the way the five-year development plans have been formulated and executed. The plans assume that the capital-output ratio and the marginal propensity to save are exogenously determined. A given target rate of growth then determines the required investment. If the domestic savings expected to be available during the plan period cannot meet the required investment, then planners make up the shortfall by foreign capital inflows rather than by adjusting the target rate of growth.

5. Compared with other developing countries, Korea may not have a higher degree of industrial concentration, but the rapid rate at which concentration was taking place troubled at least one outsider (Jones 1981). Despite the continuing efforts on the part of the government to slow down the concentration, newspaper accounts suggest that there has been little, if any, moderation in economic concentration.

16

Mexico

Eliana A. Cardoso
and
Santiago Levy

DURING THE LAST half century, Mexico has both benefited from and been hurt by changes in the world economy. Different economic policies have been tried, and their usefulness and consequences have been intensely debated. In this chapter we will consider the Mexican economic development as the result of the interaction between external shocks and economic policies. We will begin with an overview of the main growth periods since 1935 before describing the process of import-substituting industrialization and trade policies of Mexico. We will then provide an analysis of exchange rates, describe the consequences of their behavior for trade and capital flight, discuss the two-tier system implemented at the end of 1982, and examine the relationship between fiscal policies and inflation. In conclusion we will review the recent stabilization programs.

1. From 1935 to 1982

During the past fifty years, the Mexican real GDP has grown on average at 6 percent a year, notwithstanding periodic recessions. Table 16-1 summarizes the behavior of growth per capita, inflation, and real wages between 1935 and 1985. The period is divided into intervals corresponding to the duration of each administration, thus eliminating the variations of economic cycles, which in Mexico coincide with the presidential political cycle of six years. The Mexican political system promotes a strong expansion of aggregate demand in the last year of a sexenio, as government spending increases to finish public investment programs, and thus corrective policies are required in the beginning of the new sexenio; Koehler (1986) shows the coincidence of political and business cycles in Mexico.

Table 16-1. Real Wages, Inflation, and Growth in Mexico

			Percentage change during the period		
Period	*President*	*Political position*	*GDP per capita*	*Prices*	*Real minimum wage*
1935–40	Cárdenas	Left	2.8	5.9	−2.0
1941–46	Camacho	Center	3.5	17.7	−7.3
1947–52	Alemán	Right	3.1	11.2	3.8
1953–58	Ruíz Cortines	Center	3.5	6.7	0.5
1959–64	López Mateos	Center-Left	3.3	2.3	11.1
1965–70	Díaz Ordaz	Right	3.4	3.6	4.0
1971–76	Echeverría	Left	2.7	14.1	2.3
1977–82	López Portillo	Center	3.1	30.5	−3.3
1983–85	de la Madrid	Center-Right	−2.0	68.0	−8.9

Sources: Economic and financial statistics prepared by the Secretaria de Hacienda, Comisión Nacional de Salarios Mínimos, table 2; and García-Alba and Serra-Puche (1983).

To judge from growth rates per capita, Mexican development has been a success story. But there are many flaws in its success: notwithstanding the reduction in poverty during the last half century, income distribution has not improved. Futhermore, growth has been fragile, as indicated by recent events: growth rates turned negative in the early 1980s, inflation has increased, the external debt is huge, and capital flight testifies to the lack of confidence of savers and investors in the Mexican economy.

Although Mexico is still a middle-income developing economy, it is an industrial urban society. Dramatic changes in the rural-urban composition of the population took place in the last forty years. Between 1940 and 1960 the share of the urban population doubled, and more than 60 percent of Mexicans now live in cities.

The period after World War II marks the beginning of Mexico's modern economic history. Institutional seeds were planted before the war with the creation of the central bank in 1925 and a development bank, the Nacional Financiera, in 1934. Even more important was the process of political consolidation following the land redistribution programs of the Cárdenas presidency (1934–40). Nevertheless, at the end of World War II and at the beginning of President Miguel Alemán's administration (1947–52) the private and public sectors reached the formal and informal agreements which established the political and social structure that was to permit fast economic growth in the following decades (see Vernon 1963; Hansen 1971).

Yearly growth rates of population and output over the past four decades are shown in table 16-2. In a marked upward trend, population

Table 16-2. Growth Rates of Population, Output, and Prices in Mexico, 1945–85

(percent)

Year	Population	GDP	CPI	Year	Population	GDP	CPI
1945	2.7	2.7	7.4	1966	3.4	6.9	4.4
1946	2.7	5.9	24.7	1967	3.4	6.3	2.6
1947	2.7	3.7	11.9	1968	3.5	8.1	2.6
1948	2.7	4.5	6.4	1969	3.5	6.3	3.5
1949	2.7	6.0	5.0	1970	3.6	6.9	4.9
1950	2.6	9.4	6.7	1971	3.5	4.2	5.6
1951	2.9	7.3	13.6	1972	3.5	8.5	4.8
1952	2.8	4.1	14.1	1973	3.5	8.4	12.1
1953	2.8	0.4	−0.9	1974	3.5	6.1	23.5
1954	2.8	10.5	4.8	1975	3.5	5.3	15.4
1955	2.9	8.7	13.8	1976	3.6	4.5	15.7
1956	2.9	6.2	4.8	1977	3.6	3.4	29.0
1957	3.0	7.6	6.2	1978	3.2	8.3	17.5
1958	3.3	5.4	11.6	1979	3.0	9.2	18.1
1959	3.4	3.0	1.9	1980	2.8	8.3	26.4
1960	3.4	8.1	5.1	1981	2.6	7.9	27.9
1961	3.4	4.9	1.8	1982	2.5	−0.6	59.0
1962	3.4	4.7	1.2	1983	2.8	−5.3	101.8
1963	3.4	8.0	0.6	1984	2.2	3.5	65.5
1964	3.4	11.7	2.3	1985	2.1	2.9	57.8
1965	3.5	6.5	3.4				

Sources: IMF, *International Financial Statistics;* Banco de Mexico, *Informe Anual, Acervo Historio,* and *Statistical Abstract of Latin America.*

growth reached 3.6 percent a year in 1977 but then decreased to its present level of 2.1 percent a year.

Annual inflation rates, also shown in table 16-2, and real growth figures suggest five different stages in modern Mexican economic history. The first, running from 1945 to 1954, is characterized by erratic growth rates, currency devaluations, and price instability.

A second period, from 1955 through 1970, is the "stabilizing development" period, also called the "Mexican miracle." This period was later criticized because of a worsening of income distribution, an antiexport bias, and price distortions that favored the use of capital in place of abundant labor. A discussion of different growth periods appears in Solís (1981) and García-Alba and Serra-Pache (1983).

A third stage, misleadingly called "shared development," runs from 1972 to 1977 and ends with high inflation and a negative growth in per capita income. During these years, industrial production increased and agricultural growth deteriorated.

Oil discoveries in 1978 altered the situation in a dramatic way, and for the next four years the economy experienced a new era of prosperity. The rapid expansion was flawed, however, by real and financial vulnerability that became apparent at the outbreak of the 1982 crisis. On the real side, the sectoral pattern of investment was strongly biased in favor of the oil industry and the service sector and against manufacturing. On the financial side, the fiesta of spending of the late 1970s was based on money printing and external borrowing because current oil revenue was in fact insufficient to finance the boom.

Starting with the debt crisis of 1982, the Mexican economy has suffered severe shocks; a strong domestic contractionary policy in 1983, an earthquake in 1985, and a fall in international oil prices in 1981 and at the end of 1985. All played an important role in the stagflation of the mid-1980s.

Stabilizing Development, 1955–70

In the ten years that followed World War II, there was neither steady growth nor price stability. Ortiz Mena (1970), one of the chief architects of the stabilizing development period that was to follow, attributed the price instability to the vicious circle created by devaluations and consequent increases in prices. Budget deficits and investment in excess of savings had induced growth, current account deficits, and inflation. Devaluations necessary to correct for overvaluation and the deficits in external accounts created more inflation and the need for other devaluations.

A change in strategy was called for because confidence in the past government policies had been eroded. Policymakers claimed that a small, open economy bordering on the largest financial market in the world could develop only with a fixed exchange rate and price stability. Luckily for the new strategy, it was to coincide with a period of uninterrupted growth in the rest of the world. The main ingredients of the stabilizing development program were:

- A fixed nominal exchange rate
- A low ratio of government budget deficits to GDP
- A stable ratio of the public external debt to GDP. External borrowing was seen as a mechanism to help support the fixed exchange rate.
- Subsidies and tax exemptions for reinvested profits as well as promotion of import substitution through tariffs and selective licensing
- A positive real return to savers, to be achieved through positive real interest rates and low taxes on income from interest. Real interest

rates net of taxes were positive during the whole period. Taxation calculated as a percentage of taxes plus inflation with respect to nominal interest rate was above the maximum marginal personal income tax in only eight out of seventeen years (see Gil Días 1984).

- Reserve requirements of financial intermediaries set by the Bank of Mexico were used not only as an instrument of monetary policy but also as a technique to absorb government paper and thus provide compulsory loans to the government. In addition, they were a way of allocating credit between the public and private sectors. Funds available to the government in the mid-1970s through these reserve requirements represented about one-third of the liabilities of the financial system.

The macroeconomic performance during the stabilizing development period was spectacular. From 1955 to 1970, real GDP grew on average 6.7 percent a year, whereas the annual inflation rate was only 3.8 percent. At the same time, the share of investment in output increased from 14.3 percent in 1955 to 22.7 percent in 1970.

The macroeconomic framework of stabilizing development worked because the fixed exchange rate was consistent with the fiscal and monetary policies. But, the policy moved the economy further and further away from free trade. To justify protection, policymakers used arguments based on infant-industry models, dependency theory, and evidence regarding deteriorating terms of trade in developing countries.

Public sector investments were tilted toward industry with the exception of irrigation projects in the northwest region. The lag in agricultural output and the decline in the supply of agricultural products in the 1980s was reinforced by price controls on basic agricultural products. Lower incomes in the agricultural sector coupled with the increase in the rate of growth of population exacerbated the process of rural-urban migration. It gave rise to poverty belts around the big cities and also increased illegal immigration into the United States.

By the late 1960s, the weaknesses of the stabilizing development policy had become apparent. Output growth was not sufficient to accommodate the growing labor force. Solís (1981) estimated that GDP had to grow at 7.5 percent a year to absorb the growing labor force with the existing output mix and ruling factor prices. Given the real exchange rate, faster growth would imply unsustainable current account deficits (for a detailed discussion, see Levy 1980).

The external sector was not doing well. The drop in agricultural output was turning the country into a net importer of foodstuffs. Nontraditional exports were not growing because of the strong antiexport bias of the trade regime.

In addition to balance of payments problems, there were the social and economic disparities, as shown by data on income distribution among households in Mexico (Aspe and Berlstain 1984).

	Percentage share in total income		
	1963	*1968*	*1977*
Poorest 20 percent	3.5	3.4	2.9
Richest 20 percent	58.9	58.0	54.5

Because the strategy required small budget deficits, public investment had to be reduced. The cuts came in the form of reductions in public investment in agriculture and education (see Gil Díaz 1985). Such fiscal policy and the preexisting unequal distribution of productive assets maintained a skewed income distribution.

In the early 1960s, about 59 percent of national income was received by families in the top two deciles, whereas those in the poorest two deciles received only about 3.5 percent. In the same period, half the households in Mexico had an income lower than the yearly minimum wage. See Bergsman (1980).

Shared Development, 1971–77

Echeverría's administration (1971–76) started a period of shared development. Although stabilizing development had subsidized private sector investment, the shared development policy envisioned the public sector as the engine of growth. Regulations concerning foreign private investment were changed, with all foreign ventures requiring at least 51 percent of national equity participation. Ambitious public sector investment programs in industry, agriculture, and transportation were designed. As a consequence, the share of public investment in total investment, as well as the share of investment in GDP, increased.

	1950	*1955*	*1960*	*1965*	*1970*	*1975*	*1980*	*1984*
Total investment/GDP	11.7	14.3	16.7	17.5	22.7	23.7	28.1	21.6
Public investment/total investment	0.49	0.31	0.33	0.37	0.37	0.44	n.a.	n.a.

The active government spending policy pushed the growth rate in 1972 to 8.5 percent. For political reasons, a tax reform that was supposed to take place in 1972 was not carried out, and the budget deficit increased from 1 percent to 10 percent of GDP. Monetary policy turned expansionary. With negative real interest rates, the share of financial assets in GDP started to decline. There were fewer resources for the government to tap via reserve requirements. Prices responded quickly. Together with the inflation tax, it was necessary to obtain additional resources from abroad. As shown below (in billions of U.S. dollars), the public sector external debt increased from $6.6 billion in 1971 to almost $21 billion in 1976 (Serra-Puche and Ortiz 1986).

	1960	1965	1971	1976	1980	1983
Public external debt	3.25	4.18	6.66	20.84	33.87	63.41

By 1973–74 the rise in Mexican prices in excess of the rise in prices of the main trade partners had caused overvaluation. Afraid of more inflation, policymakers kept the exchange rate fixed. External imbalances began to accumulate.

The critical destabilizing decision of the Echeverría administration was to opt for expansion to correct inequality while keeping an inadequate tax structure. The shared development policy thus broke the fragile macroeconomic equilibrium that characterized the preceding period. At the same time, it kept two fundamental flaws of stabilizing development: the sluggishness of agricultural growth and the lack of foreign competitiveness of the industrial sector. The rates of growth in agricultural output averaged a negative 0.5 percent between 1971 and 1976, compared with a positive 3.7 percent between 1960 and 1970. The share of manufactured exports in foreign currency earnings fell from 27 percent in 1970 to 21 percent in 1976, with an unchanged share of total exports in output.

The shared development policy ended in an agreement with the International Monetary Fund (IMF) and an orthodox stabilization program that held back spending for the next two years in an attempt to lower inflation, build up reserves, and regain stability. The first year of López Portillo's administration (1977–82) was characterized by a negative growth rate of income per capita and the highest inflation rate in twenty-five years.

The Oil Boom, 1978–82

The 1977 recession was short-lived. Oil discoveries soon altered the whole picture. The IMF program coincided with news of huge oil deposits in the south of Mexico and increases in world prices of oil.

Oil brought a dramatic change both in Mexico's balance of payments and in its expectations concerning future growth. By early 1978, private capital had started to flow in. IMF resources were no longer needed, and the IMF program was abandoned. The second oil price increase in 1980 further improved Mexican terms of trade. Public sector investment soared, and the share of investment in GDP rose to 30 percent in 1981.

The investment boom was associated with a huge rise in imports, mostly of capital goods and intermediates. Imports increased at 50 percent a year on average between 1978 and 1981. Projected surpluses in the trade account never materialized, and the country continued to accumulate external debt. At the same time, waste entered the picture as some projects were not screened carefully.

Fiscal policy was expansionary and monetary policy accommodating. Inflation picked up after 1978, but public sector prices were adjusted at a slower pace, and the exchange rate crawled at a pace lower than the inflation differential between Mexico and its trade partners.

Faced with a domestic market expanding at 9 percent a year and an appreciating real exchange rate, enterpreneurs had no incentive to sell abroad. As a consequence, the oil share in total exports increased from 15 percent in 1976 to 78 percent in 1983. The current account now depended on the world price of one commodity. And because taxes on oil revenues were the chief source of government revenue, the budget deficit was also chiefly determined by the behavior of internationnal oil prices. The reversal of the behavior of oil prices in the second half of 1981 made the difficulties inherent in such a situation dramatically clear. A detailed analysis of the origins of the 1982 crisis appears in Looney (1985).

2. Industrialization and Trade Policy

As with many other Latin American countries, industrialization in Mexico was partly a choice of policymakers and partly the result of changing world conditions. World War II increased the demand for primary products in the world market and reduced the supply of manufactured goods to the developing countries. Mexican entrepreneurs faced increasing profits in a growing and protected domestic market. By the early 1950s, industrialization had become an explicit policy based on the influential thinking of Raúl Prebisch and the Economic Commission for Latin America.

Trade policy was the key tool in the host of instruments used to promote industrialization. Tariffs, whose chief aim before the war had been to collect revenue for the government, represented 40 percent of the taxes in 1930 and were switched from specific to ad valorem duties in the 1950s. Tariffs were designed to tax goods more heavily at a higher stage of processing.

Import permits were to play the key protective role. As time went by, increasing percentage of all imports became subjected to prior permits: 25 percent in 1956, 60 percent in 1965, and 100 percent in 1975. The basic criteria for granting import permits were:

- The good was not produced at home or could not be substituted.
- Domestic production was insufficient to meet demand.

Table 16-3. Nominal and Effective Protection Rates in Mexico, 1960
(percent)

Sector	Nominal protection	Effective protection		Antiexport bias
		Balassa	Corden	
Agriculture and livestock	6.7	3.9	3.7	9
Processed food	21.2	23.0	23.0	71
Tobacco and beverage	69.8	157.8	204.5	84
Mining and oil extraction	4.2	−6.6	−5.9	13
Intermediate products	24.4	58.0	49.8	67
Chemicals	33.5	67.0	59.3	75
Nondurable consumption goods	63.9	129.2	112.0	65
Durable consumption goods	40.8	86.7	68.3	963
Machinery	10.5	10.0	9.5	59
Transport equipment	18.0	29.6	26.3	74
Construction equipment	26.3	97.0	72.6	−6

Note: The rates of protection quoted are based on explicit tariff rates. In the presence of import permits, however, tariff rates need not reflect the difference between domestic and world prices. Actual protection rates thus probably differ from the ones reported here. For more details on protection in Mexico, see Aspra (1977); Ros (1980).

Source: Bueno (1971).

- There was a need to accumulate stocks of a strategic good under special circumstances.

In practice, these criteria were insufficient to secure a captive market for domestic producers. Efficiency and opportunity costs were not taken into account.

Import substitution started with consumer goods such as textiles and chemicals and moved to durables such as household appliances, cars, and electronics. Capital goods and intermediates were granted import permits almost automatically.

Table 16-3 shows the structure of protection in 1960. Nominal and effective protection was highest for consumer goods, somewhat lower for intermediates, and lowest for machinery and transport equipment.

Aside from tariffs and import permits, other pieces of legislation were also aimed at promoting industrialization. Accelerated depreciation was granted for fixed investment. Incentives were given for purchases of machinery and equipment. Public enterprises conceded subsidized prices for key inputs such as fuels and electricity.

Not surprisingly, manufacturing output grew at 7.6 percent a year between 1950 and 1977. Distortions introduced by protection became particularly important in two areas. First, relative factor prices were skewed, thus cheapening the use of capital goods against the use of labor and damaging employment growth. Second, the antiexport bias of the trade regime, shown in table 16-3, reinforced by an overvalued exchange rate, undermined export growth.

The composition of the country's exports and imports reflected the structure of incentives. Manufactured exports rarely accounted for more than 25 percent of total exports, and their share decreased considerably after the oil boom. Although export promotion has been a subject of much discussion, particularly since the 1970s, implementation has never taken place. Export subsidies were never sufficient to counterbalance the antiexport bias of the trade regime. Only in 1985 did the introduction of a system of drawback for import duties start to be discussed.

An opportunity for change came with the devaluation in 1976, when it was realized that the foreign sector was a key bottleneck in the growth process. Liberalization of import permits was attempted, but because it was perceived as only temporary, it triggered overstocking of imported goods. In contrast, oil soon eliminated any need for radical changes during the following four years.

The oil crisis convinced the administration that a more outward-looking and efficient industrial sector was needed. In a weak economy, however, liberalization policies are more costly to implement.

3. Exchange Rates from the Mid-1920s to 1982

The behavior of Mexican exchange rates is a fascinating topic for research. From the mid-1920s until the early 1930s, the exchange rate was fixed in terms of gold, but silver coins were the main medium of exchange, and they fluctuated against gold. Cárdenas (1982) compared this system with one of flexible exchange rates. Between 1925 and 1934, the nominal exchange rate changed every year. It was then fixed for seven years.

Starting in 1950s, with the only interruption coming in 1954, Mexico had a fixed nominal rate for twenty-five years. Figure 16-1 shows the

Figure 16-1. Effective Real Exchange Rate in Mexico, 1948–82

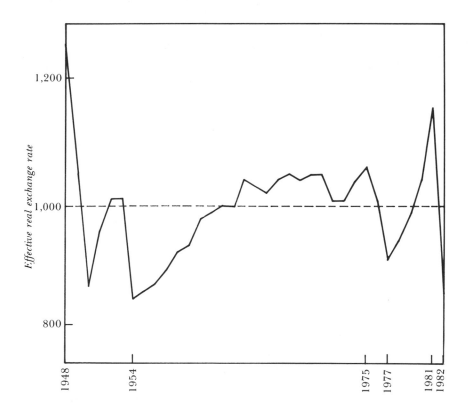

Note: The effective real exchange rate equals the Mexican wholesale price index divided by the wholesale price index of Mexican trade partners in pesos (weighted average of twenty-one countries that account for more than 95 percent of Mexico's trade).

Source: Gil Díaz (1984).

effective real exchange rate, defined as the ratio of domestic prices to the foreign prices of main trade partners, between 1948 and 1982. In the twenty years between 1955 and 1975, the real exchange rate appreciated slowly but continuously.

In 1975, overvaluation started to become a serious issue. Inflation increased because of government spending and later because of the rise in oil prices. As a result of overvaluation, the current account deteriorated and the external debt increased. From 1974 to 1976, the public external debt doubled, rising from $11 billion to $21 billion. Part of the increase in the external debt went to finance capital flight. The error and omissions in the balance of payments jumped from a negative $479 millions in 1974 to a negative $2,996 million in 1976. Finally, unable to sustain the currency against capital flight, President Echeverría devalued the exchange rate for the first time in twenty-three years in 1976 from 12.5 to 19 pesos and, in 1977, to 22.6 pesos.

In the early 1980s, overvaluation and capital flight once again became major Mexican problems. The overvalued exchange rate, coupled with the greater degree of openness of the economy resulting from oil exports and a growing external debt, made the economy especially vulnerable to external shocks. The first one came with the rise in world interest rates. The second was the fall in oil prices in 1981.[1] The fall in oil prices was made worse by the government's attitude. Instead of cutting the price of crude oil as other producers were doing, the authorities refused to lower the prices of Mexican oil for several months; the volume of exports from May to August fell to 55 percent of their level during the first four months of the year. The current account deficit exploded to reach $12 billion in 1981.

An adjustment in macroeconomic policy, particularly a reduction in spending and a realignment of the exchange rate was thus in order. The government opted to do otherwise. Access to foreign capital was plentiful, and foreign borrowing increased. Expectations regarding the sustainability of these policies were negative, and capital flight increased once again. The external public debt jumped to $52 billion in 1981.

By early 1982, the parity could be sustained no longer. The central bank pulled out of the foreign exchange market, causing an immediate devaluation of 70 percent. The devaluation was followed by an economywide wage increase, which was then followed by another devaluation. Public sector prices, in particular prices of energy and foodstuffs, were then adjusted in an attempt to reduce the budget deficit. The exchange rate depreciated again.

Faced with the erosion of the country's reserves and trying to avoid the inflationary pressures of large devaluations, the government adopted a two-tier exchange rate system on August 5, 1982. The system established a preferential rate of 49.13 pesos to the dollar to be used in transactions related to debt servicing and to high-priority imports. A second exchange rate, determined by market forces, was to apply to all other transactions. On August 13, 1982, dollar-denominated accounts in Mexican banks were made payable only in pesos. The foreign exchange market was temporarily closed for six days. Foreign exchange transactions were resumed at 69.5 pesos to the dollar for mexdollars and a free market rate that fluctuated between 100 and 120 pesos to the dollar.[2] In September 1982, banks were nationalized. Exchange controls were established for the first time since the failed attempt to impose exchange controls in 1930, and a black market developed. Thereafter, the peso continued to drift downward, first in the black market and then in the official market until its value stabilized with the new administration and an IMF program.

Exchange rate and political risks are recognized to be the main determinants of substitution between domestic and foreign assets. It is well known that people shift out of domestic currency to avoid the inflation tax. In 1980, expectations of a devaluation led to growing dollarization, measured as a share of mexdollar deposits in total financial assets, as shown in figure 16-2. Capital flight also increased, because domestic bonds and dollar-denominated deposits are not preferred to capital flight if the risk factor is associated with the overall financial solvency of the public sector.

Table 16-4 shows estimates of capital flight in Mexico. Devaluations, induced by capital flight, increase the domestic cost of external debt service, causing the budget to deteriorate further. They prompt the fear that the government might default on the domestic debt. This concern leads people to expect more inflation and devaluations and thereby generates another cycle of capital flight.

Capital flight was made possible by massive government intervention financed by short-term borrowing. More than $10 billion was raised in the second half of 1981 in international markets. Most of the funds were used to sustain the peso. Mexico's apparent inability to adjust taxes and expenditures in the face of external shocks created the fear that the country would not be able to service the debt in the future and made for a halt of capital inflows. International capital inflows declined from a peak of more than $21 billion in 1981 to less than $7 billion in 1982. Estimated capital flight reached about $8 billion in 1981 and $6 billion in 1982. The severe liquidity crisis finally forced the government to devalue and move into a dual-exchange-rate regime.[3]

Preference for a dual-exchange-rate regime rather than a fixed-exchange system is usually justified on the grounds that it would allow a country to maintain control over international reserves in times of speculation against the domestic currency and at the same time to avoid large fluctuations of the commercial rate and hence of domestic prices

**Figure 16-2. Ratio of Foreign Currency Deposits
to Total Money Stock in Mexico, 1970–82**

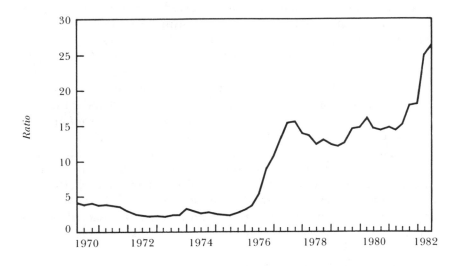

Source: Ramirez-Rojas (1985).

Table 16-4. Estimates of Foreign Debt and Capital Flows
(billions of U.S. dollars)

Estimate	1974–82	1976–82	1983–85	1976–85
Change in gross external debt	82.6	n.a.	n.a.	n.a.
Current account deficit	46.4	n.a.	n.a.	n.a.
Implicit capital outflow	36.3	n.a.	n.a.	n.a.
Capital flight	32.7	36	17	53

n.a. Not available.
Note: All estimates are of accumulated amounts.
Sources: 1974–82: Khan and ul Haque (1985); other periods: Morgan Guaranty.

in times of massive capital outflow. Early analytical work conveyed the
impression that a dual-exchange regime could isolate the production
side of the economy from disturbances in the financial market. It is now
known that dual rates affect wealth and hence income and spending.
Dual rates also have other important effects via interest rates and relative prices, especially if some goods such as nonessential import and

exports are traded along with capital in the free market. In equilibrium the two rates will have to depreciate at the same rate. The merits of the dual-exchange-rate regime will thus depend on whether it provides a better adjustment mechanism during a period of crisis by reducing the number of private bankruptcies and by isolating the budget deficit from further worsening; see Dornbusch (1986) for references.

In the Mexican case, the first effect seemed to have been present: private businesses had access to the controlled exchange rate to service their external debts. The question of impact on the budget remains to be investigated. The fact that external debt was serviced under the controlled rate does not help the budget because the public sector must still buy the exchange in the free market to service its own debt.

The purchase of essential imports with the controlled rate might have precluded the costs of large subsidies to imported foodstuffs, whose prices would have skyrocketed otherwise. But to determine whether the dual-rate system actually favored the budget, one would have to calculate the government balance for goods and services transacted in each category. This investigation remains to be undertaken.

4. Budget Deficits and Inflation

The Mexican recurrent crises of 1976, 1982, and 1986 were all preceded by real-exchange-rate overvaluation and increases in the budget deficit. Overvaluation and budget deficits proved to be a deadly combination: they induced capital flight every time people came to believe that the parity was not sustainable, thereby provoking an exchange collapse, igniting inflation, and causing the budget to deteriorate further.

Budget deficits in developing countries are commonly associated with money creation and inflation. Table 16-5 show inflation rates and the shares of the budget deficit and of seignorage in GDP.

In most years there is a positive association between the budget deficit, seignorage, and inflation. In 1983, however, the fact that the budget deficit was cut in half and money creation was contained, inflation almost doubled, in part because of the exchange collapse of the preceding year. The analysis in this section stresses the fact that the cause-and-effect relationship between budget deficits and inflation is not unidirectional.

Table 16-6 shows different measures for the share of budget deficit in output between 1950 and 1985. The government budget surpluses of the 1950s turned into small deficits in the 1960s. Until 1972, they did not exceed 2 percent of GDP. By 1975, the share of the budget deficit of the public sector in output had increased to 9 percent. With it came current account deficits, exchange devaluations, and inflation.

Table 16-5. Budget Deficits, Seignorage, and Inflation in Mexico, 1970–85

Year	Public sector budget deficit / GDP	Seignorage	Inflation
1970	2.0	0.4	5.0
1975	9.1	3.2	15.2
1980	6.7	4.9	26.3
1981	13.2	5.5	28.0
1982	17.4	10.9	58.9
1983	9.1	6.7	101.8
1984	7.0	5.8	65.0
1985	8.3	1.8	57.8

Sources: Secretaría de Hacienda, Mexico, and IMF, *International Financial Statistics.*

Table 16-6. Budget Deficit as Share of GDP in Mexico, 1950–85
(percent)

Year	Federal government	Public sector	Public sector borrowing requirements	Operational[a]	Noninterest budget deficit
1950	−1.1	n.a.	n.a.	n.a.	n.a.
1955	−0.2	n.a.	n.a.	n.a.	n.a.
1960	1.7	n.a.	n.a.	n.a.	n.a.
1965	1.7	n.a.	n.a.	n.a.	n.a.
1970	2.0	2.0	2.3	n.a.	n.a.
1975	4.2	9.1	10.5	n.a.	n.a.
1976	4.8	10.3	11.7	n.a.	n.a.
1977	3.5	7.0	8.4	n.a.	2.3
1978	3.0	4.9	6.1	n.a.	2.4
1979	3.1	6.1	7.5	n.a.	2.6
1980	3.0	6.7	7.7	n.a.	3.4
1981	6.7	13.2	14.4	11.4	8.4
1982	12.5	17.4	18.8	6.2	3.9
1983	n.a.	9.1	9.5	−4.1	−4.9
1984	n.a.	7.0	8.3	0.04	−4.8
1985	n.a.	8.3	9.9	−0.4	−3.9

n.a. Not available.
a. Excludes inflation from interest payments.
Source: Secretaría de Programación y Presupuesto, Mexico.

Although the public sector budget deficit was large, it appeared to be under control until 1980 because high oil prices favored revenues. In 1981, the budget was badly affected by both the fall in oil prices and the increase in interest rates. Everything combined to explode the deficit. With the increase in interest rates, expenditures increased. External revenue dropped because Mexico's state oil company, PEMEX, priced itself out of the world market, and oil exports dived. Domestic revenue fell because the real price of public sector goods did not rise with inflation and food products were exempt from value added taxes. When López Portillo left office in 1982, the budget deficit had reached 17 percent of GDP.

5. Recent Policies

The technocrats in de la Madrid's government, inaugurated in 1983, blamed the populism of the past administration for mismanagement, deficit spending, and corruption and signed an agreement for a three-year IMF stabilization program. The program had four main policy goals: to reduce by half the public sector deficits as a share of GDP in 1983; to institute a restrictive wage policy; to reduce inflation gradually from 100 percent in 1982 to 18 percent in 1985; and to consolidate the two exchange rates that existed alongside a black market during the crisis period.

Fiscal adjustment was seen as the main instrument for eliminating excess demand, which was supposedly behind the high inflation and external imbalance. The actual reduction of the budget deficit was close to target and came mainly from a 32 percent cut in public investment and a sharp reduction in real wages and salaries in the government sector. Social development programs declined by more than the budget as a whole (education was one of the areas hardest hit). There was also an increase in indirect taxes and an upward adjustment in public sector prices. Direct taxes declined as a result of both the economic contraction and the erosion in the real value of tax collections that happens in times of rapid inflation.

Between 1983 and 1985 the whole improvement in the noninterest budget went to finance increased interest payments, which in large part reflected the ongoing inflation. The contractionary policies induced high interest rates and recession, which further enlarged the deficit share in output, so that further cuts in government expenditures were required and more recession ensued.

The program instituted a restrictive wage policy to reduce inflation and modify relative prices. A fall in real wages was seen as necessary for the reduction of the budget deficit and for a gain in external competitiveness. Real wages did fall dramatically, as shown in figure 16-3, and the working class and the population at large did suffer from the adjustment program. Unemployment has been more serious than official publications in Mexico acknowledge, given the size of the urban informal sector and the absence of unemployment benefits. The current crisis came at a particularly bad time because of demographic dynamics. The

Figure 16-3. Real Minimum Wage in Mexico, 1977–85

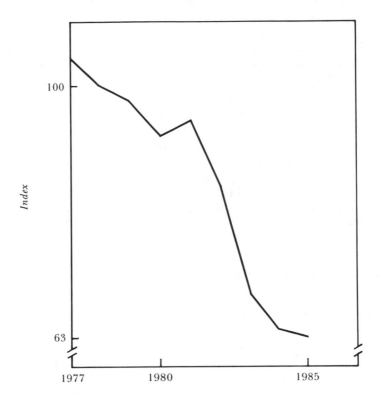

Source: Comisión Nacional de Salarios Mínimos.

rate of population growth peaked in the mid-1970s at 3.6 percent, but the rate of growth in the labor force will be the highest in the mid-1980s, rising to as much as 3.8 percent, depending on the assumptions made about participation rates. Just when the economy needed to grow fastest to absorb the labor force, the opposite occurred.

Although economic activity fell by more than 5 percent in 1983, achievements on the inflation front were minor: in 1986, inflation was still about 80 percent and rising. The inability to achieve further reductions in inflation was due not to an expansionary management of demand but to inertia and expectations. Continuing large budget deficit shares in output are not the best indicator for evaluating fiscal adjustment because interest payments on the domestic public debt contain a large component of inflation-induced expenditures that correspond to amortization of the principal. The budget deficit is large because inflation is high.

By mid-1983, the current account target was already overfulfilled as a consequence of the real devaluation and the reduction in aggregate demand. The reason for improvement was a sharp fall in imports caused by an unprecedented decline in real GDP. The dramatic shift of the trade account toward surplus appears in figure 16-4. The IMF policies worked and generated trade surpluses by creating economic contraction.

The fact that in 1983 de la Madrid and his team had halved the budget deficit and had turned a trade deficit of $5 billion into a surplus of $14 billion led many to consider Mexico a model debtor. By mid-1985, the fragility of the adjustment program became obvious as the trade surplus and the budget started to deteriorate. Falling international oil prices and a strong speculation against the peso once again led the exchange rate to collapse. The crisis of 1982, which itself was reminiscent of the one in 1976, had returned once more.

Shocks coming from the world economy in 1986 have created further difficulties for the Mexican economy. Although lower interest rates

Figure 16-4. Mexico's Trade Balance, 1970–85

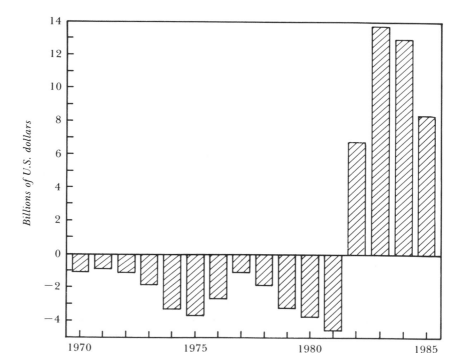

Source: IMF, *International Financial Statistics.*

have diminished the cost of servicing the debt, the much lower price of oil has cut export earnings substantially, and the net effect has been the deterioration of the current account. The inflation rate has increased and is accelerating, whereas growth is projected to be negative.

Negative growth, zero net investment, capital flight, and falling real wages make the current restrictive policies unsustainable. They generated trade surpluses to service the external debt, but such surpluses are becoming more and more difficult to obtain. Exports, particularly of manufactured goods, are not doing well. The restrictive fiscal policies and the cut in real wages have not reduced inflation. After three full years of adjustment, stability has not been achieved. Public investment fell by 60 percent in real terms between 1982 and 1986. Public investment in the non-oil sectors is now equivalent to its level in 1975. If the government fails to increase investment, bottlenecks in the supply of energy and transportation will soon hinder growth.

Growth rates and economic welfare have not been the only victims of the crisis in the 1980s. The institutional understanding between the public and private sectors has been called into question. The accumulation of assets abroad is an indicator of the existing malaise.

In a way, de la Madrid's administration has tried to solve conflicts with the business people by selling some of the stock of the banking system back to the private sector, lifting exchange controls, attempting to modify the rules governing foreign private investment, and undertaking the privatization of nonstrategic public enterprises. Regardless of whether these are the more necessary actions, it cannot be denied that a pragmatic understanding between the government and the business sector, together with an innovative economic policy and responsible cooperation from abroad, will be necessary to bring back investment and growth in Mexico.

In July 1986, Mexico reached an unprecedented agreement with the IMF. The Fund accepted the concept of the deficit corrected for inflation as the best indicator for evaluating the country's fiscal policy and approved a program that treats the foreign debt as a problem to be solved by growth rather than by recession. The program also includes two mechanisms for compensatory financing. The first protects the Mexican economy against erratic fluctuations in the price of oil, and the second, which goes into effect if the economy does not show signs of recovery in the first quarter of 1987, provides resources for a public investment program. These provisions are good news for Mexico, but they might prove insufficient if measures to rid the economy of inertial inflation are not implemented also.

If there is a lesson to be learned from the Mexican experience, it is that imbalances allowed to accumulate for too long are extremely painful to correct. The oil discoveries in the late 1970s permitted Mexico to postpone the correction of overvaluation, price distortions, and misallocation of resources. The adjustment to the adverse shocks in the early 1980s came too late and in an extremely costly way. Real wages have already fallen by 40 percent, and signs of recovery are still to be seen.

Selected Bibliography

Aspe, Pedro, and Javier Beristain. 1984. "Toward a First Estimate of the Evoluton of Inequality in Mexico." In Pedro Aspe and Paul E. Sigmund, eds., *The Political Economy of Income Distribution in Mexico*. New York: Holmes & Meier.

Aspra, L. A. 1977. "Import Substitution in Mexico: Past and Present," *World Development*, January, pp. 111–22.

Bergsman, Joel. 1980. *Income Distribution and Poverty in Mexico*. World Bank Staff Working Paper 395. Washington, D.C.: World Bank.

Bueno, Gerardo. 1971. "The Structure of Protection in Mexico." In Bela Balassa and associates, *The Structure of Protection in Developing Countries*. Baltimore, Md.: Johns Hopkins University Press.

Cárdenas, E. 1982. "Mexico's Industrialization during the Great Depression." Ph.D. diss. Yale University, New Haven, Conn.

Dornbusch, Rudiger. 1986. "Special Exchange Rates for Capital Account Transactions." *World Bank Economic Review*, vol. 1, no. 1 (September), pp. 3–33.

García-Alba, P., and Jaime Serra-Puche. 1983. *Financial Aspects of Macroeconomic Management in Mexico*. Tokyo: Asian Economic Press.

Gil Díaz, F. 1984. "Mexico's Path from Stability to Inflation." In A. C. Harberger, ed., *World Economic Growth*. San Francisco, Calif.: Institute for Contemporary Studies.

———. 1985. "Changing Strategies." In Peggy B. Musgrave, ed., *Mexico and the United States: Studies in Economic Interaction*, Boulder, Colo.: Westview Press.

Hansen, Roger D. 1971. *The Politics of Mexican Development*. Baltimore, Md.: Johns Hopkins University Press.

Ize, Alain, and Guillermo Ortiz. 1985a. "Fiscal Rigidities, Public Debt, and Asset Substitution: The Case of Mexico." Washington, D.C.: International Monetary Fund; processed.

———. 1985b. "The Exchange Rate and Stabilization Policies in Mexico, 1983–1985." Paper prepared for the Conference on Exchange Rate and Inflation, Jerusalem; processed.

Khan, Moshin, and Nadeem ul Haque. 1985. "Foreign Borrowing and Capital Flight." *IMF Staff Papers*, vol. 3, no. 4 (December), pp. 606–28.

Koehler, J. E. 1986. "Economic Policy Making with Limited Information: The Process of Macro Control in Mexico." Memorandum. Santa Monica; Calif.: Rand Corporation; processed.

Levy, S. 1980. *El problema del empleo en Mexico*. Estudios Economicos. Mexico City: Banco Nacional de Mexico.

Looney, R. E. 1985. *Economic Policymaking in Mexico: Factors Underlying the 1982 Crisis*. Durham, N.C.: Duke University Press.

Ortiz Mena, A. 1970. "Desarrollo Estabilizador." *El Trimestre Economico*, no. 146.

Ramirez-Rojas, C. L. (1985). "Currency Substitution in Argentina, Mexico and Uruguay." *IMF Staff Papers*, vol. 32, no. 4 (December), pp. 629–67.

Ros, Jaime. 1980. "Pricing in the Mexican Manufacturing Sector." *Cambridge Journal of Economics*, vol. 4 (September), pp. 211–32.

Serra-Puche, Jaime, and Guillermo Ortiz. 1986. "La Carga de la Deuda Externa." *Estudios economicos del Colegio de Mexico.*

Solís, Leopoldo. 1981. *Economic Policy Reform in Mexico: A Case Study for Developing Countries*. New York: Pergamon.

Solís, Leopoldo, and Ernesto Zedillo. 1985. "The Foreign Debt of Mexico." In Gordon W. Smith and John T. Cuddington, eds., *International Debt and the Developing Countries*. Washington, D.C.: World Bank.

Vernon, Raymond. 1963. *The Dilemma of Mexico's Development: The Roles of the Private and Public Sectors*. Cambridge, Mass.: Harvard University Press.

Notes

1. See Solís and Zedillo (1985) for an account of the contributions of domestic and external factors to debt accumulation in Mexico.

2. Until August 1982, mexdollars were dollar-denominated bank deposits available in the Mexican banking system that offered returns comparable to those available in the eurodollar market.

3. An analysis of dollarization and capital flight in Mexico is found in Ize and Ortiz (1985a and 1985b).

Appendixes

A

Sources of Current Data

Rudiger Dornbusch

THERE IS NOW a large volume of information available on the open economy.

- The *Economist* of London includes a weekly two-page sheet of information on interest rates, commodity prices, and macroeconomic statistics for the main industrial countries.

- The Morgan Guaranty and Trust Company of New York issues a monthly publication, *World Financial Markets*, which includes highly topical literature (sometimes controversial, such as the April–May 1986 discussion of capital flight) and data on real-exchange-rate trends in the industrial, countries and in some semiindustrial countries. The publication also provides extensive information on interest rates and on the Eurodollar market.

- The International Monetary Fund (IMF) has a wide range of publications that are available as a package. The *International Financial Statistics* (IFS) and the *International Financial Statistics Yearbook* are a must. These include more than a hundred time series of the chief macroeconomic data for each member country and a large number of aggregate time series (for example, on interest rates, industrial production, commodity prices, and so forth). The IFS is also available on tape.

  The IMF also publishes monthly trade statistics, *Directions of World Trade*, and two very useful *Manuals*, one dealing with government finance statistics and the other with balance of payments statistics. A number of supplements have been issued. Among these, *Economic Indicators* is a particularly useful historical survey for each country.

  The IMF publishes the *World Economic Outlook* twice a year. This exceptionally well-documented report on the world economy is essential reading.

- The Organisation for Economic Co-operation and Development (OECD) publishes *Economic Outlook* in June and December of each year. This review of macroeconomic developments for the industrial countries has forecasts that are well worth reading because developments in industrial countries have an important bearing on developing countries.
- The General Agreement on Tariffs and Trade (GATT) publishes *International Trade*, an annual report that reviews trends in world trade and provides good aggregate trade statistics.
- The White House publishes the *Annual Report on the Trade Agreements*, which reviews U.S. commercial policy issues.
- The World Bank publishes every other year or so the *World Tables* (Baltimore, Md.: Johns Hopkins University Press, 2 vols.), which contain comprehensive economic time series data for individual countries, and the *World Debt Tables* (Washington, D.C.: World Bank, annual with three supplements), which contain statistics on the external debt of more than 100 countries. Also well worth reading is the World Bank's annual *World Development Report* (New York: Oxford University Press). It reviews recent trends in the world economy and also has each year an interesting discussion of a different policy issue. In addition, the World Bank publishes from time to time well-documented reports on individual countries and problem areas.
- The Statistical Office of the United Nations publishes, with a time lag of several years, the *Yearbook of National Account Statistics*. The standard reference on the concepts is *A System of National Accounts*, published by the United Nations in 1968.

There are many more sources, but the above list provides the chief information on the international economy. One must next consult local agencies such as planning departments, central banks and finance ministries, which publish monthly and annual reports.

To keep abreast of ideas is much harder. A good job is being done by the series of *Essays* and Studies issued by the International Finance Division, Princeton University, although much of this material concentrates on the international financial system and on exchange rate problems of advanced countries.

B

National Accounting Identities

F. Leslie C. H. Helmers

THIS APPENDIX addresses three subjects: the concepts of gross domestic product (GDP) and gross national product (GNP); the balance of payments equation; and practical examples of the balance of payments equation.

1. Gross Domestic Product and Gross National Product

Perhaps the most central of all national accounting concepts asks what the market value is of all the final goods and services a country produces annually. This concept of gross domestic product (GDP) covers all the marketable goods and services produced in a country (or region) during a year. It can be conceived of in alternative ways. One is through an accumulation of the separate amounts of value added in different stages of production. The other is as the value of all *final* goods and services produced. Generally, when one is concentrating on the *production* of the GDP, one adopts the first concept; when one thinks of the demand side, one adopts the second. Under the first concept, all sorts of primary and intermediate goods sectors come into play, each contributing its own value added. Under the second concept, these primary and intermediate contributions are submerged, and the GDP is classified according to the nature or use of the final products generated by the economy in the period in question.

Under the second concept the value of GDP consists of domestic expenditures on consumption goods and services and on capital goods, plus the cost value of changes in inventories, plus the receipts for all the goods and services sold abroad, minus the payments made for imported goods and services. In this identity equation, payments for imports are a minus item because imports may be found in consumption goods, capital goods, stock changes, or even exports.

Because an increase in inventories adds to a nation's wealth and vice versa, changes in inventories may be considered changes in a nation's capital stock. Hence gross investment is defined to include additions to a nation's fixed capital as well as changes in inventories.

Thus this approach identifies gross domestic product, GDP, as the sum of expenditures on consumption, C, and gross investment, I (fixed capital investment plus changes in inventories), plus exports, X, and minus imports, M. In algebraic form

$$\text{GDP} = C + I + X - M$$

To make the system of national accounts consistent, a common set of rules and definitions has been adopted. Some of the definitions appear below.

Intermediate products are those goods that have been purchased (or received for free) by profit-making organizations (private firms and public enterprises) or by the government (central, regional, and local) within the country, which are used up in the production of other goods and services. The market values of these products are not to be included in GDP to avoid double counting.

Consumption goods are goods purchased or received free of charge by households or nonprofit organizations within the country (which include labor unions, charitable organizations, swimming clubs, and the like) as well as by the government to provide government services. By convention, the definition of private consumption goods comprises both nondurable goods, such as food, drink, some clothes, water, and heat, and durable goods, such as refrigerators, television sets, and automobiles. Examples of private consumption services include the services provided by household personnel, physicians, telephone companies, and so on. The government's current expenditures on goods and services—for road maintenance, office supplies, civil servants, teachers, policemen, and so forth—are considered government consumption. Again by convention, all defense expenditures by the government, including expenditures on durable items such as aircraft, tanks, and aircraft carriers, are considered consumption. Investment in plants producing tanks, aircraft, and so forth is considered investment, not consumption. Furthermore, housing, including housing for the armed services, is considered not a consumption good but an investment good.

Fixed capital goods, or *investment goods*, are goods purchased or received for free by profit-making organizations and the government to help produce other goods and services for a period of more than one year. Work in progress, such as a half-built bridge, is considered to be an investment. Expenditure on dwellings is considered to be a capital expenditure.

Inventories consist of intermediate products, semifinished products (excluding work in progress), consumption and investment goods, and export goods that have not yet been sold. They are valued at cost—that is, at the actual expenditures incurred on them—not at the price they can fetch in the market.

Exports are goods and services purchased by the rest of the world. They may be considered intermediate products, consumption goods, or capital goods if they remain in the country. By convention, the free-on-board (f.o.b.) value of exported goods is considered the value of merchandise exports; any other export receipts (for instance, payments received for shipping abroad carried out by residents) are considered exports of services. Goods and services acquired in a country by tourists and business travelers during their stay in the country are considered exports. Thus tourism may be considered an export industry. Other examples of exported services are those rendered by resident companies to nonresidents. These are the direct counterpart of imported services rendered by nonresident companies to residents, examples of which are given below.

Imports consist of all the goods and services purchased from the rest of the world. Merchandise imports are often valued at their cost, insurance, and freight (c.i.f.) values. The difference between c.i.f. imports and f.o.b. imports consists of services. Trade balance data, as reported by international organizations, concern merchandise exports and imports, both measured in f.o.b. values.[1] Other examples of import services are payments for (a) international air transport of residents by nonresident carriers, (b) communication services (post, telegraph, radio, satellite, and television) rendered to residents by nonresident companies, and (c) payments of insurance premiums to nonresident companies for insuring residents against such events as fire or storm damages.

The concept of GDP needs to be elucidated further. GDP is the final output produced by residents (nationals as well as foreigners) of the country within the territory of the country. Thus payments for final products produced by foreign enterprises residing in the country, or for services rendered by foreign consultants, are included in GDP. If Pavarotti were to give a concert in Sri Lanka, for instance, the expenditures incurred by residents to hear him would properly be considered consumption expenditures and should be included in the consumption part of GDP. It does not matter whether nationals of the country or foreigners residing in it or tourists visiting it pay for the output.

There are, by convention, four exceptions to the definition of GDP. First, services of housewives are not considered output. Second, illegal activities (for instance, black marketing in foreign currency, prostitution, or the production of illegal drugs) are not included in the GDP.[2] Third, the activities of foreign diplomats residing in the country are not included; their services—computed on a cost basis—are considered consumption expenditures of their governments. Fourth, shipping and air transport services abroad are, strictly speaking, services rendered outside the boundaries of the home country, but by convention, they are included in gross domestic output if these services are provided by resident companies.

The rule that gross domestic output should be measured by adding up expenditures has two major amendments. First, domestically produced goods and services given away free of charge must be included in GDP at their imputed market values. In the national accounts, these values are included in the expenditure side as well as the income side of the party concerned. Second, as was mentioned above, expenditures for dwellings are considered expenditures for fixed capital goods. Because housing is considered to be part of a nation's capital stock, we must include imputed rent on owner-occupied housing in GDP. We do so by adding estimates of market rents to expenditures as well as to income.

The reader may say "so far so good." The concept of gross domestic product clearly concerns the flow of goods and services that a country produces. From this statement it also follows that expenditures for the purchase of secondhand goods or equity shares and bonds have nothing to do with domestic output because such expenditures do not add to the flow of goods or services. Still, dealers in secondhand goods, brokers, banks, insurance companies, and the like perform services. How should the value of these services be measured? In principle, the answer is not difficult: only service charges are to be considered output. In practice, of course, such items may need to be imputed. In general, the imputed service charge should be set at such a level that it covers the payments for labor and capital. As an aside, notice that recycled products, such as scrap and waste, should be considered not secondhand goods but intermediate products.

A distinction must be made between gross domestic product and net domestic product (NDP) because fixed assets are used up in the production of final goods and services. By deducting an imputed amount for depreciation of a nation's capital stock we reach the net value of final goods and services—that is, the net domestic product. For balance of payments accounting, however, the subject we are interested in, we must work with flows of receipts and expenditures, and the concept of gross domestic product therefore remains relevant.

Many more details could be discussed if space were not a constraint. I hope, however, that the reader now has an overview of how gross domestic product can be determined, and I therefore recommend the manuals mentioned in appendix A for further details. The rest of this overview may now proceed more quickly.

Gross domestic product must be distinguished from gross national product. GDP concerns the final output produced by residents of the country. GNP includes not only final output produced by residents but also payments received by residents for factor services (services of capital and labor) rendered abroad, minus payments made to other countries for factor services rendered by nonresidents. When residents work abroad and remit part of their earnings to their country of residence, for instance, the so-called workers' remittances should be added to gross domestic product to arrive at gross national product. The opposite also applies: if a foreigner remits part of his earnings abroad, then this part should be deducted from the gross domestic product to reach the concept of gross national product. If Pavarotti chose to remit abroad part of his earnings from his concert in Sri Lanka, for instance, then in Sri Lanka his remittance would be considered a factor payment to abroad. The same applies to dividends and interest on capital. If a country is a creditor country, the interest and dividends it receives from its foreign investments should be added to GDP to arrive at GNP. If a country is a debtor country, as so many developing countries are at present, then the opposite holds. For such countries, it is quite common for interest payments on their foreign debts to surpass by far the workers' remittances and other factor incomes, so that net factor payments (NFP) need to be deducted from GDP. Hence we may write GNP = GDP − NFP.

Another way of looking at GNP is to regard it as the sum (including indirect taxes) of returns on the factors of production (labor and capital) that are employed within the country, plus the returns on the factors of production of the residents that are employed abroad, minus the returns that must be paid abroad to nonresidents for their factors of production employed within the country. This statement must be so because the value of gross domestic output minus indirect taxes equals wages, salaries, and gross profits (including depreciation), that is, the returns on the factors of production located within the country. For a debtor country, we must deduct the net factor payments made abroad (for instance, interest) for the use of factors of production within the country (for example, capital) owned by nonresidents. In principle then, the difference between GNP and GDP amounts to the balance between what nonresidents earn in the country and what residents earn abroad. Another useful definition states that GDP is what is produced within the country's borders, whereas GNP concerns what accrues to the residents of a country. GNP has nothing to do with the "nationals" of a country.

Finally, to compute the gross national income of a country, we must add to or subtract from GNP any unrequited transfers that the government or residents of a country receive or make. For most developing countries, aid grants received from foreign governments or international agencies are far larger than any grants they themselves make, so that the net unrequited transfer (NTR) is a positive item. The gross national income of a developing country may thus be defined as:

$$\text{Gross national income} = \text{GDP} - \text{NFP} + \text{NTR}.$$

2. The Balance of Payments Equation

For a country as a whole, the gross national income may be divided into two components: expenditures on consumption goods, C, and gross national savings, S.

$$\text{GDP} = C + I + X - M$$
$$\text{GDP} - \text{NFP} + \text{NTR} = (C + I + X - M) - \text{NFP} + \text{NTR} = C + S$$

Total domestic expenditures for final products consist of expenditures on consumption goods and on investment goods. Hence if we deduct total domestic expenditures from gross national income, we obtain, after rearranging terms,

$$\text{GDP} - \text{NFP} + \text{NTR} - (C + I) = (C + S) - (C + I) = (X + \text{NTR}) - (M + \text{NFP})$$
$$= \Delta\text{NFA}$$

In this identity, ΔNFA stands for increase or decrease in a country's net foreign assets position.

The equation tells us that a country's total national income minus its domestic expenditures on final products is equal to foreign exchange receipts minus foreign exchange expenditures—that is, it is equal to the surplus in the current account of the balance of payments. This statement is self-evident. When total national income, including net income from abroad, exceeds total domestic expenditures on final products, then the country will have a surplus with the rest of the world. This surplus manifests itself in the form of an increase in the net foreign assets position, NFA, which may be either an increase in foreign exchange reserves or an increase in other foreign assets, such as direct investments abroad.

In contrast, when total national income falls short of total domestic expenditures on final products, then foreign exchange receipts also fall short of foreign exchange expenditures, and the country experiences a deterioration in its net foreign assets position. This situation may arise from the drawdown of foreign exchange reserves, from the sale of some foreign assets, or from additional foreign borrowing.

Another way of considering the identity equation is to write it as $S = I + \Delta$NFA. Again, this statement is self-evident: gross national savings are equal to gross investments in domestic assets plus gross investments in foreign assets.

Although the above identity equation provides some useful insights, it does not explicitly consider the role of government. To do so, define C_g as government consumption, S_g as government saving, I_g as government investment, and similarly C_p, S_p, and I_p as consumption, saving, and investment, respectively, of the private sector. Hence, we obtain

$$
\begin{bmatrix} \text{Gross national} \\ \text{income} \\ (C+S) \end{bmatrix} - \begin{bmatrix} \text{Domestic} \\ \text{expenditures} \\ \text{on final products} \\ (C+I) \end{bmatrix} =
$$

$$
\begin{bmatrix} \text{Government} \\ \text{income} \\ (C_g+S_g) \end{bmatrix} - \begin{bmatrix} \text{Government} \\ \text{expenditures} \\ (C_g+I_g) \end{bmatrix} + \begin{bmatrix} \text{Private} \\ \text{income} \\ (C_p+S_p) \end{bmatrix} - \begin{bmatrix} \text{Private} \\ \text{expenditures} \\ (C_p+I_p) \end{bmatrix}
$$

The definition of government saving, S_g, needs some elaboration. In principle, government savings are equal to the difference between government current revenues and government current expenditures. Current revenues include direct and indirect taxes, social security contributions, profits of public enterprises accruing to the government, and grants. Current expenditures include outlays for goods and services (for instance, government consumption, C_g) as well as social security payments, subsidies, payments to cover operating losses of public enterprises, and interest payments on the national debt.

We may thus write $S_g = R_g - (C_g + C_t)$, where S_g = government saving, R_g = government current revenues, C_g = government consumption, and C_t = government transfer payments. If we consider government current revenues net of transfer payments, we obtain

$$
S_g = (R_g - C_t) - C_g = T - C_g
$$

or

$$
T = C_g + S_g
$$

In other words, government revenues, T, as defined here, consist of current revenues minus transfer payments and are equal to government consumption, C_g, and a remainder that represents government saving, S_g.

Similarly, we may define government expenditures, G, as being net of transfer payments, so that it consists of government consumption, C_g, and government investment, I_g. On a net basis we therefore obtain for government revenues minus expenditures:

$$
(C_g + S_g) - (C_g + I_g) = T - G
$$

We have now reached the balance of payments equation, which is essential for an understanding of external balance issues. The equation is presented in table B-1 together with the main policy instruments.

Table B-1. Basic National Accounting Identities and Policy Instruments

National accounting equations

$$\left[\begin{array}{l} \text{Gross national income} - \text{domestic expenditures on final products} \\ \quad (\text{GDP} - \text{NFP} + \text{NTR}) \quad - \quad\quad\quad (C + I) \end{array} \right] =$$

$$\left[\begin{array}{l} (\text{Domestic consumption} + \text{gross national saving}) - (\text{domestic consumption} + \text{gross domestic investment}) \\ \quad\quad\quad (C + S) \quad\quad\quad\quad - \quad\quad\quad\quad\quad\quad (C + I) \end{array} \right] =$$

$$\left[\begin{array}{l} [\text{Government income} - \text{Government expenditures}] + [\text{private income} - \text{private expenditures}] \\ \quad [(C_g + S_g) - (C_g + I_g)] \quad\quad + \quad\quad\quad [(C_p + S_p) - (C_p + I_p)] \end{array} \right]$$

Balance of payments equation

$$\left[\begin{array}{l} \text{Government budget surplus} + \text{private budget surplus} \\ \quad (T - G) \quad\quad + \quad\quad (S_g - I_p) \end{array} \right] =$$

$$\left[\begin{array}{c}\text{Foreign exchange receipts} \\ (X + \text{NTR})\end{array}\right] - \left[\begin{array}{c}\text{foreign exchange expenditures} \\ (M + \text{NFP})\end{array}\right] = \left[\begin{array}{c}\text{Increase in net foreign assets} \\ \Delta\text{NFA}\end{array}\right]$$

Policy instruments

$$\left[\begin{array}{l}\textit{Expenditure-changing policies} \\ \text{Fiscal policies} \\ \text{Monetary policies}\end{array}\right] \qquad \left[\begin{array}{l}\textit{Expenditure-switching policies} \\ \text{Trade policies} \\ \text{Exchange rate policies}\end{array}\right] \qquad \left[\begin{array}{l}\textit{Financial policies} \\ \text{Capital controls} \\ \text{Debt policies}\end{array}\right]$$

The balance of payments equation helps to focus on the different policy measures that a government can initiate to redress external imbalances. If the current account shows a deficit, a government can take three classes of measures corresponding to the three explanatory parts of the equation. The first class is expenditure-changing policies, which consist of fiscal and monetary policies. By raising taxes or reducing government expenditures, for instance, government saving can be increased and a current account deficit reduced. Similarly, by restricting bank credit to the private sector, private investment can be curtailed; this will increase private saving relative to investment and will again reduce the current account deficit.

The second class of measures is expenditure-switching policies, which operate directly on the foreign exchange flows. Trade policies such as quantitative restrictions, tariffs, and export subsidies all lead to a switching of expenditures among home goods, imports, and exports. Similar effects are felt when the real exchange rate is changed (see chapter 2).

The third class is financial policies, which are concerned with capital inflows and outflows. Once a certain level of current account deficit is considered acceptable, for instance, it can be financed either by drawing down foreign exchange reserves or by borrowing.

It should be emphasized that the classification of the three main policy instruments by area of economic influence is not as clear-cut as policymakers might hope, because there are always indirect effects. Expenditure-changing policies, for instance, will not only directly affect saving, consumption, and investment but may also affect imports, exports, or the exchange rate. Similarly, expenditure-switching policies, such as a devaluation, also affect saving, consumption, and investment. Finally, financial policies that permit large inflows of capital will also affect the exchange rate.

In fact, in the final outcome, the balance of payments equation must be the same under all three definitions: private plus government saving minus investment, foreign exchange receipts minus expenditures, and net foreign asset acquisition. Thus a policy which appears to work only in one of these definitions *must* have indirect effects on the other two or else end up being frustrated in its own purpose. For this reason, too, it is often advisable to attack a balance of payments deficit from different sides simultaneously. Professional economists thus often advise expenditure-curtailing policies as a needed complement to a devaluation.

3. Examples of the Basic Balance of Payments Equation

Table B-2 presents basic data for the five countries whose policies are discussed in Part III of this study. The table provides an overview of the situation in which the five countries found themselves at the end of

1980. By expressing the variables of the basic equation as percentages of GDP, we make the country data comparable and provide useful insights on the different structural relationships. Investment $(I_p + I_g)$, for instance, is at about 28–30 percent of GDP in Korea and Mexico but only at 20–23 percent of GDP in Argentina, Brazil, and Indonesia. The tax burden, T, is almost 22 percent in Indonesia and about 15 percent in the other countries. Exports are highest in Korea (33 percent) and lowest in Argentina (7 percent) and Brazil (8.5 percent). Four countries have a current account deficit of 3–8.5 percent of GDP; only Indonesia has a surplus of almost 4 percent of GDP.

The second half of may also need further explanation. When a country has a current account deficit—in other words, when the inflow of foreign exchange from current transactions falls short of the outflow of foreign exchange from current transactions—the country will have to finance this deficit by an inflow of foreign exchange from capital transactions. The capital inflow may consist of equity investments by foreigners; it may also consist of borrowing by private residents or the government. When the capital inflow is greater than the current account deficit, the surplus will appear in the form of an increase in the country's international reserves. In Brazil, for example, in 1980, the current account deficit was 5.1 percent of GDP, and the increase in international reserves amounted to plus 1.3 percent. We know, therefore, that the inflow of foreign capital amounted to 6.4 percent of GDP.

Data on the capital position of a country are generally not available. The only thing we do know is what changes have occurred in foreign assets over a year. For Brazil, the capital position deteriorated (that is, its net foreign indebtedness grew) by 6.4 percent of GDP in 1980 because of the inflow of foreign capital. When we include the increase in the international reserves of 1.3 percent of GDP, we thus find that the net foreign assets position of Brazil decreased by 5.1 percent of GDP.

Although data on the capital position of a country are not available, comprehensive data on foreign debt are published by the World Bank in the *World Debt Tables*. These data as well as international reserves are presented in table B-2. Thus we see that the external debt (including the undisbursed portions) of the five countries varies from 18 percent to 48 percent, the debt service (interest and repayment of principal) varies from 1.3 percent to 4.3 percent, and the international reserves from 2 percent to 10 percent of GDP.

The data in table B-2, being for one year, present only a snapshot. For any analysis of real growth rates, or how successful a country has been, we must work with a time series of real data. Real data are found by deflating the current value components of the basic equation by appropriate price indexes. The IMF *International Financial Statistics* reports indexes for wholesale prices, consumer prices, wages, unit values of

Table B-2. Examples of the Basic National Accounting Identities, 1980

Item	Argentina Thousands of australes	Percentage of GDP	Brazil Billions of cruzeiros	Percentage of GDP	Indonesia Billions of rupiah	Percentage of GDP	Korea Billions of won	Percentage of GDP	Mexico Billions of pesos	Percentage of GDP
GDP	28,265	100.0	13,164	100.0	45,446	100.0	37,830	100.0	4,276	100.0
NFP	−278	−1.0	−404	−3.1	−2,011	−4.4	−625	−1.7	−117	−2.7
NT	4	0.0	9	0.0	34	0.0	273	0.7	6	0.0
Income	27,991	99.0	12,769	97.0	43,469	95.6	37,478	99.1	4,165	97.4
Income and domestic expenditures										
C_g	3,739	13.2	1,153	8.8	4,688	10.3	4,247	11.2	463	10.8
C_p	18,702	66.2	9,323	70.8	27,503	60.5	24,828	65.6	2,651	62.0
S_g^a	531	1.9	746	5.7	5,183	11.4	1,096	2.9	239	5.6
S_p	5,019	7.8	1,547	11.8	6,095	13.4	7,307	19.3	812	19.0
Income	27,991	99.0	12,769	97.0	43,469	95.6	37,478	99.1	4,165	97.4
C_g	3,739	13.2	1,153	8.8	4,688	10.3	4,247	11.2	463	10.8
C_p	18,702	66.2	9,323	70.8	27,503	60.5	24,828	65.6	2,651	62.0
I_g^a	1,384	4.9	357	2.7	4,934	10.9	470	1.2	316	7.4
I_p	5,056	17.9	2,610	19.8	4,552	10.0	11,160	29.5	887	20.7
Domestic expenditures	28,881	102.2	13,443	102.1	41,677	91.7	40,705	107.5	4,317	100.9
Income − domestic expenditures	−890	−3.1	−674	−5.1	1,792	3.9	−3,227	−8.5	−152	−3.6
Saving and domestic investment										
$T = C_g + S_g$	4,270	15.1	1,899	14.4	9,871	21.7	5,343	14.1	702	16.4
$G = C_g + I_g$	5,123	18.1	1,510	11.5	9,622	21.2	4,717	12.5	779	18.2
$T - G = S_g - I_g$	−853	−3.0	389	3.0	249	0.5	626	1.7	−77	−1.8

S_p	5,019	17.8	1,547	11.8	6,095	13.4	7,307	19.3	812	19.0
I_p	5,056	17.9	2,610	19.8	4,552	10.0	11,160	29.5	887	20.7
$S_p - I_p$	−37	−0.1	−1,063	−8.1	1,543	3.4	−3,853	−10.2	−75	−1.8
$(T - G) + (S_p - I_p)$	−890	−3.1	−674	−5.1	1,792	3.9	−3,227	−8.5	−152	−3.6
Current account receipts and expenditures										
X	1,944	6.9	1,121	8.5	13,849	30.5	12,520	33.1	537	12.6
NTR	4	0.0	9	0.0	34	0.0	293	0.7	6	0.1
Receipts	1,948	6.9	1,130	8.6	13,883	30.5	12,793	33.8	543	12.7
M	2,560	9.1	1,400	10.6	10,080	22.2	15,395	40.7	578	13.5
NFP	278	10.1	404	3.1	2,011	4.4	625	1.7	117	2.7
Expenditures	2,838	10.1	1,804	13.7	12,091	16.6	16,020	42.3	695	16.2
Current account	−890	−3.1	−674	−5.1	1,792	3.9	−3,227	−8.5	−152	−3.6
Current account and capital flows										
Current account	−890	−3.1	−674	−5.1	1,792	3.9	−3,227	−8.5	−152	−3.6
Capital flow	1,395	4.9	849	6.4	−3,143	−6.9	3,014	8.0	128	3.0
Change in International reserves	505	1.8	175	1.3	−1,351	−3.0	−213	−0.6	−24	−0.6
Change in foreign assets position										
Change in foreign assets	−1,395	−4.9	−849	−6.4	3,143	6.9	−3,014	−8.0	−128	−3.0
Change in International reserves	505	1.8	175	1.3	−1,351	−3.0	−213	−0.6	−24	−0.6
ΔNFA	−890	−3.1	−674	−5.1	1,792	3.9	−3,227	−8.5	−152	−3.6

(Table continues on the following page.)

Table B-2 (continued)

Item	Argentina		Brazil		Indonesia		Korea		Mexico	
	Thousands of australes	Percentage of GDP	Billions of cruzeiros	Percentage of GDP	Billions of rupiah	Percentage of GDP	Billions of won	Percentage of GDP	Billions of pesos	Percentage of GDP
International reserves and debts										
International reserves	1,708	6.0	424	3.2	4,626	10.2	1,884	5.0	96	2.2
Debt (long and short term)	5,017	17.7	3,691	28.0	13,097	28.8	17,814	47.1	1,311	30.7
Debt service	365	1.3	362	2.7	1,103	2.4	1,637	4.3	180	4.2
Millions of U.S. dollars										
International reserves and debts										
International reserves	9,296	6.0	8,039	3.2	6,803.3	10.2	3,101	5.0	4,176	2.2
Debt (long and short term)	27,309	17.7	70,025	28.0	20,888.3	28.8	29,327	47.1	57,142	30.7
Debt service	1,987	1.3	6,875	2.7	1,758.5	2.4	2,694	4.3	7,856	4.2

Percentage of exports (X)

Internation.al reserves, debt, and current account

International					
reserves/exports	87.9	37.8	33.4	15.0	17.8
Debt/exports	258.1	329.3	94.6	142.3	244.1
Debt service/exports	18.8	32.3	8.0	13.1	33.5
Current account/exports	−45.8	−60.1	12.9	−25.8	−28.3

a. Consolidated general government data except for Korea, for which only consolidated central government data are available.

Sources: The data for GDP, NFP, C_g, C_p, X, and M were taken from IMF, *International Financial Statistics* (IFS) lines 90 through 99. The net unrequited transfers, NTR, are reported in U.S. dollars in lines 77 afd and 77 ag d as private and official unrequited transfers, respectively. To reach the value in domestic currency, the total was multiplied by the corresponding annual average exchange rate in the rf line. The change in foreign exchange reserves in U.S. dollars in line 7.9 cd was similarly converted. In lines 93 e and 93 i, IFS reports gross fixed capital formation and changes in inventories: the sum of these two figures yields gross investment, I.

Data on gross government, I_g, and gross private investment, I_p, the two components of I, are difficult to find. As a proxy for gross government investment, I_g, we take from the IMF, *Government Finance Statistics* (GFS), table for consolidated general government (central plus state and local), the reported figures for capital expenditure minus capital revenue. For Korea the GFS reports only consolidated central government figures, and we therefore use, line 13—gross capital formation, central government—as a proxy for total gross government investment, I_g. Gross private investment is found by deducting I_g from I. To estimate government saving, we deduct current expenditures from current revenues, including grants as reported in GFS, consolidated general government accounts. In the case of Korea, which reports only central government accounts, we take from the GFS, consolidated central government table, the data for current account surplus, to which we add the data for grants, if any. The level of gross private saving, S_p, is simply the difference between total gross income (GNP + NTR) on the one hand and total consumption, C, plus government saving, S_g, on the other hand.

The international reserves and debt data in U.S. dollars were taken from *World Debt Tables* and were converted into domestic currency following the procedure described above.

exports and imports, and the GDP deflator. Unfortunately, it reports only the time series data for real GDP and not for its components. The World Bank produces a comprehensive set of real data for more than a hundred countries in the *World Tables*, but there is always a time lag of a few years, so that for up-to-date information one must go to domestic sources.

Much has been written about the debt crisis. Does table B-2 bear out the prevailing wisdom? Is there really a crisis? If we regard the debt data as a percentage of GDP, the situation does not appear serious at all. Many private households have mortgage debts amounting to four or five times their income, and mortgage payments often surpass 30 percent of family income. In comparison, the highest ratios of debt and debt service to GDP in the table are 47.1 percent and 4.3 percent, respectively (both for Korea). Thus if one were to go by these data, there should be no serious problems.

Some economists, however, do not consider the comparison of a country with a private household valid. They believe that, if a comparison is to be made, then it should be with a subsistence farmer, the bulk of whose activities takes place in the internal sphere. In their opinion, just as the cash inflows and outflows of a subsistence farmer determine his creditworthiness, so should foreign exchange receipts and expenditures determine a country's creditworthiness. This approach is expressed in the bottom part of table B-2, where international reserves, debt, debt service, and current account deficits, appear as percentages of export receipts. These data give an entirely different picture. In Brazil, for instance, debt service in 1980 amounted to 32 percent of exports. The total debt stood at 329 percent of exports, and if the current account deficits were to continue at the same rate, Brazil's debt would increase by some sixty percentage points each year.

This type of analysis can also be criticized, however, because it is static. Economies grow, and countries with low levels of exports can, if they are prepared to open up their economies, attain relatively high levels of exports and overall growth rates within a reasonable time span.[3] In other words, creditworthiness and the ability to service debt can be determined only country by country, depending on the type of policies a country follows. We must therefore not impose arbitrary rules, such as that debt service should never exceed 25 percent of exports or 4 percent of GDP.

Notes

1. The International Monetary Fund, for instance, reports trade balance data in current dollars in line 77 ac d of the respective country pages of *International Financial Statistics*.

2. Another matter is whether unofficial market activities should be included in GDP. Tax evasion is quite common in many countries. A dentist charges less when paid in cash, for instance, with the understanding that expenses will not be recorded. According to some estimates, such transactions could total 25 percent of GDP in some countries.

3. For detailed reviews of the benefits of an open approach to foreign trade, see Ian Little, Tibor Scitovsky, and Maurice Scott, *Industry and Trade in Some Developing Countries: A Comparative Study* (London: Oxford University Press, 1970). A series of studies organized by Jagdish N. Bhagwati and Anne O. Krueger make the point that export-oriented strategies result in superior growth performance. For an overview study, see Anne O. Krueger, *Trade and Development in Developing Countries: Synthesis and Conclusions* (Chicago, Ill.: University of Chicago Press, 1983). Many individual country studies by Bela Balassa arrive at the same conclusion. See Bela Balassa, "Adjustment Policies in Developing Countries: A Reassessment," World Bank, Development Research Department, Washington, D.C., June 1984; processed.

C

Real-Exchange-Rate Indexes

F. Leslie C. H. Helmers

AN EXCHANGE RATE may be defined, first, as the price of a foreign currency unit in terms of domestic currency units (for example, rupiah per dollar) and, second, in the inverse manner (for example, dollars per rupiah). In the *International Financial Statistics*, 114 countries from a total of 137 report their exchange rates in the first way; the remainder use the second way. Industrial countries in the latter group include Australia, New Zealand, Switzerland, and the United Kingdom; developing countries include Botswana, Fiji, Ghana, Iraq, and Nigeria. Economists have no established preference for one or the other of these measures, and the choice is inconsequential as long as the measure is well defined and consistent.

Let us first review the definition most often used. As an example, consider Indonesia, which reported (see rf line in IFS) that in 1980 its average exchange rate was Rp627 per U.S. dollar. In 1984 it was Rp1,025.9 per U.S. dollar. Thus the price of the U.S. dollar in terms of rupiah increased by 64 percent (Rp1,025.9/Rp 627 = 1.64).

In real terms, however, the story is different. According to the Indonesian consumer price index (line 64 in IFS), the consumer had to pay 151.7 in 1984 for a basket of goods that cost 100 in 1980. Thus if we had to pay Rp1,025.9 per U.S. dollar in 1984, then we need to deflate this price by the Indonesian consumer price index to find the relevant consumer price in 1980 rupiah. In doing so, we find that in 1984 the price in 1980 rupiah for one U.S. dollar amounted to Rp676.3 (Rp1,025.9 · 100/151.7). But this is not yet the end of the real-exchange-rate story because, worldwide, U.S. dollars had become less valuable. To measure this price effect on the U.S. dollar, the U.S. wholesale price index is often used. Indeed, in 1984 the U.S. wholesale price index stood at 115.4 compared with 100 in 1980. Thus in 1984 the value of one U.S. dollar measured in 1980 U.S. dollars was $0.867 ($1 · 100/115.4). We have now found the 1984 real exchange rate. It is simply the price in 1980 rupiah that was paid for one 1980 U.S. dollar. Thus in 1984 the real exchange rate was Rp780.4 (Rp676.3/$0.867) and the real exchange rate index was 124.5 (Rp780.4/Rp627). In other words, whereas between 1984 and 1980 the appreciation of the U.S. dollar in rupiah in nominal terms was 64 percent, it was only 24.5 percent in real terms.

In its general form, the real exchange rate can be defined as follows:

$$E = \frac{E_n/P_d}{\$1/P_w}$$

where E is the real exchange rate, E_n is the nominal exchange rate expressed in units of domestic currency per U.S. dollar, P_d is the appropriate price deflator for the domestic currency, and P_w is the appropriate price deflator for U.S. dollars.

Simply put, the real exchange rate is the price in real terms of a real dollar a country uses for its international transactions. In the example, it is found by deflating the domestic currency by the consumer price index (CPI) and the dollar by the U.S. wholesale price index. The CPI is an appropriate deflator because it measures the overall loss in purchasing power of the domestic currency. Furthermore it is published regularly. The GDP deflator can sometimes be used, but it is not a good index for countries with high inflation rates and is inevitably reported with a time lag.[1] As regards the deflator for the U.S. dollar, the U.S. CPI, in principle, would not be a good deflator to use because this index includes the prices of many domestic services and home goods. We are more interested in a measure of the price level of international goods. Because it is heavily weighted with tradable goods, the U.S. wholesale price index may be considered a proxy for such an index. More refined deflators for the price of international goods expressed in dollars can of course be constructed by taking a weighted average of the wholesale price indexes of several major countries expressed in terms of the dollar. Unfortunately, such an index is not published regularly.[2]

Many variants of the real exchange rate are possible, depending on what the analyst wants to emphasize. If the tariff system of a country changes over the years, for instance, the analyst may wish to work with the following formula, which presents the real exchange rate that importers face:

$$E = \frac{F_n(1 + t_m)/P_d}{\$1/P_w}$$

where t_m stands for the level of import duties as a fraction of c.i.f. values.

Table C-1. Examples of Real Exchange Rates

Item	Argentina (australes)	Brazil (cruzeiro)	Indonesia (rupiah)	Korea (won)	Mexico (peso)
Real exchange rate index based on domestic CPI (1980 = 100)[a]					
Nominal exchange rate, 1980	0.00018	52.71	627.0	607.4	22.95
Nominal exchange rate, 1984	0.06765	1,848.03	1,025.9	806.0	167.83
Domestic consumer price index, 1984	17,462.0	2,922.5	151.7	137.6	679.0
U.S. wholesale price index, 1984	115.4	115.4	115.4	115.4	115.4
Real exchange rate, 1984	0.00045	73.0	780.4	676.0	28.52
Real-exchange-rate index, 1984	243.3	138.4	124.5	111.3	124.3
Real-exchange-rate index, 1980	100.0	100.0	100.0	100.0	100.0
Real exchange rate index based on domestic GDP deflator (1980 = 100)[b]					
GDP deflator, 1984	n.a.	2,923.6	n.a.	133.1	654.2
Real exchange rate, 1984	n.a.	72.9	n.a.	699.0	29.60
Real-exchange-rate index, 1984	n.a.	138.4	n.a.	115.1	129.0
Real exchange rate index based on domestic wage index (1980 = 100)[c]					
Domestic-wage-rate index, 1984	n.a.	n.a.	n.a.	167.3	494.2
Real exchange rate, 1984	n.a.	n.a.	n.a.	556.0	39.19
Real-exchange-rate index, 1984	n.a.	n.a.	n.a.	91.5	170.8

n.a. Not available.

Note: E_n = domestic currency units per nominal dollar. CPI = domestic consumer price index. WPI, USA = wholesale price index in the United States.

a. $E = \dfrac{E_n/\text{CPI}}{\$1/\text{WPI, USA}}$

b. $E = \dfrac{E_n/\text{GDP deflator}}{\$1/\text{WPI, USA}}$

c. $E = \dfrac{E_n/\text{domestic wage index}}{\$1/\text{WPI, USA}}$

Source: IMF, *International Financial Statistics.*

Similarly, a real exchange rate can be constructed for exporters by using the formula

$$E = \frac{E_n(1 - t_x)/P_d}{\$1/P_w}$$

where t_x represents the export duties as a fraction of f.o.b. value.

Sometimes analysts may want to concentrate on the competitive position of the country with regard to its main trading partners. Gillis and Dapice in their study of Indonesia, for instance, work with a trade-weighted real exchange rate, which is defined as

$$E = \frac{2}{3} \ \frac{\text{Rp}/\text{CPI}_{rp}}{\text{Yen } 1/\text{CPI}_{yen}} + \frac{1}{3} \ \frac{\text{Rp}/\text{CPI}_{rp}}{\$1/\text{CPI}_{\$}}$$

As mentioned earlier, in principle it is preferable to use wholesale price indexes rather than consumer price indexes to deflate the yen and the dollar because wholesale prices are more representative of the prices of the internationally traded goods.

Finally, another interpretation of the real-exchange-rate concept is useful for analyzing the resource reallocation effects of real-exchange-rate changes. We reach this interpretation by noting that $E_n \cdot P_w$ presents the domestic price of imports and exports (that is, the price of tradables) and that P_d, the domestic price deflator, may be considered a proxy for the price of home goods. In other words, the real exchange rate may also be considered a measure of the price of tradables to the price of home goods.

$$E = \frac{E_n \cdot P_w}{P_d} = \frac{\text{Price of tradables}}{\text{Price of home goods}}$$

A variant of this index is used by Krugman in chapter 4. He uses the world export prices in dollars for P_w and the Brazilian wholesale price index for P_d. Because he works with the reciprocal definition of the real exchange rate, he writes his index also in reciprocal form (see below). Cardoso and Levy use a similar index in chapter 16.

In addition, a wage index, W_d, can be used to deflate the domestic currency:

$$E = \frac{E_n \cdot P_w}{W_d} = \frac{\text{Price of tradables}}{\text{Domestic cost}}$$

This index measures the competitive position of industries that produce internationally traded goods.

Some examples of real exchange rates and the corresponding indexes appear in table C-1. The real exchange rates for the five countries have been calculated for 1984 using 1980 as the base year. Three domestic price deflators have been used: the consumer price index, the GDP deflator, and the wage index. To deflate the dollar, the U.S. wholesale price index has been used.

For Brazil, Korea, and Mexico, countries for which GDP deflators are available, there is almost no difference between the real-exchange-rate indexes based on domestic CPI and the GDP deflator. For several countries, however, there is a substantial difference when one compares the CPI- or GDP-deflated real-exchange-rate indexes with the wage-deflated indexes. In Mexico, for instance, the real-exchange-rate index based on the domestic CPI was 124.3 in 1984; the real-exchange-rate index based on domestic wage movements was 170.8 in 1984. The reason is that the wage index did not rise as much as prices (the 1984 wage index was 494 compared with the consumer price index of 679).

Let us now briefly consider the reciprocal definition of the exchange rate. This definition expresses foreign currency units in terms of the domestic currency unit. Thus for Indonesia in 1980, the nominal exchange rate was $1/Rp627 = $0.001595/Rp1, and in 1984 it was $1/Rp1,026 = $0.000975/Rp1. From this statement it follows that in nominal terms the price of the rupiah in U.S. dollars decreased by 39 percent ($0.000975/$0.001595 = 0.61). In other words, between 1980 and 1984, the rupiah was devalued by 39 percent against the U.S. dollar. This definition tells us immediately by what proportion the domestic currency has devalued or revalued, whereas with the first definition we see immediately by how much the price level of international goods has risen or fallen relative to domestic prices. Recall that under the first definition we found the U.S. dollar price in rupiah increased by some 64 percent between 1980 and 1984. Thus to find the devaluation we need to take the reciprocal of 1.64, which is 0.61, and deduct it from 1.0. It should be clear that the various types of real exchange rates discussed above are found in the second type of analyses in the form of reciprocals.

Dornbusch uses a mixture of the two ways of expressing the exchange rate. On the one hand, he defines the nominal exchange rate as consisting of pesos per dollar. On the other hand, he uses several types of reciprocal indexes to measure the real exchange rate. Dornbusch's use of the domestic wage rate as a deflator is very illuminating. In this definition, the real exchange rate is written as

$$E^* = \frac{1}{E} = \frac{W_d}{E_n \cdot P_w} = \frac{W_d / E_n}{P_w}$$

where E^* is Dornbusch's definition of the real exchange rate, W_d is the domestic wage rate index, and the other terms are as defined earlier.

This definition of the real exchange rate simply presents the domestic wage measured in real dollars. Suppose that in 1984 the wage rate is

Rp720 per week and the nominal exchange rate is Rp60 for a dollar. Then the wage per week in 1984 is $12. Suppose a basket of international goods that cost $100 in 1980 costs $120 in 1984. Then in terms of 1980 dollars, the domestic wage rate is $10 ($12 · 100/120). By analyzing the domestic wage in real dollars over time, we thus see how the international competitiveness of a country develops.

Other variations of this definition can be obtained by using the U.S. wage index, or a weighted wage rate index of trading partners, to deflate the dollar. In fact, Dornbusch's index is constructed in this way. For expository purposes, however, Dornbusch assumes that the foreign wage index does not change (see note 2 in chapter 5). In other words, the foreign index remains at 100.

Notes

1. The GDP deflator is not an appropriate index for countries with high inflation rates because it is based on factor prices. It therefore does not capture the underlying inflation rate except in cases of wage indexation.

2. Harberger has recently published such an index. See Arnold C. Harberger, "Applications of Real Exchange Rate Analysis," paper prepared for the Economic Development Institute of the World Bank, Washington, D.C., June 1986; processed.

D

Effective Protection

F. Leslie C. H. Helmers

IN VARIOUS PARTS of this book, reference is made to effective protection or domestic resource cost. What do these phrases mean? Let us consider first the level of import and export duties in the five countries reviewed in Part II of this study.

Table D-1 gives the details. Import duties may be found in line 6.1 of *Government Financial Statistics* (GFS); merchandise imports (c.i.f. values), in line 71 of *International Financial Statistics* (IFS). Export duties appear in line 6.2 of GFS, merchandise exports (f.o.b. values), in line 70 of IFS.

In 1980, import duties were 20 percent of the c.i.f. value of imported goods in Argentina, the highest among the five countries. Export duties as a share of f.o.b. value were highest in Mexico at 38 percent. In most developing countries, export duties generally amount to only a few percentage points. The high rate in Mexico occurs because exports of petroleum, which account for more than 60 percent of exports, are heavily taxed.

Developing countries levy import and export duties because they are an important source of revenue and can easily be imposed. For the developing countries as a whole, taxes on international transactions accounted for more than 16 percent of total central government revenues in 1980 (see table D-2). For the industrial countries, the figure was only 1.5 percent. Import duties are also often used to protect domestic industries. Typically, the rates of duty vary widely, so that even if a country has an average import duty of, say, 20 percent, some of its industries—often those producing luxury goods—may well receive nominal protection of 100 percent or higher. The level of the nominal tariff is, however, not a good indicator of the actual protection an industry enjoys. For this purpose, economists have developed the concept of effective protection. Out of several possible variants, in the following paragraphs we use the one that most closely ties in with the discussion in chapter 2.[1]

Table D-1. Import and Export Duties, 1980

Duty	Argentina (thousands of australes)	Brazil (billions of cruzados)	Indonesia (billions of rupiah)	Korea (billions of won)	Mexico (billions of pesos)
Import duties	393.0	88.3	448.0	1,014.0	48.3
Merchandise imports (c.i.f.)	1,937.0	1,228.6	6,793.0	13,541.0	447.0
Import duties (percent)	20.3	7.2	6.6	7.5	10.8
Export duties	36.0	64.2	305.0	—	136.5
Merchandise exports (f.o.b.)	1,474.0	1,038.1	13,737.0	10,633.0	357.5
Export duties (percent)	2.4	6.2	2.2	—	38.2

Source: IMF, GFS *Yearbooks* and *International Financial Statistics.*

Table D-2. Central Government Revenue by Category for Developing and Industrial Countries, 1980
(percent)

Category	Share of central government revenue	
	Developing countries	Industrial countries
Taxes on income and profits	24.74	39.60
Social security contributions	10.95	31.89
Domestic taxes on goods and services	26.45	17.09
Taxes on international trade transactions	16.35	1.47
All other taxes, revenues, and grants	21.51	9.95
Total	100.00	100.00

Source: GFS *Yearbook,* 1985.

The upper half of table D-3 presents a practical example. Suppose refrigerators can be imported at a c.i.f. price of $300. At an exchange rate of Rp10 per dollar, the c.i.f. value is Rp3,000. Suppose the import duty is 20 percent, or Rp600. Then a domestic manufacturer can spend as much as Rp3,600 to produce a refrigerator and still be competitive with imports. Notice that indirect taxes are not added in because imports as well as domestically produced goods are subject to these taxes.

Table D-3. Example of Effective Protection Rates on Refrigerators

Item	Domestic content in domestic prices (rupiah)	Domestic content in world prices	
		Rupiah at official rate	Dollars at official rate
Effective protection rate of 57 percent			
Output price of refrigerator			
Import price c.i.f.	3,000	3,000	300
Import duties 20%	600	—	—
Maximum domestic output price	3,600	—	—
Imported intermediate products			
Import of motor			
(Rp1,500 + 2%)	1,530	1,500	150
Depreciation of imported			
machinery (Rp500 + 0%)	500	500	50
	2,030	2,000	200
Available for wages, domestic capital, and domestic intermediate products	1,570	1,000	100
Effective protection rate of 20 percent			
Output price of refrigerator			
Import price c.i.f.	3,000	3,000	300
Import duties 20%	600	—	—
Maximum domestic output price	3,600	—	—
Imported intermediate products			
Import of motor			
(Rp1,500 + 20%)	1,800	1,500	150
Depreciation of imported			
machinery (Rp500 + 20%)	600	500	50
	2,400	2,000	200
Available for wages, domestic capital, and domestic intermediate products	1,200	1,000	100

Suppose now that the refrigerator motor cannot yet be produced domestically and that the domestic manufacturer must import the motor for a total price of Rp1,530 (c.i.f. value Rp1,500 + 2 percent import duty). Suppose also that the domestic manufacturer needs a plate-bending machine. This machine needs to be imported, but there is no import duty on it. Suppose the annual depreciation on the machine is Rp500. The total import content of the refrigerator may then be set at Rp2,030, whereas the domestic output price will be Rp3,600. The remainder of Rp1,570 will be available to cover wages, depreciation of domestic capital, normal profits, and domestic intermediate products.

Furthermore, this margin may also include any "rents" the domestic manufacturer makes (more on this point later).

Consider now what the country has saved in foreign exchange by having the refrigerator produced domestically. First, the refrigerator itself is no longer imported, and there is thus a saving of $300. There are inputs with an import content of $200, however. Thus the actual saving is $100. As discussed, the domestic manufacturer can use as much as Rp1,570 of domestic resource cost to produce the refrigerator competitively with imports. In other words, to save one dollar, the domestic resource cost of Rp15.70 can be used, which is 57 percent more than the exchange rate. The nominal tariff of 20 percent on imported refrigerators is thus in reality an effective protection rate of 57 percent.

In formula form, the effective protection rate may be written as:

$$\begin{bmatrix} \text{Effective} \\ \text{protection} \\ \text{rate} \end{bmatrix} = \frac{\begin{bmatrix} \text{Domestic content at} \\ \text{domestic prices in} \\ \text{rupiah} \end{bmatrix} - \begin{bmatrix} \text{Domestic content at} \\ \text{world prices in} \\ \text{rupiah} \end{bmatrix}}{\begin{bmatrix} \text{Domestic content at} \\ \text{world prices in} \\ \text{rupiah} \end{bmatrix}} \cdot 100$$

Thus to check our example we find that

$$\begin{bmatrix} \text{Effective protection} \\ \text{rate} \end{bmatrix} = \frac{\text{Rp1,570} - \text{Rp1,000}}{\text{Rp1,000}} \cdot 100 = 57\%$$

Similarly, we have

$$\begin{bmatrix} \text{Domestic} \\ \text{resource cost} \end{bmatrix} = \frac{\begin{bmatrix} \text{Domestic content at} \\ \text{domestic prices in} \\ \text{rupiah} \end{bmatrix}}{\begin{bmatrix} \text{Domestic content at} \\ \text{world prices in} \\ \text{dollars} \end{bmatrix}} = \frac{\text{Rp1,570}}{\$100} = \text{Rp15.70}$$

Thus the concept of domestic resource cost is just another way of expressing the effective protection a domestic manufacturer enjoys.

The term "import content of a domestic product" refers to either the import value or the depreciation component of products that are imported at the margin. "Domestic intermediate products" are defined as intermediate products that are produced either by domestic manufacturers producing potentially tradable but not actually internationally traded goods (in other words they are producing only for the domestic market) or by producers producing the pure home goods. The definition of domestic intermediate products is thus consistent with the discussion in chapter 2, where we distinguished between four types of domestic producers.

The above example shows that nominal rates of 20 percent or 30 percent can result in effective protection rates on the order of several hundred percent. Unfortunately, there are few recent studies on the effective protection rates in the five countries taken as examples. Available studies have shown effective protection rates in manufacturing for Argentina at 162 percent (1958) and 111 percent (1969); for Brazil at 184 percent (1963) and 63 percent (1967); for Indonesia at 66 percent (1971) and 30 percent (1975); for Korea at 38 percent (1978); and for Mexico at 27 percent (1960).[2]

Why does a variety of effective protection rates for different industries make no sense from an economic point of view? The reason is, of course, that the incentive structure becomes completely distorted. Why should one producer be allowed to spend up to, say, Rp30 to save or earn a dollar, whereas another producer must make do with Rp10 to earn a dollar? Of course, large gains can be made by the owners of the resources used to produce highly protected products. In some countries, the pursuit of effective protection has become an art, leading to the term "rentseekers." In these countries, manufacturers may spend a substantial part of their time not on increasing the efficiency of their production processes but on obtaining special protection, which allows them to make extraordinary profits (the "rent").

What can one do to eliminate what is sometimes called the hothouse atmosphere of the rentseekers? The answer is a tariff unification program. If every import—consumption goods, intermediate products, or capital goods—has the same level of import duty, then all domestic manufacturers will have the same level of protection. Furthermore, the government will not suffer any loss in revenues. Consider the lower part of table D-3, which reproduces the previous example but now with an import duty of 20 percent on all imports. The result is that the nominal rate of 20 percent has now also become an effective rate of protection of 20 percent. Under a tariff unification program some import duties may need to be lowered but some others may need to be increased. Often such a program cannot be implemented immediately and needs to be undertaken over a period of five to seven years.

If all export duties were at the same level, and all duties on imports used for the production of export goods were rebated when the goods were leaving the country, then the domestic resource cost used to earn a dollar through exporting would be the same for all exporters. Again, such a program of incentive unification can often be implemented only gradually over several years.

Several arguments have been brought forward against tariff unification. First, why should not luxury goods, such as automobiles, air conditioners, or even refrigerators, be subjected to a high import duty? The answer is simple. If the government really wants to curtail the consumption of such goods, it should impose an excise tax on imports as well as on the domestically produced luxury goods. No distortions would then be created because the incentives for domestic producers would remain the same. Consumption, however, would be curtailed because of the excise tax.

Second, why should not infant industries receive high protection? The problem is how to determine which industries should be considered to be in an infant stage. The argument has always been used in countries with a very small industrial base. If one wants to follow the protection route, then it is better to give relatively high uniform protection to all industries rather than to select a few industries for special favors.

Finally, why should not special sectors, say, steel producers or farmers, obtain high protection for strategic (defense or food security) reasons? If steel is given a high import duty, then the price of domestically produced steel will be way above the import price. Such special protection will jeopardize the overall industrialization effort. If for one reason or another the domestic steel sector needs special treatment, then it would be much better for the government to subsidize the losses the steel industry might incur than to raise the domestic output price. As regards food, the policy in many developing countries has been one not of high protection but of negative protection. Food imports have been subsidized, which makes it difficult for farmers to compete with imports. The negative effects of such policies have now become well known, and incentives for farmers are gradually being increased. It would, of course, be just as bad to overdo the incentives by giving high protection, for then food prices and wages would increase excessively, thereby reducing the real exchange rate and making the economy again uncompetitive with the rest of the world.

Notes

1. The most common methods of calculating effective protection rates have been devised by Corden and Balassa. For the Corden method, see W. M. Corden, "The Structure of a Tariff System and the Effective Protection Rate," *Journal of Political Economy,* no. 74 (June 1966), pp. 221–37. The Balassa method is discussed in Bela Balassa and Associates, *The Structure of Protection in Developing Countries* (Baltimore, Md.: Johns Hopkins University Press, 1971). A detailed discussion of effective protection rates appears in Ian Little, Tibor Scitovsky, and Maurice Scott, *Industry and Trade in Some Developing Countries: A Comparative Study* (London: Oxford University Press, 1970), chap. 5 app. Another detailed discussion, which also deals with export goods as inputs (they are to be treated as imports) in production processes for which effective protection rates are calculated, appears in Arnold C. Harberger, "Issues of Tariff Policy," paper prepared for the Economic Development Institute of the World Bank, Washington, D.C., April 1985; processed.

2. The 1958 estimate for Argentina and the 1960 estimate for Mexico have been taken from Little, Scitovsky, and Scott, *Industry and Trade in Some Developing Countries*, chap. 5 app. They were calculated by following the Corden method. The Indonesia data are reported by Gillis and Dapice in chapter 14. The 1969 Argentina estimate and the two Brazil estimates are from Anne O. Krueger, *Trade and Development in Developing Countries: Synthesis and Conclusions* (Chicago, Ill.: University of Chicago Press, 1983), pp. 34,36. The Korea estimate (Corden method) is by Soogil Young and Yoo Jungho, "The Basic Role of Industrial Policy and a Reform Proposal for the Protection Regime in Korea," Korea Development Institute, Seoul, December 1982. Not all estimates are calculated in the same manner. They do provide, however, indicators of the extent of protection in the different countries.

Index